Praise for *Business Model Innovation Strategy*

Grounded in decades of rigorous research, Amit and Zott provide THE definitive guide to innovating a winning business model. Brimming with timely illustrations, the authors use the latest in "design thinking" to apply their crisp ideas to real-life situations. Perfect for the boardroom or the classroom!

—Kathleen M. Eisenhardt, Stanford W. Ascherman M.D. Professor, Professor of Strategy, and coauthor of *Simple Rules*, School of Engineering, Stanford University

Amit and Zott give us a timely and important road map for dealing with the two intense challenges that we face as we climb out of the pandemic: surviving the shock and building a better future. The book clears the fog on finding a way forward through business model innovation, engaging the right partners, and making astute commitments – all while keeping the lights on.

—Anita McGahan, University Professor, George E. Connell Chair in Organizations and Society, and Professor of Strategic Management, Rotman School of Management, University of Toronto

A business model is a core element of every entrepreneur's and senior manager's strategy. Amit and Zott's book is an up-to-date, comprehensive, insightful, and action-oriented manuscript on business model innovation strategy. Anchored in decades of research, filled with illustrations from around the world, and containing tools to help with formulating and implementing strategy for business model innovation, it is a valuable guide for practitioners and a teaching resource for faculty and students.

—Garth Saloner, Botha-Chan Professor of Economics, Dean, Stanford Graduate School of Business (2009–2016), Stanford University

At last an excellent book on business model innovation . . . the crucial step that technology wizards often get wrong.

—David J. Teece, Thomas W. Tusher Professor in Global Business, Walter A. Haas School of Business, University of California, Berkeley

Blockbuster Video. Borders Books. Sears. Yahoo. Encyclopedia Britannica. These were household names that were killed by innovative business models (that leveraged disruptive technologies). In their new book, Professors Amit and Zott provide entrepreneurs with actionable and hands-on frameworks to help founders build and implement innovative, robust, and disruptive business models.

—Josh Kopelman, Founding General Partner, First Round Capital; Founder, Half.com; Co-Founder, Infonautics Corporation

The rapidly changing world demands constant innovation and necessitates persistent revision and adaptation of existing strategies. This rigorous and insightful book by Amit and Zott features concrete business model innovation strategy techniques that complement the traditional scope of how to conduct business – a topic every company must urgently address to sustain itself long term.

—Dr. Johannes Sommerhäuser, Senior Vice President Innovation, Bosch Management Consulting; Robert Bosch, GmbH

Through a systematic approach with a structured framework and various case studies, the authors shed light on how to build and execute innovative business models in the real world. The broad coverage of this book offers fantastic practical knowledge whether you are an entrepreneur or an academic researcher.

—Gang Yu, Ph.D., Co-Founder and Executive Chairman of 111 Inc. Former corporate executive at Dell and Amazon

Two of the pioneers in thinking about business models have now produced an invaluable book that brings the latest research to business model innovation. You will learn how business models can be innovated, and also why many times they are not. This will be an essential reference for years to come. Every business manager should buy and read it now.

—Henry Chesbrough, Professor at UC Berkeley-Haas, and author of *Open Innovation*

Finally we have a book on business models that is both conceptual and practical, and which fits exceptionally well in business strategy courses. Amit and Zott have brought all the essential elements together in a way that provides a useful guidepost for entrepreneurs starting a new business as well as those seeking to innovate their business model within established companies.

—Marvin Lieberman, Professor of Strategy; Harry and Elsa Kunin Chair in Business and Society; Senior Associate Dean, Anderson School of Management, University of California, Los Angeles

This is the go-to book on the art-and-science of designing and implementing innovative, scalable, and robust business models. Amit and Zott, the widely cited global thought leaders, offer a cutting edge, holistic understanding of what business models are, how to design them to create and capture value, and how to implement and modify them in light of changing business conditions. I highly recommend this book to business school professors, students, managers, and entrepreneurs.

—Quy Huy, The Solvay Chaired Professor of Technological Innovation. INSEAD, Fontainebleau, France

As a business model innovation (BMI) consultant to many leading companies around the world, I realize the importance of anchoring my advice on actionable frameworks and tools that are based on rigorous state of the art research. Amit and Zott's timely and pioneering book provides such a perspective and is therefore a must read for any manager.

—Edward H.B. Giesen, IBM Global Business Services, Global Partner, European Growth Leader Digital Strategy/Global CBM Leader

This is essential reading and a practical handbook for entrepreneurs starting a new venture, or those charged with corporate innovation. A thoughtful, erudite, and fascinating read. I sincerely wish this book had been available when I started my first venture.

—Steve Jackson, Co-Founder and Group COO, Xoomworks

Business model innovation has been central to my social entrepreneurship efforts in the last ten years. The authors' profound insights into effective business model design and strategy explained in this book have been instrumental for the success of my projects, some of which serve millions of beneficiaries. I am thrilled to see the authors' breakthrough thinking in action-oriented form in this book; thousands of entrepreneurs will benefit greatly from it, just as I have.

—Gopala Krishnan, Founder and CEO,
Inditech Technology Services Pvt Ltd.

Amit and Zott have written a must-read primer on business model innovation. If your objective is not only surviving the crisis but thriving in the "new normal" then you found the right source of inspiration.

—Bruno Lea, Entrepreneur and President,
Performer CNC, France

Based on a comprehensive set of cutting-edge research projects, Raffi Amit and Christoph Zott turn what was the black art of business model innovation into a pragmatic and reliable framework for the managerial toolbox. Their concepts will become the benchmark for strategy and innovation consulting, teaching, and research.

—Dietmar Harhoff, Director, Max-Planck Institute for Innovation and Competition, Germany; Honorary Professor, University of Munich

The business model construct has fundamentally changed how firms – small and large, young and established – create and appropriate value . . . and how they innovate! With *Business Model Innovation Strategy*, Raffi Amit and Chris Zott have created a book that strikes just the right balance: in a highly inspiring manner they combine action-oriented insights with thorough analysis of the primary factors shaping business model design and implementation. Let them be your expert guides on your business model innovation journey!

—Marc Gruber, Chaired Professor of Entrepreneurship and Technology Commercialization, Swiss Federal Institute of Technology, Lausanne, Switzerland

As a company in the process of digitalizing its business models, we are facing exceptionally challenging times. Based on our ambidextrous strategy, it is of utmost importance to adopt a comprehensive, holistic approach to our innovation activities. By offering scientific concepts and practical examples, this book is an essential guide for incumbent firms seeking to develop a successful business model innovation strategy.

—Dr. Uwe Kirschner, Vice President Bosch Management Consulting, Partner Business Model Innovation

My team at Next47, a Siemens backed accelerator, is helping Siemens identify and create its next generation of high-growth businesses. Amit and Zott's rigorous and insightful analysis provides invaluable guidance for the mission-critical business model innovation strategy that every market leading company must adopt.

—Dr. Matthias Roth, Director at Next47, Siemens AG

I am a big fan of business model innovation. Done right, as we did at Dianping, it creates a much larger, sustainable, and defensible business that can have a huge impact on society at large. Amit and Zott's groundbreaking book has a very practical orientation and is a must-read for every entrepreneur and manager.

—Tao Zhang, Chairman, Internet Plus Holdings Ltd. Founder, CEO and Chairman, Dianping.com

BUSINESS MODEL INNOVATION STRATEGY

RAPHAEL AMIT AND CHRISTOPH ZOTT

BUSINESS MODEL INNOVATION STRATEGY

TRANSFORMATIONAL CONCEPTS AND TOOLS FOR ENTREPRENEURIAL LEADERS

WILEY

Published by John Wiley & Sons, Inc., Hoboken, New Jersey.
Published simultaneously in Canada.

Library of Congress Cataloging-in-Publication Data:
Names: Amit, Raphael, 1947- author. | Zott, Christoph, 1967- author.
Title: Business model innovation strategy : transformational concepts and tools for entrepreneurial leaders / Raphael Amit, Christoph Zott.
Description: Hoboken, New Jersey : Wiley, [2020] | Includes index.
Identifiers: LCCN 2020023350 (print) | LCCN 2020023351 (ebook) | ISBN 9781119689683 (hardback) | ISBN 9781119689669 (adobe pdf) | ISBN 9781119689676 (epub)
Subjects: LCSH: Business planning. | Strategic planning. | Management.
Classification: LCC HD30.28 .A445 2020 (print) | LCC HD30.28 (ebook) | DDC 658.4/063–dc23
LC record available at https://lccn.loc.gov/2020023350
LC ebook record available at https://lccn.loc.gov/2020023351

Cover Design: Wiley
Cover Images: Colorful business model strategy © Raphael Amit and Christoph Zott
Author Images: (Amit) courtesy of Raphel Amit, (Zott) © Jordi Estruch Massana

Printed in the United States of America

SKY10082938_082724

To our parents, wives, and children, who have inspired and motivated us and supported us firmly in our scholarly endeavors for many years.

Contents

Preface

We completed the writing and editing of our book during the height of the global COVID-19 pandemic, which triggered a severe and multifaceted global crisis. The crisis included simultaneous, interrelated, and unprecedented shocks relating to public health, global transportation, individual freedom, international collaboration, and the world economy. The global economy suffered from both supply- and demand-side shocks that generated extraordinary economic upheaval and widespread unemployment. The coronavirus pandemic also caused a major shock in global capital markets and extreme volatility in domestic and international financial systems. Uncertainty regarding the future reached the highest level in over a century. Temporary and permanent business closures, along with bankruptcies, resulted in the loss of millions of jobs. Many people lost their lives to the pandemic, especially the old and vulnerable.

A catastrophe of this scale is likely to alter the preferences, habits, and risk attitudes of consumers, in part because of long stay-at-home and social distancing measures; the strategies of managers; and economic, social, and political policies. While this crisis will have profound and broad social and economic implications, and the exact nature of the so-called "new normal" will only be revealed in the coming months and years, what seems very likely at this time is that many companies – large and small, public and private, for-profit and social – will be prompted to reinvent and reimagine themselves to be able to survive and prosper. Executive leaders around the world will have to take a hard look at how to do business in the post COVID-19 era, since the shocks caused by this pandemic will affect every aspect of a company's business model and the technologies used to enable business operations.

Prior to the coronavirus pandemic, many companies focused on finding the most efficient architecture for their activity systems. That resulted in outsourcing many activities to partners and vendors, often located abroad, which led to the formation of complex global supply chain networks. The shock to these global supply chains that resulted from the abrupt and comprehensive shutdown of economies in Asia, Europe, and the U.S. caused enormous disruptions in a broad range of industries; most notable during the coronavirus crisis were medical equipment and hospital supplies. As a result of the shock to supply chains, coupled with likely changes in the preferences of consumers, numerous challenges arose for established companies. These challenges may, however, reveal new opportunities. The "new normal" that may follow the crisis and the uncertain pace of recovery from the current global recession will incentivize startup entrepreneurs and corporate leaders alike to rethink the design of their business models; to adopt a system-level approach to business model design; and to embrace a preference for resilience over efficiency in the conceptualization and the design of their business models along with enhanced use of digital technologies. These developments will drive substantial structural changes in the architecture of the activity systems of firms. In other words, they will likely spur business model innovations, and thus heighten the need for entrepreneurial leaders to develop a business model innovation strategy, as outlined in this book.

Our book is targeted at both the academic and professional markets and is intended for a global audience. Faculty and students use it as a textbook in both degree and non-degree programs; entrepreneurial leaders in both new and established businesses (both for-profit and non-profit) use this book as a rigorous, comprehensive, and detailed guide to enable the design and implementation of innovative, scalable, and robust business models for their companies. While the book is deeply anchored in theory and rigorous empirical research, it has a very pragmatic orientation and is filled with examples and illustrations from around the world. We draw on over 20 years of pioneering research that originated in 1999 on the 8th floor of Angus Hall at the University of British Columbia in Vancouver, Canada, where we met in 1995. The book is a true team effort involving thousands of hours of collaboration and brainstorming sessions in person and via electronic communication technologies. Our extensive joint publications on all aspects of business model innovation strategy have been widely cited by scholars and practitioners around the world. At the same time, we draw on the impressive and rapidly growing body of collective scientific research on business models generated by colleagues at notable academic institutions. In our teaching and consulting work, the concepts and in particular the processes that are contained in the book have proven effective at enabling entrepreneurial leaders in both startups and established incumbent firms to conceptualize, design, and implement innovative and value-creating business models for their companies.

The book content is organized into three parts as follows:

Part I: Foundation and Mindset for Business Model Innovation

The first part of our book lays out the conceptual foundation of the business model construct. In Chapter 1 we define the business model as a system of interdependent activities and present the framework that we developed through our research, which serves as the common thread throughout the book. In Chapter 2 we lay the theoretical foundations of the business model construct and show that the business model is a new strategic issue that complements traditional corporate and business strategy issues. Chapter 3 highlights the importance of adopting a holistic business model mindset, which is crucial for understanding, developing, and implementing business model innovations. Finally, Chapter 4 formally defines business model innovation and illustrates it through a series of real-world examples.

Part II: Strategic Design and Evaluation of Business Model Innovation

Part II of the book presents practical strategies and hands-on tools to help managers and entrepreneurs obtain real, workable skills for business model innovation. Chapter 5 introduces important concepts from the field of design, a methodology that is highly applicable to the development of novel business models, and Chapter 6 offers a dynamic process method for business model design. Other relevant methods for business model design, including received processes of venture design, are surveyed in Chapter 7, and the related key concepts of value drivers and value propositions are covered in Chapter 8. Chapter 9 offers an essential toolkit for conducting business model analysis and designing new business models.

Part III: Making Business Model Innovation Happen

To create lasting capabilities to adopt a business model innovation – and continue innovating through time – it is crucial to be aware of business model implementation challenges and how to successfully address them. This is the focus of Part III of the book. Chapter 10 focuses on the implementation of business model innovation in established firms and the specific challenges such firms are faced with. Chapter 11 discusses the specific barriers that can arise in new ventures and the associated mitigation strategies. Finally, Chapter 12 highlights the important role of the business model in the context of digital transformation and lays out the different steps involved in developing a business model innovation strategy.

Our hope is that the book will become a helpful companion for faculty who wish to teach business model innovation strategy, a vital tool for students who study the subject in degree and non-degree courses, and, very importantly, an essential guide for entrepreneurial managers who seek to develop a winning business model innovation strategy for their firm.

Raphael Amit (Philadelphia, USA) and **July 2020**
Christoph Zott (Barcelona, Spain)

PART I

Foundation and Mindset for Business Model Innovation

1 Why Do Business Models Matter? The "What, How, Who, and Why" Framework for Understanding Any Business Model

Why Do Business Models Matter?

In the past few decades, innovations in computing and information technologies have accelerated, instigating a fundamental shift in the economic and competitive landscapes. The changes that this shift has been fueling are pervasive, comprehensive, and disruptive. Often touted as the "digitalization of business," they go far beyond increasing firm efficiency and profitability through digitizing individual processes or functions within firms. They are profound, holistic, and may shake firms to their core. They encompass every industry in every corner of the world. They present new and exciting business opportunities in industries that were considered all but immune to attacks from newcomers. These developments present enormous opportunities for aspiring entrepreneurs whose innovative business models can disrupt entire industries, as Airbnb did in the hospitality industry, or Uber did in the industry for personal transportation. Managers of incumbent firms need to explore new possibilities for value creation that are anchored in the redesign of their firms' business models, as Charles Schwab, the financial services firm, did when it transformed its business model from call center-assisted trades to enabling clients to trade electronically themselves using a web-based platform. On the flip side, every manager of every well-performing firm needs to take seriously the possibility of eroding margins that result from competitors' business model innovations.

A business model is about "how to do business," and business model innovation is about "how to do business in new ways." Together, they have become crucial strategic issues for general managers, entrepreneurs, investors, and all those aspiring to assume any of these important roles at some point in their professional careers. Hardly recognized or talked about until the end of the last century, the concept of the business model suddenly became "en vogue" in the mid-1990s, emerging as a key topic in conversations about new business opportunities and how to capture them (see Exhibit 1.1). It has since become a core ingredient for opportunity analysis and development, and has yielded the development of important new tools such as the Business Model Canvas.[1] Our book presents an important step forward in several aspects: first, by offering a unique blend of scientific concepts and insights with practical tools and examples; second, by providing an actionable framework for business model innovation that focuses on needs and activities; third, by highlighting the strategic aspects of business model innovation; and, last but not least, by adding a dynamic dimension that considers the entire process – from inspiration to implementation of business model innovation.

[1] Osterwalder and Pigneur (2010)

Exhibit 1.1 Interest in Business Models as Measured by Published Articles

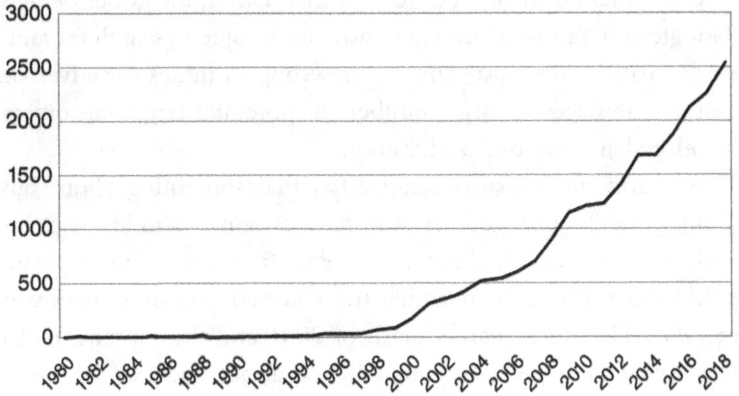

The "take-off" of the business model as an important determinant of a company's financial performance occurred in parallel with the introduction of the internet, the development of the first browsers (such as Netscape) that made the internet technology accessible to the broader public, and the ability to monetize business model innovation, as evidenced by the sky-high valuations of IPOs (Initial Public Offerings)[2] in the second half of the 1990s and the early 2000s. This period saw the first wave of companies, including Amazon, eBay, Google, and Yahoo, that used internet technology to power their innovative business models and thereby reach millions of customers. Three of these firms had their IPOs in 1996–98 (Google went public in 2004). Compared to their established competitors, these companies introduced entirely new ways of doing business.

Amazon began as an online bookseller, which fundamentally changed the way customers shopped for books. eBay established an online platform

---

[2]The term Initial Public Offering refers to the issuance of shares to the public during the first listing of a company on a stock exchange. It marks a change in the shareholding structure of a company from being closely held and privately owned to being a widely held public company. An IPO is often carried out for the purpose of raising a significant amount of capital relatively cheaply to finance the growth of the company and to eventually provide liquidity for early investors, founders, and employees through subsequent secondary share offerings.

where individuals could buy used goods from specific sellers, not unlike a flea market but on a much larger scale, and without requiring the physical presence of either buyer or seller (or, for that matter, the goods being sold). And Google and Yahoo offered new ways for people to search for and consume information, thus also offering new opportunities for advertisers to deliver their messages to large numbers of potential target customers in a highly tailored and personalized fashion.

These early success stories suggested that something about business had fundamentally changed. It was not, as some pundits had initially believed, that the world had entered a new era of boundless opportunities and goldilocks economies in which the received economic laws were no longer valid. The stock market crash of 2001 and the subsequent failures of firms that had once been much hyped about and had attained high valuations (such as Webvan or Boo.com) made this abundantly clear. Yet, despite all the skepticism that followed the initial hype in the wake of the stock market bust, Amazon, eBay, Google, and Yahoo managed to survive, and with them the insight that technology-enabled business model innovations had become a new reality for managers to be reckoned with; that is, managers realized that leveraging and deploying advanced computing and communication technologies in order to create value for a firm's stakeholders presented a fundamental challenge to the status quo of their firms. So, what exactly had changed? What was new?

Quite simply, the business model had become one of the core strategic choices that general managers and entrepreneurs (and those who support and invest in them) need to consider. It answers the question: How should the firm do business?[3] For decades, the key strategic decisions that managers and entrepreneurs were asked to address, which were also highlighted in management courses, centered on: (i) corporate strategy issues, and (ii) business strategy issues. Corporate strategy issues concern the scope of the firm and include such questions as: What industries and product market segments should the firm be in? How should the firm enter these markets (i.e., through mergers and acquisitions, joint ventures, or de novo entry)? When should the firm enter these markets? Business strategy issues center

---

[3]Note that this is a colloquial definition meant to give you a first intuitive understanding of the concept; we will present a more formal and rigorous definition below.

on establishing and sustaining the competitive advantage of a firm. They include such questions as how to compete in a particular product market (e.g., compete on the basis of differentiation or cost leadership?), and what resources and capabilities to acquire or develop.

The advent of the internet did not undermine the importance of these classic choices; they remain as valid and relevant as ever. However, it added an essential strategic choice onto the entrepreneur's and general manager's plates, namely the question of *how to do business*. This question does not replace, or diminish the importance of, any of the previously mentioned strategic issues. Rather, it complements them and thus expands the range of strategically relevant considerations for entrepreneurs and managers who are keen on pursuing and exploiting new business opportunities in addition to defending and securing their existing ones. In other words, addressing the business model question has become a strategic imperative for entrepreneurial leaders. Technological change – mainly in information and telecommunication technologies, as we will explain in more depth in Chapter 5 – has enabled the development of entirely new business models, whereas in the past technological change mainly spurred the development of new products and processes.

For example, Reed Hastings and Marc Randolph, the co-founders of Netflix, which was incorporated in 1997, utilized the internet to introduce a business model innovation in the video rental industry. Up until that point, the industry had been dominated by incumbents such as Blockbuster. Now, instead of picking up a movie at a specialized rental shop, customers could receive DVD rentals from Netflix through the mail.[4] This represented a business model innovation, as it involved an entirely new way of doing business, for which Netflix even secured a business method patent. The new model relied on customers selecting and renting movies online instead of going to a shop; burning DVDs in partnership with DVD manufacturers just-in-time as customers ordered the movies; and shipping the DVDs via the United States Postal Service with a pre-paid return envelope directly to the customers.

Senior managers are well aware of the threat posed by disruptive digital newcomers. A survey conducted among C-level executives finds that "competition isn't just coming from new permutations of old industries . . . it's

[4]Teece (2010)

also coming from digital invaders with totally different business models."[5] One of these digital invaders, Uber, was created in 2009. In its last pre-IPO private equity financing round on August 27, 2018, Uber raised $500 million at a pre-money valuation of $71.5bn with reported 2017 revenues of $7.5bn.[6] This compared with a market valuation of about $34bn (about half of Uber's) for Ford Motor Company in late 2018, on annual revenues of approximately $160bn (about 20 times Uber's 2017 revenues).[7] Ford, a pioneering car manufacturer, was founded in 1903, over a century before Uber. Clearly, investors expected Uber to do well in the market for personal transport, estimated at $10tr annually.[8] Another digital invader, Airbnb, a home-sharing company founded in 2008, was valued in 2018 at $31bn on estimated annual revenues of $3.5bn for 2017.[9] This company, which does not own or operate any real estate, was widely considered a challenger to the hotel industry, which had not seen any significant innovation for decades until the rise of home-sharing business models. In comparison, Hilton, an established hotel chain with a well-known global brand, had a market valuation of $21bn that was about 30% lower than that of Airbnb.[10] The differences between the valuations of incumbents such as Hilton and Ford, and the new entrants into their industries such as Airbnb and Uber, respectively, can be attributed in part to their vastly different business model designs. More specifically, it can be attributed to their technology-driven business model innovations. Airbnb did not just invent a new hotel format; it introduced an entirely new method for providing a place to stay for those in need of accommodation.

In a nutshell, business models and in particular business model innovations matter because they are a source of opportunity for entrepreneurs and for entrepreneurially minded managers (who are sometimes called *intrapreneurs*) in established firms. They also matter because they have financial performance consequences. Business model innovation refers to

---

[5]IBM Institute for Business Value (2015, p. 5)
[6]Bond and Fontanella-Khan (2018), Hook (2018), and Crunchbase website. Uber. Funding rounds.
[7]Ford Motor Company (2019)
[8]The Economist (2016)
[9]Lex (2018)
[10]Lex (2018)

the conceptualization and implementation of new ways of doing business in order to better address the imperfectly met needs of customers and other market participants such as suppliers. Business models are a locus of innovation and value creation, as the founders of Uber – Garrett Camp and Travis Kalanick – or the founders of Airbnb – Brian Chesky, Joe Gebbia, and Nathan Blecharczyk – can testify. For new ventures as well as for established firms, they open new paths for exploiting market opportunities, beyond coming up with new products or services.

Car manufacturers like Volkswagen (VW) have clearly understood the strategic importance of business model thinking for their own future market positioning and success. Volkswagen's decisive move into the electric car business with a €30bn investment program announced in 2018 is not just product-driven but goes beyond the automobile industry's classic paradigm of competing on product characteristics such as car design, performance, quality, or price.[11] The German company seeks to emulate in the auto industry Apple's platform-driven business model by providing a unifying chassis that serves as a basic building block for different electric car models. Powered by a proprietary operating system that will allow for over-the-air software updates and support various apps, much like an iPhone, the platform is intended to provide a new digital in-car experience. Like the Apple Store or Google Play, the IT infrastructure will be open to third-party apps and so create a "shopping mall" for new digital services.[12] The key idea behind VW's strategy, therefore, is not just to make the production of electric cars cheaper and to establish an industry standard (a goal is for their chassis to eventually be licensed to other car manufacturers), but to get closer to the customer and sell them new digital services on an ongoing basis, much like Apple is doing in the mobile phone business. Like Tesla, VW even aims at replicating Apple's retailing model, bypassing traditional car dealerships and setting up company-owned stores that function as showrooms.[13] These measures go beyond mere product or service innovations; instead, they represent a business model innovation. In the section

---

[11]McGee (2019)

[12]VW chief operating officer Ralf Brandstätter quoted in the *Financial Times* (McGee, 2019)

[13]Ramsey (2018)

that follows, we offer a more formal and precise definition of our core concepts.

What Is a Business Model?

In what follows we briefly review a range of approaches to defining a business model and identify common themes that form the foundations for our definition of a business model as an interdependent activity system that may span both firm and industry boundaries. The way we define it, a business model is designed to capture a perceived market opportunity in a way that creates value for all stakeholders. We proceed to identify the four dimensions of a business model, namely, (i) its content, i.e., *what* activities the business model is composed of; (ii) its structure, i.e., *how* these activities are linked in the business model; (iii) its governance, i.e., *who* performs the activities that are enabled by the business model; and (iv) its value logic, i.e., *why* does the business model create value and *why* does it also enable value appropriation through a revenue model.

Approaches Towards Defining Business Models

In the academic literature, different conceptualizations of the term "business model" have been proposed.[14] Broadly speaking, some business model concepts center on value creation, while others focus more on mechanisms for value appropriation.

The value creation perspective of the business model, which is the one we embrace in this book, has been advanced to capture the essence of "how firms do business."[15] It describes the business model as a source of innovation when, for example, it connects previously unconnected parties (such as private drivers and passengers in the case of Uber), links stakeholders in new ways, or introduces new transaction mechanisms (as in the case of eBay). Not surprisingly, this view of the business model focuses on activities, and the ways these activities are linked with one another,

[14] Zott, Amit, and Massa (2011)
[15] See Amit and Zott (2001); and Zott and Amit (2007, 2008)

to address the "how to" question. Others have advocated a more encompassing definition of the term, with greater emphasis on value appropriation.[16]

Despite the absence of a clear consensus in the academic literature on a universally accepted definition, researchers have converged on some important common themes that characterize business models. Specifically,

- Business models center on the logic of how value is created for all stakeholders, not just how it is captured by one firm.
- Activities performed by the focal firm play an important role, but so too do the activities performed by partners, suppliers, and even customers.
- Business models emphasize a system-level, holistic approach to explaining how firms "do business."
- The business model is emerging as a new focal point for analysis.[17]

Taken together, these four themes represent a common denominator that points toward the business model as a concept that builds on that of the well-established value chain, which represents the firm's "collection of activities that are performed to design, produce, market, deliver, and support its product."[18] Although the notion of the business model draws on arguments that are central to the value chain framework, in particular that activities and multiple sources of value matter, it extends those arguments in important ways. The business model extends the concept of the value chain by (i) emphasizing value creation and delivery dynamics, (ii) spanning firm and industry boundaries, and (iii) allowing for a non-linear sequencing

[16]For example, see Osterwalder and Pigneur (2010), or Chesbrough and Rosenbloom (2002, p. 529) who link the business model to the technology management literature and define it as the "heuristic logic that connects technical potential with the realization of economic value," emphasizing its role in linking technology to market outcomes. Consistent with this perspective, Casadesus-Masanell and Ricart (2010) posit that one important component of business models is the set of choices made by management regarding how the organization operates, such as compensation practices, procurement contracts, location of facilities, or assets employed. Another component of business models, according to this view, is reflected in the consequences of these choices, such as low cost or a culture of frugality. For other definitions, see Zott, Amit, and Massa (2011).

[17]Zott, Amit, and Massa (2011)

[18]Porter (1985)

Exhibit 1.2 From Value Chain to Business Model

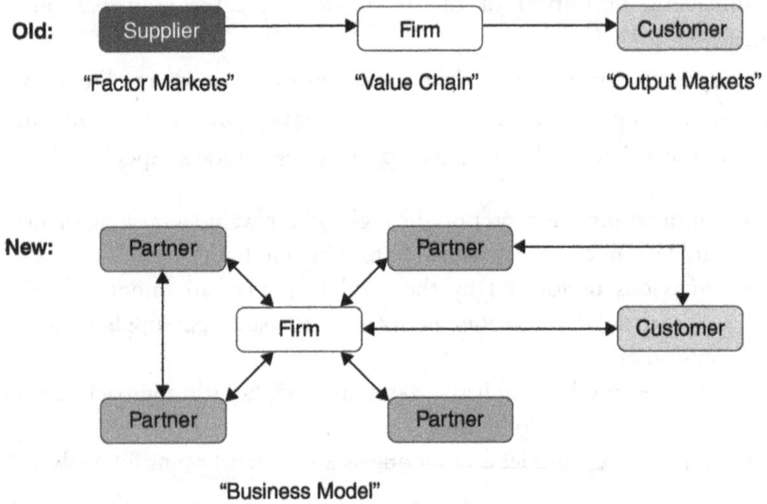

of interdependent activities. (See Exhibit 1.2.) These are each explained in more detail below.

- *Emphasizing value creation and delivery dynamics*: Amazon has widely deployed artificial intelligence (AI) across its business to help build and deliver value for its customers and partners.[19] Since its early years, for instance, it has used AI algorithms to provide customized product recommendations for customers. These algorithms more generally help Amazon learn about customer preferences and behavior, then dynamically implement this knowledge. This is reflected in a product offering that not only better meets current consumer demand but also anticipates *future* demand. Anticipating demand in turn leads to faster delivery times, as goods can be proactively stocked in strategic locations. In Amazon's model, value creation and delivery therefore become *circular* rather than strictly *linear*. Over time, and as its number of customers (and therefore transactions) has increased, Amazon's algorithms have become more advanced, helping it build a product and product delivery activity system that is highly responsive to customer needs.[20]

[19]Levy (2018) and Terdiman (2018)
[20]Terdiman (2018)

- *Spanning firm and industry boundaries*: In the early 1980s, TradePlus (today known as E★TRADE) introduced a groundbreaking online direct brokerage platform that enabled the execution of the "first-ever electronic trade by an individual investor."[21] As this new platform removed the need to go through a stockbroker, and made trading significantly more cost-effective, individuals could trade stocks at a highly affordable price. E★TRADE's platform model connects an expansive, industry-spanning range of participants: individual investors, small business owners, companies that are publicly traded, and large market makers such as Citadel.
- *Allowing for a non-linear sequencing of interdependent activities*: On eBay's auction platform, the pricing of individual items is determined via a dynamic auction process. Customers browse product listings, then interact with each other to set the final price of an item (by setting interdependent bids). These customer activities – browsing and bidding – occur simultaneously and interactively, i.e., in a non-linear fashion.

Our Definition: The Business Model as an Activity System

Building on the four themes identified above, we formally define the **business model** as *the system of interdependent activities that are performed by a focal firm and by its partners and the mechanisms that link these activities to each other*. An **activity** in a focal firm's business model can be viewed as *the engagement of human, physical, and/or capital resources of any party to the business model (the focal firm, end customers, vendors, etc.) to serve a specific purpose toward the fulfillment of the overall objective*. An **activity system** is a *set of interdependent and interconnected activities that are centered on a focal firm; it encompasses activities that are conducted either by the focal firm or by partners, customers, or vendors*.[22]

Business models are created by entrepreneurial leaders who shape and design organizational activities as well as the links (transactions) that weave activities together into a system. Such purposeful design – within and across firm boundaries – is the essence of the business model.[23] The architecture of the firm's activity system – shaped by the choice of activities, how they are

[21] E★TRADE (2019)
[22] Zott and Amit (2010)
[23] Zott and Amit (2009)

Exhibit 1.3 Architecture of Business Model Participants

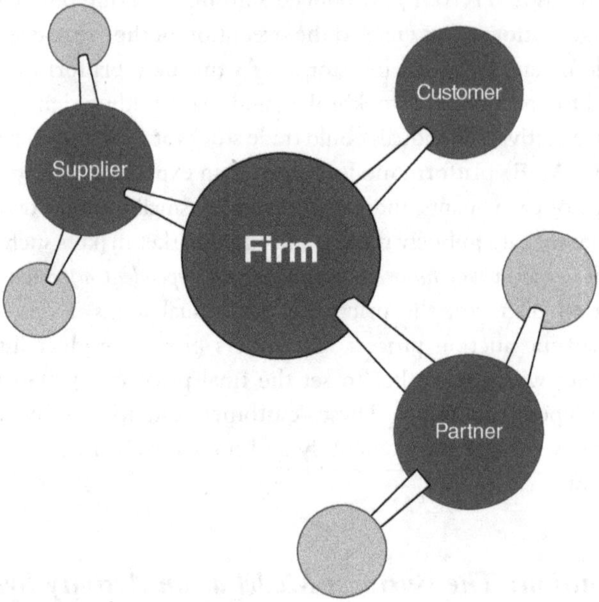

linked, and who performs them – captures how the focal firm is embedded in its "ecology," i.e., in its multiple networks of suppliers, partners, and customers. (See Exhibit 1.3.)

To fully address a market opportunity, a firm's business model (a.k.a. activity system) may transcend the focal firm and span across the firm and its industry boundaries, but it remains centered on a focal firm, enabling the focal firm not only to create value with its partners through the activities they perform, but also to appropriate a share of the value created. The firm's *revenue model* plays an important role in value appropriation. Akin to a pricing strategy for specific products or services, the revenue model refers to the specific modes in which a business model enables revenue generation.[24]

The conceptualization of the business model as a dynamic activity system that is orchestrated by a focal firm, yet involves external participants (other firms and customers) who carry out some of the activities in the business model system, suggests that a business model can be described by four dimensions that are introduced next. We refer to these as the

---

[24]Amit and Zott (2001)

What, How, Who, and ***Why*** of the activity system. These mutually exclusive dimensions not only allow us to analyze, understand, and evaluate existing business models, but they also help illuminate what makes an innovative business model truly novel. Taken together, they constitute the foundational conceptual framework for this book.

The "What, How, Who, and Why" Framework

As mentioned in the previous sections, we conceive of the business model as a value-centered activity system that is designed and enabled by a focal firm in order to meet perceived market needs. The key dimensions of a business model, depicted in Exhibit 1.4, are

1. Its content, i.e., *what* activities the business model is composed of (***What***)
2. Its structure, i.e., *how* these activities are linked in the business model (***How***)
3. Its governance, i.e., *who* performs the activities that are enabled by the business model (which activities are performed by the focal firm, versus those performed by partners, suppliers, or customers) (***Who***)
4. Its value logic, i.e., *why* does the business model create value and *why* does it enhance value appropriation (***Why***)[25]

The What *Dimension*

All business models are comprised of a set of activities. Most of the core activities are generally performed by the focal firm, but relevant activities carried out by other stakeholders in the business model (such as customers and partners) are also included. These activities, which make up the ***What*** dimension, can – and often do – change over time, and they can represent a source of business model innovation. Apple's set of activities evolved, for example, when it introduced music downloads through iTunes in the early 2000s – a novel activity for the firm. Similarly, IBM was for decades principally focused on producing and delivering hardware, such as large

[25]See Zott and Amit (2001, 2007, 2008, 2010)

Exhibit 1.4 Business Model Framework

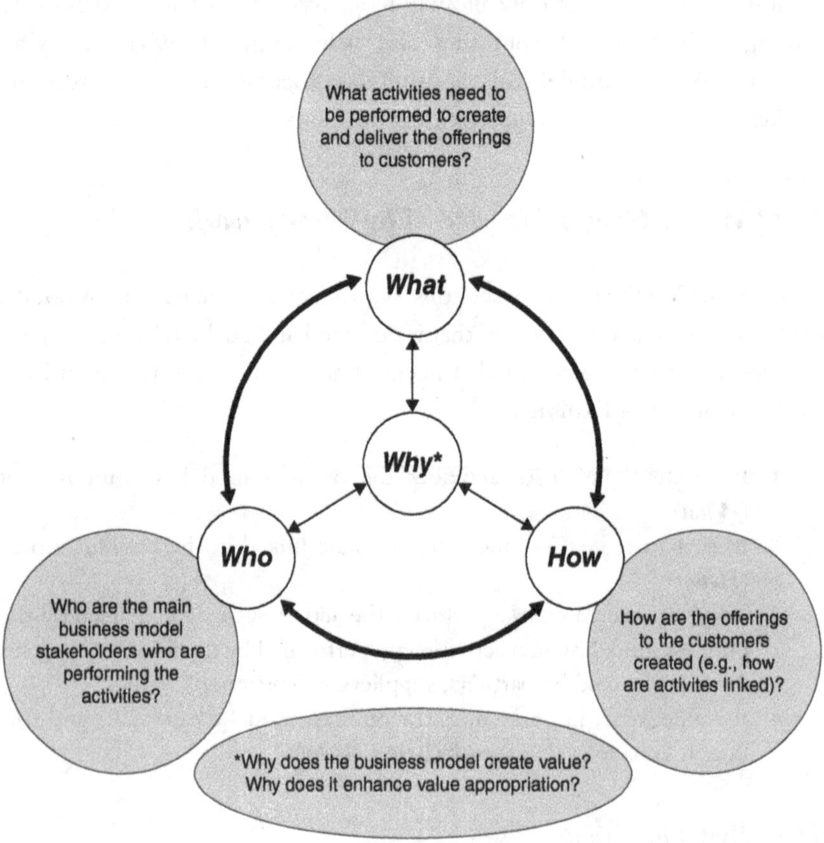

mainframe computers. In the early 1990s, however, the company's business model started to shift towards providing services, utilizing the firm's extensive experience and knowledge to provide consulting services, software, and IT maintenance. By 2006, half of IBM's revenues came from this new set of service-oriented activities.[26] Today, IBM is one of the global powerhouses in developing cutting-edge software and cloud computing solutions, such as IBM Watson.

---

[26]Zott and Amit (2010)

The How *Dimension*

The structure of the business model describes how its various activities are linked, including the *mechanisms* that link them and the *sequence* in which they are linked. This dimension – the ***How*** of the business model – also refers to the relative position of the various activities within the architecture of the entire system. For example, are they core activities central to the business model? Or, are they peripheral activities playing a supporting role? Established in the 1980s, computer manufacturer Dell introduced a highly innovative business model in its space, which met with great success. The company was a pioneer in the direct-to-customer approach for selling computers, and also became known for its build-to-order model. Up until then, the dominant model in the computer industry had been a build-to-stock one that was dependent on retail brick-and-mortar stores. Instead of building computers from scratch – which would have meant not only assembling computers, but also building all components from scratch, as early computer companies had done – Dell assembled them using components built by suppliers. It also utilized connectivity in its customer-driven supply chain to increase production coordination and agility. The sequencing and prioritization of the activities in its activity system allowed Dell to avoid the retailer markups and stocking costs facing other computer manufacturers.[27]

The Who *Dimension*

The third dimension of a business model is its governance – the ***Who*** of the business model. Governance identifies which stakeholders in the business model perform which activities. Like the other dimensions of the business model, governance can also be a source of innovation and competitive advantage. Going back to the example of Dell, the focal firm (Dell) innovated its business model governance by designing computers, coordinating the production supply chain, and selling the computers directly to consumers. Suppliers, who are essential partners of the focal firm, perform the manufacturing of computer parts. This contrasts with the governance of the

[27] Magretta (1998)

previous dominant model of personal computer manufacturing, in which the focal firms designed and built component parts themselves, and then sold the assembled computers through retail partners.

Or consider LetGo, an app launched in 2015, which is an internet-based platform that connects local buyers and sellers of secondhand goods. Consider as a point of contrast the now-antiquated mode of taking out classified ads in a local newspaper, a model which had existed for decades, if not centuries. In the case of LetGo (or Craigslist, a competitor with a web-based product for local classifieds listings), the platform is now provided not by a newspaper, but by a digital firm. Some of the stakeholder activities are the same (sellers place ads, and local buyers browse through these ads), but the governance (at the level of the platform) is different in that important activities (such as creating listings) are performed by customers, not the firm that owns and operates the platform.

The Why *Dimension*

Finally, the ***Why*** dimension of the business model refers to its value logic, i.e., how it helps the focal firm create and capture value. This dimension is closely related to the concept of the revenue model, which is defined as the modes in which a business model enables revenue generation.[28] Hilti, for instance, is a provider of professional-grade tools primarily for the construction industry. The Liechtenstein-based company, which was founded in 1941, offers a broad range of products such as drilling and demolition, cutting, sawing, and grinding systems, as well as installation and firestop systems. These are delivered by its logistic partners and sold by Hilti vendors, through its website as well as in retail stores. Hilti is one of the most successful B2B direct vendors in the construction industry. In 2016, two-thirds of the company's 24,000-plus employees were employed in sales and technical service, dealing personally with customers on a daily basis.[29] Yet, despite its success with selling products, at the beginning of the twenty-first century the company decided to additionally offer customers the possibility of renting tools. Complementing this shift, the firm's revenue model changed from

[28] Amit and Zott (2001)
[29] Hilti (2016)

one-time transactional sales income to recurring rental income. In other words, the value creation logic – and hence the ***Why*** dimension – inherent in Hilti's business model changed. Hilti's interaction with the customer in the new model does not end with the successful sale of a tool. Instead, the new rental activity implies a necessary, ongoing exchange of information between Hilti and the client on, for instance, tool usage and damages. Hilti then uses that information to identify, offer, and perform new value-creating activities such as tool maintenance, repair, and inventory management.

Implications of the Framework

It is important to emphasize that the business model is about the what, how, who, and why *of the activity system* orchestrated by a focal firm, not about any other possible what, how, who, or why question, insofar as the question is not directly related to a specific activity within the system or the set of activities that comprise the system. For example, what products to sell is an excellent and important question, but the ***What*** dimension of a business model is not about this question. Many firms sell similar products, yet through different (indeed, sometimes vastly different) business models. A consumer loan product (*what product?*), for instance, can be engineered and sold through a classic retail banking model, which relies on customers making deposits (*what activity?*) and the bank running physical branch offices (*what activity?*). Alternatively, it can be sold through a peer-to-peer model that brings together individual participants who buy and sell loans (*what activity?*) on an internet-based platform that is being maintained (*what activity?*) by a focal firm.

We consider the business model of a (new or existing) firm or business unit to be innovative when its activity system is novel in the product-market space in which the firm or business unit operates.[30] For an existing firm, this may imply a significant strategic shift, in particular when the new business model creates new sources of revenues, or when it redefines the rules of competition for an entire industry.

For example, by leveraging connectivity, Michael Dell implemented a customer-driven, build-to-order business model that challenged the

[30] Amit and Zott (2012)

traditional build-to-stock model of selling computers through retail stores. His main idea, in other words, was a business model innovation. And when Apple introduced the iPhone in 2007, and subsequently the App store, it revolutionized the smartphone handset industry, primarily through its business model innovation. Apple's business model shifted from being a product-centric firm – developing, manufacturing, and marketing stylish and expensive bundled hardware and software – to one focused on a powerful platform based on the iOS operating system. The shift enabled Apple to create more value for all business-model stakeholders, such as app developers, telecommunication companies that operate wireless networks around the world, and, of course, users, while capitalizing on the use of its hardware and thereby substantially enhancing its own market value. In other words, innovating its business model complemented Apple's capabilities in product innovation and design. This substantially enhanced value creation for all Apple stakeholders, as well as Apple's own value capture, as evidenced by the enormous increase in the company's stock price and enterprise value after 2007.

Value Creation vs. Value Appropriation in Business Models

As already mentioned, a business model is geared toward total *value creation* – for all parties involved, not just the firm whose business model is under consideration. Total value creation can be thought of as a "value pie." The greater the total value created, the larger the proverbial value pie. Value appropriation, in turn, is the amount of value that is captured by individual stakeholders. In other words, value appropriation can be thought of as the proportionate size of individual slices of the value pie. So not only do you want a bigger value pie – as it means there's more to go around – but you also want a bigger individual slice of that pie (see Exhibit 1.5).

The business model lays the foundations for the focal firm's value capture by co-determining (along with the firm's products and services) the overall "size of the value pie," which can be thought of as an upper limit to the firm's value capture. In addition, the business model also co-determines the focal firm's ability to receive a sizeable slice of the pie by influencing its bargaining power vis-à-vis other business model stakeholders. The greater the total value created, and the greater the focal firm's bargaining

Exhibit 1.5 Value Created vs. Value Appropriated

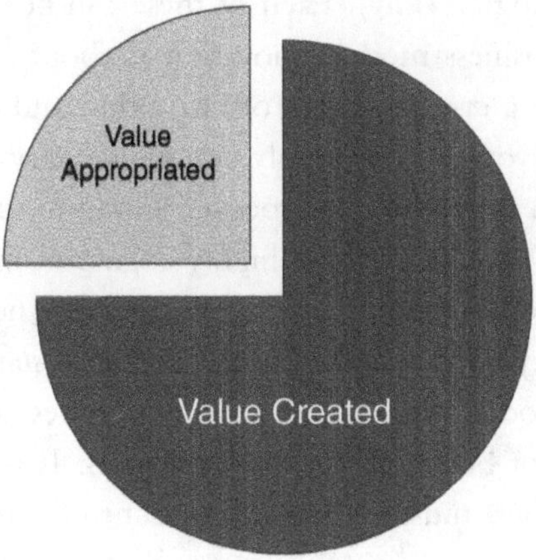

power, the greater the amount of value that the focal firm may be able to appropriate.[31] This will be explained in greater detail in Chapter 8.

Summary of Key Takeaways and Outlook

In this chapter, we have introduced our definition of the business model as a purposefully designed and value-centered activity system, where an activity is the *engagement of human, physical, and/or capital resources of any party to the business model (the focal firm, end customers, vendors, etc.) to serve a specific purpose toward the fulfillment of the overall objective*, which is typically an unmet or suboptimally met customer need. The concept of the business model first came about in parallel with the proliferation of internet-based technologies and platform businesses in the 1990s. Disruptive new firms pointed to the existence of a new – and fundamental – strategic choice facing managers and entrepreneurs. This choice, of *how to do business*, complements long-standing strategy issues, such as questions of corporate strategy and business strategy.

We have also introduced our business model framework that will be developed in more depth throughout the course of this book. According to our conceptualization, a business model can be described in terms of

[31] Zott and Amit (2007)

four interrelated dimensions: content (***What***), structure (***How***), governance (***Who***), and value logic (***Why***). Each of these can be a source of innovation for a firm. Business model innovation is about *how to do business in new ways*. It can be a crucial source of disruption and competitive advantage, and it goes beyond (but is highly complementary to) existing sources of innovation, such as product or process innovation. Both new firms and established corporations need to be highly cognizant of the opportunities, and challenges, posed to their industries by innovative new business models. In other words, they need a *business model innovation strategy*.

A business model innovation strategy enables an organization to generate a stream of business model innovations. It refers to the choices entrepreneurial leaders must make with respect to the following:

- The design of a new system of activities (***What? How? Who? Why?***); this dimension of a business model innovation strategy is addressed in detail in Chapters 1 through 4 of the book;
- The processes, including their antecedents, by which a new activity system is created; this dimension of a business model innovation strategy is addressed in detail in Chapters 5 through 9 of the book;
- The implementation and ongoing adaptation of the new activity system to ensure coherence (i.e., internal, external, and strategic fit), with the objective of sustaining and improving the focal organization's key performance metrics; this dimension is addressed in Chapters 10 through 12 of the book.

The set of ideas and tools introduced in this book will allow you to adopt a business model mindset, rigorously analyze business models, and learn how to implement business model innovation. Beyond these formal concepts and tools, however, you will also learn to *think as a business model designer*. One of the most important skills needed to become a good business model designer is the ability to think *holistically* about your firm's current or future business model. This ability to "see the big picture" will allow you to conceptualize and innovate at a *system* level. Adopting a design-oriented business model mindset, you will be equipped to design a firm that is ready to meet expected future trends (for example, in technology). Just as importantly, you will also be equipped to design a dynamic activity system that can quickly respond and adapt to the trends you *don't* expect. If you are an entrepreneur developing an exciting new product, how do you then embed this product in a responsive (and perhaps equally new) activity system that protects you from the competition? If you build an innovative new digital platform, how can you think about maximizing value for *all* members of the activity system? These are just some of the questions of high strategic relevance that we will address in this book.

References

Amit, R. & Zott, C. (2001). Value creation in e-business. *Strategic Management Journal,* **22**(6–7), 493–520.

Amit, R. & Zott, C. (2012). Creating value through business model innovation. *MIT Sloan Management Review,* **53**(3), 41–49.

Bond, S. & Fontanella-Khan, J. (2018, December 8). Uber speeds towards stock market listing. *Financial Times.* Retrieved from https://www.ft.com/content/79560992-fa8c-11e8-af46-2022a0b02a6c

Casadesus-Masanell, R. & Ricart, J. E. (2010). From strategy to business models and onto tactics. *Long Range Planning,* **43**(2–3), 195–215.

Chesbrough, H. & Rosenbloom, R. (2002). The role of the business model in capturing value from innovation: Evidence from Xerox Corporation's technology spin-off companies. *Industrial and Corporate Change,* **11**(3), 529–555.

Crunchbase website. Uber. Funding rounds. Retrieved from https://www.crunchbase.com/organization/uber/funding_rounds/funding_rounds_list

E*TRADE (2019). Retrieved from https://about.etrade.com/home

Ford Motor Company (2019). *Ford Motor Company reports fourth quarter and full year 2018 results.* Retrieved from https://s22.q4cdn.com/857684434/files/doc_financials/2018/4Q/Q4-FY-2018-Earnings-Release-FINAL-(1).pdf

Hilti (2016). *Company report.* Retrieved from https://www.hilti.group/content/dam/documents/Media-Release/publications/Hilti_2016_Company-Report_EN.pdf

Hook, L. (2018, February 14). Uber pares quarterly losses and lifts revenues. *Financial Times.* Retrieved from https://www.ft.com/content/a0f2af96-1117-11e8-940e-08320fc2a277

IBM Institute for Business Value (2015). Redefining boundaries: insights from the global C-suite study. Retrieved from https://www.ibm.com/downloads/cas/VJEP6Z9D.

Levy, S. (2018, January 2). Inside Amazon's artificial intelligence flywheel. *Wired.* Retrieved from https://www.wired.com/story/amazon-artificial-intelligence-flywheel/

Lex (2018, December 27). Airbnb: Sharing is wearing. *Financial Times.* Retrieved from https://www.ft.com/content/af217efa-eb85-11e8-89c8-d36339d835c0

Magretta, J. (1998). The power of virtual integration: An interview with Dell Computer's Michael Dell. *Harvard Business Review,* **76**(2), 73–84.

McGee, P. (2019, February 30). Volkswagen's plan to kill off Tesla. *Financial Times.* Retrieved from https://www.ft.com/content/a2b8cf3a-1e14-11e9-b126-46fc3ad87c65

Osterwalder, A. & Pigneur, Y. (2010). *Business Model Generation: A Handbook for Visionaries, Game Changers, and Challengers.* Hoboken, NJ: Wiley.

Porter, M. E. (1985). *The Competitive Advantage: Creating and Sustaining Superior Performance.* New York, NY: Free Press.

Ramsey, M. (2018, September 27). VW trying hard to follow the Apple business model. *Forbes.* Retrieved from https://www.forbes.com/sites/mikeramsey/2018/09/27/vw-trying-hard-to-follow-the-apple-business-model/#229436934737

Teece, D. J. (2010). Business models, business strategy and innovation. *Long Range Planning,* **43**(2–3), 172–194.

Terdiman, D. (2018, October 5). How AI is helping Amazon become a trillion-dollar company. *Fast Company.* Retrieved from https://www.fastcompany.com/90246028/how-ai-is-helping-amazon-become-a-trillion-dollar-company

The Economist (2016, September 3). Uberworld. *The Economist.* Retrieved from https://www.economist.com/leaders/2016/09/03/uberworld

Zott, C. & Amit, R. (2007). Business model design and the performance of entrepreneurial firms. *Organization Science,* **18**(2), 181–199.

Zott, C. & Amit, R. (2008). The fit between product market strategy and business model: Implications for firm performance. *Strategic Management Journal,* **29**(1), 1–26.

Zott, C. & Amit, R. (2009). The business model as the engine of network-based strategies. In P. R. Kleindorfer, Y. R. Wind, & R. E. Gunther (Eds.), *The Network Challenge: Strategy, Profit, and Risk in an Interlinked World* (pp. 259–275). Upper Saddle River, NJ: Wharton School Publishing.

Zott, C. & Amit, R. (2010). Business model design: An activity system perspective. *Long Range Planning,* **43**(2–3), 216–226.

Zott, C., Amit, R. & Massa, L. (2011). The business model: Recent developments and future research. *Journal of Management,* **37**(4), 1019–1042.

2 How Business Models Create Value in New Ways – Case Studies and Theory

Value Creation Through Business Models

This chapter situates the business model as a new theoretical construct that is centered on an activity perspective on value creation. It is anchored in a rich body of prior academic work on value creation. We start with two motivating examples (Uber and Michelin) to show how value creation through business models is distinct from other sources of value creation, such as products and services. Next, we describe five foundational theories of value creation – Schumpeterian innovation, the resource-based view, transaction costs economics, Porter's value chain analysis, and strategic network theory – showing how they provide a robust intellectual underpinning for the concept of the business model. We then explain how the business model is distinct from traditional business and corporate strategy, and why it is not all-encompassing – two common misconceptions.

Uber: A Star Is Born

Following the successful sale of his first start-up to eBay in 2007, Garrett Camp, a Canadian tech entrepreneur living in San Francisco, bought himself a luxury sports car. He quickly ran into a problem, however. It was highly inconvenient to drive – and park – his new car in the city. Transportation alternatives, he found, were limited. A long-standing policy capping the number of taxi licenses in San Francisco meant, for instance, that taxi demand in the city almost always ran ahead of supply.[1]

Noting the presence of unmarked sedans, which were common in touristic areas, but had difficulty connecting with customers, Camp started to develop an idea for an on-demand ride service that would work via a smartphone app. An early slide deck shows sleek high-end cars available to book in "1-click."[2] Camp pitched his idea to friends and acquaintances. One of these friends, fellow entrepreneur Travis Kalanick, liked the idea but was not initially convinced he should join the new venture.

In December 2008, Kalanick and Camp were in Paris for a tech conference. One night, after an evening out, they were berated and cursed in French by a cab driver. It was enough to convince Kalanick, who was left infuriated by the incident, to join Camp's new venture. Crucially, he insisted that the company not buy a fleet of cars, as Camp had envisioned, but instead onboard existing drivers. Kalanick would later state, "We don't own cars and we don't hire drivers. . . . I want to push a button and get a ride. That's what it's all about."

In July 2010, the first rider took an "UberCab" in San Francisco. Capturing early enthusiasm, a journalist gave UberCab a glowing review, stating that it "eliminates everything bad about a taxi experience."[3] Uber quickly

---

[1]This section draws on *The Upstarts* by Stone (2017)
[2]Camp (2017); see also Mannes (2017)
[3]Arrington (2010)

began operations in other markets, launching in New York in 2011.[4] User adoption was rapid, among both riders and drivers eager to join the emerging gig economy. In 2012, the company debuted UberX, a more affordable option that could directly target taxis.[5] Taking on such a deep-seated industry was a bold move anywhere, but this was especially true in New York City, where regulations on the city's iconic yellow taxis had created a high barrier to entry for would-be drivers. Through its innovative digital business model, Uber bypassed these regulations altogether.[6]

Its efforts paid off. By 2016, Uber was the world's most valuable startup.[7] In July 2018, the company hit the milestone of 10 billion rides.[8] Few firms ever achieve the level of recognition Uber has managed to attain worldwide. Fewer still manage to achieve it in under ten years. How did the company do it? After all, offering a ride, from point A to point B, was not a fundamentally new idea. The basic elements of soliciting a driver, who picks you up and drives you to your location for a variable fee, all exist whether you take an Uber, book a private chauffeur, or hail a cab.

But Uber somehow managed to connect people with rides in new ways that made the whole process faster, cheaper, and more reliable. And it did so without physically owning cars or hiring drivers, which was unheard of for a company in the transportation industry. Despite the many controversies that have tracked its rapid growth, it's impossible to deny the influence Uber has had in defining the market for personal transportation. By better meeting customer needs, it has reshaped a time-worn industry, even leading taxi companies to improve their notoriously poor service standards.[9]

Simply stated, Uber is a matching platform. Its data-driven digital business model is very efficient, as captured, for example, by the capacity utilization rate, which is 30% higher for UberX drivers than taxi drivers

---

[4] Uber (2011)
[5] Melendez (2014)
[6] Wallsten (2015)
[7] The Economist (2016)
[8] Uber (2018)
[9] Wallsten (2015)

when measured by time, and 50% higher when measured by miles.[10] This can be attributed to several features that undergird Uber's business model: its matching platform technology; scale; inefficient regulations on taxis; and the use of freelance drivers and surge pricing, which help match supply with demand throughout the day.[11]

Uber's business model thus ensures that both riders and drivers do not lose time trying to connect with the other party. Consider a potential Uber rider, whose alternative is attempting to hail a cab on the street. This involves time and effort – and may not even be successful. The Uber business model also reduces payment frictions by making paying significantly easier. A given taxi may be hesitant to accept credit cards (or its card reader could be broken). However you choose to pay for your cab ride, it takes time to collect and process the payment. With Uber, this whole process is made seamless and automatic.

Another feature of Uber's business model is its easy signaling of quality.[12] Unlike taxis, Uber drivers are rated by their riders; these ratings are easily accessible and allow future riders to quickly decide whether to accept a particular driver. The converse applies to passengers, who are rated by drivers. Passengers with a problematic history can be rejected by drivers in advance, avoiding potential issues. With taxis, there is no way of knowing beforehand if a driver is good, or a passenger potentially troublesome.

The efficiency of Uber's business model is compounded by network effects, where value builds as the network (in this case, the number of people who use the Uber app) grows. As it is easy to join Uber – for riders, all you need to do is download the app and enter your credit card information – the network has grown quickly globally. From the perspective of riders, Uber is not bound to their particular "home" region. You can pull out your phone whether you are in Paris or New York City, open the Uber app, and coordinate a ride. As the number of riders increases, more drivers are encouraged to also join, as the size of the opportunity has grown. More

[10]The capacity utilization rate in personal transportation either refers to the fraction of time that drivers have a fare-paying passenger in the car or by the fraction of miles that drivers log in which a passenger is in the car (Cramer and Krueger, 2016).
[11]Cramer and Krueger (2016)
[12]Wallsten (2015)

drivers mean faster pick-up times and higher overall efficiency. This, in turn, encourages more riders to join the service. And so on.

Following Uber's IPO in May 2019, questions remain regarding its long-term wealth creation. But it's impossible to deny that Uber's influence has been transformative. And Uber's value creation story isn't a product or service story – it's largely a business model one.

Michelin: Not Tired of Tire Rental

In 1889, Michelin was founded in Clermont-Ferrand, France, by two brothers, Édouard and André Michelin. The Michelin brothers started off making tires for bicycles, inventing the detachable bike tire in 1891.[13] Quickly, they saw another emerging opportunity. With good foresight, they switched their focus to what was then a sensational novelty – automobiles.

When Michelin was founded, there were fewer than 3,000 cars in the whole of France.[14] Just fifteen years later, in 1904, France was producing an estimated 16,000 cars annually. By 1906, Michelin had grown enough to open its first factory located outside of France.[15] The ensuing explosion in new means of road and air transport provided the company with opportunities to outfit not only cars, but also trains, trucks, buses, planes, and motorcycles, with tires. Today, Michelin is recognized as a leading firm in the global tire business; in 2018, it had full-year revenues of over 22 billion euros.

Throughout the twentieth century, Michelin largely relied on a strong product focus supported by a conventional, manufacturing-based business model. Core activities were designing and manufacturing tires, then selling these to customers via a network of distributors; the distributors also often took care of ongoing servicing. Michelin developed a reputation for the high quality of its products, as well as its product innovations (such as developing the radial tire in 1946)[16] and complementary side businesses including the production of road maps and the prestigious Michelin Guide.

---

[13]Michelin website. Businesses.
[14]Flink (1988, p. 19)
[15]Michelin website. History.
[16]Michelin website. Innovation.

Value creation for Michelin's customers was therefore mostly concentrated in its products (tires) and services (e.g., road guidance).

Despite its long-standing focus on manufacturing, toward the end of the twentieth century Michelin had for some time been aware of the potential of developing an ongoing relationship with its clients, for example, with a few isolated programs providing tire management to select customers. The success of these small-scale endeavors led the company to more formally launch a new business model solution in 2000. Instead of selling a new tire, the company offered certain customers (specifically, transportation companies in Europe) the possibility of renting tires by *buying kilometers*.[17] The truck tires would be entirely managed by Michelin for the duration of the rental period. Customers would be paying for *usage* rather than for the *ownership* of a physical product.

This new offering, Michelin Fleet Solutions, represented an innovative extension of Michelin's hitherto straightforward business model. Notably, it established an ongoing interaction between Michelin and its end customers in a particular market segment. The physical product (tires) remained unchanged, although it was not sold to customers anymore, and Michelin performed the additional activities of tire management and maintenance. This changed key aspects of its activity system, notably its governance (the ***Who*** of the business model), as servicing would previously have been the responsibility of customers. Importantly, Michelin's new business model enhanced value for all parties involved.

First, it enhanced value for customers, going beyond the value created by the stand-alone product. Trucking companies no longer had to worry about handling unforeseen tire-related events on the road, as they could call on Michelin. The transaction costs of coordinating servicing, a complex process requiring specific capabilities, were also significantly reduced. Having Michelin extend its expertise to tire management would help ensure that tire life be prolonged as much as possible. By regrooving and retreading tires, for instance, Michelin can make a single tire last significantly longer, in effect giving it several lives.[18] Optimally serviced tires can have a positive

[17]Renault, Dalsace, and Ulaga (2010)
[18]Michelin. (2015, November 30). The 4 lives of a truck tire [video file]; and Renault, Dalsace and Ulaga (2010)

impact on safety and decrease fuel consumption – major concerns for transportation firms. Beyond the clear cost savings, this also has a broader environmental benefit.[19]

Second, the new business model created the potential for Michelin, the focal firm, to create more value by establishing a closer relationship with its customers. Michelin could thus increase the likelihood of locking them in, instead of switching to buying tires from competitors; it could also more directly market new products to them. In short, Michelin's innovative new business model, of *tires as a service*, enabled value creation *beyond* its high-quality products; the business model in and of itself became a source of value creation.

The next section will briefly review what we know about the business model as a source of value. We will refer to it as a "unit of analysis" for understanding how value is created.[20]

Standing on the Shoulders of Giants: Theoretical Foundations

Early research on business models conducted at the end of the 1990s and during the first decade of the twenty-first century was motivated primarily by the desire to explain the phenomenon of e-business. Scholars, as well as managers and entrepreneurs, were keenly interested in understanding how value was created through new ventures that harnessed digital technologies and operated in virtual markets, a relatively new phenomenon at the time.[21] Received theories of value creation in entrepreneurship and strategy seemed relevant for understanding that phenomenon better, although they were also found to be limited in that each theory only captured part of the story. The various theories also relied on different units of analysis, none of which seemed entirely satisfactory for capturing

[19]Renault, Dalsace, and Ulaga (2010)
[20]A unit of analysis refers to who or what is being analyzed in a study. In management research, typical units of analysis include the firm or business units, groups, or individuals within a firm.
[21]Shapiro and Varian (1999)

precisely how interesting new startups, like Amazon, eBay, Google, or Netflix, were proposing to rewrite the rules of business. With their novel technology-driven, boundary-spanning, customer-centric, and global approaches, these ventures were defying established categorizations. What industry was Amazon in? What business was Google in? Who did the actual work for eBay? What was the essence of Netflix's new method of DVD rentals? In other words, what was the appropriate unit of analysis for looking at this new breed of companies and their new ways of doing business? Since none of the established categories (e.g., industry, firm, business unit, or process) seemed fully satisfactory, a new one was developed: the business model.

One of the earliest definitions states that "a business model depicts the content, structure, and governance of transactions designed so as to create value through the exploitation of business opportunities."[22] The key ideas captured in this definition are that (i) a digitally driven business model reduces transaction costs and enables new transaction architectures or systems; and (ii) these new systems can address customer needs in new or superior ways and therefore create superior value. For example, eBay was the first company to introduce customer-to-customer auctions on a large scale. In this business model, even low-value items can be successfully traded between individual consumers. Priceline.com introduced reverse market auctions, whereby individual buyers indicated their purchase needs and reservation prices to sellers who then submitted their bids for these customers who could choose among the best offers. Autobytel.com revolutionized the automobile-retailing process in the U.S. by linking potential buyers, auto dealers, finance companies, and insurance companies,

---

[22]See Amit and Zott (2001, p. 511). In their definition, "*transaction content* refers to the goods or information that are being exchanged, and to the resources and capabilities that are required to enable the exchange. *Transaction structure* refers to the parties that participate in the exchange and the ways in which these parties are linked. Transaction structure also includes the order in which exchanges take place (i.e., their sequencing), and the adopted exchange mechanism for enabling transactions. . . . Finally, *transaction governance* refers to the ways in which flows of information, resources, and goods are controlled by the relevant parties. It also refers to the legal form of organization, and to the incentives for the participants in transactions."

thus enabling around-the-clock, one-stop car shopping from home. Like the aforementioned Uber and Michelin, these companies all introduced new ways of conducting and aligning commercial transactions. They created value by connecting previously unconnected parties, eliminating inefficiencies in the buying and selling processes, adopting innovative transaction methods, capturing latent consumer needs (such as haggle-free car purchasing from the convenience of your home), and/or by creating entirely new markets (e.g., auctions for low-ticket items). Priceline.com has even been granted a business method patent on its innovative "name your own price" method.[23]

Based on the insight that transactions link activities, and therefore transactions and activities can be viewed as two sides of the same coin,[24] this early transaction-based view of the business model evolved into the activity-based framework that forms the conceptual backbone of this book (see Chapter 1). This evolutionary step provided several advantages.[25] First, managers and entrepreneurs tend to think more naturally in terms of activities than in terms of transactions, so an activity-based framework is easier to learn and apply than a transaction-based one. Second, in the academic literature transactions are often considered in isolation and not as part of a system, as business model thinking requires. Activities, in contrast, are typically associated with a higher-order structure (such as a value chain or network or system), of which they form a part. Third, the notion of a transaction has a rather mechanistic connotation, whereas the notion of activity (at least implicitly) acknowledges the possible involvement of people and thereby invites social considerations.

While advancing the notion of the business model along those dimensions, the shift toward an activity-based perspective on business models preserved the key early ideas of the construct, in particular the idea of a system of activities and the main design elements (content, structure, and

---

[23]In a reverse market, customers post desired prices for sellers' acceptance.

[24]For an analogy, consider graph theory in mathematics with its dual perspectives on nodes and arcs. One can describe a graph either by focusing on its nodes and by listing all the other nodes to which they are linked, or by focusing on the arcs and by describing which nodes pertain to each arc. Both foci are equivalent in that they yield a complete description of the graph.

[25]For more detail, see Zott and Amit (2010).

governance). Consistent with the early research on the theoretical underpinnings of a business model, the activity system perspective is anchored in five received theories of value creation: Schumpeterian innovation, the resource-based view, transaction cost economics, the value chain, and strategic network theory.

Schumpeterian Innovation

Austrian economist Joseph Schumpeter (1883–1950) pioneered the theory of economic development and new value creation through the process of technological change and innovation.[26] He identified several sources of innovation for entrepreneurs, including the introduction of new goods or production methods, the creation of new markets, the discovery of new supply sources, and the reorganization of industries. Schumpeter introduced the idea of "creative destruction," noting that following technological change, rents stemming from risky initiatives in uncertain and complex environments become available to entrepreneurs. These rents (now named *Schumpeterian rents*) later diminish as knowledge diffuses and innovations become established practices in economic life.[27]

According to Schumpeter, the primary source of value creation is innovation, i.e., novel combinations of resources (and the services they provide) as the foundations of new products and production methods. Schumpeter's notion of innovation is relatively broad and extends beyond products and processes as sources of innovation to encompass novelty in factor markets; distribution channels; marketing methods; and, in a stroke of genius, many decades before the introduction of mobile phones and the internet, new ways of utilizing information. In a sense, then, Schumpeter's thinking paved the way for considering the entire business model as a source of innovation and value creation, beyond the products or services sold to customers (which is how most people think about innovation). Schumpeter's theoretical developments urge business model designers to consider how novelty in each and every one of the different dimensions of a business model can enhance the total value created.

---

[26] Schumpeter (1934)
[27] Schumpeter (1942)

Resource-Based View

The resource-based view (RBV) of the firm, which builds on Schumpeter's perspective on value creation, views the firm as a bundle of resources and capabilities. The RBV states that marshalling and uniquely combining a set of complementary and specialized resources and capabilities (which are heterogeneous within an industry, scarce, durable, not easily traded, and difficult to imitate) may lead to value creation.[28] Since it was developed in the 1980s and 1990s, the RBV has been widely applied; it has reached maturation as a theory.[29] Several extensions emerged such as the "demand-side" view to address the fact that the RBV initially focused largely on the supply side.[30] Demand-side scholars point out that demand (which comes from customers) is what makes resources valuable; they also typically make a distinction between value creation, which is determined by consumers' willingness to pay, and value appropriation, which is determined by market structure and resource ownership. Another extension to RBV, the dynamic capabilities approach, explores how valuable resource positions are built and acquired over time.[31] Dynamic capabilities are rooted in a firm's managerial and organizational processes, such as those aimed at coordination, integration, reconfiguration, or transformation.[32] These capabilities enable firms to create and capture Schumpeterian rents.

Traditionally, the RBV takes the firm as the level of analysis, and its resources as the unit of analysis. Resources include physical assets and human capital, as well as managerial and organizational capabilities; they enable activities and the links among them. Resources can therefore be considered the micro-foundations of business models. In particular, *digitally enabled* business models allow firms to tap into new resource-based sources of value creation. For example, instead of owning or controlling resources and capabilities (either through building or acquiring them), accessing such resources through partnering and resource sharing agreements has

[28] Penrose (1959); Wernerfelt (1984); Barney (1991); Peteraf (1993); Amit and Schoemaker (1993)
[29] Barney, Ketchen, and Wright (2011)
[30] Priem (2007); Adner, and Zemsky (2006)
[31] Teece, Pisano, and Shuen (1997); Teece (2009)
[32] Eisenhardt and Martin (2000)

become more prevalent in digitally enabled business model designs. RBV informs such boundary-spanning business model designs by highlighting the importance of resource combinations, in particular of those that exhibit complementarities.

According to RBV, the qualities of resources co-determine the value creation potential of the individual activities that they enable (***What***). The sequence in which they are deployed (***How***), moreover, determines the extent to which potential complementarities among them can be leveraged. At the same time, the RBV suggests that business model designers need to strike a careful balance between value creation and appropriation, which are interdependent: value creation provides the basis for value appropriation, and the prospect of value appropriation is an important incentive for value creation. Therefore before reaching out to partners (***Who***) and inviting them to conduct activities within one's business model to cocreate the offerings, a careful analysis of the simultaneous effects on value creation and appropriation (***Why***) is necessary. In an increasingly digital world, the preservation of value is generally becoming more challenging because rivals may also enjoy easy access to substitute resources. Furthermore, since information-based resources and capabilities have a higher degree of mobility than other types of resources and capabilities, value migration is likely to increase, and the sustainability of newly created value may be reduced.

Transaction Cost Economics

The central question addressed by transaction cost economics (TCE) is why firms internalize transactions that might otherwise be conducted in markets.[33] The main theoretical framework was developed by Oliver E. Williamson, who received the Nobel Prize in Economics in 2009 (together with Elinor Ostrom) for his ideas.[34] Although Williamson refers primarily to transactions (*the* unit of analysis in TCE), his theory applies equally to the analysis of activities. Indeed, TCE has been applied extensively to examine whether it is advantageous to conduct an activity (such as manufacturing a product) in-house, or whether it is better to outsource it to another

[33]Coase (1937)
[34]Williamson (1975, 1979, 1983)

party (the "make-or-buy" choice). Williamson developed TCE prior to the emergence of the internet, in an age characterized by the prevalence of physical goods and services, when transactional inefficiencies were abundant and transaction costs were high.

At its core, transaction cost theory is concerned with explaining the choice of the most efficient governance form (e.g., make or buy) given a transaction that is embedded in a specific economic context. Transaction costs include the costs of planning, adapting, executing, and monitoring task completion. Williamson identified bounded rationality coupled with uncertainty and complexity, asymmetric information, and opportunism in small-numbers situations as conditions under which transactional inefficiencies may arise that vary with the governance mechanism adopted. Transaction cost economics consequently identifies transaction efficiency (and the attenuation of the above factors) as a major source of value, as enhanced efficiency reduces costs. Moreover, reputation, trust, and transactional experience can lower the cost of idiosyncratic exchanges between firms, and investment in information technology can reduce coordination costs and transaction risk.[35]

Most business models today are at least partly digital, and one of the main advantages of digitization is the reduction in transaction costs it engenders. Hence, the transaction cost approach critically informs our understanding of value creation in business models. In addition to decreasing the direct costs of economic transactions and their associated activities, digital business models may also reduce indirect costs, such as the costs of adverse selection, moral hazard, and hold-up. This may result from an increased frequency of transactions (through open standards), a reduction in transaction uncertainty (by providing a wealth of transaction-specific information), and a reduction in asset specificity (the next site is only "one click away"). The small-numbers bargaining problem may be mitigated because previously unconnected parties (e.g., buyers and sellers) can now easily connect and interact electronically, as the previously mentioned example of Uber illustrates.

We note that in the context of business models, the interdependencies and complementarities among activities further enhance the value creation of the system of activities. While TCE focuses on cost minimization

---

[35] Clemons and Row (1992)

by parties in a bilateral transaction (***Who***), the business model includes numerous interdependent stakeholders (i.e., focal firm, suppliers, partners, and customers), and the opportunities for joint value maximization are significant.[36] Furthermore, while the governance modes that are highlighted by TCE, namely hierarchies (make) and markets (buy), are foundational, developments in computing and information technologies have enabled new hybrid forms of governance that are encapsulated by novel business models (***How***). Lastly, while transaction efficiency is an important source of value, there are other forms of value creation that are leveraged by busness models, such as innovation and the reconfiguration of resources (***Why***).[37]

Value Chain Analysis

Michael Porter's value chain framework analyzes value creation at the business unit (BU) level.[38] Value chain analysis includes four steps: (i) defining the strategic BU, (ii) identifying critical activities, (iii) defining products, and (iv) determining the value of distinct activities. The main questions that the value chain framework addresses are as follows: (i) What activities should a firm perform, and how? and (ii) What is the configuration of the firm's activities that would enable it to add value to the product and to compete in its industry? Value chain analysis explores primary activities, which involve the creation of physical products and have a direct impact on value creation, and support activities, which affect value only through their impact on the performance of the primary activities.

Porter defines value as "the amount buyers are willing to pay for what a firm provides them. Value is measured by total revenue . . . A firm is profitable if the value it commands exceeds the costs involved in creating the product."[39] Value can be created by differentiation along every step of the value chain, through activities resulting in products and services that lower buyers' costs or raise buyers' performance (or both). Drivers of product

[36] Zajac and Olsen (1993)
[37] Goshal and Moran (1996)
[38] Porter (1985)
[39] Porter (1985, p. 38)

differentiation, and hence sources of value creation, are policy choices (what activities to perform and how), linkages (within the value chain or with suppliers and channels), timing (of activities), location, sharing of activities among BUs, learning, integration, scale, and institutional factors.[40]

Value chain analysis can be helpful in examining value creation in business models, in particular regarding specific activities. For example, Amazon utilizes logistics activities based on artificial intelligence and autonomous driving technologies in order to increase the speed and reliability of the delivery of products ordered online. By doing so, it aims to increase the value created for customers through order fulfillment activities. However, the value chain model may be more suitable for the analysis of traditional production and manufacturing firms than for service firms or digital businesses where the resulting "chain" (if there is one) does not fully capture the essence of the value creation mechanisms of the firm. For example, in an insurance company, "what is received, what is produced, what is shipped?"[41] Similar questions can be asked about mostly digital business models (such as Amazon's), in which key activities and transactions are anchored in complex information flows.

Concepts such as open innovation, innovation value chain, industry architecture, and value networks came about in response to the limitations embedded in the value chain framework that were revealed by the digital transformation of the business landscape.[42] Much of this body of work has been focusing on the emergence and evolution of structures and dynamics at the network or industry levels.[43] The notion of the business model, in contrast, represents another extension of the value chain idea. The business model concept draws on arguments that are central to the value chain framework, in particular that activities (***What***) and multiple sources of value matter. It extends those arguments in important ways, however: by focusing on total value creation for all stakeholders involved in a business model (***Why***);[44] by emphasizing value creation and delivery dynamics, and

[40]Porter (1985, p. 124–127)
[41]Stabell and Fjeldstad (1998, p. 414)
[42]Chesbrough and Appleyard (2007); Jacobides, Knudsen, and Augier (2006); Normann and Ramirez (1993)
[43]Brusoni, Jacobides, and Prencipe (2009)
[44]Brandenburger and Stuart (1996)

allowing for a non-linear sequencing of interdependent activities (***How***); and lastly by allowing for the possibility that certain key activities in a business model are performed by third parties, rather than by the focal firm (***Who***).

Strategic Network Theory

Strategic networks are "stable interorganizational ties which are strategically important to participating firms. They may take the form of strategic alliances, joint-ventures, long-term buyer-supplier partnerships, and other ties."[45] The main questions that strategic network theorists seek to answer are as follows: (i) Why and how are strategic networks of firms formed? (ii) What is the set of inter-firm relationships that allows firms to compete in the marketplace? (iii) How is value created in networks (for example, through inter-firm asset co-specialization)? and (iv) How do firms' differential positions and relationships in networks affect their performance?

Traditionally, network theorists with a background in sociology or organization theory have focused on the implications of network structure for value creation. The configuration of the network in terms of density and centrality, for example, has been considered an important determinant of network advantages, such as access, timing, and referral benefits.[46] Moreover, the size of the network and the heterogeneity of its ties have been conjectured to have a positive effect on the availability of valuable information to the participants within that network.[47] In addition to enabling access to information, markets, and technologies, strategic networks offer the potential to share risk, generate economies of scale and scope,[48] share knowledge and facilitate learning,[49] and reap the benefits that accrue from interdependent activities. Other sources of value in strategic networks include shortened time to market, enhanced transaction efficiency, reduced asymmetries of information, and improved coordination between the firms involved in an alliance.[50] These network-based advantages, along with

[45]Gulati, Nohria, and Zaheer (2000, p. 203)
[46]Freeman (1979); Burt (1992)
[47]Granovetter (1973)
[48]Katz and Shapiro (1985); Shapiro and Varian (1999)
[49]Anand and Khanna (2000); Dyer and Nobeoka (2000); Dyer and Singh (1998)
[50]Kogut (2000); Gulati, Nohria, and Zaheer (2000)

basic network effects, have spurred the rising popularity of platform-based business models.[51]

A network effect occurs when a technology, product, or service becomes more valuable as the number of people using it increases; value is derived from the "connections that enable communications, content exchange, commerce, cooperation (cocreation), coopetition, and coordination"[52] among users. An example is a social media platform such as Instagram or Facebook, where the chances of connecting with someone you know – which boosts the value you derive from the product – becomes likelier as the user base increases.

The network perspective is clearly relevant for understanding value creation in business models because of the importance of digitally connected firms, suppliers, customers, and other partners. However, it may not fully capture the value-creation potential of innovative business models that enable entirely new possibilities for value creation through the structuring of activities and novel ways to transact. For instance, strategic network theory and the formal tools provided by network analysis only partially explain the value-creation potential of a company such as online marketplace Groupon. Groupon connects businesses with budget-conscious (and often local) consumers (the ***Who***), who buy products or coupons for services (for example, haircuts and exercise classes) that are redeemed later by the customers (the ***How***). Once businesses have signed up for Groupon, they benefit from the exposure of a large and well-advertised site; in turn, Groupon takes a cut of everything sold through its site (the ***Why***). Groupon was at one time the fastest startup to reach a $1 billion valuation.

Business Model: New Unit and Level of Analysis

As we have seen above, different theories focus on different units of analysis to explain how value is created: entrepreneurs (Schumpeterian innovation), resources (RBV), transactions (TCE), activities (value chain analysis), and networks (strategic network theory). The key advantage is that this allows the theorist to capture distinct ways for creating value in business,

---

[51] Cennamo and Santalo (2013)
[52] Afuah (2018, p. 86)

which works especially well in situations in which activities can be cleanly separated, are connected in a primarily linear fashion, involve mainly the flow of physical goods, and are performed by only a few actors within well-defined organizational boundaries. In other words, these perspectives are well-suited for analyzing and understanding value creation in the old offline economy. The key disadvantage, of course, is that each of these theories can only explain a part of the value creation process in a digitally interconnected economy, which calls for a more holistic, systemic, and integrative approach for understanding value creation.

The business model as a new unit of analysis satisfies these requirements. It refers to a system of activities linked through transactions designed and enabled by a focal firm, yet spanning firm and possibly industry boundaries. The business model represents a "purposeful" network of the firm, its suppliers, partners, and customers, who link and deploy their respective resources and capabilities to enable activities that are geared (that is why we call it purposeful) toward the fulfillment of specific customer needs. As such, the business model complements received units of analysis; it does not replace them. It adds a new perspective on value creation in the digital age. Embracing the concept means acknowledging that through the advent of digital and other enabling technologies, such as AI, cloud computing, and Blockchain, new ways of doing business are becoming possible that require new analytical approaches, lenses, and tools (without making established ones obsolete).[53]

The business model can be viewed as a new level of analysis, not just a new unit of analysis.[54] At a given level of analysis, different units of analysis can be examined. For example, at the firm level of analysis, one might be interested in understanding why different firms in the same industry perform differently. To do so, one might zoom in on firm-level capabilities (here, the unit of analysis) as a possible explanation. Alternatively, one might

---

[53]According to Bresnahan and Trajtenberg (1995, p. 84), enabling technologies are those that "open up new opportunities rather than offering complete, final solutions." Examples include the Internet, Blockchain, machine learning, Internet of Things, cloud computing, autonomous cars, or 5G cellular technologies.

[54]A level of analysis depicts "the unit to which the data are assigned for hypothesis testing and statistical analysis" (Rousseau, 1985, p. 4).

be interested in understanding how CEO decisions (a different unit of analysis) influence performance at the firm level. As a general rule of thumb, the level of analysis refers to what we seek to explain (in econometric analyses, this is also referred to as the "dependent" variable), whereas the units of analysis often refer to the factors that might serve as an explanation (in econometric analyses, these are referred to as the "independent" variables).

The business model is the level of analysis, for example, when one tries to understand total value creation through the business model, or seeks to understand the competitive advantage of a particular business model compared to other, rival business models. For example, a relevant question at the business model level of analysis would be: What is the value creation potential of alternative combinations of activities and partners? As a level of analysis, the business model is nested between the firm level and the levels of the network, industry, ecosystem, and the broader environment, as illustrated by Exhibit 2.1. It is centered on a focal firm, yet spans focal firm boundaries by including stakeholders with which the firm interacts when it produces and delivers value. As such, the business model is linked to other levels of analysis, yet it is distinct.

Although we have already explained what a business model is, to develop a really thorough understanding of the concept it is useful to also explain how it relates to, and, more importantly, differs from, other concepts that might be perceived as similar, such as ecosystem or organizational form. You can find this discussion in an online appendix to this chapter (see www.BMIStrategy.com). In addition, it might be useful to explain what a business model is not.

Exhibit 2.1 The Business Model vs. Other Levels of Analysis

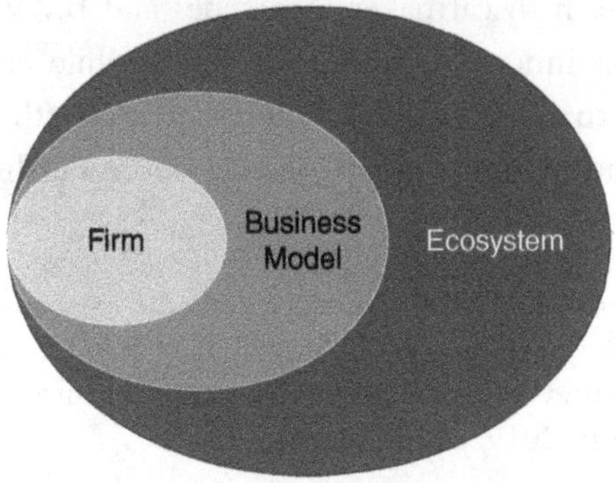

What the Business Model Is Not

In order to further sharpen the concept of the business model, we address in this section two common misperceptions about the business model, namely that the business model is the same as strategy, and that the business model is an all-encompassing aggregation of firm elements.

The Business Model Is Not Traditional Strategy

As noted in Chapter 1, the traditional strategic management literature distinguishes between business strategy issues that relate to the product market positioning of a firm (or its business unit) and corporate strategy issues that relate to the scope of the firm. More specifically, business strategy answers the question of how to position the firm (or business unit) vis-à-vis its competitors and customers in the product market space. Corporate strategy issues answer such questions as in what businesses to be in, or when and how to enter and exit these businesses. The business model complements (but of course does not replace) these classic strategy questions. It adds an important, hereto unanswered, question of "how to do business" in each product market segment in which a firm chooses to compete. (See Exhibit 2.2 for a distinction between business model and product market strategy.)

Firms with innovative or less-innovative business models, respectively, can pursue product market strategies such as cost leadership and/or product differentiation (Porter 1985). Lidl and ALDI, for instance, are two leading budget supermarket chains. Neither has a particularly innovative business model, and they both are pursuing a low-cost strategy. For most of their history, German carmakers Mercedes and BMW have also relied on traditional, non-innovative business models while embracing product market strategies that are based on differentiation (through innovation in technology and design) rather than cost leadership.[55] Conversely,

---

[55]BMW and Mercedes-Benz have joined a wave of experimentation with new business models in the car industry. Traditional manufacturers are consolidating by launching joint ventures to speed the development of autonomous vehicles, for example. See Traugott (2019) and Masters (2019).

Exhibit 2.2 Business Model vs. Product Market Strategy

	Business Model	Product Market Strategy
Definition	Value-centered system of interdependent activities that is designed by a focal firm and is operated by the focal firm and by its partners in order to meet perceived market needs.	Pattern of choices that explains how a firm achieves and maintains competitive advantage through its positioning in product markets.
Main Questions Addressed	How to connect with factor and product markets. ▪ ***What*** activities to perform? ▪ ***How*** to link the activities? ▪ ***Who*** conducts the activities? ▪ ***Why*** should the activities be performed (value creation and appropriation logic)?	What positioning to adopt against rivals. ▪ What kind of generic strategy to adopt (i.e., cost leadership and/or differentiation)? ▪ When to enter the market? ▪ What products to sell? ▪ What customers to serve? ▪ Which geographic markets to address?
Level of Analysis	Business model of the focal firm (which may span its boundaries and include its exchange partners)	Firm

American firms Southwest Airlines and Apple are two companies with innovative business models. They have pursued a low-cost product market strategy and a differentiation product market strategy, respectively.

The design of the business model in terms of the ***Who, How, What,*** and ***Why*** of the activity system thus represents an important new set of strategic decisions a firm has to make in addressing the question of how to do business. We note that competition in the twenty-first century is not just among products and services in the market anymore; it is also among business models of focal firms. Importantly, the design choices that focal firms make with respect to their business models are distinct, but they complement product market positioning decisions (business strategy) and scope choices (corporate strategy). For example, a firm needs to decide what type of product market positioning to adopt, i.e., cost leadership and/or product/service differentiation;[56] or when to enter the market.[57] As well, a firm needs to determine how to do business in its chosen market segment so as to maximize value creation and appropriation. The answers to these questions are central to our understanding of how firms that operate in competitive product markets create and appropriate value.

The Business Model Is Not All-Encompassing

Business models are sometimes seen as something comprehensive, comprised of nearly everything related to the firm. An example of this thinking is exemplified by the Business Model Canvas, a methodology for drawing out and describing the key elements of a firm or new venture on a pre-formulated schema (or "canvas"). It has nine essential building blocks: customer segments, value propositions, channels, customer relationships, revenue streams, key resources, key activities, key partnerships, and cost structure.[58] As we will explain in Chapter 9, this bottom-up approach can be helpful for fleshing out a business model, and moving it toward a business plan and finally toward implementation. However, it does not fully coincide with the more parsimonious and holistic framework introduced in Chapter 1 – the ***What, How, Who,*** and ***Why*** of the firm's activity system. If the business model is conceived as an all-encompassing concept, it becomes difficult to distinguish it from other "big" concepts such as the firm, or its organizational structure.

---

[56] Porter (1985)
[57] Lieberman and Montgomery (1988)
[58] Osterwalder and Pigneur (2010)

Similarly, the business model should not be confused with a business plan. These two concepts are not interchangeable. Unlike a business model, a business plan is a static, forward-looking document that is prepared, for example, by entrepreneurs seeking funding. A good business plan is a snapshot of the future; it discusses people, opportunity, market trends, technology, operations, business model, competitive strategy, marketing strategy, and financials, among other things, as a moving target that is likely to change over time.[59] The new venture's business model is thus depicted in the business plan, and it is distinct from the much broader in scope business plan. For example, the business plan commonly spells out key assumptions, such as projections regarding future sales. The business model, in contrast, is just a description of the activity system that is envisioned.

Summary of Key Takeaways for the Effective Business Model Designer

In this chapter, we have explored the theoretical foundations of the business model concept, situating it against established theories of value creation. We briefly explained these theories, which include Schumpeterian innovation, the resource-based view, transaction cost economics, Porter's value chain analysis, and strategic network theory. Applied alone, any one of these can individually explain certain *aspects* of how a business model creates value, such as through novelty, or increased efficiency. As demonstrated by the example of Uber, however, no one theory can fully explain how digitally enabled, and highly innovative new business models, create value.

This overview confirms the business model as a new and important construct that is well-anchored theoretically. It is separate from other sources of value creation, such as the product(s) and/or service(s) offered by a firm. It can, however, closely complement and enhance the value created by a product, as in the case of Michelin. This is similar to a crucial point made in Chapter 1, namely that the business model is a distinct source

---

[59]Sahlman (1997)

of competitive advantage that goes beyond existing sources of innovation such as product-based innovation.

To further clarify our concept, we identified a few misconceptions to address what a business model is *not*. First, broadly speaking, it is not business or corporate strategy. It would be fair to say, though, that the business model represents an important new dimension of firm strategy that complements the more traditional dimensions of strategy. Second, the business model is not a comprehensive aggregation of elements that comprise every essential aspect of the firm.

References

Adner, R. & Zemsky, P. (2006). A demand-based perspective on sustainable competitive advantage. *Strategic Management Journal,* **27**(3), 215–239.

Afuah, A. (2018). *Business Model Innovation: Concepts, Analysis, and Cases* (2nd ed.). New York, NY: Routledge.

Amit, R. & Schoemaker, P. J. H. (1993). Strategic assets and organizational rent. *Strategic Management Journal,* **14**(1), 33–46.

Amit, R. & Zott, C. (2001). Value creation in e-business. *Strategic Management Journal,* **22**(6–7), 493–520.

Anand, B. N. & Khanna, T. (2000). Do firms learn to create value? The case of alliances. *Strategic Management Journal,* **21**(3), 295–315.

Arrington, M. (2010, August 31). What if Ubercab pulls an Airbnb? Taxi business could (finally) get some disruption. *TechCrunch.* Retrieved from https://techcrunch.com/2010/08/31/what-if-ubercab-pulls-an-airbnb-taxi-business-could-finally-get-some-disruption/

Barney, J. B. (1991). Firm resources and sustained competitive advantage. *Journal of Management,* **17**(1), 99–120.

Barney, J. B., Ketchen, D. J., Jr., & Wright, M. (2011). The future of resource-based theory: Revitalization or decline? *Journal of Management,* **37**(5), 1299–1315.

Brandenburger, A. M. & Stuart, H. W., Jr. (1996). Value-based business strategy. *Journal of Economics & Management Strategy,* **5**(1), 5–24.

Bresnahan, T. F. & Trajtenberg, M. (1995). General purpose technologies 'engines of growth'? *Journal of Econometrics,* **65**(1), 83–108.

Brusoni, S., Jacobides, M. J., & Prencipe, A. (2009). Strategic dynamics in industry architectures and the challenges of knowledge integration. *European Management Review,* **6**(4), 209–216.

Burt, R. S. (1992). *Structural Holes: The Social Structure of Competition.* Cambridge, MA: Harvard University Press.

Camp, G. (2017, August 23). The beginning of Uber. *Medium.* Retrieved from https://medium.com/@gc/the-beginning-of-uber-7fb17e544851

Cennamo, C. & Santalo, J. (2013). Platform competition: Strategic trade-offs in platform markets. *Strategic Management Journal,* **34**(11), 1331–1350.

Chesbrough, H. W. & Appleyard, M. M. (2007). Open innovation and strategy. *California Management Review,* **50**(1), 57–76.

Clemons, E. K. & Row, M. C. (1992). Information technology and industrial cooperation: the changing economics of coordination and ownership. *Journal of Management Information Systems,* **9**(2), 9–28.

Coase, R. H. (1937). The nature of the firm. *Economica, New series* **4**(16), 386–405.

Cramer, J. & Krueger, A. B. (2016). Disruptive change in the taxi business: The case of Uber. NBER working paper 22083, National Bureau of Economic Research, Cambridge, MA. Available at: https://www.nber.org/papers/w22083.pdf

Dyer, J. H. & Nobeoka, K. (2000). Creating and managing a high-performance knowledge-sharing network: The Toyota case. *Strategic Management Journal,* **21**(3), 345–367.

Dyer, J. H. & Singh, H. (1998). The relational view: Cooperative strategy and sources of interorganizational competitive advantage. *Academy of Management Review,* **23**(4), 660–679.

Eisenhardt, K. M. & Martin, J. A. (2000). Dynamic capabilities: What are they? *Strategic Management Journal,* **21**(10–11), 1105–1121.

Flink, J. J. (1988). *The Automobile Age.* Cambridge, MA: The MIT Press.

Freeman, L. C. (1979). Centrality in social networks conceptual clarification. *Social Networks,* **1**(3), 215–239.

Ghoshal, S., & Moran, P. (1996). Bad for practice: A critique of the transaction cost theory. *Academy of Management Review,* **21**(1), 13–47.

Granovetter, M. S. (1973). The strength of weak ties. *American Journal of Sociology,* **78**(6), 1360–1380.

Gulati, R., Nohria, N., & Zaheer, A. (2000). Strategic networks. *Strategic Management Journal,* **21**(3), 203–215.

Jacobides, M. G., Knudsen, T., & Augier, M. (2006). Benefiting from innovation: Value creation, value appropriation and the role of industry architectures. *Research Policy,* **35**(8), 1200–1221.

Katz, M. L. & Shapiro, C. (1985). Network externalities, competition, and compatibility. *American Economic Review,* **75**(3), 424–440.

Kogut, B. (2000). The network as knowledge: Generative rules and the emergence of structure. *Strategic Management Journal,* **21**(3), 405–425.

Lieberman, M. B. & Montgomery, D. B. (1988). First-mover advantages. *Strategic Management Journal,* **9**(S1), 41–58.

Mannes, J. (2017, August 23). Here is Uber's first pitch deck. *TechCrunch.* Retrieved from https://techcrunch.com/gallery/here-is-ubers-first-pitch-deck/slide/8/

Masters, B. (2019, July 1). Self-driving car companies find that going it alone is difficult. *Financial Times.* Retrieved from https://www.ft.com/content/39c01b56-9be5-11e9-9c06-a4640c9feebb

Melendez, S. (2014, January 3). How Uber conquered the world in 2013. *Fast Company.* Retrieved from https://www.fastcompany.com/3024236/how-uber-conquered-the-world-in-2013

Michelin (2015, November 30). The 4 lives of a truck tire. [Video file]. *YouTube.* Retrieved from: https://www.youtube.com/watch?v=Iwi6ZLkV4Sw

Michelin website. Businesses. Retrieved from https://jobs.michelinman.com/eng/get-to-know-us/Key-Information#c-products-and-services

Michelin website. History. Retrieved from https://www.michelin.com/en/michelin-group/about-us/history/

Michelin website. Innovation. Retrieved from https://www.michelin.com/en/innovation/

Normann, R. & Ramirez, R. (1993). Designing interactive strategy. *Harvard Business Review,* **71**(4), 65–77.

Osterwalder, A. & Pigneur, Y. (2010). *Business Model Generation: A Handbook for Visionaries, Game Changers, and Challengers.* Hoboken, NJ: Wiley.

Penrose, E. T. (1959). *The Theory of the Growth of the Firm*. Oxford, UK: Oxford University Press.

Peteraf, M. A. (1993). The cornerstones of competitive advantage: A resource-based view. *Strategic Management Journal*, **14**(3), 179–191.

Porter, M. E. (1985). *The Competitive Advantage: Creating and Sustaining Superior Performance*. New York, NY: Free Press.

Priem, R. L. (2007). A consumer perspective on value creation. *Academy of Management Review*, **32**(1), 219–235.

Renault, C., Dalsace, F., & Ulaga, W. (2010). Michelin Fleet Solutions: From selling tires to selling kilometers. HEC Paris case no. 510-103-1.

Rousseau, D. M. (1985). Issues of level in organizational research: Multi-level and cross-level perspectives. *Research in Organizational Behavior*, **7**, 1–37.

Sahlman, W. A. (1997). How to write a great business plan. *Harvard Business Review*, **75**(4), 98–108.

Schumpeter, J. A. (1934). *The Theory of Economic Development: An Inquiry into Profits, Capital, Credit, Interest, and the Business Cycle*. Cambridge, MA: Harvard University Press.

Schumpeter, J. A. (1942). *Capitalism, Socialism and Democracy*. New York, NY: Harper & Brothers.

Shapiro, C. & Varian, H. R. (1999). *Information Rules: A Strategic Guide to the Network economy*. Cambridge, MA: Harvard Business School Press.

Stabell, C. B. & Fjeldstad, O. D. (1998). Configuring value for competitive advantage: On chains, shops, and networks. *Strategic Management Journal*, **19**(5), 413–437.

Stone, B. (2017). *The Upstarts: How Uber, Airbnb, and the Killer Companies of the New Silicon Valley are Changing the World*. New York, NY: Little, Brown and Company.

Teece, D. J. (2009). *Dynamic capabilities and strategic management: Organizing for Innovation and Growth*. Oxford, UK: Oxford University Press.

Teece, D. J., Pisano, G., & Shuen, A. (1997). Dynamic capabilities and strategic management. *Strategic Management Journal*, **18**(7), 509–533.

The Economist. (2016, September 3). From zero to seventy (billion). *The Economist*. Retrieved from https://www.economist.com/briefing/2016/09/03/from-zero-to-seventy-billion

Traugott, J. (2019, March 1). BMW And Mercedes-Benz join forces on new project. *CarBuzz*. Retrieved from https://carbuzz.com/news/bmw-and-mercedes-benz-join-forces-on-new-project

Uber (2011, May 4). Uber NYC has launched. *Uber Blog*. Retrieved from https://www.uber.com/blog/new-york-city/uber-nyc-launches-service/

Uber (2018, July 24). 10 Billion. *Uber Newsroom*. Retrieved from https://www.uber.com/newsroom/10-billion/

Wallsten, S. (2015). The competitive effects of the sharing economy: How is Uber changing taxis? Technology Policy Institute, Washington, DC. Available at: https://www.ftc.gov/system/files/documents/public_comments/2015/06/01912-96334.pdf

Wernerfelt, B. (1984). A resource-based view of the firm. *Strategic Management Journal,* **5**(2), 171–180.

Williamson, O. E. (1975). *Markets and hierarchies: A study in the internal organizations: Analysis and antitrust implications*. New York, NY: Free Press.

Williamson, O. E. (1979). Transaction-cost economics: The governance of contractual relations. *Journal of Law & Economics,* **22**(2), 233–261.

Williamson, O. E. (1983). Credible commitments: Using hostages to support exchange. *American Economic Review,* **73**(4), 519–540.

Zajac, E. J. & Olsen, C. P. (1993). From transaction cost to transactional value analysis: Implications for the study of interorganizational strategies. *Journal of Management Studies,* **30**(1), 131–145.

Zott, C. & Amit, R. (2010). Business model design: An activity system perspective. *Long Range Planning,* **43**(2–3), 216–226.

3 Adopting a Business Model Mindset – A Prerequisite for Transformative Innovation

Toward a Business Model Mindset

Consider the case of FriCSo, a young Israeli engineering company that had achieved a significant technological breakthrough in the area of friction reduction.[1] Friction is the archenemy of mechanical systems – it reduces the power of machines; leads to overheating; and causes wear, breakdown, and seizure in moving parts. FriCSo's technical invention reduced friction by over 15,000%. Surely such a staggering technology – with clear and wide applicability in industries with products and industrial applications that involve moving parts (such as machine manufacturing, automobile, shipbuilding, etc.) – would be a sure bet for commercial success. Or would it?

[1] Loch, Zott, Guttman, Jokela, and Nahminas (2008)

Once a target industry (say, automobile) had been defined, what kind of company would you have built in order to commercialize the intellectual property? What business model would you have adopted in order to embed the new firm into the existing ecology of original equipment manufacturers (OEMs), and the myriad of tier one, two, and three suppliers to the industry? Would you have chosen to become a machine manufacturer, building machines embedded with the new technology, and selling them to the OEMs? Or, would you rather have built and operated a factory (what the founders of the firm called a "job-shop") that would perform the surface treatment of moving parts for clients who would outsource that step in their commercial production line to you? Alternatively, would you rather have opted for a pure R&D firm that sells its technology (e.g., via licensing agreements) to third parties such as machine manufacturers?

Each of these choices involved a fundamentally different business model. That is, they each implied a different set of activities, as well as different resources and capabilities to perform them – either within the firm, or outside it, through cooperation with partners, suppliers, or customers. Each of these choices also had implications for the performance potential of the venture. They would affect what capital expenditures were necessary, what prices could be charged, what margins would be earned, and, perhaps most importantly, the customers and competitors the new firm would deal with. In other words, the design of the business model was a key decision for the entrepreneurs who created the new firm. It was of fundamental importance to FriCSo. The value that the firm would create, and (of crucial importance from an investor's perspective) the value that could be appropriated upon exit, critically hinged on this choice. The question for FriCSo was not which business model could create incrementally more value. Rather, it was: Which business model would allow them to survive and thrive?

The choice of the business model is also a crucial task for general managers who are charged with rethinking their old business model to prepare their firm for the future. Once the template is set, the activities are in place, and the resources have been developed and honed, that template will be difficult to change, due to forces of inertia (failure to change when change is needed) and resistance to change.[2]

[2]Snihur and Zott (2020)

Now, here comes the catch. Entrepreneurs and general managers often do not pay enough attention to the design of their business model, i.e., the ***What, How, Who,*** and ***Why*** of the activity system. Instead, they focus on more conventional strategic choices, such as what market segments to serve. How and when to enter into the selected markets. How to compete in the firm's selected markets. In fact, the design of the business model is not always viewed as a major strategic choice, as it is taken as a given. In other words, managers accept the received business model templates in their industry without questioning them.

What might explain this oversight? There are several factors. As we have seen in previous chapters, the business model is an activity-system-level construct, and (business) people are simply not used to thinking in terms of activities (rather than products) or organizational systems (rather than functions or business units). Therefore, the business model as a concept is not the first thing that comes to a manager's mind when pondering the future.

Instead, people tend to focus on what they are *cognitively familiar* with (such as product-market strategy choices within well-known and well-established business model templates) simply because it is easier for the human brain to make a connection to it.[3] This can leave them with mental blind spots. Because managers do not pay enough attention to these blind spots, they are not aware that they exist. For example, executives of car manufacturers first reacted to Tesla's new entry into their industry by reflecting on their own product portfolios, and whether they needed to add new hybrid or electric models to it, rather than fundamentally questioning their firms' business models in a more holistic fashion.[4] That is, they kept focusing on the car as a product – a concept with which every manager

---

[3]In psychological research, this well-known phenomenon is captured by the notions "mental models," "cognitive frames," or "schemas." In this chapter, we use these terms interchangeably. Schemas have been defined as "cognitive structures that represent knowledge about a concept or type of stimulus, including its attributes and the relations among attributes"; they refer to "people's theories and concepts of the world" (Fiske and Taylor, 1991, p. 98).

[4]For example, "Tesla was at first underestimated by Ford, where many employees dismissed the new entrant as a minor niche player with an eccentric leader" (Gundling, 2016, p. 13).

in the automobile industry was intimately familiar, which had formed the basis of competition in that industry for a century. At the same time, however, Tesla founder Elon Musk had already adopted a much broader perspective on his firm's innovation strategy, taking Apple as an inspiration for not only promoting distinctive technology and sleek product design, but also imitating and incorporating key aspects of Apple's business model, such as placing its stores in high-end malls instead of relying on dealer franchises.

Failing to question the received business model can be outright dangerous, as the case of Polaroid shows. Anchored on the strong beliefs of the company's founder, Edwin Land, Polaroid managers were so used to making money through selling film (what could be called a "razor/blade business model"), that they had difficulty imagining possible new business models involving digital photography.[5] This was despite the fact that Polaroid was one of the early players in the digital camera business, with the introduction of a digital technology, the PDC-2000 model, in 1996. However, the firm failed to capture a large enough market share in that segment, and in 2001 had to declare bankruptcy.

To avoid a similar fate, and in order to harness the value creation potential of their own business models, managers need to develop and raise their own awareness (along with the awareness of their entire organization) to the importance of business models for value creation. In other words, they need to strategically frame business models as a source of value creation and capture. In particular, when innovation is desired, firm leaders need to ensure that managers or employees who wish to innovate no longer focus solely on their firms' products and services, or on management processes, but also consider creative new ways in which the firm can engage with its stakeholders to conceive, produce, deliver, and consume the firm's products and services. In short, managers and employees need to adopt a business model mindset to acknowledge and leverage the possibility that innovation can happen at the business model level – in addition to innovation at the product/service level.

---

[5] Tripsas and Gavetti (2000); Benner and Tripsas (2012)

What Is a Business Model Mindset?

According to *Merriam-Webster's* dictionary, a mindset is "a mental attitude or inclination," or "a fixed state of mind." It is thus intricately linked with human cognition, that is, the ways in which the human brain processes thoughts, memories, and feelings. Indeed, the mindset as a fixed mental state or attitude is closely linked with the notion of cognitive frames, which are fixed "knowledge structures that help individuals to organize and interpret incoming perceptual interpretation by fitting it into already available cognitive representation from memory."[6] However, a mindset not only determines what cognitive frames people use as interpretive lenses, but also to what kind of perceptual information they apply them. In other words, a mindset determines what we expect to perceive, and what we are prepared to perceive.

This can lead to the development of analytical blind spots. If managers are set on analyzing business problems or opportunities at the product or process level, for example, they will simply not attribute these business problems to the business model, or seek a business model solution to address a business opportunity. In a similar vein, as the case of Polaroid shows, if managers are stuck on a particular business model, they may have a hard time capitalizing on new technologies or emerging customer needs. That is why a business model mindset is needed in organizations. It denotes a state of mind, attitude, or inclination that helps someone consider the firm's entire activity system, along with its associated dimensions of content (***What***), structure (***How***), governance (***Who***), and value logic (***Why***), as a potential solution for a business problem or opportunity. Those with a business model mindset do not just take the business model as a given, nor do they simply focus on more familiar units of analysis, such as the product, or a function of the business such as sales. Instead, they think proactively and holistically about "how to do business." That is, when analyzing business problems and opportunities, they think about their firm's system of activities. (For founders and entrepreneurial managers, problems and opportunities are two sides of the same coin. A problem represents an opportunity

[6]Cornelissen and Werner (2014, p. 187).

to come up with a better solution, and an opportunity is only present when there is a real problem to solve.)

Just as cognitive frames act as lenses for interpretation, notably when people are confronted with novelty, a business model mindset can help managers better understand and react to changes in the business environment. This is especially true when these changes enable or involve the development of new business models, such as those of Uber or Airbnb, and managers are gripped by the fear of being "out-Ubered." Indeed, a business model mindset used as a cognitive frame to confront environmental changes can "have broad and far reaching implications for the ability and willingness to acquire, assimilate and reconfigure knowledge and resources to adapt to [the] changes."[7] These implications range from making better decisions in a change management context to improving one's ability to explain the need for business model-related change to others and thereby enlisting their support.

The good news for leaders of business model change initiatives is that, as an attitude or inclination, a business model mindset can be developed and sharpened. That is, managers can do something about it: they can work to improve their own business model mindset, and that of other team and organization members.

Why Is a Business Model Mindset Needed? Mindset Traps

As the term "mind*set*" implies, once a mind is set on something, it is rather fixed and rarely subject to change; mindsets are sticky and difficult to alter. This is hardly surprising because their raison d'être is to make cognitive processes more efficient by simplifying a complex reality, filtering out noisy information, and facilitating connections with existing knowledge. As a result, discrepant (though possibly important) information gets ignored, data gaps are filled with typical information, and mental models are hardly ever revised. In other words, mindsets tend to be self-fulfilling.[8] As a result, one might fall into one of two mindset traps:

---

[7]Eggers and Park (2018, p. 369)

[8]Gioia (1986) cited in Martins, Rindova and Greenbaum (2015)

1. The trap of focusing on the product, technology, or process as a source of innovation instead of the business model, which requires a more system-level, holistic perspective. In other words, this refers to the risk of getting trapped in the wrong "level of analysis."
2. The trap of taking the business model as a "given" and following a dominant template, such as the prevailing and most familiar business model in an industry (e.g., Citibank in retail banking, McDonald's in fast food, or Starbucks in coffee retailing). In other words, this refers to the risk of being trapped in a specific business model template, and of failing to realize that the business model in and of itself is a variable that can (and perhaps should) be subject to change, too.

Level-of-Analysis Trap

Because of their holistic, system-level nature, business models are often unfamiliar cognitive schemata, and therefore not "easy to see" for everyone. Examining how established companies deal with their respective business model challenges, researchers have found that the managers in these companies regularly pay more attention to individual components of the business model rather than to the business model as a whole.[9] In other words, they do not see the forest for the trees – and fall into the level-of-analysis mindset trap. As a result, they have difficulty "unlearning" the old model and adopting a new one.

Improvements made to their business models are more of an incremental nature, dubbed "local unlearning," which prevents a more fundamental business model overhaul. Focusing on the trees instead of the forest, that is, rejuvenating individual business model components, is practical and understandable from a cognitive point of view, but often leads to overlooking and postponing out-of-the-box exploration. "The attention to and unlearning of business model components not only might fail to trigger attending to the whole business model, but could also hinder such holistic reflection. This highlights the importance of Gestalt cognitive processes, which reveal that recognizing and attending to the whole is different from the processes of attending to the parts and pieces."[10]

---

[9] Mehrizi and Lashkarbolouki (2016)
[10] Mehrizi and Lashkarbolouki (2016, p. 316)

There are three distinct aspects of the level-of-analysis mindset trap:

- Failure to pay attention to fundamental questions and worries about the overall business logic.
- Failure to pay attention to long-term trends in markets and core technologies.
- Failure to think strategically about the business model.

Taken together, this could yield a vicious circle of pinpointing problems at the business model *component* level and taking renewal actions through local enhancements, while failing to address and possibly change the overall business system. Especially when such renewal efforts yield short-term improvements, it might give managers a false sense of security with their old business models.

Take as an example package holiday and vacation tour operator Thomas Cook. The company had a long history stretching back to 1841, when founder Thomas Cook, a British cabinetmaker, organized a train ride for supporters of the Victorian temperance movement who wanted to travel to a meeting held in a nearby town.[11] From there, Thomas Cook's namesake company expanded to leisure travel and grew to become one of the top holiday package operators in the UK and Europe, at some point operating as many as 60 brands. Its core product was package vacations, but it also offered travel components (such as flights) and tailored vacations. As selling package tours required the operator to book capacity (e.g., hotel rooms and flight seats) in advance, Thomas Cook's business model was highly dependent on careful capacity management.[12]

Despite its long history and expertise in the travel industry, by 2010 Thomas Cook faced serious financial pressure, and bankruptcy seemed increasingly likely. In 2011, a year during which multiple profit warnings were issued, the company merged its British retail arm with another firm that also had a large network of travel shops, a move that was criticized

[11]Thomas Cook website. The temperance social movement swept through Britain in the nineteenth century; proponents advocated abstention from alcohol consumption (Collins, 2011).
[12]Esty, Gilson, and Sesia (2014, p. 3–4)

at the time as "bizarre . . . given travel's rapid shift online."[13] A new CEO, Harriet Green, was appointed in 2012 to craft a turnaround. Under Green's leadership, Thomas Cook aggressively undertook a series of crisis measures, centered around cost cutting and maintaining operations,[14] a restructuring that was widely praised.

The success of this restructuring, however, likely helped entrench Thomas Cook's core business model, instead of leading executives to consider a more comprehensive and holistic change. Thomas Cook had "led Brits into the era of cheap Mediterranean package holidays in the sunburnt sixties. Sticking with that formula in the noughties [1990s] – and doubling down on bricks-and-mortar travel agencies – blinded the group to growing digital competition."[15] In 2017, the firm's long-standing core activity of buying spare capacity ahead of time – which allowed it to arrange discounts but was also heavily dependent on customers actually then making those bookings – again showed its fundamental vulnerability, when Thomas Cook needed "to offer margin-eroding discounts when bookings did not go as expected."[16] In 2019, Thomas Cook, mired in debt, abruptly closed shop and declared bankruptcy following the collapse of rescue talks. The sudden shuttering of this once-pioneering firm, which repeatedly failed to innovate its business model in the face of digital disruption, left an estimated half-million holidaymakers stranded at resorts around the world.[17]

Familiarity Trap

Realized business models refer to actual activities embedded in procedures, contracts, relationships, and tacit routines. Cognitive business models are their corresponding collective cognitive representation.[18] Because of their

---

[13] *The Sunday Times* cited in Esty, Gilson, and Sesia (2014, p. 4); see also Provan (2019) for citation on profit warnings.
[14] Esty, Gilson, and Sesia (2014)
[15] Lex (2019)
[16] Eley (2018)
[17] Hancock and Thomas (2019)
[18] Doz and Kosonen (2010)

highly structural nature, realized business models (as well as their cognitive representations) are likely to be inertial, stable, and difficult to change. There may even be a reinforcing relationship between realized and cognitive business models, where the business model structure gets imprinted in firms through two parallel yet interlinked and mutually reinforcing paths (see Exhibit 3.1). The first is the *structural imprinting* path, where managers as business model designers determine and set business model features (***What, How, Who, Why***). The second is the *cognitive imprinting* path, where the managers' business model design practices are passed on to and adopted by others in the firm.[19] Especially in new business ventures, important characteristics of business models are shaped during the sensitive period of early founding. These characteristics can persist for long periods of time despite subsequent environmental changes. Hence, the importance of the founders' mindset is displayed in this early period.

In addition, business models can be difficult to change due to path dependencies, dominant logics, managers' cognitive limitations, and resistance to change.[20] The dominant logic within Polaroid, for example,

Exhibit 3.1 Familiarity Trap through Business Model Imprinting in Organizations

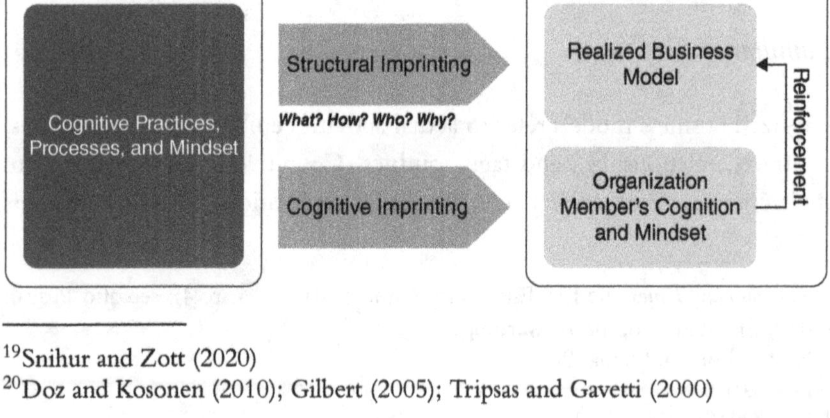

[19]Snihur and Zott (2020)

[20]Doz and Kosonen (2010); Gilbert (2005); Tripsas and Gavetti (2000)

dictated that Polaroid made money on consumables, not hardware (the razor/blade model in instant imaging). This logic created cognitive inertia with corporate executives (although not with the managers directly involved with digital imaging, who developed a more adaptive representation of the emerging competitive landscape). In the early 1990s, these executives discouraged "search and development efforts that were not consistent with the traditional business model." The company did not at that time develop the critical capabilities that would have allowed it to successfully move into digital imaging with an alternative business model, "e.g., as a low-cost/high-quantity hardware producer."[21]

Cognitive Underpinnings of Business Models

Given the importance of mindset for business model design and innovation, business models have a strong cognitive underpinning. Cognition can be defined as the set of processes through which human beings pursue conscious intellectual activities such as thinking, reasoning, or remembering.[22] These processes precede and enable human behavior. Cognition also refers to the content of a person's knowledge, thoughts, and beliefs. This is captured by the expression "knowledge structure," which refers to the structural relationships among the various components of the knowledge stored and processed in our brains.[23] In short, cognition is about what kind of information our brains process and how they do so.

Regarding the relationship between cognition and business models, researchers distinguish between *business models as cognitive structures*, and *cognition as an antecedent to business model design and implementation*, with a particular emphasis of the latter on cognitive processes promoting business model change and innovation.

[21] Tripsas and Gavetti (2000, p. 1158)
[22] See *Merriam-Webster's Dictionary*
[23] Cowan (1990)

Business Models as Cognitive Structures

Business models can be conceived of as mental models that "consist of concepts and relations among them that organize managerial understandings about the design of activities and exchanges that reflect the critical interdependencies and value-creation relations in their firms' exchange networks."[24] These mental models are organized by a logic of value creation that guides the structuring of activities and transactions within the realized business model.

Business models as mental models have been described as design logics that delineate the activity system's architecture in terms of its content, structure, governance, and value logic. These can be characterized via design themes (novelty, lock-in, complementarities, and efficiency).[25] According to this perspective, business models can be viewed as cognitive structures that embody a theory of how to set boundaries to the firm, and of how to create value.[26]

Taken to the extreme, the cognitive perspective suggests that business models are mere models, that is, representations of reality, just like models in science, mathematics, or economics.[27] This school of thought sees the business model as something abstract, a "mental construct that resides in the head of the employees as schemas" (Gassmann et al. 2016). This contrasts with the view that a business model is real, can be observed and described, and has perceivable consequences in the world. While a firm's business model may of course *reflect* the ideas and design aims of managers, it does not exist solely in the intangible sphere of their minds.

Cognition as Antecedent: Cognitive Practices and Processes Underpinning Business Model Design and Innovation

Another perspective on business models and cognition views business models as realized activity systems, but acknowledges their cognitive antecedents.

---

[24]Martins, Rindova, and Greenbaum (2015, p. 105)
[25]These themes will be explained in detail in Chapter 8; see also Zott and Amit (2007, 2010).
[26]Doz and Kosonen (2010, p. 371)
[27]Baden-Fuller and Morgan (2010)

However, some empirical studies on business model emergence tend to portray it simply as a matter of the founders' imagining and implementation. For instance, Walmart founder Sam Walton has been credited with imagining and implementing new practices, such as regarding pricing, pressure on vendors, and technology use, that enabled a new retailing business model.[28] The founder of Xerox, Joe Wilson, has been said to have imagined a new business model anchored on leasing instead of selling expensive copying machines.[29] But what does founders' imagining and implementation of business models, especially novel ones, actually mean? Recent research has begun to address this question and has uncovered a number of cognitive practices involved in this process. (See Exhibit 3.2 for a summary.)

Cognitive Practices

Two cognitive practices stand out that are used by founders of firms with highly innovative business models: *industry-spanning search* and *complex system*

Exhibit 3.2 Business Models and Cognition

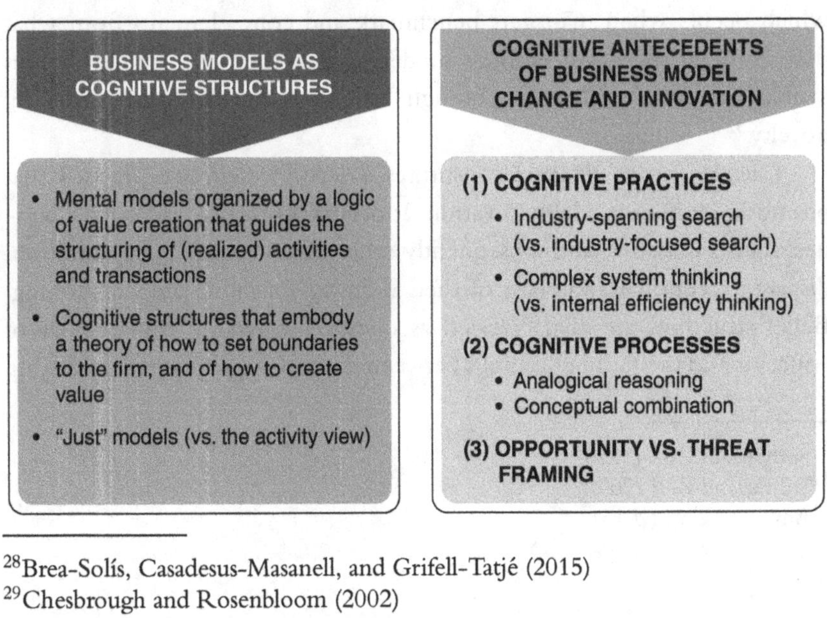

[28] Brea-Solís, Casadesus-Masanell, and Grifell-Tatjé (2015)
[29] Chesbrough and Rosenbloom (2002)

thinking.[30] Together, they could be viewed as constituting elements of a "business model innovation mindset."

Industry-spanning search occurs when managers actively search outside their industry for the stimulus to develop a novel business model. This cognitive practice involves long jumps to search other industries for inspiration to design novel business models. The founders of a venture in the healthcare industry in Spain, for example, realized that the hospital they served lacked a centralized depository for information about patients' medical records that could be accessed by doctors and nurses. To solve this problem, they developed a new business model anchored on a platform to share clinical knowledge around patient-centric healthcare. More specifically, they provided a depository that would connect patients, doctors, hospitals, insurance providers, and other companies. The inspiration for doing so came from Twitter. As one of the founders explained: "During the initial period, I was thinking about Twitter, where you have followers. The more you give, the more you get. It is then that I decided that this company is going to be like Twitter, this is the point of how to engage medical doctors."[31] This illustrates how looking outside your industry and "thinking outside the box" can help generate new business models.

The opposite of industry-spanning search is *industry-focused search,* which occurs when managers benchmark and copy elements from what they consider successful business models within their own industry. This enables improved efficiency through imitation, but without increasing novelty.[32]

Complex system thinking constitutes a second cognitive practice that promotes business model innovation. It occurs when the leaders of a business model initiative, and subsequently other members of the organization, display exceptional awareness of their industry structure and functioning. Belief structures are characterized as complex based on the number of concepts and the number of links between them. Complex system thinking

---

[30] Snihur and Zott (2020)
[31] Snihur and Zott (2020)
[32] Amit and Zott (2015)

manifests itself through deep reflections about the different types of participants in an industry and about their manifold interactions. For instance, in the health industry it is important to understand how value-creating activities are divided between industry actors, what exchanges (of physical goods, information, etc.) take place, and what incentives motivate participants to participate in these exchanges. The complexity of managers' belief structures facilitates appropriate strategic actions due to better information processing.[33] And, systemic thinking promotes a holistic understanding of where novelty lies at the system level, thereby fostering business model innovation.[34]

The opposite of complex system thinking is *internal efficiency thinking*, which manifests itself through a preoccupation with internal issues such as cost control and operational efficiency, as with the Thomas Cook restructuring. This cognitive practice promotes incremental rather than radical innovation (if any at all).[35]

Interestingly, while some of the cognitive practices mentioned above help with the design of new, innovative business models, their successful implementation also hinges on the question of power. Power is defined as unilateral control over resources, which enables key business model decision

---

[33] Nadkarni and Narayanan (2007)

[34] Health systems have many interdependent elements that create a dynamic complexity, whereby "a system response occurs as a result of the interactions among the system's elements rather than the result of a change in one component" (Atun, 2012, p. iv5). More generally, systems theory takes a broad view of systems, with a parallel to the holistic thinking needed for a business model mindset. In one definition, systems thinking has been described as a mindset that "recognizes the interrelatedness of things" and is increasingly relevant in the Big Data era (Vasallo, 2018). According to Donella Meadows, the late systems theorist, environmentalist, and author of *The Limits to Growth* (1972) (see The Donella Meadows Project website), a system is defined as "a set of things – people, cells, molecules, or whatever – interconnected in such a way that they produce their own pattern of behavior over time. The system may be buffeted, constricted, triggered, or driven by outside forces. But the system's response to these forces is characteristic of itself, and that response is seldom simple in the real world" (Meadows, 2015, p. 2).

[35] Gurtner and Reinhardt (2016)

makers "to get things done the way one wants them to be done."[36] High degrees of business model innovation seem particularly likely in cases where, in addition to the presence of industry-spanning search and complex system thinking, one individual (who could be considered the key business model decision maker) has considerable power regarding business model-related decisions.

In contrast, under a power regime that favors organic decentralized decision-making, in which key actors in the venture jointly exercise control in relation to important decisions about business model design, business model innovations are less likely. When several team members (and sometimes even investors and board members) actively participate in business model design decisions, the degree of business model innovation stays low or is even lowered. This is because, in order to reach consensus, radical proposals are filtered out, and often the lowest common denominator prevails.

Cognitive Processes

Building on the idea of a close link between human cognition and business model design, researchers have highlighted two generative cognitive processes – *analogical reasoning* and *conceptual combination* – that can be used to design innovative business models.[37] Each of these processes has a similar sequential structure consisting of the following steps: (i) identification of another business model that serves as a template ("source model") for the business model that needs to be innovated ("target model"); (ii) comparison of the source with the target business model to determine what elements of the source may create value in the target; (iii) integration of the elements from the source into the target business model; and (iv) modification of these elements to fit the target model better.

Analogical reasoning involves the choice of a source model from a domain that serves as an analogy in order to create novelty in another domain

[36]Salancik and Pfeffer (1977, p. 14)
[37]Martins, Rindova, and Greenbaum (2015)

through a comparison at the system level. For example, Tesla chose Apple Computers as an analog "to position its distinctive technology (electric motors) favorably relative to the dominant design technology (internal combustion engines) in the auto industry."[38] Aravind Eye Hospital chose McDonald's as an analog to enable standardization of operational processes, product recognition, accessibility, and scale for cataract eye surgeries to the poor in India.

Specific subprocesses used in analogical reasoning augment the effectiveness of this methodology, and make even imperfect analogies (that possibly result from previously described industry-spanning search) work in the context of business model innovation. Researchers have examined, for example, the use of financial market analogies for the development of online advertising exchanges.[39] Their analysis revealed three distinct types of activities that organizational actors use: stretching, bending, and positioning.

- **Stretching**: Applying an analogy to a new context, even in cases when there are significant differences with the old context or source model (hence the analogy must be "stretched").
- **Bending**: Changing firm activities to better fit the analogy invoked through stretching. This creates better correspondence between the target and source domains. The bending process focuses on changing the context of the analogy rather than the analogy itself.
- **Positioning**: Utilizing stretching and bending as a source of differentiation and to develop a competitive position in the market.

A second cognitive process besides analogical reasoning is *conceptual combination,* which involves comparing one or more source models with a target business model, then focusing on the differences among them to generate ideas for modifying the target model, or for creating an entirely new one. For example, the founder of Starbucks, Howard Schultz, conceptually combined the concepts of specialty coffee retailer (target

[38]Martins, Rindova, and Greenbaum (2015, p. 107)
[39]Glaser, Fiss, and Kennedy (2016)

model), café (source model), office (source model), and gallery (source model) to create the core of the Starbucks business model. In contrast with analogical reasoning, conceptual combination relies less on system-level comparisons and more on comparisons of specific features, while keeping the whole in mind. For example, the important feature of "displaying a unique ambiance" within the Starbucks concept apparently resulted from a conceptual combination of "diversifying merchandise into a wide range of coffee-making and drinking accessories" (from the classic specialty retail store business model), "aestheticizing coffee and the coffee drinking experience" (from the gallery model), "offering possibilities for comfortably sitting down and enjoying freshly brewed coffee" (from the café model), and "providing a work environment for professionals" (from the office model).[40]

Opportunity vs. Threat Framing

How firms deal with business model issues also depends on how these issues are framed and presented internally. When issues are framed as threats, this typically engenders a tendency among individuals, groups, or organizations to behave rigidly, which promotes inertia and thus prevents the adoption of business model innovation. This is due to two effects. First, threats result in the restriction of information processing, narrowing the field of attention and reducing the number of channels used for information processing. Second, power and influence become more concentrated at higher levels of the corporate hierarchy, which reduces both flexibility and variation.[41] By contrast, when issues are cognitively framed and presented to others as opportunities, they are often associated with positive projected outcomes and expectations of gain, which in general

[40]Martins, Rindova, and Greenbaum (2015, p. 111)
[41]Staw, Sandelands, and Dutton (1981)

helps overcome inertia, motivate change, and promote business model innovation.[42]

The effects of threat and opportunity perception on inertia (i.e., failure to change when change is called for), however, are subtler than meets the eye. Two types of inertia can be distinguished: failure to change resource investment patterns ("resource rigidity"), and failure to change organizational processes that use these resources ("routine rigidity"). In a study that examined the reaction of traditional print media to the emergence of digital technologies, it was observed that opportunity framing was necessary, yet insufficient, to trigger an adaptive organizational response to the onslaught of digital media to the traditional newspaper business; such framing alone did not overcome newspaper firms' resource rigidity.[43] Only additional threat framing motivated a forceful response that increased firms' resource commitment to experimenting with and developing new business models. That response, however, was rigid, top-down, and narrow in scope; it involved replicating newspaper content online without developing new sources of revenues. In other words, it fostered routine rigidity. Only when the offices and employees of the new digital corporate ventures were separated physically from the newspaper offices and staff, did the digital initiatives finally take off. The physical separation helped decouple the threat perception prevalent in the parent company from the opportunity perception prevalent in the online initiative. Threat and opportunity framing, meanwhile, coexisted simultaneously at the corporate level, where they were cognitively integrated by members of the top management team.

Thus, both opportunity and threat perception are important cognitive enablers of business model change and innovation, which are also fostered by the involvement of outsiders in the business model change initiative and

---

[42]See Thomas, Clark, and Gioia (1993). Research suggests, furthermore, that managers are more likely to frame a new technology or business model as an opportunity when they have experienced prior success with a similar technology or business model (Martins and Kambil, 1999). Events framed as opportunities often serve as time signals to shift an actor's focus from the past or present to the future (Dutton, 1993).

[43]Gilbert (2005)

the structural differentiation of the initiative from the parent organization. (In Chapter 10, we will talk more about the organizational enablers and barriers to implementing new business models in established firms.)

Ways to Foster a Business Model Mindset

There are also tangible and targeted actions to strengthen business model mindsets. The first category is managerial leadership actions to foster employees' business model mindset. The second category of actions can help foster one's own business model mindset. These two categories of actions are covered in more detail below.

Leadership Actions to Foster Employees' Business Model Mindset

In this chapter, we have argued so far that adopting a business model mindset is crucial for successful business model design and innovation. A business model mindset often involves a shift in mindset from the product to the business model level of analysis. This is not necessarily intuitive for managers and employees (e.g., R&D workers) who have spent much of their working life dealing with product- and technology-related issues.

A mindset shift can be facilitated, however, by clear communication and specific training. Top management needs to send a strong awareness-enhancing message about the importance of the topic. Volkmar Denner, the CEO of German engineering firm Bosch (which in 2018 had sales revenues of 78.5 billion euros and employed 68,700 R&D associates worldwide[44]), for example, has stated, "In the future, we will focus on more than just products. . . . we want to encourage people to turn more of their attention to new types of business models. Product innovations alone won't be enough to ensure our company's continuing success."[45] Top management also needs to endorse targeted training measures, such

[44]Bosch (2019)
[45]Bosch (2011, p. 12)

as awareness-creating workshops that explain and illustrate to managers and employees from the rank and file the underlying concepts (e.g., what is a business model, why is it important, etc.). These workshops can also provide vivid examples of business model innovations from within the firm's own ecosystem or (to promote boundary-spanning search) from completely unrelated industries.

In addition to such immediate and tactical measures, leaders can also take more long-term strategic actions in order to foster and establish a business model mindset among their employees. Three have been identified and described in the literature: employee selection, memorable mentoring, and role modeling.[46]

Employee Selection

Leaders need to develop particular criteria for selection decisions about which employees to hire. These criteria should take into account the candidate's willingness and ability to adopt a business model mindset and engage in business model thinking. Some of these criteria could be about openness and learning, for example. When a new venture has a novel business model, or when an established firm seeks to renew its current one, many things related to the business model still need to be figured out and fine-tuned. Employees should therefore pay attention to these aspects and be open to learning more. Job candidates could be probed, for example, about their recent learning experiences, which could give valuable hints about how they would approach a business model challenge. Such a selection approach, which emphasizes more openness toward business model issues and less expertise with a particular product and/or in a particular industry, could lead to recruitment of individuals with little work experience in the given product-market domain of a focal firm but high long-term potential for valuable contributions to business model development.

---

[46]Snihur and Zott (2020)

Memorable Mentoring

Employees internalize managers' behavioral and thinking patterns through formal and informal interactions in meetings or business trips, during which managers can convey specific business model-related cognitive practices. For example, the founder of a European healthcare startup organized regular future-oriented meetings where everyone was encouraged to share examples from other industries to solve problems related to the startup's business model. Employees were actively encouraged by the founder to think about business model issues by comparing how things were done in different domains such as medicine and software. Many years later, the COO of the firm recalled that, "My first month [in the startup] was eventful, the first meeting was about revolutionizing healthcare, something I expected in Silicon Valley, but not here."[47] The COO's memories about his first month at the startup, almost six years after he had been hired, suggested that his learning through mentorship had become a deep and lasting influence on his thinking; he did not simply execute the founder's orders but had embraced the founder's way of thinking. Another manager from the same firm explained how a memorable business trip to China had enabled him to generate novelty through industry-spanning search.

Role Modeling

A third leadership action that fosters a business model mindset among employees is role modeling, which occurs when leaders display behaviors that employees perceive as exemplary or inspiring. This action is distinct from mentoring, which involves leaders' purposeful (inter)actions to teach employees something specific. In contrast, role modeling is neither necessarily based on direct interaction nor does it necessarily have an explicit teaching purpose. For example, through casual observation employees might perceive their CEO as hard-working, interested in business

[47] Snihur and Zott (2020)

model issues, and always open to what is new. They might learn just by observing the CEO's way of thinking and acting. Role modeling thus enables the assimilation of leader business model-oriented practices by key employees.

Ways to Foster One's Own Business Model Mindset

Managers and employees can, of course, develop their own business model mindset without having to rely on the actions of their superiors or coaches. First and foremost, it is helpful to acquire and enhance knowledge of key business model concepts (such as the ones explained in Chapters 1 and 2). Furthermore, a person's sensitivity to business model issues can be fostered through a set of distinct cognitive actions, such as anticipating, distancing, abstracting, and reframing (see Exhibit 3.3).[48]

- **Anticipating**: Exploring future business model concepts. Anticipating ideally allows a manager to implement business model innovations far enough in advance that the firm can maintain its competitive position. At the same time, managers should not be overreliant on formal strategic foresight tools, which can invite complacency about an inherently unknown future. This is a fine line between thinking enough about future possibilities, and not becoming mentally "stuck" in static (imagined) scenarios.
- **Distancing**: Gaining perspective about the current business model through nurturing an "outside-in" perspective. When engaged in the everyday business of a firm, it can be easy to lose sight of the bigger picture; however, it is important to keep a distance in order to have a holistic view of the business model. This can be achieved by stepping away from this for a certain amount of time, for example through participating in a strategy workshop. Another way to achieve distancing is by leveraging the view of a firm outsider (external hires or outside advisors, for example), or of existing employees who have been working at the "periphery" of the firm and therefore have a broader perspective.

[48] See Doz and Kosonen (2010, p. 371–376)

- **Abstracting**: Restating business models in conceptual terms. Once a manager has been able to step back and achieve distancing, it is easier to think about the business model in abstract and generalizable terms. This can be helpful in identifying and applying elements of an existing business model to a new domain, or vice versa. However, it is also a balance, because being too abstract (and oversimplifying) can lead one to ignore important elements tied to the underlying context of an existing business model.
- **Reframing**: Generating new perspectives and new business model alternatives. Once distancing and abstracting have been achieved, new possibilities or "strategic frames" for the business model can be considered. Firms that have strong communication processes, flexibility, consistency in approaching change, and multiple diverse perspectives can more easily consider and reframe their business model. In firms that lack this flexibility, however, it often takes a crisis before alternatives are considered.

These actions help executives of a firm to be more precise and accurate in their perceptions of the (external) ecosystem and of the (internal as well as boundary-spanning) activity system.[49] They also help organization members develop an increased awareness of, and a keener attention to, the

Exhibit 3.3 Ways of Fostering a Business Model Mindset

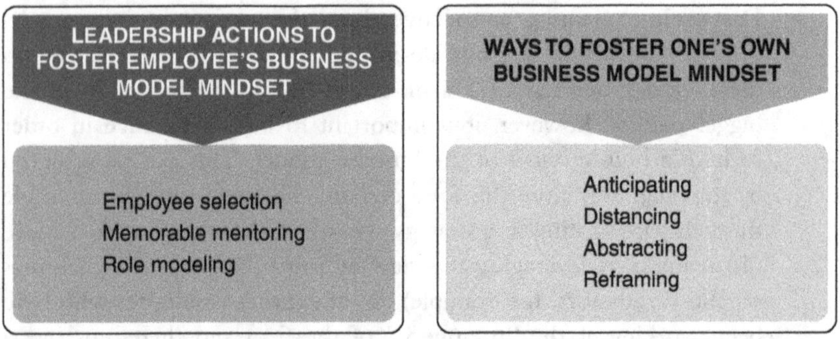

Source: Doz, Y. L, & Kosonen, M. (2010). Embedding strategic agility: A leadership agenda for accelerating business model renewal. *Long Range Planning,* **43**(2–3), 370–382.

[49]See Doz and Kosonen (2010, p. 381)

business model as a key strategic issue. Such attention-enhancing efforts can be further accentuated through consciously considering the *targets* of attention that are closely related to the business model level of analysis, such as the dominant industry logic, or distant business methods.[50]

Summary of Key Takeaways for the Effective Business Model Designer

In this chapter, we examined business models through a cognitive lens: conceiving of business models as mental structures, how to develop a business model mindset, common mental "traps" that impede business model innovation, and the cognitive antecedents of business model innovation.

Because of inertial forces, realized business models (as well as their corresponding cognitive representations), are difficult to change once set in place. For example, managers often accept received business model templates in their industries, without critically considering alternatives, or they simply do not question their firm's existing model. This thinking can endanger the firm's very survival, as illustrated by the case of Polaroid.

We defined a *business model mindset* as a state of mind, attitude, or inclination that helps someone consider the firm's entire activity system as a potential solution for a business problem or opportunity. Such a mindset can help you understand, and prepare for, changes in your industry or business environment, by thinking proactively and holistically about how to do business. Thinking holistically is not easy, and it is not something managers are used to doing. Luckily, business model thinking, particularly as it relates to innovation, can be taught, learned, and developed.

First, it's important to be aware of several mindset traps. The first is getting stuck in the wrong level of analysis, and focusing on product, technology, or process innovation rather than the business model. (It is much easier to focus on improving individual components, rather than the whole activity system.) The second mindset trap happens when you follow the dominant business model template in your industry, forgetting that the business model is something that can, and often should, be (re)designed.

---

[50] Frankenberger and Sauer (2019)

Second, we described two cognitive practices that promote business model innovation: *industry-spanning search* and *complex system thinking*. The first, industry-spanning search, is when managers search outside their industry for inspiration in developing innovative business models. It contrasts with industry-focused search, where existing templates are used (which can boost efficiency, but not novelty). The second cognitive practice that promotes business model innovation is complex system thinking. This is contrasted with internal efficiency thinking, which promotes incremental innovation (or no innovation). These two cognitive practices are more likely to be successfully implemented when one individual has more control over decisions related to the business model.

Third, we described two cognitive processes that are used to generate innovative business models: *analogical reasoning* and *conceptual combination*. These two processes follow a similar sequence, starting with the identification of a business model that will serve as a template, or source model, for the target model. These two models are then compared, and elements that are identified as useful are then integrated into the target business model and modified accordingly. Fourth, cognitive framing is also important. When issues are framed solely as threats, rigidity is promoted; when they are framed as opportunities, they are more likely to ultimately encourage business model innovation.

Lastly, a mindset change can be instigated through targeted training and workshops. Longer-term actions managers can take to develop a business model mindset among their employees include: employee selection (finding employees who exhibit traits that may enable them to develop business model thinking); memorable mentoring (purposeful actions through which managers can transmit business model-related cognitive practices to employees); and role modeling (where employees are inspired to adopt specific mindsets and behaviors from managers). We also discussed strategies to help you foster your own business model mindset. The most important thing to acquire is knowledge of key business model concepts. These can be enhanced by specific actions, such as anticipating, distancing, abstracting, and reframing.

References

Amit, R. & Zott, C. (2015). Crafting business architecture: The antecedents of business model design. *Strategic Entrepreneurship Journal,* **9**(4), 331–350.

Atun, R. (2012). Health systems, systems thinking and innovation. *Health Policy and Planning,* **27**(Suppl. 4), iv4–iv8.

Baden-Fuller, C. & Morgan, M. (2010). Business models as models. *Long Range Planning,* **43**(2–3), 156–171.

Benner, M. & Tripsas, M. (2012). The influence of prior industry affiliation on framing in nascent industries: The evolution of digital cameras. *Strategic Management Journal,* **33**(3), 277–302.

Bosch (2011). Bosch Group anniversary magazine: 125 years of "knowing how, thinking beyond" innovation. Retrieved from http://c-career-bosch-de.resource.bosch.com/media/en/public/de/documents/innovationen/innovation_de.pdf

Bosch (2019, May 5). *Bosch invests billions in climate action and air quality* [Press release]. Retrieved from https://www.bosch-presse.de/pressportal/de/en/bosch-invests-billions-in-climate-action-and-air-quality-188736.html

Brea-Solís, H., Casadesus-Masanell, R., & Grifell-Tatjé, E. (2015). Business model evaluation: Quantifying Walmart's sources of advantage. *Strategic Entrepreneurship Journal,* **9**(1), 12–33.

Chesbrough, H. & Rosenbloom, R. (2002). The role of the business model in capturing value from innovation: Evidence from Xerox Corporation's technology spin-off companies. *Industrial and Corporate Change,* **11**(3), 529–555.

Collins, N. (2011, January 28). The temperance movement. *The Telegraph.* Retrieved from https://www.telegraph.co.uk/foodanddrink/foodanddrinknews/8287027/The-temperance-movement.html

Cornelissen, J. P. & Werner, M. D. (2014). Putting framing in perspective: A review of framing and frame analysis across the management and organizational literature. *Academy of Management Annals,* **8**(1), 181–235.

Cowan, D. A. (1990). Developing a classification structure of organizational problems: An empirical investigation. *Academy of Management Journal,* **33**(2), 366–390.

Doz, Y. L. & Kosonen, M. (2010). Embedding strategic agility: A leadership agenda for accelerating business model renewal. *Long Range Planning,* **43**(2–3), 370–382.

Dutton, J. E. (1993). The making of organizational opportunities: An interpretive pathway to organizational change. In B. M. Staw & L. L. Cummings (Eds.), *Research in Organizational Behavior* (Vol. **15**, pp. 195–226). Greenwich, CT: JAI Press.

Eggers, J. P. & Park, F. P. (2018). Incumbent adaptation to technological change: The past, present, and future of research on heterogeneous incumbent response. *Academy of Management Annals,* **12**(1), 357–389.

Eley, J. (2018, November 30). Thomas Cook faces deeper challenges than hot summer and late bookings. *Financial Times.* Retrieved from https://www.ft.com/content/702e3a48-f48c-11e8-9623-d7f9881e729f

Esty, B. C., Gilson, S. C., & Sesia, A. (2014). Thomas Cook Group on the brink (A). Harvard Business School Case 215-008, August 2014. (Revised March 2016.)

Fiske, S. T. & Taylor, S. E. (1991). *Social Cognition* (2nd ed.). McGraw-Hill Series in Social Psychology. New York, NY: McGraw-Hill.

Frankenberger, K. & Sauer, R. (2019). Cognitive antecedents of business models: Exploring the link between attention and business model design over time. *Long Range Planning,* **52**(3), 283–304.

Gassmann, O., Frankenberger, K., & Sauer, R. (2016). *Exploring the field of business model innovation.* Switzerland: Springer International Publishing AG.

Gilbert, C. G. (2005). Unbundling the structure of inertia: Resource versus routine rigidity. *Academy of Management Journal,* **48**(5), 741–763.

Gioia, D. A. (1986). Conclusion: the state of the art in organizational social cognition. In D. A. Gioia & H. P. Sims, Associates (Eds.), *The Thinking Organization* (pp. 336–357). San Francisco, CA: Jossey-Bass.

Glaser, V. L., Fiss, P. C., & Kennedy, M. T. (2016). Making snowflakes like stocks: Stretching, bending, and positioning to make financial market analogies work in online advertising. *Organization Science,* **27**(4), 801–1064.

Gundling, E. (2016). Disruption in Detroit: Ford, Silicon Valley, and beyond (A). *Berkeley – Haas School of Business Case Series, University of California, July 1, 2016.*

Gurtner, S. & Reinhardt, R. (2016). Ambidextrous idea generation – antecedents and outcomes. *Journal of Product Innovation Management,* **33**(S1), 34–54.

Hancock, A. & Thomas, D. (2019, September 24). 130,000 still stranded as Thomas Cook repatriations continue. *Financial Times.* Retrieved from https://www.ft.com/content/b1bf1cec-dea2-11e9-9743-db5a370481bc

Lex (2019, April 23). Thomas Cook/Fosun: Beached wail. *Financial Times.* Retrieved from https://www.ft.com/content/20f9aac6-6501-11e9-9adc-98bf1d35a056

Loch, C., Zott, C., Guttman, A., Jokela, P., & Nahminas, D. (2008). FriCSo (A): How to translate a new technology into a business (model)? [Case Study.] Fontainebleau, France: INSEAD.

Martins, L. L. & Kambil, A. (1999). Looking back and thinking ahead: Effects of prior success on managers' interpretations of new information technologies. *Academy of Management Journal,* **42**(6), 652–666.

Martins, L. L., Rindova, V. P., & Greenbaum, B. E. (2015). Unlocking the hidden value of concepts: A cognitive approach to business model innovation. *Strategic Entrepreneurship Journal,* **9**(1), 99–117.

Meadows, D. H. (2015). *Thinking in Systems: A Primer.* White River Junction, VT: Chelsea Green Publishing.

Meadows, D. H., Meadows, D. L., Randers, J., & Behrens, W. W. (1972). *The Limits to Growth.* New York, NY: Universe Books.

Mehrizi, M. H. & Lashkarbolouki, M. (2016). Unlearning troubled business models: From realization to marginalization. *Long Range Planning,* **49**(3), 298–323.

Merriam-Webster's Dictionary. Retrieved from https://www.merriam-webster.com

Nadkarni, S. & Narayanan, V. K. (2007). Strategic schemas, strategic flexibility, and firm performance: The moderating role of industry clockspeed. *Strategic Management Journal,* **28**(3), 243–270.

Provan, S. (2019, February 7). Travel agent Thomas Cook weighs sale of airline as losses widen. *Financial Times*. Retrieved from https://www.ft.com/content/518456e6-2a6e-11e9-a5ab-ff8ef2b976c7

Salancik, G. R. & Pfeffer, J. (1977). Who gets power – and how they hold on to it: A strategic-contingency model of power. *Organizational Dynamics*, **5**(3), 3–21.

Snihur, Y. & Zott, C. (2020). The genesis and metamorphosis of novelty imprints: How business model innovation emerges in young ventures. *Academy of Management Journal*, **63**(2), 554–583.

Staw, B. M., Sandelands, L. E., & Dutton, J. E. (1981). Threat rigidity effects in organizational behavior: A multilevel analysis. *Administrative Science Quarterly*, **26**(4), 501–524.

The Donella Meadows Project website. Retrieved from http://donellameadows.org/staff/

Thomas Cook website. Retrieved from https://www.thomascook.com/

Thomas, J. B., Clark, S. M., & Gioia, D. A. (1993). Strategic sensemaking and organizational performance: Linkages among scanning, interpretation, action, and outcomes. *Academy of Management Journal*, **36**(2), 239–270.

Tripsas, M. & Gavetti, G. (2000). Capabilities, cognition, and inertia: Evidence from digital imaging. *Strategic Management Journal*, **21**(10–11), 1147–1161.

Vassallo, S. (2018). *The Way to Design*. San Francisco, CA: Foundation Capital.

Zott, C. & Amit, R. (2007). Business model design and the performance of entrepreneurial firms. *Organization Science*, **18**(2), 165–335.

Zott, C. & Amit, R. (2010). Business model design: An activity system perspective. *Long Range Planning*, **43**(2–3), 216–226.

4 Business Model Innovation – A Fundamentally New Source of Innovation

What Is Business Model Innovation?

Companies often make substantial efforts to innovate their processes and products to achieve revenue growth and to maintain or improve profit margins. Innovations to improve processes and products, however, are often expensive and time-consuming. They require a considerable upfront investment in everything from research and development (R&D) to specialized resources, new plants and equipment, and even the creation of entire new business units. Yet future returns on these investments are uncertain. Hesitant to make such big bets, more and more companies are turning toward business model innovation (BMI) as a lower-cost, lower-risk alternative, or to complement product or process innovation.

A global survey of over 2,000 CEOs by IBM (part of IBM's 19th Global C-Suite study) found that 50% of CEOs interviewed see their existing business model as under threat by competitors who utilize technology to "create more compelling value propositions." Only 18% of these CEOs view their business model as safe from threat.[1] And in another global study, conducted by KPMG, in which 530 executives were interviewed, researchers found that a majority of companies surveyed (58%) "are developing new – or rethinking existing – business models."[2] But what is business model innovation precisely? How does it differ from other forms of innovation, such as technological innovation or product innovation? Does it complement these other forms of innovation, and if so, how? Before formally defining the concept, let us consider an example.

Imagine you are a graduate student and one day, during an intramural rugby game, you break your leg, which requires an emergency operation. While your student health insurance covers some of the costs, there is still a significant co-payment. You have a part-time job to cover your living expenses, but your savings were depleted when you paid your final tuition installment. What do you do? You can try to obtain a personal loan at your local bank. Despite your excellent credit score, this choice comes with a high interest rate, as you are not currently working full-time. Seeking a better option, you can call your grandmother to ask if she would be willing to lend you the $5,000 you owe the hospital. Knowing you are responsible and hard-working, and that you have a job lined up after you graduate in a few months, she agrees to lend you the money.

This interpersonal system of lending is informal, small-scale, and operates in parallel to institutional banking. Up until recently, there have been few other options other than going through a bank or through such an informal system (such as asking a parent or your grandmother) for obtaining a small personal loan with a manageable rate of interest (i.e., excluding predatory lending avenues). This is especially true for freelancers and others without a steady income.

In 2005, however, four individuals – Richard Duvall, James Alexander, David Nicholson, and Giles Andrews – created an alternative. That year,

[1] IBM Institute for Business Value (2018, p. 9)
[2] KPMG (2018, p. 21)

Zopa, the first peer-to-peer online lender, was born in the UK.[3] It took the long-standing idea of an individual, person-to-person loan and scaled it, creating a fintech platform that matched people who needed a loan with favorable terms, especially those poorly served by institutional banking, and people who had money to loan out. Unlike traditional banks, Zopa did not itself lend out money.

Nevertheless, the financial product traded on the Zopa platform looked very much like a standard loan. Zopa loans have to be paid back during a well-defined period, with regular monthly installments and a fixed interest rate payment. Individuals taking out a loan have to pass an online credit score check, and then submit additional documentation to Zopa to prove they can afford the loan. There is therefore no fundamental innovation in the financial product per se. The business model, however, is quite different from the model of traditional banks, which operate through consumer-facing retail branches. With Zopa, everything happens online; it is a BMI.

Individual investors, who want to earn a higher rate of interest on their money than with a traditional savings account, place money that is spread out over several borrowers; as a way to decrease the risk, no single individual borrower is assigned more than 1% of an investor's total amount. Furthermore, investors hold contracts directly with borrowers – not with Zopa.[4]

Zopa, and the peer-to-peer lending industry that quickly followed, saw strong growth. By 2012, Zopa had approximately 700,000 members.[5] In January 2018, Zopa hit the milestone of 3 billion pounds lent.[6] As of 2019, Zopa's target return rates for its investors (i.e., individuals who are lending out money via pooled loans) were 4.5% and 5.2%, respectively, for different kinds of products.[7] By comparison, in June 2018, the average interest rate for a one-year fixed-rate individual savings account in the UK was 1.22%.[8]

---

[3]INSEAD (2012)
[4]Zopa website. FAQs.
[5]Kupp and Anderson (2006)
[6]O'Neill (2018)
[7]Zopa website. Invest.
[8]Beioley (2018)

Business Model Innovation Formally Defined

This section presents our definition of business model innovation. To clarify the definition, an illustration (with two examples, of a startup and an established company, respectively) is provided. In addition, three points are highlighted that illustrate what business model innovation is *not.*

Definition

As stated earlier, *a business model is a boundary-spanning system of interdependent activities that centers on a focal firm, yet may encompass activities performed by its partners, suppliers, and customers in the pursuit of value creation and capture.* The following elements characterize the business model:

i) Its content (***What*** are the activities that encompass the business model?)
ii) Its structure (***How*** are these activities linked, both the sequencing of the activities and the exchange mechanisms among the activities?)
iii) Its governance (***Who*** performs the activities, i.e., which activities are performed by the focal firm, versus those performed by partners, suppliers, or customers?)
iv) Its value logic (***Why*** does the business model create value and ***Why*** does it enhance value appropriation?)

Firms can innovate their business model along any of these dimensions. They can, for example, add or eliminate activities, possibly resulting in new-to-the-industry activity systems (novel content); bring in new partners to perform specific activities (novel governance); link activities in new ways (novel structure); or adopt a new revenue model (novel value logic).

Consider Netflix and the business model innovation it introduced to the movie rental space.[9] At the end of the 1990s, Netflix adopted a business model that differed significantly from the business models of existing movie rental incumbents such as Blockbuster. Netflix partnered with movie studios to rent movies recorded on DVDs, instead of VHS tapes, to customers through its website instead of rental stores. To deliver DVDs, Netflix partnered with the U.S. Postal Service (USPS) to ship DVDs with a pre-paid return envelope to

[9] Ahuja and Novelli (2016)

customers' homes. Netflix thus introduced novel business model content by adding the new activities of burning and shipping DVDs. It also introduced novel business model governance by bringing in USPS as a partner for DVD delivery. Moreover, Netflix introduced a novel structure by allowing customers to order online. Finally, the firm also changed the prevailing value logic in the movie rental industry by adopting a subscription pricing model, which allowed customers to choose and rent three movies at any point in time. As a result of all of these choices, its business model was not just new to the movie rental business in the United States, but new to the world.

This brings us to the question of when to call a business model change "new," "novel," or "innovative."[10] The answer depends on who you ask, because novelty is in the eye of the beholder. For startups, the term *business model innovation often refers to the introduction of a business model that is novel (in terms of its content and/or structure and/or governance and/or value logic) to the product-market space in which the firm competes.* For example, Netflix was presumably the first firm globally that introduced a subscription-based DVD rental model without physical stores; its business model was truly "new to the state of the art."[11] Established firms like Ford or IBM, however, may not have such high hurdles and often label a business model change an innovation when it is simply new to their firm; it does not necessarily have to be new to the world or even to their industry. Therefore, in this book we consider a *business model design of an incumbent firm to be innovative when the firm changes its activity system so that the new system is novel for the firm and possibly also in the product-market spaces in which it competes.*[12]

---

[10]We use these terms interchangeably.

[11]Birkinshaw, Hamel, and Mol (2008, p. 825)

[12]There are other differences between new and established firms regarding business model innovation that are addressed in other chapters of this book. For example, conceiving of a business model innovation might be more challenging for established firms than for new firms because of mindset traps (see Chapter 3). Also, new and established firms face different challenges in implementing business model innovations (see Chapters 10 and 11). For example, established firms need to overcome internal organizational hurdles (i.e., resistance to change), whereas new firms often struggle with their lack of resources and their liability of newness.

Illustrating the Definition

To determine whether a business model is innovative or not, two questions need to be addressed. First, is the activity system novel in any of its key dimensions (***What, How, Who, Why***)? And second, for whom is it novel? In this section, we offer two illustrations, one for a startup (Zopa, introduced above) and another for an incumbent firm (Hilti, a European power tool manufacturer introduced in the first chapter).

Let's first look at Zopa and consider whether (and in what sense) the business model it introduced was novel, keeping in mind the four key dimensions. Its business model was novel in its governance (***Who***); customers perform activities such as lending, previously performed by banks. Zopa enables loans, but without retail banking locations (as would be necessary for a traditional loan), and this entails a change in the activities performed (no retailing). In addition, a credit allocation mechanism allows the risk for investors to be dispersed among several borrowers, a novel transaction mechanism (***How***). In sum, Zopa designed a business model that was new in its product-market space (the relevant criterion for determining the innovativeness of a startup's business model).

Second, let's look at Hilti, a power tool manufacturer based in Lichtenstein. Hilti introduced a business model innovation when it allowed select customers to sign up for what it called fleet management. This entailed renting instead of selling power tools (a new activity and revenue model) and maintaining customers' power tools, an activity previously often performed by the customers themselves. From its own point of view, Hilti's business model change was an innovation. But it was also an innovative approach in the market for large power tool manufacturers.

What Business Model Innovation Is NOT

It is important to highlight the types of changes or innovations that should *not* be considered business model innovation (BMI). Below are three changes that do not constitute BMI: (i) modified activities or exchanges; (ii) product or service innovations; and (iii) corporate venturing.

Business Model Innovation vs. Modified Activity/Exchange

First, modifying an activity by making it faster, cheaper, or higher quality is not a business model innovation. As an illustration, consider the introduction of automated news article writing by local news outlets in the UK. Robot journalism, where an algorithm writes pieces based on templates, has been used by major outlets to write, for example, sports results, which are easy to automatize. To increase their output, local UK news outlets have started to use automated news article writing to produce more stories, relieving the time constraint imposed on their human journalists. Journalists can add to these automatically generated articles, or focus on other aspects of their work, such as conducting more in-person interviews.[13] This has substantially enhanced overall productivity (allowing the publication of more pieces), but has left the business models of the news outlets essentially unchanged. It represents a process innovation, but does not constitute a business model innovation, as virtually no aspect of the overall activity system (with its key dimensions of ***What, How, Who,*** and ***Why***) has been changed substantially.

Another type of change that should not be considered a business model innovation is the modification of an exchange mechanism among activities, such as an upgrade in a firm's communication system, which allows for better coordination among activities. While such a change might improve the performance (e.g., efficiency) of the business model, the basic architecture of the activity system (along with its key aspects of ***What*** activities it is made up of, ***How*** these activities are linked, ***Who*** performs them, and ***Why*** they allow for value creation and capture) is essentially left unchanged. Indian budget hotel chain OYO, for example, was founded in 2013 and can be found today in 80 countries. OYO has adopted a franchising model, which is not novel in the hotel industry. The company franchises existing hotels, helping boost occupancy by deploying technology-driven solutions.[14] It has implemented a number of process innovations, for example, such as instant booking and virtual check-in through a comprehensive guest app. While

---

[13]Nilsson (2019)
[14]Parkin (2019)

these measures have helped OYO land significant investment and expand at an impressive rate, they do not per se constitute business model innovations.

Business Model Innovation vs. Product/Service Innovation

According to one definition, a product "is anything that can be offered to a market to satisfy a want or need, including physical goods, services, experiences, events, persons, places, properties, organizations, information, and ideas."[15] A business model, in contrast, describes ***How*** a product is created through a set of interrelated activities in factor markets and also ***How*** it is offered to customers in the respective product market. One area where this distinction is clear is in plant-based meat alternatives, which have become increasingly popular as consumers become more attuned to the high environmental costs of industrial meat production. Two of the most visible companies in this area are Impossible Foods and Beyond Meat, which are competing on product innovation rather than business model innovation; both companies are racing to create the (highly engineered) plant-based burger that most effectively attains the taste, look, and consistency of beef.[16]

The distinction between product innovation and business model innovation is easiest to see when the product is purely a physical good, and the business model refers to the underlying activities involved in creating the good and putting it in front of the customer. Pharma companies such as Pfizer or Novartis, for example, aim at developing new, innovative drugs that can be used as effective medications by patients all around the world, and they have done so by relying on standard business models anchored on strong in-house R&D. In other words, they aim at product innovation, not business model innovation. However, when some Pharma firms decided to complement (or even replace) in-house product R&D with R&D done by partner firms (such as biotech startups), creating entirely new exchange mechanisms, these firms innovated their business models.

---

[15]Kotler and Keller (2009, p. 358). French economist Jean-Baptiste Say argued that services were distinct from products in that with services production and consumption cannot be separated.
[16]Terazono (2019)

They changed their activity systems by adding or removing activities (the ***What***), adding exchange mechanisms (the ***How***), or adding new partners (the ***Who***), bringing about a change in the entire activity systems. One example is Belgian Pharma company UCB, which has innovated its business model toward a "patient-centric" service model. Some of the changes it implemented included developing free holistic health management tools for patients, and strategically partnering with firms from both within and outside the industry.[17]

The distinction between business model innovation and product innovation, however, can become conceptually more challenging the greater the service component of the product is. Services, like business models, rely on activities, and this tends to blur the distinction between these concepts. Sometimes, a business model innovation may involve a service innovation, and vice versa. Hilti's idea of integrating fleet management activities within its business model, for example, changed the way it served its customers by selling them services (rental and inventory management of power tools) instead of merely products (power tools).

However, business model and service innovation do not always go hand in hand. Consider, for example, the aforementioned peer-to-peer (P2P) lending company Zopa. The venture started with a highly innovative business model, yet the financial service it delivered through that model (namely, issuance of unsecured personal loans) was the same as the comparable financial service delivered by a standard bank. Both entail issuance of a loan granted to an individual without provision of collateral. Just like with a regular bank, this loan had to be paid back during a well-defined period (e.g., five years) through an amortization scheme, with a fixed interest payment due every month.

Conversely, there can be service innovations that do not involve business model innovations. For example, when airline flight attendants sing a happy song after a safe landing, this represents a (certainly incremental) service innovation, but it has nothing to do with the airline's business model. Every airline in the world can introduce this new element to its customer service by training employees accordingly, without making any changes to its underlying business model.

---

[17] Rasmussen and Foss (2014, p. 12–13)

Business model innovation is therefore neither a sufficient nor a necessary condition for product/service innovation, and vice versa. To satisfy their consumption needs, customers are buying products and services, not business models, but the business models (i.e., "how" the products and services are engineered and delivered to the customers) can critically influence the customer experience (as we will see in greater detail in Chapter 8).

Business Model Innovation vs. Corporate Venturing

Business model innovation in established firms is often embedded in corporate venturing initiatives.[18] Corporate venturing refers to business-building initiatives taken in those firms. German engineering giants Bosch and Siemens, for example, are large, well-established multinational conglomerates that not only focus on R&D in technology and engineering, but have also embraced systematic efforts to foster corporate venturing. Bosch has formed an internal incubator, *grow*, an independent company that is part of the Bosch Group. Through this initiative and Bosch employee "intrapreneurs," the company seeks to systematically identify and promote innovations, including business model innovations. Participating startup teams get specific coaching on the business model and startup methodologies, as well as support from the *grow* platform team and (if successful) funding from Bosch. Siemens, through its *Next47* venture capital arm and a separate technology accelerator, aims to identify promising ventures that fit within its ecosystem. Siemens seeks to unlock and augment the value of technology by pairing it with strong (and sometimes highly innovative) business models, based on a proprietary business model pattern database.

---

[18]See Frankenberger and Zott (2018). In contrast, a few companies like Apple or Amazon have managed to embed business model innovation and entrepreneurial initiative into the very DNA of their firms. They therefore do not need to rely exclusively on separate corporate venturing programs. Jeff Bezos, the founder and CEO of Amazon, exemplified this thinking in his 2016 letter to shareholders where he explained that "Day 2 is stasis. Followed by irrelevance. Followed by excruciating, painful decline. Followed by death. And *that* is why [at Amazon] it is *always* Day 1."

However, despite the deep linkages between corporate venturing and business model innovation-oriented activities, these two sets of activities are not completely inseparable. Sometimes corporate venturing is performed in the classic sense, i.e., with a focus on new products, services, processes, or technologies, and without much regard to business model innovation. In practice, with few exceptions such as *grow* or *Next47*, the application of the business model concept within corporate venturing initiatives is often loose.

A Framework for Business Model Innovation

In this section, we present a framework for business model innovation. It is based on the basic business model framework introduced in Chapter 1 and on the definitions given above.[19] Our innovation framework (see Exhibit 4.1) suggests a range of questions that can be helpful for identifying possible levers for business model innovation.

As Exhibit 4.1 suggests, business model innovation can occur in a number of ways, such as:

Exhibit 4.1 Six Questions About Business Model Innovation

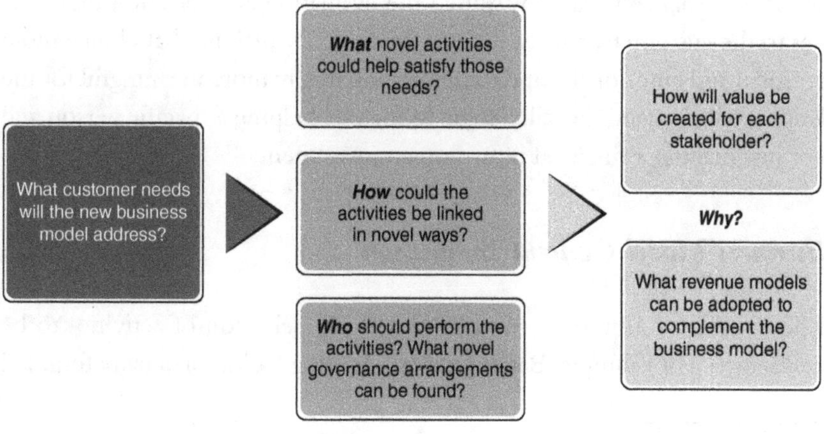

[19]This section draws on Amit and Zott (2012).

i) By adding novel activities. We refer to this form of business model innovation as new activity system content, or content innovation – a change along the ***What*** dimension. This could be through forward or backward integration, for example.[20]
ii) By linking activities in novel ways. We refer to this form of business model innovation as new activity system structure, or structure innovation – a change along the ***How*** dimension.
iii) By changing one or more parties that perform any of the activities. We refer to this form of business model innovation as new activity system governance, or governance innovation – a change along the ***Who*** dimension.
iv) By changing the value logic of the business model, in particular by adopting a novel revenue model. We refer to this form of business model innovation as value logic innovation – a change along the ***Why*** dimension.

Innovations in business model content, structure, governance, and value logic are often highly interdependent. Take the U.S.-based P2P lending company Prosper, for example. The venture, which was founded in 2005 (just like Zopa), aims at enabling direct, small, unsecured loans between individual lenders and borrowers. The founders made the conscious early decision to let lenders choose the borrowers to whom they wanted to lend their money. This was a structural choice (settling the question of how lending and borrowing activities were linked), but it also constituted a decision about governance because it shifted the evaluation and selection of activities to the customers, and away from the firm. By making that choice more personal and emotional – and therefore potentially more meaningful for the lenders – it changed the value logic to include helping a specific person and not just making a financial return on an investment.

Business Model Content Innovation

The content of a business model refers to the selection of activities to be performed. For example, Bancolombia, a leading Colombian bank founded

[20]We note in this context that even if the ***What*** of the business model may change (i.e., what activities are included), the "what" of the customer offering (i.e., what product or service the customer buys) may or may not remain unchanged.

in 1875, began offering microfinance services in 2001.[21] Offering microfinance, or "financial services to households and micro-enterprises that are excluded from traditional commercial banking services,"[22] required adopting activities beyond those of a traditional retail bank. The perceived market need for these activities was the demand for microcredit among the more than 60% of Colombians who did not have access to banking services. To perform these new activities – an innovation in the content of its business model – the bank needed to train its top management, hire and train new staff, and link the new activities to its existing system (platforms, applications, and channels).[23]

Business Model Structure Innovation

The structure of a business model describes how the activities are linked, in other words the sequencing of activities and the exchange mechanisms among the linked activities. To illustrate structure innovation, consider Pokémon GO, an augmented reality smartphone app that was rolled out worldwide in the summer of 2016.[24] When compared to the traditional business model of console and game manufacturers such as Nintendo, which were faced with stagnating growth amid the increasing popularity in smartphones, the business model of Pokémon GO was highly innovative. It linked the virtual world and the real world in ways that were unheard of. Anyone could download the smartphone app and hunt monsters "in real life," with virtual Pokémon characters that could be found in real spaces. Using augmented reality, millions of people started to "chase" Pokémon in public areas. The game turned real locations, like parks and monuments, into Pokémon gyms, where you could defend or attack rival groups with your own team of pocket monsters.

The Pokémon franchise has always been about wandering a virtual world collecting, training, and fighting Pokémon against other players. In the past, all you needed was a console and a screen. With the new business

[21] Berger, Goldmark, and Miller-Sanabria (2006, p. 90) and Grupo Bancolombia website.
[22] Beck (2015)
[23] Banerjea, Kahn, Petit, and White (2006)
[24] See Zott and Amit (2017)

model, however, the only thing that remained the same were the Pokémon characters and universe. Now, Pokémon no longer merely inhabit gaming consoles but a mixed reality created by mobile devices, mapping interfaces, and the physical world. The business model structure was completely innovated.

Business Model Governance Innovation

The governance of a business model refers to who performs the activities. Franchising, for example, represents one (possibly novel) approach to activity system governance, which can be the key to unlocking value. In the early 1970s, the Japanese retail market was defined by the presence of large "general merchandising stores," as well as many small mom-and-pop stores. To protect small independent stores, the Japanese government implemented strict regulations on larger retail outlets, such as limiting their size and opening times.[25] Spotting an opportunity, Japanese businessman Toshifumi Suzuki, an employee of Ito-Yokado, one of the dominant Japanese general merchandising store chains, led an initiative to convert small independent stores to 7-Eleven convenience store franchises (just like OYO is doing today in the hotel business). Because of their smaller size, these franchises did not face the same regulations as larger stores.[26]

By licensing the American 7-Eleven brand and creating a network of franchised stores in Japan, Suzuki was an early adopter of what was then a novel type of activity system governance (new to Japan, but not to the rest of the world) specifically in the area of convenience store retailing. He managed to create value through professional management, supply chain innovation, and local adaptation.[27] Others followed his lead, and there are today around 58,000 convenience stores (which are known as *konbini* in Japanese) in Japan, many of which are open 24/7 and stock a wide variety of items, including fresh bento boxes and other quality food items.[28]

---

[25]Stecker, Martinez-Jerez, Hill, Egawa, and Yamazaki (2009)
[26]Stecker, Martinez-Jerez, Hill, Egawa, and Yamazaki (2009); Han and Lal (2005); Uranaka and Shimizu (2016)
[27]Nagayama and Weill (2004)
[28]Nakamura (2019)

Starting with Toshifumi Suzuki's business model innovation in the 1970s, which introduced a novel governance type in the Japanese convenience store retailing space, the concept has become a retailing phenomenon in Japan.

Business Model Value Logic Innovation

The value logic of a business model explains how the business model helps the focal firm create and capture value. A key aspect is the revenue model, i.e., the specific ways a business model enables revenue generation for the firm and its partners.[29] Just as a pricing strategy complements product design, a revenue model complements the design of a business model's structure, content, and governance.

Consider, for example, Nespresso, a division of Swiss-based Nestlé Corporation, which introduced a low-cost espresso machine that uses custom, Nespresso-produced coffee capsules. After buying an affordable Nespresso machine, a customer needs to use Nespresso's premium coffee capsules, which creates a lock-in effect.[30] By selling consumables to espresso machine owners, Nestlé profits from both the initial sale of the machine and the ongoing use of the machine. This type of revenue model is known as the razor/blade model, after Gillette's model of selling (cheap) razors and (expensive) razor blades.

Another frequent revenue model innovation is the switch from transaction-based to subscription-based pricing (adopted, for example, by streaming video and music providers Netflix, Apple Music, and Spotify), or the switch from one-time sales of expensive products to pay-for-use schemes (e.g., Xerox, which switched from selling machines to charging customers for the number of copies made).

As an illustration for value logic innovation that goes beyond revenue model innovation, consider again Pokémon GO. The new business model created entirely new possibilities for revenue generation. Initially, Pokémon

---

[29] Amit and Zott (2001)

[30] In 2014, antitrust action (in France) removed this obligation. Previously, Nestlé placed a notice on its products that informed consumers they should only use branded Nespresso pods; furthermore, the company did not extend product warranties if customers used non-Nespresso pods. Ferdman (2014); Jolly (2014)

GO's monetization was fairly simple – gamers could buy in-game virtual goods, such as Poké Balls or lure modules to attract and catch Pokémon, which enhanced gameplay. Since then, it has also allowed for sponsored locations. For example, it partnered with Starbucks stores in the U.S. in 2016 to make some coffee shops PokéStops and Gyms.[31] Following its launch in 2016, Pokémon GO has maintained its popularity worldwide, hitting over $2 billion in in-app purchases in September 2018, according to an analyst estimate.[32] It has added new features and increased engagement by organizing events like the Pokémon GO Fests and Community Days, which bring together large groups of players in outdoor spaces such as parks.

Measuring Business Model Innovation

Measures of business model innovation either seek to dimensionalize the degree of novelty of a business model, or the scope of the business model innovation, or both.[33] We distinguish among quantitative and qualitative measures.

Quantitative Measures

Quantitative measures of business model innovation seek to numerically capture the innovativeness of a business model. This is not straightforward, because business model innovation is essentially a qualitative phenomenon. To reduce a business model's innovativeness to a number, researchers have developed various measurement scales.[34] One of these scales was used to assess the innovativeness of young entrepreneurial internet-based firms that

---

[31] Carman (2017) and Pokémon Go website.
[32] Blacker (2018)
[33] See Foss and Saebi (2015, p. 211)
[34] Clauss (2017) proposes several different approaches to capture business model innovation, including multi-item scales, a hierarchical measurement model, and a meta construct. In his paper, he also surveys relevant previous work, including Patzelt et al. (2008), Bock et al. (2012), and Brea-Solís et al. (2015).

went public in the second half of the 1990s.[35] It contains the following items:

Survey Item	Scale*
1. The business model offers new combinations of products, services, and information	SA, A, D, SD
2. The business model brings together new participants	SA, A, D, SD
3. Incentives offered to participants in transactions are novel	SA, A, D, SD
4. The business model gives access to an unprecedented variety and number of participants and/or goods	SA, A, D, SD
5. The business model links participants to transactions in novel ways	SA, A, D, SD
6. The richness (i.e., quality and depth) of some of the links between participants is novel	SA, A, D, SD
7. Number of patents that the focal firm has been awarded for aspects of its business model	0, 1–2, 3–4, >4
8. Extent to which the business model relies on trade secrets and/or copyrights	R, S, B, N
9. Does the focal firm claim to be a pioneer with its business model?	Y, N
10. The focal firm has continuously introduced innovations in its business model	SA, A, D, SD
11. There are competing business models with the potential to leapfrog the firm's business model	SA, A, D, SD
12. There are other important aspects of the business model that make it novel	SA, A, D, SD
13. Overall, the company's business model is novel	SA, A, D, SD

* SA – Strongly Agree (coded as 1), A – Agree (0.75), D – Disagree (0.25), SD – Strongly Disagree (0); Y – Yes (1), N – No (0); R – Radically (1), S – Substantially (0.66), B – a bit (0.33), N – not at all (0); 0 (0), 1–2 (0.33), 3–4 (0.66), >4 (1)

These survey questions can be applied to company-specific documents, which are easier to obtain if the company is already public, or in the process of going public, in which case the IPO prospectus can be analyzed. As a

[35] Zott and Amit (2007)

first step, the answers to the questions can be written up in a text format. Analysts can then apply the respective scale (e.g., "strongly agree" that "the business model brings together new participants"), exercising their judgment based on their in-depth understanding and knowledge of the focal firm's business model. The scales are subsequently transformed and coded into standardized scores (e.g., 1 for "strongly agree"). Following that step, all the individual item scores are aggregated into an overall score for the composite scale using specific (e.g., equal) weights. This process yields a distinct quantitative measure of the extent to which a business model is innovative.[36] Due to the nature of the questions, and the scales applied to assess them, the measure captures both the degree of novelty of the business model and the scope of the business model innovation.

Qualitative Measures

Qualitative measures of business model innovation are in line with the qualitative nature of the phenomenon. As such, they are often involved as an early step in the process of establishing quantitative measures. However, qualitative measures are not straightforward to obtain either, because they require a sound understanding and thorough analysis of a firm's business model. This often involves time-consuming and cumbersome data collection from multiple sources, such as: (i) interviews with top executives, founders, employees, investors, board members, and customers; follow-up emails; and phone calls with these parties to clarify questions;

---

[36]The internal consistency and reliability of the measure has been validated using standard econometric procedures, such as the calculation of Cronbach alpha coefficient and partial least squares analysis (for details, see Zott and Amit, 2007). It should be noted that this specific scale has been developed to measure the degree of business model innovation of a particular type of firm – young, internet-enabled firms on the verge of going public in the United States and Europe. For other types of firms, the items will likely have to be adapted. For example, Frankenberger and Zott (2018) use a subset of the items to measure the novelty of business model initiatives in established firms. Their four-item scale captures (i) the extent to which the resulting business model design offers new combinations of products, services, and information; (ii) the extent to which it brings together new participants; (iii) the extent to which it links existing participants in novel ways; and (iv) the extent to which the novel business model design is considered to be a pioneer in its industry.

(ii) on-premises real-time observation of board meetings and key firm activities; (iii) firm documents such as detailed business plans, investment memoranda, or minutes of board meetings; and (iv) archival data, including firms' websites, press coverage, blogs, and video excerpts.[37]

The collected data can be analyzed to establish the degree and/or scope of business model innovation by examining and assessing the various key dimensions of a firm's business model: content (i.e., new activities that are performed within the business model), governance (i.e., which new participants are in charge of what activity), structure (i.e., new links among activities), and value logic (e.g., new revenue model). For example, firms that innovate all four elements simultaneously exhibit a broad scope of business model innovation, and those that do so compared to their industry peers exhibit a high degree of novelty.

Illustrating the Upside of Business Model Innovation

The basic premise of business model innovation is that it can increase value creation and/or value capture for the focal firm, and thus enhance firm performance. To illustrate this upside, consider the cases of Apple and HTC. For most of its history, Apple had been focused on the production of innovative hardware and software, mostly personal computers. By creating the iPod and the associated music download business of iTunes, its legal online music download service, Apple introduced an innovation of its business model. Apple was the first computer company to include music distribution as an activity, linking it to the development of the iPod hardware and software. By adding this new activity to its business model, which links the music label owners with end users, Apple transformed music distribution by enabling users to legally download single songs. Rather than growing by simply bringing innovative new hardware to the market, Apple transformed its business model to encompass an ongoing relationship with its customers (similar to the razor/blade model of companies such as Gillette), enabling Apple, and its business model partners, to extract ongoing value from the use of the Apple hardware and software. In this way, Apple expanded the

---

[37]For an application of this method, see Snihur and Zott (2020).

locus of its innovation from the product space to the business model space. Exhibits 4.2 and 4.3 illustrate, respectively, the revenue, profit, and stock price change at Apple Inc. after the introduction of its business model innovations (e.g., iPod/iTunes, iPhone/App Store).

Exhibit 4.2 Apple Revenues and Net Income (Before/After Business Model Change)

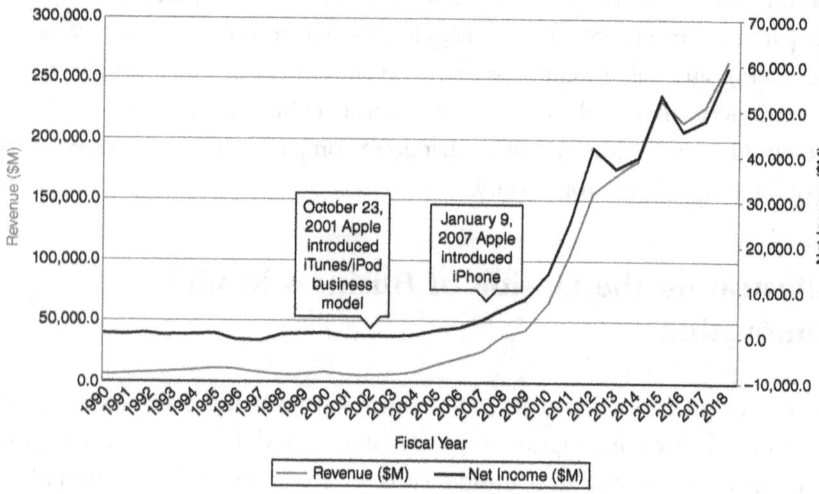

Exhibit 4.3 Apple Stock Price (Before/After Business Model Change)

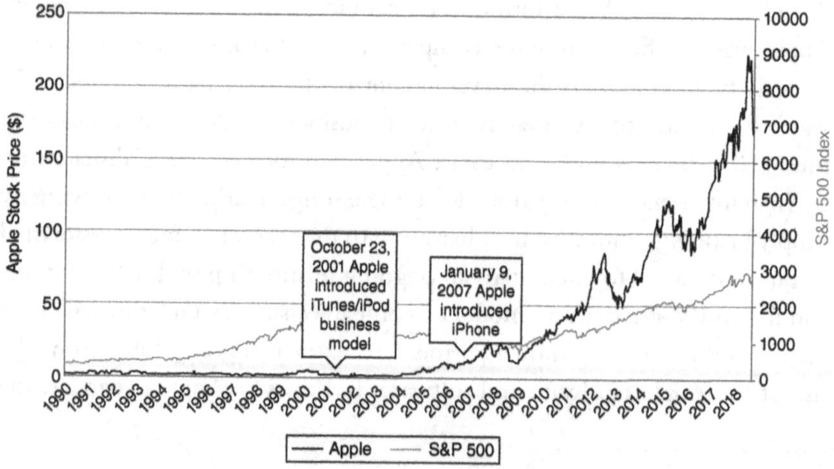

By contrast, even some otherwise high-performing companies can struggle if they rely solely on product innovation. Since it was founded in 1997, Taiwanese company HTC has been an innovative original equipment manufacturer (OEM). Initially, HTC manufactured handsets for Microsoft-powered mobile phones for companies such as Palm, HP, and T-Mobile. In 2006, it changed its product-market strategy from being a contract OEM manufacturer to selling its own HTC-branded smartphones to wireless network operators and the general public through various distribution channels. HTC excelled in many ways, recording several firsts in the smartphone product-market space and winning numerous awards for its technological innovations. Yet HTC struggled as its business model remained centered on hardware design and product innovation. In 2018, it had the weakest sales in its history as a public company. HTC sells great razors, but no razor blades: its business model allows it to only benefit from the sale of its innovative, state-of-the-art smartphones, 5G home hubs, and VIVE virtual reality headsets – but not their use.

The relatively poor financial performance of HTC stock in the past few years (see Exhibit 4.4) highlights the fact that in the fast-moving technology marketspace, product innovation that is not coupled with business model innovation may not be enough to compete. In contrast to Apple, HTC has not been involved in the creation or delivery of mobile content

Exhibit 4.4 Stock Price of HTC vs. Apple

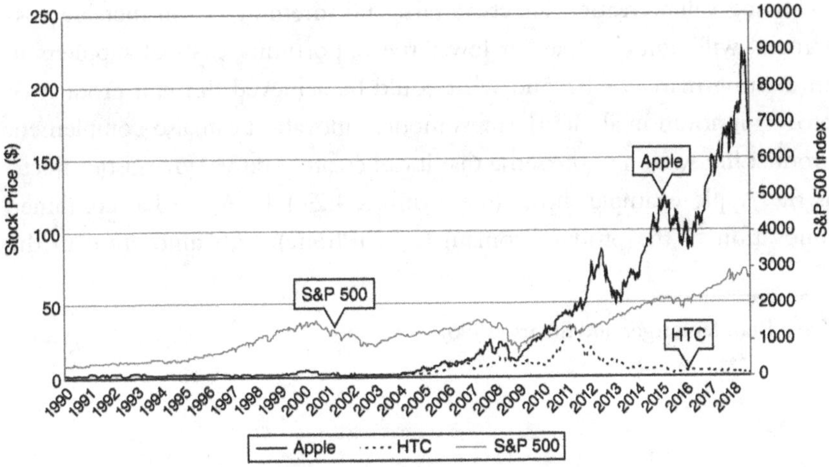

or services, and its devices function on third-party operating systems (i.e., Google and Microsoft), generating revenues for HTC only from the hardware sales. Apple, on the other hand, benefits from economies of scope due to the interoperability of its software base (iOS, iTunes, App Store, iCloud) for its various products, such as computers (MacBooks and iMacs), tablets (iPads), and phones (iPhones). In addition, Apple benefits from the direct ownership of the distribution channels (online App Store, offline Apple retail stores). Furthermore, Apple's business model enables it to derive revenue from the App Store sales of third-party applications and iTunes songs, and from AT&T for the use of its iPhone for voice and data.

Pros of Business Model Innovation

Business model innovation entails several distinct benefits for the innovating focal firm. First, it complements other forms of innovation. Second, it does not usually require large upfront investment (e.g., into developing technological expertise and capabilities). Third, it can serve as an effective barrier to imitation. Finally, business model innovation can be a disruptive force in an industry. We will elaborate on each of these advantages next.

Value Creation Beyond Process or Product Innovation

As a source of innovation, business model innovation can have any of the following value creation effects.[38] First and foremost, it can increase customers' willingness to pay, or lower the opportunity costs of suppliers in an existing market – beyond what could be achieved through product or process innovation alone. Business model innovation can also complement product innovation in the sense that it can create positive synergistic effects, as the Apple example shows (see Exhibits 4.2–4.4). Apple has combined innovation in the product domain (e.g., iPhone) with innovation in the

[38] See Brandenburger and Stuart (1996)

business model domain (e.g., App Store). In this case, one form of innovation enhances the value created by the other. The value created through the introduction of new hardware is enhanced by the value of exciting new content that can be played on the device, and vice versa.[39] Business model innovation can thus help companies stay ahead in the product innovation game and mitigate the product innovator's problem that "you're always one innovation away from getting wiped out by a new competing innovation that eliminates the need for your product."[40] A good product that is embedded in an innovative business model is less easily shunted aside. Someone might come up with a better smartphone than Apple's tomorrow, but few of the hundreds of millions with iPhones and App Store accounts will be open to switching brands.

What is more, business model innovation can create an entirely new market or allow a firm to create and exploit new opportunities in existing markets. Dell, for example, implemented a customer-driven build-to-order business model, which replaced the traditional build-to-stock model of selling computers through retail stores.[41] This represented an enormous value creation opportunity in an existing market. Or consider the firm Taco Bell, the restaurant chain offering Mexican-style fast food. In the late 1980s, Taco Bell decided to turn restaurant kitchens into heating and assembly units. Most chopping, cooking, and clean-up activities were transferred to corporate headquarters. The food was sent pre-cooked in plastic bags to restaurants, where it could be quickly heated, assembled, and served.[42] This incremental business model innovation (a change in the ***What***, as new activities were added, and in the ***Who***, as the governance structure changed) was not game-changing for the fast food industry, but it allowed Taco Bell to realize economies of scale and improvements in efficiency and quality control, as well as increase space for customers within the restaurants.[43]

---

[39] Zott and Amit (2008)
[40] The Economist Intelligence Unit (2005)
[41] Brynjolfsson and Hitt (2004, p. 27-48)
[42] See Applegate, Schlesinger, and Delong (2001)
[43] Santos, Spector, and Van Der Heyden (2009)

Low Capital Expenditure

Resource configurations in the digital economy have enabled the creation of a broad range of asset-light business model innovations, such as eBay, Priceline, and more recently the Airbnb, Uber, and DiDi platforms in the so-called sharing economy. Digitization has substantially expanded the scope of resources a firm can utilize in conceptualizing and implementing a novel business model, thereby reducing capital expenditures (or CapEx for short). To illustrate, consider again Netflix's movie streaming business. Rather than spending its own capital to build and operate server farms, cloud computing technology enables Netflix to utilize the physical infrastructure of cloud computing services (e.g., from Amazon's AWS) to store movies and enable streaming. The digitization of businesses thus allows entrepreneurs and managers alike to reimagine the boundaries of their resource configurations with minimal CapEx, thereby enhancing the value creation potential of resources.[44] Specifically, the novelty of a digitally powered low-CapEx resource configuration may come from several sources:

1. The newness of the needs to be met, as illustrated by the business model of Open Table, the digital restaurant reservation system that enables instant online restaurant reservations and enhanced utilization of dining capacity. Digitization in and of itself created the new need for online restaurant reservations. It also created the resources to be more effectively utilized, as illustrated by the business model of Instacart, an online grocery shopping platform. The founders of Instacart identified the unmet need of working urban residents to save time on grocery shopping, as well as the underutilized time and labor of other urban residents (e.g., those who are unemployed).
2. The innovative ways through which the matching of resources and needs is enabled and more efficiently and effectively managed. This is illustrated by the low-CapEx business models of Airbnb and Uber. Digitization enables Airbnb to reach underutilized, privately owned hospitality capacity, and Uber to utilize privately owned vehicles for providing taxi-like services.
3. The uniqueness of the complementarity among all value co-creators that the focal firm bridges and involves in the value-creation process.

[44] Amit and Han (2017)

Value is created for all co-creators when new value co-creators with distinct yet complementary resources and needs are added into the configuration. This enhances the overall complementarity of the resource configuration. American company Square, which provides mobile payments processing, point-of-care solutions, and other financial services to small businesses, has been experimenting with connecting its retail store clients to other value co-creators that have not had effective connections with retail stores. This process is known as grafting, whereby a focal firm experiments with new combinations of hereto unconnected (or less connected) resources and needs. For Square, such value co-creators include, but are not limited to, financial service providers (e.g., credit report services), business service providers (e.g., tax services), and logistics service providers (e.g., on-demand delivery services). The objective of grafting is to identify unique complementarities between resources and needs, and enhance the value creation of the resource configuration.

Effective Barriers to Imitation

Due to interdependencies among activities, competitors might find it more difficult to imitate and/or replicate an entire novel activity system than a single novel activity, product, or process. Interdependencies exist when activities, taken together, have a different impact on an objective function (e.g., performance) than each of the activities considered in isolation. Interdependencies are created by entrepreneurs or managers in several ways: when they choose the set of organizational activities they consider relevant to satisfying a perceived market need; when they design the links that weave activities together into a system; and when they shape the governance mechanisms that hold the system together.

Research on imitation suggests three factors that facilitate imitation: identification of what to imitate, ability to imitate, and motivation to imitate.[45] Business model innovations present effective barriers to imitation when they lower competitors' identification, ability, and motivation to imitate. Competitors can *identify* new elements of a business model design

[45]Chen (1996)

sometimes only by examining publicly available information on corporate websites, in media descriptions, or by learning about it directly from the focal firm's customers and suppliers (and sometimes even employees).

Competitors' *ability* to imitate a business model innovation will depend on the particular features underlying the innovation design, their ability to recognize and understand all activities and their interdependencies, the accompanying necessary contractual arrangements, and their own resources and capabilities and existing contractual arrangements. Finally, competitors' *motivation* to imitate the business model innovation will depend on a number of factors, such as the additional profit potential, the degree of innovation legitimacy, compatibility with the existing business model, and the degree of organizational inertia and resistance to change.

Industry Disruption

Business model innovation can also entail industry disruption, which is typically understood as a process in which established incumbents (e.g., U.S. incumbent steel firms such as now defunct Bethlehem Steel) focus on improving their offering to the most demanding customers, and new entrants (e.g., mini-mills processing low-grade steel from industrial waste) target overlooked segments, often at a lower price and with less sophisticated products and/or technology. Over time, the entrant gradually improves its offering, and more and more mainstream customers switch to the entrant away from the incumbent; in other words, disruption occurs. This hypothesis is also known as the Theory of Disruptive Innovation.[46]

An increasing number of leading business thinkers argue that today we live in an age of disruption that re-orders how organizations and ecosystems operate. An IBM (2018) report that summarizes interviews with CEOs

---

[46]Christensen (1997, 2006); Christensen, Raynor, and McDonald (2015). According to Clayton Christensen's website, "Disruptive Innovation describes a process by which a product or service initially takes root in simple applications at the bottom of a market—typically by being less expensive and more accessible—and then relentlessly moves upmarket, eventually displacing established competitors."

states that, "CEOs today recognize the criticality of disruption . . . . They've grown accustomed to the barrage of sudden change and have factored that reality into their day-to-day operations and strategies." Furthermore, "a growing number are embracing radically new models. Instead of going it alone, they're innovating with partners on new business platforms in new ecosystems."[47]

Indeed, while the theory of disruptive innovation was originally formulated with product or technological innovations in mind, it also applies to business model innovations. In his elaboration of the theory, the late Harvard Professor Clayton M. Christensen pointed out that the term "disruptive innovation" refers to the disruption of existing incumbents through new business models rather than through new technologies alone.[48] As Christensen emphasizes, "it was a business model problem. I made a mistake when I labeled the phenomenon as a disruptive technology; the disruptive business model in which the technology is deployed paralyzes the incumbent leader . . . [disruption often] is a business model problem, not a technology problem."[49]

Examples such as low-cost airlines fit the idea of a disruption based on innovations in the business models rather than in new technologies or new products.[50] Southwest Airlines introduced the low-cost model in aviation, trimming down on services and focusing on a few key routes. In a similar vein, the business model of Netflix became highly disruptive to the video rental ecosystem when customer adoption rapidly picked up. Customers were attracted because they did not have to spend time going to a video rental store or pay additional fees if they forgot to return a video in time. They could devise wish lists and consult movie reviews on the Netflix website, at the same time providing Netflix with useful information about their tastes. Its business model innovation generated a different value proposition to customers, delivered with a different configuration of activities from the way Blockbuster and other video rental stores functioned. If Netflix

---

[47] IBM Institute for Business Value survey (2018, p. 1)
[48] Christensen (2006, p. 49)
[49] Christensen (2006, p. 43 and 48)
[50] Markides (2006)

had failed to attract a significant number of customers, its partners (DVD manufacturers, USPS, movie studios) would probably have ended their collaboration, and the disruption might not have occurred.

The business model as a potential source of disruption also implies that new entrants can immediately target the most profitable, mainstream market segments rather than focusing only on less profitable niche segments, as Christensen's original theory would suggest. In the case of Netflix, mainstream customers were dissatisfied with late return fees and the limited selection of movies in video rental stores that only carried blockbusters. These customers switched to Netflix for reasons beyond the low price of its offering. Thus, in contrast to the theory's original focus on slow and gradual disruption from the low-end to mainstream customers, business model innovation that immediately attracts mainstream customers could happen relatively quickly, when increasing numbers of customers start adopting the new model, especially in a digital age that favors quick diffusion of online content and promotes strong network effects. De novo firms, as well as existing firms from other industries, might be tempted by the lure of rapidly attracting numerous mainstream customers, and launch business model innovations. Thus, disruptors can be both small de novo firms as well as large established firms from other industries; this is another extension of Christensen's original theory.

Conversely, for the disrupted firm, failure to adapt the business model can entail serious negative performance consequences. As mentioned in Chapter 3, Polaroid's managers never updated the firm's analog razor/blade business model (making money on the consumables, not the hardware) despite having developed an excellent technological understanding of digital imaging.

Illustrating the Downsides of Business Model Innovation

Business model innovation, like all other forms of innovation, also has its downsides – challenges, costs, and risks. Chief among these is the risk of business failure. In 2013, Israeli entrepreneur Shai Agassi's Better Place, a de novo entrant in the automobile space that attempted to introduce a new business model for electric cars, declared bankruptcy. The company, which was founded in 2007, had raised nearly $1 billion and was once touted as a leader among Green Tech startups. Its spectacular demise can be seen as a case study in business model innovation gone wrong. The founder had envisioned providing heavily subsidized electric cars, with users paying a variable monthly fee to have their electric car batteries quickly swapped out at a network of automated stations – eliminating the need to wait for a battery to charge. Agassi saw Better Place as providing a path to widespread adoption of electric cars, by reducing "range anxiety" and increasing the affordability of electric cars. He compared its business model to that of wireless phone carriers, which subsidize an expensive phone when users sign up for a multiyear phone contract. While Better Place set laudable – and lofty – goals, these goals ultimately did not match up to the reality of building its business model.[51]

First, Better Place massively underestimated the cost of building its electric car fleet and charging network. Second, customers did not enthusiastically embrace the offering. To sustain its risky, scale-dependent revenue model, Better Place would have needed a rapid, widespread rate of user adoption. Before ending operations, Better Place had sold under 1,500 cars. It was forced to declare bankruptcy within only a year of opening its charging network to its first Israeli clients.[52]

Another fatal flaw of the Better Place business model was that it had proven difficult to convince essential business model value co-creators about the legitimacy of the new business model. This might have been one of the factors that contributed to the company's failure to generate enough demand. Renault was the sole supplier of electric cars to Better Place, but when the startup failed to deliver high-volume sales, Renault left the partnership. Breaking the implicit industry norm of high-volume production precipitated the bankruptcy of Better Place the following year. Another problem was the difficulty of persuading other car manufacturers, who were alienated by Agassi's approach and overly optimistic projections, to partner

---

[51] Chafkin (2014); Woody (2013) and Gunther (2013)
[52] Woody (2013); Chafkin (2014)

with the company. Better Place had simply assumed that car manufacturers would produce cars that could work with its battery system.[53]

Cons of Business Model Innovation

Besides the general risks that any innovation carries (e.g., insufficient customer adoption, small market size, lack of feasibility, liability of newness, costs of organizational change, and other implementation risks), business model innovation involves a number of specific challenges inherent in its systemic and holistic nature.

Lack of Protection from Imitation by Competitors

Business model innovations are hard to protect legally. Although business method patents exist in the U.S. (but not in Europe), they are difficult to enforce. With the exception of natural monopolies such as social networks (in 2019, Facebook had a market share of 67%), most markets addressed by business model innovators present low barriers to entry. As pointed out by *The Economist*, "If Uber really is worth $100bn, after investing only $15bn or so, why wouldn't its rivals keep trying their luck, or an established tech giant be tempted in?"[54] The risk of imitation by competitors increases: (i) the more attractive the business model innovation is in terms of its market potential; (ii) the more legitimate the innovation is in the eyes of customers, regulators, and other ecosystem players; and (iii) the more loosely coupled the underlying activity system is.[55]

For example, greater legitimacy makes the business model innovator a more serious threat to existing incumbents and increases their incentive to retaliate early in the competitive process. Incumbents can retaliate in many ways, such as imitating the new business model, engaging in

[53] Gunther (2013)

[54] The Economist (2019)

[55] According to Rivkin (2000), a loosely coupled system is more responsive to change, but also more prone to imitation from competitors.

a price war, or lobbying regulators.[56] In 2004, for example, incumbent Blockbuster (unsuccessfully) imitated Netflix's BMI by launching its own line of online DVD rentals. In the market for shaving products, two large incumbents – Unilever and Edgewell Personal Care – have made business model moves by acquiring disruptive subscription-based startups (Dollar Shave Club and Harry's, respectively).[57]

Generally speaking, the incentives for incumbents to imitate the new entrant increase under conditions of uncertainty: the greater the uncertainty, the more incumbents will engage in social comparisons with other firms in all aspects of their business, which in turn increases the likelihood of imitation.[58] Imitation is therefore a major concern for managers operating under uncertainty, which is often characteristic of markets in which disruptive business model innovation occurs.

Legitimacy Risk

To gain support from customers and other stakeholders, a company introducing business model innovation needs high legitimacy, as stakeholders usually expect socially acceptable designs.[59] If the innovator is an existing company – for instance, Apple when it introduced the iPod/iTunes business model – the company might be recognized by customers and other ecosystem participants as legitimate on the basis of its previous achievements. When the innovator is a new venture like Uber or Better Place, however, the legitimacy challenge will be more acute, due to the combined novelty of its business model, the young firm's liability of newness, and (possibly, as in Uber's case) the lack of acceptance of the new business model by parts of society.[60]

Consider once again the example of Netflix. Before it became profitable and successful, Netflix struggled to convince customers and other participants in its business model about the legitimacy of the business

---

[56] Ahuja and Novelli (2016); Casadesus-Masanell and Zhu (2013)
[57] Georgiadis and McCormick (2019)
[58] DiMaggio and Powell (1983)
[59] Aldrich and Fiol (1994); Suchman (1995)
[60] Stinchcombe (1965)

model innovation. The general public was not accustomed to renting videos online, and there were no norms, rules, or precedents for letting customers choose movies, pay online, and receive DVDs through the mail. It was also difficult for Netflix to convince other partners, such as DVD manufacturers or movie studios, to participate in its business model innovation, presumably because "there was no proven financial model for a subscription-based online entertainment rental company . . . no one had ever done it."[61] It took Netflix several years to negotiate revenue-sharing agreements with movie studios. The studio response was summarized in one representative's quote: "I don't understand that concept – this is not how people get VHS tapes."[62] Netflix's legitimacy issues were compounded by the unprecedented number and variety of participants in its business model innovation, e.g., customers, DVD manufacturers, movie studios, and the USPS.

Risk of Increased Complexity

As previously emphasized, the business model is a system of interdependent activities, some of which are carried out by partners. The robustness and stability of such an activity system depends in part on the sustained alignment of incentives among all partners (stakeholders). As the competitive landscape evolves and/or as technologies evolve, new opportunities for business model innovation emerge. This may in turn lead to a focal firm adding activities to its business model that are carried out by new partners. The greater the number of partners in the business model of a focal firm, the greater the number of interdependencies that need to be managed. In turn, this increases the complexity of the system, which may adversely affect its stability and viability. As the bargaining power of partners may change over time with the evolution of technologies and consumer preferences, incentives among the partners can diverge. This raises the risk of collapse due to unmet incentive compatibility constraints.

---

[61] Keating (2012, p. 80)
[62] Keating (2012, p. 38)

The complexity of a business model, and hence the risk to its viability, is also increased through new and more complex exchange mechanisms among existing partners. In other words, changes to the architecture of linkages among existing partners may also adversely affect the viability of a business model. For example, a bidding exchange mechanism is more vulnerable to failure than a fixed-price exchange mechanism. The complexity of the value capture mechanism, which is depicted by the focal firm's revenue model, may also adversely affect the robustness of the business model, and hence its viability.

Risk of Path Dependency

A new business model can create new path dependencies and thereby sow the seeds of future inertia, especially if it involves the introduction of a tightly coupled activity system, which is more prone to inertia and may be harder to change than a loosely coupled one. As we have seen in Chapter 3, making changes to a company's whole activity system, rather than optimizing individual activities such as production, requires systemic and holistic thinking, which can be demanding. When responding to a crisis, operating in tough economic times, or taking advantage of a new opportunity, rethinking an entire business model may not always be the first thing on a manager's mind. This is particularly true when the level of internal resistance to change is high. As a result, choices on business model design often go unchallenged for a long time.

Summary of Key Takeaways for the Effective Business Model Designer

Companies are increasingly turning toward business model innovation as an alternative or a complement to product and process innovation, which can be expensive and risky. A firm can innovate any of the four key dimensions of its business model.

First, it can add or eliminate activities (novel content, or content innovation) – a change in the ***What*** dimension of its business model.

Second, it can bring in new partners to perform specific activities (novel governance, or governance innovation) – a change in the ***Who*** dimension of its business model.

Third, it can link activities in new ways (novel structure, or structure innovation) – a change in the ***How*** dimension of its business model.

Fourth, it can adopt a new revenue model (novel value logic, or value logic innovation) – a change in the ***Why*** dimension of its business model. Innovations in one or more of these four dimensions are often highly interdependent.

The meaning of business model innovation may differ across firms, for example, in startups versus larger incumbent firms. For a startup's business model to be considered innovative, it should be novel in the firm's product market space. For an incumbent's new business model to be innovative, it should be novel at the very least for the firm (and possibly also in its product-market space). When existing activities or exchanges are simply modified, this does not change the overall activity system and is therefore not considered as business model innovation. Business model innovation should also be carefully distinguished from product or service innovation. Finally, business model innovation can be embedded in corporate venturing, even though some corporate venturing programs are more focused on business model innovation than others.

The basic premise of business model innovation is that it can increase value creation and/or value capture for the focal firm, and thus enhance firm performance. Business model innovation entails several distinct benefits for the innovating focal firm. First, it complements other types of innovation. Second, a novel business model (for example, a digitally-powered business model) can be cost-effective. Third, business model innovation can serve as an effective barrier to imitation. Finally, business model innovation can create a new market or allow a company to uncover new opportunities in existing ones. In some cases, it can lead to industry-wide disruption.

Business model innovation also has downsides, some of which are due to its systemic and holistic nature. The greatest risk is that the business will fail. A second key risk is the lack of protection from imitation by incumbents.

Companies introducing business model innovations also need high legitimacy, which may be harder for new ventures to achieve. The robustness and stability of the business model is furthermore partially dependent on the sustained alignment of incentives among all stakeholders. As the complexity of a business model increases, so does the risk to its viability. Another risk to a new business model is the possibility that path dependencies become entrenched.

To conceive of possible business model innovations, we suggest that entrepreneurial leaders and managers ask themselves the following six key questions:

- What perceived customer needs can be satisfied through the new model design?
- What novel activities are needed to satisfy these perceived needs?
- How could the required activities be linked to each other in novel ways?
- Who should perform each of the activities that are part of the business model (e.g., the focal firm or a partner), and what novel governance arrangements could enable this structure?
- How can value be created in novel ways through the business model for each of the participants?
- What novel revenue model fits with the firm's business model to appropriate part of the total value it helps create?

Addressing these six questions can help managers see their firms' business models more clearly, in the context of the networks and ecosystems in which they operate. Without a business model perspective, a firm is a mere participant in a dizzying array of networks and passive entanglements. Adopting the business model perspective can help managers purposefully structure the activity systems of their firm in the context of other firms and economic agents in their ecosystems. This purposeful design and structuring of business models, which encompasses internal as well as boundary-spanning activities, are key tasks for general managers and entrepreneurs and can be an important source of innovation, helping the company look beyond its traditional sets of partners, competitors, and customers. Most importantly, perhaps, this approach encourages systemic and holistic thinking when considering innovation instead of concentrating on isolated, individual choices. The message to managers is the following: when you innovate, look at the forest, not the trees – and get the overall design of your activity system right before optimizing the details.

References

Ahuja, G. & Novelli, E. (2016). Incumbent responses to an entrant with a new business model: Resource co-deployment and resource re-deployment strategies. *Advances in Strategic Management* **35**, 125–153.

Aldrich, H. E. & Fiol, C. M. (1994). Fools rush in? The institutional context of industry creation. *The Academy of Management Review* **19**(4), 645–670.

Amit, R. & Han, X. (2017). Value creation through novel resource configuration in a digitally enabled world. *Strategic Entrepreneurship Journal* **11**(3), 228–242.

Amit, R. & Zott, C. (2001). Value creation in e-business. *Strategic Management Journal* **22**(6-7), 493–520.

Amit, R. & Zott, C. (2012). Creating value through business model innovation. *MIT Sloan Management Review* **53**(3), 41–49.

Applegate, L. M., Schlesinger, L. A. & Delong, D. (1998). Taco Bell, Inc.–1983–94. HBS No. 398-129. Harvard Business Publishing.

Banerjea, S., Kahn, R., Petit, C. & White, J. (2006). *Dare to Be Different: Why Banking Innovation Matters Now*. Somers, NY: IBM Global Services.

Beck, T. (2015). Microfinance: A critical literature survey. IEG working paper 102284, 2015/No.4, World Bank Group, Washington, D.C. Retrieved from: http://documents.worldbank.org/curated/en/588931467993754857/Microfinance-a-critical-literature-survey

Beioley, K. (2018, August 31). Popularity of Isas drops to 18-year UK low. *Financial Times*. Retrieved from https://www.ft.com/content/d2f1c806-ad0c-11e8-89a1-e5de165fa619

Berger, M., Goldmark, L. & Miller-Sanabria, T. (Eds.) (2006). *An Inside View of Latin American Microfinance.* Washington, DC: Inter-American Development Bank.

Birkinshaw, J., Hamel, G. & Mol, M. J. (2008). Management innovation. *Academy of Management Review* **33**(4), 825–845.

Blacker, A. (2018, September 25). Pokémon GO catches $2 billion since launch. *Apptopia.* Retrieved from https://blog.apptopia.com/pok%C3%A9mon-go-catches-2-billion-since-launch

Brandenburger, A. M. & Stuart, H.W., Jr. (1996). Value-based business strategy. *Journal of Economics & Management Strategy* **59**(1), 5–24.

Brynjolfsson, E. & Hitt, L. (2005). Intangible assets and the economic impact of computers. In Dutton, W. et al. (Eds.), *Transforming Enterprise* (pp. 27–48). Cambridge, MA: MIT Press.

Carman, A. (2017, June 1). Niantic earns up to 50 cents per visit to sponsored Pokémon Go stops. *The Verge.* Retrieved from https://www.theverge.com/2017/6/1/15724196/niantic-pokemon-go-sponsorship-app

Casadesus-Masanell, R. & Zhu, F. (2013). Business model innovation and competitive imitation: The case of sponsor-based business models. *Strategic Management Journal* **34**(4), 464–482.

Chafkin, M. (2014, July 4). A broken place: The spectacular failure of the startup that was going to change the world. *Fast Company.* Retrieved from https://www.fastcompany.com/3028159/a-broken-place-better-place

Chen, M. J. (1996). Competitor analysis and interfirm rivalry: Toward a theoretical integration. *The Academy of Management Review* **21**(1), 100–134.

Christensen, C. M. (1997). *The Innovator's Dilemma: When New Technologies Cause Great Firms to Fail.* Boston, MA: Harvard Business School Press.

Christensen, C. M. (2006). The ongoing process of building a theory of disruption. *Journal of Product Innovation Management* **23**(1), 39–55.

Christensen, C. M., Raynor, M. & McDonald, R. (2015). What is disruptive innovation? *Harvard Business Review* **93**(12), 44–53.

Clayton Christensen website. Retrieved from http://claytonchristensen.com/key-concepts/

Clauss, T. (2017). Measuring business model innovation: Conceptualization, scale development, and proof of performance. *R&D Management* **47**(3), 385–403.

DiMaggio, P. J. & Powell, W. W. (1983). The iron cage revisited: Institutional isomorphism and collective rationality in organizational fields. *American Sociological Review* **48**(2), 147–160.

Ferdman, R. A. (2014, April 17). Someone is finally forcing Nespresso to open-source its coffee pods. *Quartz*. Retrieved from https://qz.com/200161/someone-is-finally-forcing-nespresso-to-open-source-its-coffee-pods/

Foss, N. & Saebi, T. (Eds.) (2015). *Business Model Innovation.* Oxford, UK: Oxford University Press.

Frankenberger, K. & Zott, C. (2018). The role of differentiation, integration, and governance in developing innovative business models. *Academy of Management Proceedings* **2018**(1).

Georgiadis, P. & McCormick, M. (2019, May 9). Edgewell to buy shaving start-up Harry's in $1.4bn deal. *Financial Times*. Retrieved from https://www.ft.com/content/70c421cc-7243-11e9-bbfb-5c68069fbd15

Grupo Bancolombia website. Retrieved from https://www.grupobancolombia.com/wps/portal/acerca-de/informacion-corporativa/quienes-somos

Gunther, M. (2013, March 5). Better Place: What went wrong for the electric car startup? *The Guardian*. Retrieved from https://www.theguardian.com/environment/2013/mar/05/better-place-wrong-electric-car-startup

Han, A. & Lal, R. (2005). Tanpin Kanri: Retail practice at Seven-Eleven Japan. HBS No. 506-002. Harvard Business Publishing.

IBM Institute for Business Value (2018). Plotting the platform payoff: Insights from the chief executive officer study. Global C-suite Study 19th edition. Retrieved from https://www.ibm.com/downloads/cas/NJYY0ZVG

INSEAD (2012). Alumnus entrepreneur profile: Giles Andrews (www.Zopa.com). Retrieved from https://centres.insead.edu/entrepreneurship/alumni-entrepreneurs/documents/giles-andrews-zopa.pdf

Jolly, D. (2014, April 17). Nestlé loses a clash over single-serve coffee. *New York Times*. Retrieved from https://www.nytimes.com/2014/04/18/

business/international/nestle-loses-a-clash-over-single-serve-coffee.html

Keating, G. (2012). *Netflixed: The Epic Battle for America's Eyeballs.* New York, NY: Penguin Group.

Kotler, P. T. & Keller, K. L. (2009). *Marketing Management 13th Edition.* Upper Saddle River, NJ: Pearson Prentice Hall.

KPMG (2018). No normal is the new normal. Global Consumer Executive Top of Mind Survey. Retrieved from https://assets.kpmg/content/dam/kpmg/xx/pdf/2018/06/no-normal-is-the-new-normal.pdf

Kupp, M. & Anderson, J. (2006). Zopa.com. Case-Reference no. ESMT-306-0065–1. European School of Management and Technology Berlin.

Markides, C. (2006). Disruptive innovation: In need of better theory. *Journal of Product Innovation Management* **23**(1), 19–25.

Nagayama, K. & Weill, P. (2004). 7-Eleven Japan Co. Ltd.: Reinventing the retail business model. CISR working paper 338, MIT Sloan School of Management, Cambridge, MA.

Nakamura, N. (2019, May 18). 58,000 shops later, Japan's convenience stores turn fresh page. *Nikkei Asian Review.* Retrieved from https://asia.nikkei.com/Business/Business-trends/58-000-shops-later-Japan-s-convenience-stores-turn-fresh-page

Nilsson, P. (2019, June 4). Robo-reporter writes front-page news. *Financial Times.* Retrieved from https://www.ft.com/content/e2cbe014-8131-11e9-b592-5fe435b57a3b

O'Neill, T. (2018, July 2). Zopa celebrates £1.5m profit as revenues climb by 40% to £46.5m. *Zopa Blog.* Retrieved from https://blog.zopa.com/2018/07/02/zopa-celebrates-1-5m-profit-revenues-climb-40-46-5m/

Parkin, B. (2019, July 19). Oyo founder triples stake with $2bn share buyback. *Financial Times.* Retrieved from https://www.ft.com/content/1f592b0a-aa21-11e9-984c-fac8325aaa04

Pokémon Go website. Retrieved from https://pokemongolive.com/en/post/starbucks/

Rasmussen, K. A. & Foss, N. J. (2014). Business model innovation in the pharmaceutical industry: The supporting role of organizational design. SMG Working Paper No. 4, Frederiksberg: Djøf Forlag.

Rivkin, J. W. (2000). Imitation of complex strategies. *Management Science* **46**(6), 824–844.

Santos, J., Spector, B. & Van Der Heyden, L. (2009). Toward a theory of business model innovation within incumbent firms. INSEAD working paper 2009/16/EFE/ST/TOM.

Snihur, Y. & Zott, C. (2020). The genesis and metamorphosis of novelty imprints: How business model innovation emerges in young ventures. *Academy of Management Journal* **63**(2), 554–583.

Stecker, E., Martinez-Jerez, F. A., Hill, L. A., Egawa, M. & Yamazaki, M. (2009). Lawson: Becoming the community store of 9,000 Japanese communities. HBS No. 409-112. Harvard Business Publishing.

Stinchcombe, A. L. (1965). Social Structure and Organizations. In March, J.P. (Ed.), *Handbook of Organizations* (pp. 142–193). Chicago, IL: Rand McNally.

Suchman, M. C. (1995). Managing legitimacy: Strategic and institutional approaches. *The Academy of Management Review* **20**(3), 571–610.

Terazono, E. (2019, May 13). Plant-based meat group Impossible Foods raises $300m. *Financial Times*. Retrieved from https://www.ft.com/content/85cc077e-757c-11e9-be7d-6d846537acab

The Economist (2019, April 17). The trouble with tech unicorns. *The Economist*.

The Economist Intelligence Unit (2005). Business 2010: Embracing the challenge of change. *The Economist*.

Uranaka, T. & Shimizu, R. (2016, April 7). Seven & i's 83-year-old CEO quits after board rejects his proposal. *Reuters*. Retrieved from https://www.reuters.com/article/us-seven-i-hldgs-managementchanges-rejec/seven-is-83-year-old-ceo-quits-after-board-rejects-his-proposal-idUSKCN0X419D

Woody, T. (2013, May 26). The lesson from Better Place's bankruptcy: Be more like Tesla. *Quartz*. Retrieved from https://qz.com/88214/the-lesson-from-better-places-bankruptcy-be-more-like-tesla/

Zopa website. FAQs. Retrieved from https://www.zopa.com/support/faqs

Zopa website. Invest. Retrieved from https://www.zopa.com/invest

Zott, C. & Amit, R. (2007). Business model design and the performance of entrepreneurial firms. *Organization Science* **18**(2), 181–199.

Zott, C. & Amit, R. (2008). The fit between product market strategy and business model: Implications for firm performance. *Strategic Management Journal* **29**(1), 1–26.

Zott, C. & Amit, R. (2017). Business model innovation: How to create value in a digital world. *Marketing Intelligence Review* **9**(1), 19–23.

PART II

Strategic Design and Evaluation of Business Model Innovation

5 Strategic Design of Innovative Business Models – How to Bring Design Thinking and Creativity to Your Business Model

Why Design Is More Than a Metaphor for Business Model Development

Unlike other forms of innovation, such as product or process innovation, business model innovation rarely requires a technological breakthrough as a precondition. Business model innovation often begins with the question: "What customer need will the new business model address?" This human-centric view suggests important connections with the concept of design. Finding novel solutions to humans' needs is a main tenet of the design profession. Indeed, careful observation of human behavior is a common starting point in any design process. Focused, insightful observation can be a powerful source of innovation. Such observation combines careful watching with questions about why things might be happening. Consequently, central ideas from the design field have been applied to business model design and innovation. Design is not just a catchy metaphor, but of high practical relevance for managers interested in coming up with new business model ideas. This is shown in the following statement, by one of the co-founders of peer-to-peer (P2P) lending startup Zopa:

> *I designed the business model; how the market was going to work. The major design piece was in actually understanding how to match up lenders and borrowers. How was that process going to work? How was the pricing going to work? How would we balance supply and demand across different markets? How would we spread liquidity across different markets? It was much more than a strategic role. It was a very design led role and it was a really interesting role. You get the opportunity to take a blank sheet of paper and design a working market and understand how the supply is going to change and how it's going to affect the price and how demand is going to change and what that's going to do to the price and understand all those implications. It was an interesting problem to solve.*[1]

The co-founder saw himself more as a designer than as a manager. Consequently, he adopted "Business Architect" as his official job title, reflecting his crucial role in designing the business model. He told us:

> *I think my role in Zopa was . . . designing how the model was going to work and how the business was going to work and creating that vision going forward. So in terms of what an architect does: designs a house, how it looks, and how it works.*

This clearly shows that entrepreneurs and managers tasked with developing a new business model consider themselves as designers, or architects.

[1]Based on a personal interview.

In fact, according to Herbert Simon, who won the 1978 Nobel Prize in Economics, every entrepreneur and entrepreneurial manager is a designer because, "everyone designs who devises courses of action aimed at changing existing situations into preferred ones."[2] That's precisely what entrepreneurs do – aim at building companies that create wealth and provide a better future for us all!

Business model scholars inspired by design thinking distinguish among distinct phases such as observation and synthesis, when business model designers identify the key customer needs to be addressed. In subsequent phases, designers generate alternative business model configurations, refine them to a smaller subset, and nurture their chosen business model until it is mature enough for implementation.[3] This "process" view of design (i.e., *how* something is being designed), is the subject of Chapter 6 (How to Design a New Business Model – A Dynamic Design Method). In the present chapter, we focus on design "content," i.e., the question *what* is being designed (namely, the ***What, How, Who,*** and ***Why*** of the business model), and in particular what drivers influence the subsequent design and its resulting outcomes. These drivers can be summarized by the acronym DESIGN that will be introduced later in this chapter; each letter in the acronym stands for a different design driver.

Exhibit 5.1 shows the main conceptual elements of business model design, and maps them onto the relevant chapters in the book in which they will be explained.

As Exhibit 5.1 indicates, one important outcome of business model design is business model innovation (explained in Chapter 4), which is consistent with the general idea that the design method is a powerful

Exhibit 5.1 Business Model Design

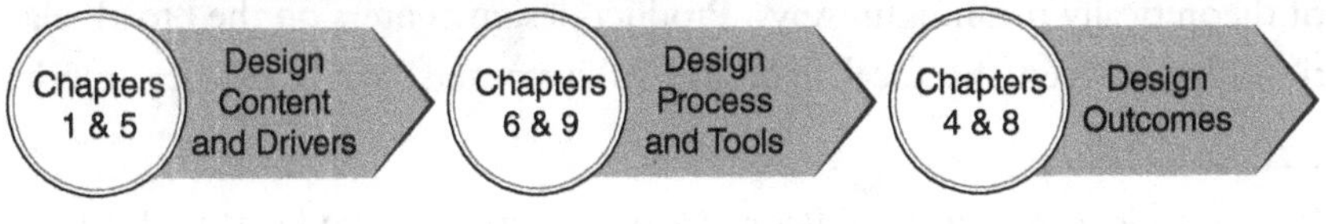

[2]Simon (1996, p. 111)
[3]Zott and Amit (2015)

approach for generating innovation. Another outcome of applying design to the business model is value creation for the various stakeholders in a business model. In Chapter 8, we refer to such value created for stakeholders as the "value proposition." Finally, we will also learn more in a later chapter of this book about visual representations of business models and other tools inspired by designers, such as the stakeholder journey, that promote the application of design thinking to business models. The existence and popularity of such hands-on tools partly explains the high level of interest in the business model concept among practitioners.[4] They are explained in Chapter 9.

What Is Design?

Design "is concerned with how things ought to be, with devising artifacts to attain goals."[5] It is a problem-solving approach that often involves multiple players from a number of disciplines and has "recognizable phases, and these, while not always in the same order, nearly always include analytic phases of search and understanding, and synthetic phases of experimentation and invention."[6] Design can therefore be "thought of as an integrated and disciplined innovation process that builds creative insight from deep knowledge."[7] Typical domains for the application of design include architecture, fashion, engineering, software, and medicine.

In the context of business, design has traditionally been associated with product and/or service design, as well as organizational design. Yet, the advances in communication and computing technologies that led to the emergence of the digital economy have created new opportunities for the application of the design methodology to business, namely the strategic design of the way the company conducts business within its ecosystem.

Business model design and product design differ, however, in a number of theoretically meaningful ways. Product design centers on the broad relationship between the focal firm and its customers, while business model

[4]E.g., Casadesus-Masanell and Ricart (2010), Osterwalder and Pigneur (2010)
[5]Simon (1996, p. 114)
[6]Owen (1993, p. 2)
[7]Dunne (2018, p. 15)

design considers multiple stakeholders such as suppliers and partners (in addition to the firm and its customers). In other words, business model design involves the conceptualization of a boundary-spanning activity system that includes the mechanisms that connect these interdependent activities and the identification of the parties that carry out each of the activities within the system. Product design, on the other hand, is ordinarily centered on identifying a set of interdependent physical components and features that characterize the firm's offerings to its clients. Relevant features of product design, such as technical functionality or aesthetic appeal, do not readily apply to business model design. Hence, any theory that links antecedents and outcomes of product design does not automatically carry over to business model design.[8]

At the organization level, design often refers to the process of grouping activities, roles, or positions in the organization to effectively (and possibly in new ways) coordinate the interdependencies that exist.[9] At the business model level, design can be conceived as the particular (and possibly novel) configuration of activities enabled by business model stakeholders and the resources they deploy.

Design has also been described as a mindset and discipline that is anchored on designers' sensitivity and their human-centered methods to discover peoples' needs and respond to them with new value propositions. It is a method for innovation that requires hard work, as well as skilled and trained human capital. It involves high degrees of coordination within and across interdisciplinary teams. It also requires time for data collection and analysis. Especially during the creative phases, it can appear chaotic, iterative, and unplanned.[10] Although its success cannot be guaranteed, design works particularly well for problems that can be characterized as "wicked."

---

[8]Traditionally, design has been considered by companies as part of the product development process. More specifically, the design focus has been mainly on the form and aesthetics of newly developed products. Increasingly, however, companies are asking designers to use their skills in order to create innovative solutions rather than to simply dress up products. Design is thus becoming more of a mainstream practice within firms aimed at crafting solutions that meet new customer needs and deliver new customer experiences.

[9]Pfeffer (1978)

[10]Brown (2008)

Wicked problems do not have an obvious solution because of incomplete, contradictory, or changing requirements; complex interdependencies; and high (social) complexity.[11] Examples of wicked problems include poverty and terrorism.[12]

Despite the pervasiveness and importance of design, a commonly accepted, unified science or theory of design does not yet exist.[13] The first approaches to formalize a design theory led scholars to think about how to decompose a complex dynamic into a set of smaller, well-defined problems. The next generation of theories conceived of design as a social process, and shifted the focus from problem-solving to problem-formulating.[14]

Business Model Strategic Design Drivers

In what follows, we highlight and describe the design drivers – captured by the acronym **DESIGN** – that enable the business model designer to strategically consider factors that frame and focus the business model design task. These design drivers include internal factors, or constraints as they are referred to in the design literature (which we specifically refer to as **D**eployable resources), the focal firm's **E**xternal environment, **S**takeholders' activities, **I**ncumbents' templates, **G**oals to create and capture value, and the perceived **N**eeds of customers).

Deployable Resources (D) and External Environment (E)

Every business model design project has constraints that give boundaries to a problem. The concept of "constraint" is indeed central to design. As Tim Brown, the Chairman of California design company IDEO, put it, "The willing and even enthusiastic acceptance of competing constraints is

[11] See Churchman (1967) for an early use of the term, and Rittel and Webber (1973) for a formal definition.
[12] Camillus (2008)
[13] Simon (1996, p. 113)
[14] Beckman and Barry (2007)

the foundation of design thinking."[15] In the case of business model design, we distinguish between internal and external constraints.

Deployable resources, which are also known as internal constraints, concern the availability of human and capital resources and capabilities that can be deployed to enable activities. If a firm does *not* own or control the deployable resources that are necessary to conduct relevant activities central to its business model, it needs to decide whether and how to develop or acquire these. It can contemplate partnering options, whereby other potential business model stakeholders could help the focal firm address its resource bottlenecks. If, on the other hand, the firm has sufficient access to resources (maybe even slack resources that make it more resilient in the face of setbacks), these very same resources could be deployed in alternative uses within the organizational structure of the focal firm. In other words, both the absence and the presence of deployable resources can constitute internal constraints for the business model designer.

External constraints refer to the conditions imposed on the business model designer by the focal firm's external environment, including its competitive market and its technological ecosystem. It also includes the macroeconomic (e.g., interest rates), legal, socio-political, regulatory, and cultural environment in which the business model will be embedded; these are therefore also often referred to as "environmental constraints." The viability of a new business model design depends in part on the degree to which it complies with important legal, regulatory, technological, and industry norms and requirements. For example, new air taxi transportation services require suitable aircraft (jets that take off and land vertically and then move into horizontal flight), but more importantly suitable public infrastructure, regulatory approval, and public acceptance. Such external factors affect the range of design alternatives that may be considered.[16] In other words, the external environment affects the feasibility of intended

---

[15]Brown (2009, p. 19)

[16]Morgan Stanley estimates the air taxi market will be worth $1.5tn annually by 2040. A trip in an air taxi from JFK Airport to downtown Manhattan would last approximately six minutes (compared to about one hour in a regular taxicab), and cost about the same as a cab ride, according to estimates from Munich-based startup Lilium, which focuses on developing and producing air jets for urban transportation services (Pfeifer, 2019).

business model designs, and it also influences the specific ways in which activities within the business model can be carried out.

The technological ecosystem of a firm is part of its external environment. Several technological trends have been converging that encourage companies to design new business models. Chief among these is the digitization of business, and the increasing numbers of digital natives who expect a brilliant and individualized digital customer experience.[17] The shift to digitally enabled social interaction enables, and even requires, firms to transform the customer experience. As a result, business model innovations, undergirded by digital technologies, are becoming the norm.[18] Top decision-makers in firms seem to be highly aware of digital technologies and the imperative (as well as the many exciting possibilities) for new customer interactions. In a survey conducted by IBM already in 2013, almost seven out of ten C-suite executives recognized the move to social and digital engagement with customers.[19] Furthermore, there is a steady flow of business model innovations that are based on new technologies, or the novel use of older technologies.[20]

A range of enabling technologies besides the internet have been introduced over the past two decades that can give rise to new business model designs. They include advanced big data analytics, mobile channels, social media, cloud computing, artificial intelligence, machine learning, blockchain, the Internet of Things, autonomous cars, and 5G cellular technologies. Some of these technologies are still in an early stage of development so that they should truly be considered as emerging technologies.[21]

---

[17] "Digital natives" refers to people born in the period between about 1980 and 2000, who grew up with the internet (The Economist, 2010).

[18] Enabling technologies are those that support "complementary innovations" and "open up new opportunities rather than offering complete, final solutions" (Bresnahan and Trajtenberg, 1995, p. 84).

[19] IBM Institute for Business Value (2013, p. 9)

[20] IBM Institute for Business Value (2015, p. 1)

[21] The following five key attributes qualify a technology as emerging: (1) radical novelty, (2) relatively fast growth, (3) coherence, (4) prominent impact, and (5) uncertainty and ambiguity (Rotolo, Hicks, and Martin, 2015).

Big data analytics: Big data analytics "examines large amounts of data to uncover hidden patterns, correlations and other insights."[22] To illustrate the enabling nature of this technology, consider the telematics devices installed in cars by insurance companies. In combination with enhanced data analytics, these devices make it possible for specific driver and car information to be turned into predictive insights, which can be used by insurance companies to personalize insurance premiums and proactively provide recommendations to drivers.[23]

Mobile channels: Mobile channels provide a way for businesses to connect with customers through their mobile devices. They have become major channels for sales and delivery. For example, established banks are now increasingly doing business with their customers over mobile channels, which are rapidly replacing physical branches. Some fintech startups, such as Germany's N26, provide entirely mobile banking solutions to its customers, choosing to forgo physical locations entirely.

Social media: Social media strategies have become imperative for firms. Companies can leverage social networking platforms to obtain data, advertise directly, and engage with their customers in new ways. For example, airlines are now in direct individual contact with their customers through various social media platforms such as Twitter.

Cloud computing: Cloud computing is "the delivery of computing services – including servers, storage, databases, networking, software, analytics, and intelligence – over the internet ('the cloud') to offer faster innovation, flexible resources, and economies of scale."[24] It is a key enabler for scalable digital business models.

Artificial intelligence: Artificial intelligence has been described as "the study of methods for making computers behave intelligently. Roughly speaking, a computer is intelligent to the extent that it does the right thing rather than the wrong thing. The right thing is whatever action is most likely to achieve the goal, or, in more technical terms, the action that maximizes expected utility. AI includes tasks such as learning, reasoning, planning, perception, language understanding, and robotics."[25] World Chess Champion Magnus Carlsen, for example, has invested in an

[22]SAS website. Big Data Analytics.
[23]Ralph (2017)
[24]Microsoft Azure website. What is Cloud computing?
[25]Berkeley EECS website. Q&A: The future of artificial intelligence.

AI-powered app that allows users to play "against" Carlsen in simulated chess games.[26]

Machine learning: Machine learning is a well-developed subset of artificial intelligence. Cassie Kozyrkov, Chief Decision Scientist at Google, describes machine learning in simple terms, as a "thing-labeler." "At its core, machine learning is just a thing-labeler, taking your description of something and telling you what label it should get."[27] It enables automated customer service chatbots, or "virtuous cycles," such as through increasingly precise insights and product or service recommendations (such as the product recommendations provided by Amazon, or the playlist recommendations provided by Spotify).

Blockchain: Blockchain is perhaps best-known today as the technology behind Bitcoin, but its applications are far-reaching and will allow novel ways of structuring transactions and information. Blockchains are a more secure method for record keeping, which is centralized rather than distributed.[28]

The Internet of Things: Broadly, the Internet of Things refers to "everything connected to the internet but it is increasingly being used to define objects that 'talk' to each other."[29] Everything from sensors to devices such as smartphones interact through a vast connected network, producing staggering amounts of interrelated data that can be analyzed through big data analytics.

Autonomous cars: Autonomous (or self-driving) cars employ a suite of sensors and technologies to drive from one point to another;[30] they today have varying degrees of autonomy from human drivers. Self-driving cars are expected to have a substantial impact on existing business models in the car industry, such as the traditional model that relies on private car ownership.[31]

5G: 5G is the "5th generation mobile network," which will power and bring online a widespread network of Internet of Things sensors and devices through much higher capacity and speeds.[32]

---

[26] Hall (2019)
[27] Kozyrkov (2019)
[28] The Economist (2018)
[29] Burgess (2018)
[30] Gartner website. IT Glossary.
[31] UMTRI (2015)
[32] Qualcomm website. Everything You Need to Know about 5G.

Thus, embedded in carefully designed business models, enabling technologies can have enormous value creation potential in a broad range of applications. The business model is the key to unlocking the value from these technologies. The rewards will go to the firms that find the smartest business model designs. Taken together, the power of the enabling technological trends can have a profound impact and offer completely new business model design opportunities.

Constraints have often been viewed by business model theorists as barriers or stumbling blocks, and only rarely linked with positive design outcomes such as innovation.[33] Key to dealing constructively with constraints by creating novelty and/or adopting elements from existing business models is therefore the adoption of a design attitude that views constraints as stimuli and creative challenges, rather than as obstacles that require taken-for-granted responses. It is akin to refusing to accept norms without questioning them. The design perspective reminds business model designers about the importance of viewing challenges as opportunities for designing innovative solutions – which, according to Austrian economist Joseph Schumpeter, is one of the basic premises of entrepreneurship.[34]

Stakeholders' Activities (S)

The next business model design driver – stakeholders' activities – is rooted in the design concept "collaboration." This concept refers both to collaboration with partners during the design process, and to collaboration as a defining characteristic of the resulting business model design. Given that the focus of this chapter is on design *content* rather than *process*, we discuss

---

[33]For an exception see Sanchez and Ricart (2010)

[34]Schumpeter (1934). Correspondingly, in entrepreneurship, such an attitude has been termed "entrepreneurial mindset." Such a mindset may be more prevalent in new firms than in established firms, which makes the emergence of novel business model designs more likely in startups than in corporate ventures. Corporate ventures often inherit structures and processes from the parent corporation, from which they borrow core competencies and resources, as well as cognitive models. This generally limits rather than fosters the emergence of business model innovation (see also Chapter 3 on cognition and its associated traps).

here collaboration embedded in the design solution. In a business model, the focal firm collaborates with business model stakeholders (partners, customers, suppliers, and financiers) and for this purpose needs to craft a unique value proposition for each business model stakeholder. Some of the activities (sometimes even many of them – see the examples of online marketplaces such as eBay or LetGo, in which customers do most of the marketing and selling) are performed by these stakeholders. Therefore, we refer to these as "stakeholders' activities."[35]

Considering how activities performed by stakeholders could enhance business model designs is important because it emphasizes the business model as a unit of analysis that is nested between the firm and network or ecosystem levels (see Chapter 2, Exhibit 2.1). Although it seems to be broadly accepted at a theoretical level that the business model is a construct that spans firm and industry boundaries, in practice some managers still underemphasize and/or underappreciate its boundary-spanning nature and tend to center on its firm-level characteristics. The stakeholders' activities design driver clearly calls for shifting the focus beyond the focal firm's boundaries. It alerts business model designers to the advantages of proactively incorporating and leveraging resources and capabilities that exist within the focal firm's ecosystem.[36]

---

[35]Stakeholder theory highlights the role of relationships among groups that have a stake in the business (model). It highlights the importance of managing the diverse interests of all the stakeholders and adopts a relational and value-based view, suggesting that business "can be understood as a set of relationships among groups which have a stake in the activities that make up the business" (Freeman, 2010, p. 7). Stakeholder theory advances a number of conditions under which the diverse interests of stakeholders are better coordinated and managed, including interest alignment, fairness, stakeholder integration, and stakeholder management. For a review of stakeholder theory, see Laplume, Sonpar, and Litz (2008).

[36]A focus on stakeholders' activities also puts into sharper relief the relationship between a business model and the ecosystem in which it is embedded. The business model describes how a focal firm taps into its ecosystem to perform the activities that are necessary to fulfill the perceived customer needs. In other words, it comprises the activities performed by the subset of actors in the focal firm's ecosystem (including the focal firm itself) that are interwoven within its own activity system.

More specifically, business model design requires the simultaneous consideration of multiple outsourcing and partnering arrangements involving stakeholders' activities. Unlike the decision of whether to outsource one particular activity or not (i.e., whether to "make or buy" it), which, given the activity, hinges mostly on transaction cost considerations,[37] the decision at the system level about the bundle of activities performed by the focal firm and its partners involves two steps. First, it requires a conceptualization of the set of activities that will encompass the activity system. This step centers on the concept of complementarities, that is, whether activities potentially reinforce each other with respect to some defined outcome. For example, should a P2P firm include a credit risk assessment of borrowers in its business model?

The second step involves considering the appropriate activity governance. If the activity is to be included in the business model, who should perform it – the focal firm, or one of its partners, vendors, or other stakeholders? For example, does the P2P lending platform leave it up to the lenders to perform a credit risk assessment of borrowers by providing them the necessary tools, or should it offer such a function as part of its platform? In the P2P lending market space, possible business model stakeholders may include banks (to ensure compliance with a country's legislation and regulations), credit data firms (to facilitate the risk assessment of borrowers), commercial lending firms (to inject liquidity into the system), payment processing firms (to enable payments), and so forth. The many different combinations of stakeholders and the activities that they could perform define a potentially vast solution space for the business model designer.

Accordingly, the co-founder of P2P lending firm Zopa described the task of putting together the firm's activity system as *value engineering*: "You're designing partners the way you would design a web page or you would design a piece of machinery, and you have to say, 'What's the value? What can I do myself? Can we use open source software for this? Do we have to make our own? Can we use a partner?'" For example, Zopa relies on information it obtains from established credit rating agencies, such as Equifax, to provide an initial quote to prospective new borrowers.[38]

---

[37] Williamson (1985)
[38] Selvam (2016)

Incumbents' Templates (I)

Designers can draw inspiration from the templates (i.e., the established business models) of incumbent firms in their industry with which they may be familiar, or from another industry that may be applicable to the design task at hand. In other words, designers routinely draw on existing templates.[39]

Being inspired by, and drawing on, business models of incumbents is common practice in business model design. Founders of new firms especially often search widely (by talking to investors, mentors, or colleagues who might be able to offer advice) for examples of other business models on which they can draw in the design of their own model. The founders of Zopa, for example, were strongly influenced by business model designs from outside their targeted domain of activity (commercial lending). In particular, they considered internet auction platform eBay, as well as the market for corporate bonds, and blended these templates to create an online marketplace for personal unsecured loans. The founders of rival P2P firms used other templates for designing their business models, such as Craigslist and Grameen bank, Wall Street and the Hoi credit system in Vietnam, online banks, and iPod and iTunes.[40] Researchers have even reported one case in which the founder of a healthcare-related new venture borrowed extensively from the business model templates of at least 32 established firms in other (i.e., non-healthcare) industries, such as Twitter, Haier, and HTC. This helped her redesign the venture's business model and increase its novelty.[41]

Templates can help business model designers find new ideas. They can also help manage the uncertainty associated with the introduction of a new business model by giving them important cues about what designs might work, and why. This is because templates are proof of successful concepts, and as such can be used for framing and benchmarking, and thus for shaping one's own and other people's perceptions.

The most familiar and expected resolution of a business model design task is the "default template," that is, the business model of the dominant incumbent firm(s) in one's core industry.[42] This suggests a tradeoff between

---

[39] Boland and Collopy (2004, p. 268)
[40] Amit and Zott (2015)
[41] Snihur and Zott (2020)
[42] Boland and Collopy (2004, p. 269–270)

efficiency (which lowers organizational risk) and novelty (which creates an advantage for the firm). Default solutions often foster efficiency at the expense of novelty (see also our discussion of mindset traps in Chapter 3: people tend to follow the dominant, efficient design).[43] Indeed, default templates provide important clues to new entrants about the efficient deployment of resources and capabilities that undergird the business model. These dominant designs are likely to link activities in a cost-reducing manner; that is, individual activities are linked with each other in a way that reduces transaction costs in the activity system as a whole, which is manifested in the structure and governance of the activity system. Hence, in the design of the structure and governance of new business models, drawing on the most prevalent designs of business models in an industry is likely to enhance the efficiency of the new models. However, this may come at the risk of path dependency, and a low degree of novelty. For example, a new fast-food chain modeled after McDonald's is likely to exhibit high efficiency in its operations, but may be lacking an innovative edge – at least as far as the business model is concerned (the product selection on the menu is another matter).

Goals (G) and Needs (N) of Customers

To be a potentially viable design, each design task must have a goal.[44] In the context of business model design, the "goal" design driver is often closely linked with customer (or, more generally, stakeholder) needs, another important design antecedent.[45] To illustrate, consider the case of P2P lending company Prosper, which was introduced in Chapter 4. The founders of Prosper, Chris Larsen and John Brown Witchel, believed that

[43]This means that if one adopts the default solution, the resulting business model is more likely to be efficient rather than novel. It does not mean, however, that a novel solution (i.e., one that departs from the default solution) cannot be more efficient. (See also Zott and Amit, 2007, who argue that novelty-centered design and efficiency-centered designs are not mutually exclusive.)

[44]Boland and Collopy (2004, p. 272)

[45]According to Boland and Collopy (2004, p. 269), "a designer always has a client and is always producing a product or service for that client. A client is indispensable to the statement of the design project and the setting of the design problem."

"one of the great social injustices of the world was lack of transparency in lending."[46] They thought that lending was a business that touched many people's lives in personally meaningful and important ways, yet it was an area of society over which consumers had virtually no control. This insight was at the heart of their efforts to design a P2P marketplace that was going to be fairer and more transparent to consumers than existing business models. They sketched out what such a web-based platform would look like, always asking themselves: "Is it the most efficient, is it the most consumer friendly, is it the most helpful?"[47] In other words, their design work centered on the goal of meeting the perceived needs of potential borrowers, in that the resulting business model should be efficient and easy to use.

A business model design should not only consider customers' needs, but the needs of all stakeholders – chief among them the focal firm, but also suppliers and strategic partners – and satisfy their incentive compatibility constraints. Put differently, it needs to fulfill the twin objectives of value creation (for all involved in the business model) and value appropriation (for the local firm). Importantly, we note that much scholarship on strategy to date has focused on explaining value appropriation (e.g., firm profits), while entrepreneurship scholars have tended to focus more on value creation. A design perspective on business models strongly suggests, however, that it is important to emphasize both. It helps achieve this integration by adding a focus on the customers and their needs, thus complementing much of the traditional strategy literature, which is characterized by a supply-side focus.

Business model designers often make great efforts to better understand their customers' needs and how to fulfill them.[48] They are deeply concerned with creating value for other stakeholders, not just for their own focal firms. This is the case for Kobo360, an African startup founded by Wharton alumnus Obi Ozor, and Ife Oyedele II. The new firm developed an "Uber for

---

[46]Based on personal interviews and research (like the other direct quotes in this section).

[47]Ditto.

[48]Boland and Collopy (2004, p. 267) note that "it is an emotional struggle with the competing forces and demands of the situation and indicates an intense level of care about the right course of action."

logistics" model that connects truck drivers and truck fleet operators with companies importing goods in some of Africa's most populated countries (Nigeria, Togo, Ghana, and Kenya). By introducing an app-based logistics platform to an industry hitherto characterized by insecurity, corruption, and inefficiency, Kobo360 not only creates value for themselves, but also gives truck drivers a means to overcome some major obstacles created by paperwork and handshake-based relationships. Specifically, the startup creates value for drivers by providing them with truck financing, discounts on diesel, healthcare and school fees assistance, per-trip insurance, and upfront payments.[49] In addition, Kobo360 enables fleet operators to track their deliveries in real time and informs them instantaneously about any problems. All of this also benefits society as a whole, as the business model promotes reliable business partnerships and boosts economic growth.

Thus, an important antecedent for adopting a particular business model design would be the goal of creating value for *all* business model stakeholders, that is, a focus on total value, rather than a focus on value capture by the focal firm alone.[50] By adopting a total value perspective, business model designers integrate the resource, i.e., supply and demand sides of the business model. By taking into account the interests of others, they also increase the opportunity cost of breaking away from the focal firm's business model and enhance the commitment of business model stakeholders.

Consider, for example, the case of a developer building an app for Apple's iOS platform. The distribution of the app is via an Apple handheld device such as a smartphone or tablet, which is powered by the iOS operating system. The value created by Apple's handheld devices for stakeholders such as users, and of course Apple (the focal firm in this example), increases with the number of applications run on its devices. Apple therefore has a strong incentive to attract app developers to its iOS digital platform. An app developer, meanwhile, has a strong incentive to ensure that the app is accessible for downloading through the App Store and that it runs smoothly on all of Apple's handheld devices. This increases the total value for users

[49] Munshi (2019)

[50] See Brandenburger and Stuart (1996). The total value created through the business model of a focal firm can be defined as the willingness-to-pay of all customers minus the opportunity cost of all suppliers and partners in the business model, including the focal firm (see Zott and Amit, 2008, and also Chapter 8).

of Apple mobile devices, the app developer, and of course Apple. Hence, in this example the incentives of both parties, namely Apple and the app developer, are compatible. The cost of breaking from Apple's digital platform for the app developer who relies on that iOS platform for distributing the service enabled by the app is high. The strong incentive compatibility between the app developer and Apple enables both parties to capture some of the value that is created through the partnership.

Thus, the business model designer needs to carefully balance potentially competing goals and objectives of various business model stakeholders, and engage with the tensions that arise from them openly and creatively.[51] To achieve this balancing act, good judgment is needed, especially in the case of complex business models that involve many different stakeholders (see Chapter 4, where complexity is mentioned as a risk factor of business model innovation). An emphasis on value creation without regard to value capture would be naïve, and put the economic viability of the focal firm at risk. Conversely, a preoccupation with value capture might unnecessarily reduce the amount of total value that could be created, and increase the likelihood that some participants might find it unattractive to participate in an assigned role in the business model. As a result, the business model might fall apart.

A case in point is the failed electric car company Better Place introduced in Chapter 4, which raised $850 million before it filed for bankruptcy in 2013.[52] The company developed and sold battery-charging and battery-switching services for electric cars produced by the French automaker Renault. Its innovative business model, which represented a radical deviation from the business models of traditional automakers, involved many partners, both private and public. The incentives of these various partners to collaborate were not sufficiently aligned, in particular since sales of the Renault Fluence electric cars were far behind original projections. This led to the withdrawal of critical partners like Renault and to the collapse of Better Place's novel business model.

In summary, designers can influence the architecture of their business models by paying close attention to the following design drivers: deployable resources, external constraints, stakeholders' activities, incumbents' templates, goals, and needs. Exhibit 5.2 summarizes these DESIGN drivers.

---

[51] Boland and Collopy (2004, p. 268 and 276)
[52] Blum (2017)

Exhibit 5.2 DESIGN Drivers

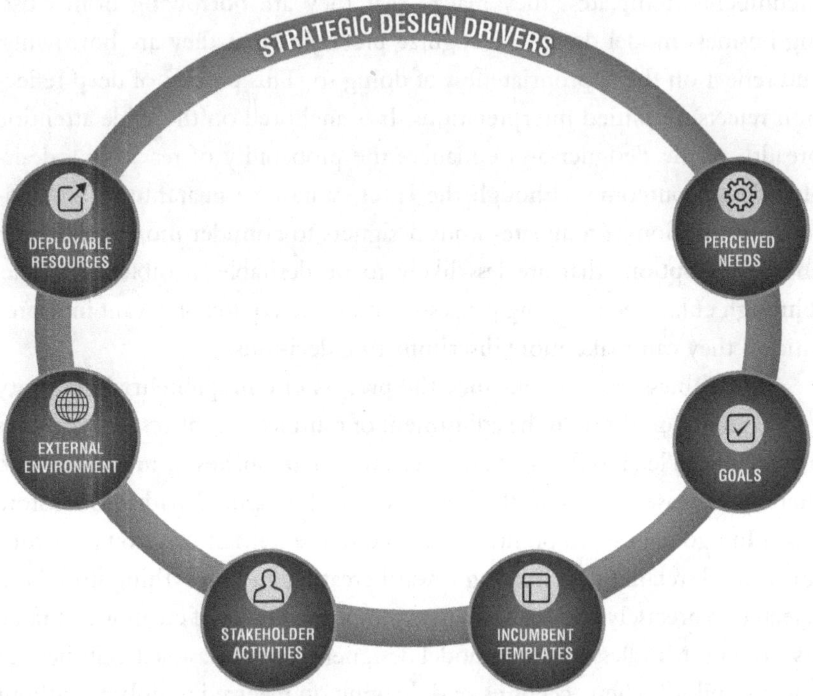

Mindfulness in Design

The preceding section highlighted that a designer's awareness influences the ways in which the DESIGN drivers shape the resulting design process and outcome. In the context of business model design, awareness refers specifically to recognition, in real time, that one is, for example, applying elements from a default design template, or that one needs to balance the value creation needs of various distinct stakeholders. It is aptly captured by the concept of *mindfulness*, which refers to a "state of active awareness characterized by the continual creation and refinement of categories, an openness to new information, and a willingness to view contexts from multiple perspectives."[53]

Mindful business model designers are keenly aware of their options when they work around constraints, engage with stakeholders, consider

[53]Levinthal and Rerup (2006, p. 502)

templates, and keep client needs in mind. For example, when considering incumbents' templates, they realize that they are borrowing from existing business model designs, recognize precisely what they are borrowing, and reflect on the appropriateness of doing so. This process of deep reflection rejects simplified interpretations. It is anchored on the wide attention breadth of the designer and enhances the probability of reaching a desirable design outcome, although the latter cannot be guaranteed.[54] Mindful consideration of templates leads designers to consider more alternatives and reject options that are less likely to be desirable, feasible, or viable. Through enhanced scanning processes and more context-relevant interpretations, they can make more discriminating decisions.

Mindfulness can also enhance the process of entrepreneurial discovery and exploitation through the adjustment of routines, templates, and business plans.[55] It can lead to the deliberate rejection of templates in an industry and thereby increase novelty in the business model design. Canadian bookstore chain Indigo is a case in point. It followed in the steps of Amazon (a disruptor in book retailing) in moving toward creating an "everything store" but rejected to precisely copy the Amazon template in favor of creating a curated assortment. Mindless business model designers, by contrast, act as if they are "on autopilot" when accepting and drawing on received templates without questioning them. This is akin to the familiarity trap of human cognition discussed in Chapter 3, which typically entails suboptimal design outcomes, because, "When people in an organization engage in mindless acts based on precedent, such behavior precludes them from even considering whether practices need to be reexamined."[56]

Mindfulness defined as a state of active awareness is related to, but distinct from, mindset. Recall our definition of a business model mindset as a state of mind, attitude, or inclination that helps someone consider the firm's entire activity system, along with its associated dimensions of content (***What***), structure (***How***), governance (***Who***), and value logic (***Why***), as a potential solution for a business problem or opportunity. Nurturing a business model mindset can help designers be more mindful (and vice versa),

---

[54]Dane (2011), Rerup (2005)
[55]Rerup (2005)
[56]Pfeffer and Sutton (1999, p. 7)

because it sharpens their awareness about what to design, and from where to seek information and inspiration.

To summarize, mindful consideration of the DESIGN drivers (i.e., their reflective, explicit, and well-reasoned application, such as borrowing from a well-honed, efficient, legitimate business model template while being fully aware of what one is doing) is a good thing. Their mindless application (e.g., automatically copying an incumbent's template), however, could be costly. Sticking to a default model because one does not know any better (e.g., due to path dependency, bias, and/or bounded rationality) might be understandable, but does not seem wise.

Robust Business Model Design

New business model designs can drive substantial value creation. There is, however, a high degree of uncertainty with respect to value appropriation from such innovations. How can innovators make sure that they (and not others) profit from them? This question has received substantial attention, in particular from technology management scholars who have pointed to the importance of the strength of the appropriability regime;[57] the importance of the timing of the innovation;[58] the types of assets that the innovating firm controls (e.g., generic, specialized, or cospecialized complementary assets);[59] and the factors of patenting or secrecy.[60]

This suggests that business model innovators need to think strategically about how to best protect the value that their innovation generates from

[57]Teece (1986) defines an appropriability regime as "the environmental factors, excluding firm and market structure, that govern an innovator's ability to capture the profits generated by an innovation." The most important aspects of an appropriability regime are "the nature of the technology, and the efficacy of legal mechanisms of protection" (p. 287).

[58]Lieberman and Montgomery (1998)

[59]Teece (1986) defines generic assets as "general purpose assets which do not need to be tailored to the innovation in question"; specialized assets as assets "where there is unilateral dependence between the innovation and the complementary asset"; and cospecialized assets as assets "for which there is a bilateral dependence" (p. 289).

[60]See, for example, Arundel (2001)

appropriation by others (for example by competitors who seek to copy the new model). Business model innovators need to do this, while at the same time ensuring that their innovation is viewed as legitimate by society, which is a precondition for its value creation. Legitimacy refers to "a generalized perception or assumption that the actions of an entity are desirable, proper, or appropriate within some socially constructed systems of norms, beliefs, and definitions."[61] The quest for legitimacy is important because newness and lack of familiarity are well-known barriers to innovation adoption.[62] That is, business model designers need to simultaneously enhance the legitimacy of their innovative designs and protect them from imitation by others. In other words, they have to ensure the robustness of the resulting business model designs. Robust business model innovations are those that are both legitimate and do not lend themselves easily to imitation.[63]

Designing Robust Business Model Content (What)

To increase the legitimacy of new business model content, business model innovators can select legitimate customer-facing activities for inclusion in their designs, built around features that are already familiar to their clients. Familiarity with particular activities ensures that customers (or other business model stakeholders) are more likely to accept a firm's value proposition and know intuitively how to evaluate it. Although familiarity is not required for legitimacy (i.e., the perception of appropriateness), it can contribute to it, as the appropriateness of familiar practices is usually questioned less, due

---

[61] Suchman (1995, p. 574)

[62] In a historic case study of Thomas Alva Edison, Hargadon and Douglas (2001) suggest how to make innovation more palatable to customers through skillful design. The authors analyze how Edison's successful introduction of the lightbulb and the associated electric lighting system (a tremendous technological innovation at the time) depended on situating the technological innovation within the context of the established gas lighting industry, with which customers were intimately familiar. The researchers refer to the balance, from the customer's perspective, between familiar and new product design elements as "robust design."

[63] This section draws on Snihur, Amit, and Zott (2020).

to repeated use.[64] For instance, when it was introduced in 2003, Apple's iTunes Store built on the specific habit of downloading music through the internet, which numerous internet-savvy customers had been cultivating for some time. The familiarity of the practice made the new model more acceptable.

Now, how do you reduce the likelihood of imitation of legitimate business model content (***What***)? One way is by generating incompatibilities with incumbents' existing business models. Perceived incompatibility arises when a firm fears that the addition of activities will either reduce revenues or increase costs, given the existing resources and capabilities that support the firm's current business model. For example, Apple developed a stronger value proposition for its customers by coupling the iPod (a product innovation) with the iTunes Store (a business model innovation). The music labels did not imitate the iPod and iTunes combination, however, because to provide music enthusiasts with sufficient content they would have had to cooperate to obtain access to each other's catalogues while simultaneously cannibalizing their profitable sales of compact discs. Thus, by accessing publicly available information about Apple's business model through the corporate website, media coverage, or customer accounts, incumbents could easily identify the content of the new business model, i.e., discern the activities that were performed within it. Nevertheless, established players from both the music and electronics industries were slow to imitate Apple's business model innovation, despite the relative ease of identifying the customer-facing activities of the iPod/iTunes business model because of perceived incompatibilities with their own models.

Designing Robust Business Model Structure (How)

Business model structure refers to how activities are linked both within the firm and across its boundaries, i.e., with its external partners (***How***). Business model structure is generally more difficult to identify for competitors than business model content (***What***) or governance (***Who***). To increase business model legitimacy, therefore, business model designers need to make

[64] Aldrich and Fiol (1994)

legitimate structural elements visible, while keeping novel elements that may lack legitimacy less visible.[65] This could help foster legitimacy and at the same time prevent imitation and thus increase the business model's robustness. For example, when making international acquisitions, Walmart's managers introduce only small changes in customer-facing activities, whereas they make significant changes to back-office activities, like procurement, information systems, and logistics, which remain less visible. There could be many reasons for this, but one of the effects is that incumbents find it more difficult to identify and replicate these structural changes.

This suggests that for designing robust business model structure, firms reveal selected aspects of their business models while concealing others. A vineyard, for example, may be comfortable telling customers about general farming practices and innovations used in grape growing, but not about the specific techniques of winemaking, thus emphasizing legitimate aspects of their business models, while keeping other practices (especially those that refer to business model structure) concealed.[66] Netflix understood this, too: "On the surface, Netflix is a massive video store, taking in cash for monthly renting rights and loaning out DVDs to the consumer. Beneath the surface, Netflix is akin to a think tank, creating algorithms to maximize the long-term value of each customer that it enlists, orchestrating a complex distribution system and finding ways to reduce its costs of service. It is the unseen aspects of Netflix's business model . . . which differentiate it from the competition"[67] – and, we would add, help protect it from imitation.

Designing Robust Business Model Governance (Who)

Business model governance refers to activity control, or who is in charge of what activity (***Who***). According to institutional theorists, forming ties with

[65]Institutional theorists have discussed the concealment or decoupling of potentially problematic practices (e.g., Pache and Santos, 2013). However, here by "less visible" we mean concealed elements of the business model that need not be problematic for business model participants but at the same time can help protect the innovative business model from imitation.

[66]Voronov, De Clercq, and Hinings (2013)

[67]Keating (2012, p. 136)

well-established organizations that perform activities within a focal firm's business model signals appropriateness by association.[68] Thus, by outsourcing some activities to legitimate partners, firms can reassure customers and other partners about the legitimacy of their new business model governance arrangements. Strong relationships with legitimate, and perhaps prominent, partners indicate that the focal firm has earned a positive evaluation from experienced and influential actors, signaling legitimacy to other participants.[69]

How is it possible to simultaneously enhance legitimacy of business model governance and prevent imitation of the new business model? As part of their effort to select legitimate partners, firms can co-opt incumbents into becoming partners by creating and offering them roles, such as supplier, buyer, or complementor, in the new business model. Partnering with incumbents contributes to reducing their willingness to imitate business model innovation by offering them a strong value proposition, for instance in terms of a revenue-sharing agreement. Spotify (a de novo entrant) partnered with music labels and the social networking sites Facebook and Twitter to provide direct streaming of its music library (constructed through resource combination with several music labels) to a mix of free users and monthly subscribers. The partnership between Spotify and the music labels, an astute balancing act on Spotify's part, subsequently became the labels' biggest source of digital music revenue, which in some countries even surpassed iTunes.[70] The arrangement significantly limited the music labels' willingness to imitate Spotify's business model innovation. Although Spotify shares knowledge about its innovation with the music labels, this knowledge flow is traded off against the cost music labels would incur if they were to launch a music streaming service themselves.

While the idea of co-opting incumbents may appear intuitive, it is not easy to establish relationships with well-known partners, or to design mutually acceptable and beneficial value-sharing agreements, especially for de novo entrants that lack credibility. Existing research shows that the skill levels of entrepreneurs vary, and that engaging in skillful "symbolic management" or providing appealing visions for the future, such as adopting "anti-leader

[68]DiMaggio and Powel (1983)
[69]Stuart, Hoang, and Hybels (1999)
[70]Greeley (2011)

positioning," might help to win over partners, especially in the case of new firms.[71]

Summary of Key Takeaways for the Effective Business Model Designer

Design offers a human-centered framework that is highly relevant for tackling a range of dynamic and complex problems situated in the real world. In this chapter, we introduced a design perspective to tackle one such task – the design of innovative new business models. A design approach to business models offers entrepreneurs and incumbent firms a content-based framework for crafting innovative, robust, and scalable new business models. It places a heavy emphasis on identifying customer and partner needs. We identified six business model design drivers summarized in the acronym DESIGN, which are taken from key design concepts (such as constraints, collaboration, templates, and goals). These DESIGN drivers can help you identify the internal and external factors underpinning your business model design. They are summarized below.

The first two design drivers are comprised of the two main sets of constraints facing the business model designer: **D**eployable resources (or internal constraints) and the **E**xternal environment (or external constraints). Constraints are integral to the design process. They present a creative challenge – and an opportunity – for innovation. Internal constraints are the resources and capabilities a firm has for various activities. The external environment (or external constraints) is important to ensure a viable business model design; it includes the competitive market and technological ecosystem, as well as the macroeconomic, legal, socio-political, regulatory, and cultural backdrop.

The third business model design driver is **S**takeholders' activities. This design driver is derived from the concept of collaboration. It

---

[71] Zott and Huy (2007), Santos and Eisenhardt (2009). See Chapter 11 for more details on symbolic management, and also on how the choice of revenue model can help with designing robust business model value logic (***Why***).

captures collaboration as a crucial attribute built into the business model. Stakeholders' activities are defined as activities in the business model that are performed by partners, customers, suppliers, or other stakeholders. Crucial to this is the firm's ability to craft distinct value propositions for the various stakeholders, as well as reach into its larger ecosystem to identify potential resources and capabilities.

The fourth business model design driver is **I**ncumbents' templates. Designers can draw inspiration from the templates (i.e., the established business models) of incumbent firms in their industry with which they may be familiar with, or from another industry. This entails a tradeoff, however, between efficiency and novelty. Dominant designs in an industry are often associated with higher efficiency, but lower novelty.

The fifth and sixth design drivers are the **G**oals of the focal firm and **N**eeds of customers. The goal of business model design is highly interconnected with the needs of not just customers, but all stakeholders in the business model. This requires emphasizing both total value creation *and* value appropriation, which needs to be balanced. Higher value creation for all stakeholders makes it less likely that partners will leave the business model. Balancing the needs of all stakeholders, and the dual goals of value creation and value appropriation, requires creativity and sound judgement.

There are two additional aspects to consider in the application of design to business models. Alongside the DESIGN drivers, these increase the likelihood of successful business model innovation. The first is mindfulness. Mindful business model designers think deeply about the design problem facing them, staying aware of their options, constraints, and stakeholder needs. They carefully consider all possibilities, including incumbent templates, in a holistic and critical way. This is contrasted to mindless business model design, which recalls the familiarity trap discussed in Chapter 3. The second important factor to consider is robustness. Robust business models should be both legitimate and difficult to imitate. Legitimacy refers to acceptance within the society the firm operates in. This is especially important for new firms with highly novel business models, which might be difficult to convey to potential customers or partners.

References

Aldrich, H. E. & Fiol, C. M. (1994). Fools rush in? The institutional context of industry creation. *Academy of Management Review* **19**(4), 645–670.

Amit, R. & Zott, C. (2015). Crafting business architecture: The antecedents of business model design. *Strategic Entrepreneurship Journal* **9**(4), 331–350.

Arundel, A. (2001). The relative effectiveness of patents and secrecy for appropriation. *Research Policy* **30**(4), 611–624.

Beckman, S. L. & Barry, M. (2007). Innovation as a learning process: Embedding design thinking. *California Management Review* **50**(1), 25–56.

Berkeley EECS website. Q & A: The future of artificial intelligence. Retrieved from http://people.eecs.berkeley.edu/~russell/temp/q-and-a.html

Blum, B. (2017). *Totaled: The Billion-Dollar Crash of the Startup that Took on Big Auto, Big Oil and the World*. Sherman Oaks, CA: Blue Pepper Press.

Boland, R. J., Jr. & Collopy, F. (2004). *Managing as Designing*. Stanford, CA: Stanford University Press.

Brandenburger, A. M. & Stuart, H. W., Jr. (1996). Value-based business strategy. *Journal of Economics & Management Strategy* **5**(1), 5–24.

Bresnahan, T. F. & Trajtenberg, M. (1995). General purpose technologies 'Engines of growth'? *Journal of Econometrics* **65**(1), 83–108.

Brown, T. (2008). Design thinking. *Harvard Business Review* **86**(6), 84–92.

Brown, T. (2009). *Change by Design: How Design Thinking Transforms Organizations and Inspires Innovation*. New York, NY: HarperCollins.

Burgess, M. (2018, February 16). What is the Internet of Things? *Wired*. Retrieved from https://www.wired.co.uk/article/internet-of-things-what-is-explained-iot

Camillus, J. C. (2008). Strategy as a wicked problem. *Harvard Business Review* **86**(5), 98–106.

Casadesus-Masanell, R. & Ricart, J. E. (2010). From strategy to business models and onto tactics. *Long Range Planning* **43**(2–3), 195–215.

Churchman, C. (1967). Wicked problems. *Management Science* **14**(4), B141–B142.

Dane, E. (2011). Paying attention to mindfulness and its effects on task performance in the workplace. *Journal of Management* **37**(4), 997–1018.

DiMaggio, P. J. & Powell, W. W. (1983). The iron cage revisited: Institutional isomorphism and collective rationality in organizational fields. *American Sociological Review* **48**(2), 147–160.

Dunne, D. (2018). *Design Thinking at Work: How Innovative Organizations are Embracing Design.* Toronto, CA: University of Toronto Press.

Freeman, R. (2010). Managing for stakeholders: Trade-offs or value creation. *Journal of Business Ethics* **96**, 7–9.

Gartner website. IT Glossary. Retrieved from https://blogs.gartner.com/it-glossary/autonomous-vehicles/

Greeley, B. (2011, July 14). Daniel Ek's Spotify: Music's last best hope. *Bloomberg Businessweek.* Retrieved from https://www.bloomberg.com/news/articles/2011-07-13/daniel-ek-s-spotify-music-s-last-best-hope

Hall, A. (2019, September 3). Magnus Carlsen buys chess platform Chessable.com. *Financial Times.* Retrieved from https://www.ft.com/content/c2a4b3a0-cd8b-11e9-99a4-b5ded7a7fe3f

Hargadon, A. & Douglas, J. (2001). When innovations meet institutions: Edison and the design of the electric light. *Administrative Science Quarterly* **46**(3), 476–501.

IBM Institute for Business Value (2013). The customer-activated enterprise: Insights from the global C-suite study. Retrieved from: https://www.ibm.com/downloads/cas/QVPRRP2E

IBM Institute for Business Value (2015). Redefining boundaries: Insights from the global C-suite study. Retrieved from: https://www.ibm.com/downloads/cas/VJEP6Z9D.

Keating, G. (2012). *Netflixed: The Epic Battle for America's Eyeballs.* New York, NY: Penguin Group.

Kozyrkov, C. (2019, October 5). The simplest explanation of machine learning you'll ever read. *LinkedIn.* Retrieved from https://www.linkedin.com/pulse/simplest-explanation-machine-learning-youll-ever-read-cassie-kozyrkov/

Laplume, A. O., Sonpar, K. & Litz, R. A. (2008). Stakeholder theory: Reviewing a theory that moves us. *Journal of Management* **34**(6), 1152–1189.

Levinthal, D. & Rerup, C. (2006). Crossing an apparent chasm: Bridging mindful and less-mindful perspectives on organizational learning. *Organization Science* **17**(4), 502–513.

Lieberman, M. B. & Montgomery, D. B. (1988). First-mover advantages. *Strategic Management Journal* **9**(S1), 41–58.

Microsoft Azure website. What is cloud computing? Retrieved from https://azure.microsoft.com/en-us/overview/what-is-cloud-computing/

Munshi, N. (2019, August 26). Tech start-ups drive change for Nigerian truckers. *Financial Times*. Retrieved from https://www.ft.com/content/c6a3d1f2-c27d-11e9-a8e9-296ca66511c9

Osterwalder, A. & Pigneur, Y. (2010). *Business Model Generation: A Handbook for Visionaries, Game Changers, and Challengers*. Hoboken, NJ: John Wiley & Sons.

Owen, C. L. (1993). A critical role for Design Technology. *Design Management Journal (Former Series)* **4**(2), 10–18.

Pache, A. C. & Santos, F. (2013). Inside the hybrid organization: Selective coupling as a response to competing institutional logics. *Academy of Management Journal* **56**(4), 972–1001.

Pfeffer, J. (1978). *Organizational Design*. Arlington Heights, IL: AHM Publishing.

Pfeffer, J. & Sutton, R. (1999). *The Knowing-Doing Gap: How Smart Companies Turn Knowledge into Action*. Boston, MA: Harvard Business School Press.

Pfeifer, S. (2019, May 15). Air taxi aimed at revolutionising urban travel unveiled. *Financial Times*. Retrieved from https://www.ft.com/content/b91706c6-7728-11e9-be7d-6d846537acab

Qualcomm website. Everything you need to know about 5G. Retrieved from https://www.qualcomm.com/invention/5g/what-is-5g

Ralph, O. (2017, August 11). Drivers put the brakes on car insurance with a black box. *Financial Times*. Retrieved from https://www.ft.com/content/894c3f5e-786c-11e7-a3e8-60495fe6ca71

Rerup, C. (2005). Learning from past experience: Footnotes on mindfulness and habitual entrepreneurship. *Scandinavian Journal of Management* **21**(4), 451–472.

Rittel, H. W. J. & Webber, M. M. (1973). Dilemmas in a general theory of planning. *Policy Sciences* **4**, 155–169.

Rotolo, D., Hicks, D. & Martin, B. R. (2015). What is an emerging technology? *Research Policy* **44**(10), 1827–1843.

Sanchez, P. & Ricart, J. E. (2010). Business model innovation and sources of value creation in low-income markets. *European Management Review* **7**(3), 138–154.

Santos, F. M. & Eisenhardt, K. M. (2009). Constructing markets and shaping boundaries: Entrepreneurial power in nascent fields. *Academy of Management Journal* **52**(4), 643–671.

SAS website. Big data analytics. Retrieved from https://www.sas.com/en_us/insights/analytics/big-data-analytics.html

Schumpeter, J. A. (1934). *The Theory of Economic Development: An Inquiry into Profits, Capital, Credit, Interest, and the Business Cycle*. Cambridge, MA: Harvard University Press.

Selvam, S. (2016, July 11). Zopa and credit score. Zopa Blog. Retrieved from https://blog.zopa.com/2016/07/11/zopa-and-credit-scores/

Simon, H. A. (1996). *The Sciences of the Artificial* (3rd ed.). Cambridge, MA: MIT Press.

Snihur, Y., Amit, R. & Zott, C. (2020). Creating and capturing value from emerging technologies: The role of strategic business model design. *Strategy Science* (forthcoming).

Snihur, Y. & Zott, C. (2020). The genesis and metamorphosis of novelty imprints: How business model innovation emerges in young ventures. *Academy of Management Journal* **63**(2), 554–583.

Stuart, T. E., Hoang, H. & Hybels, R. C. (1999). Interorganizational endorsements and the performance of entrepreneurial ventures. *Administrative Science Quarterly* **44**(2), 315–349.

Suchman, M. C. (1995). Managing legitimacy: Strategic and institutional approaches. *Academy of Management Review* **20**(3), 571–610.

Teece, D. J. (1986). Profiting from technological innovation: Implications for integration, collaboration, licensing and public policy. *Research Policy* **15**(6), 285–305.

The Economist. (2010, March 6). The net generation, unplugged. *The Economist*. Retrieved from https://www.economist.com/technology-quarterly/2010/03/06/the-net-generation-unplugged

The Economist. (2018, August 30). The promise of the blockchain technology. *The Economist*. Retrieved from https://www.economist.com/technology-quarterly/2018/08/30/the-promise-of-the-blockchain-technology

UMTRI. (2015, February 11). *Driverless vehicles: Fewer cars, more miles. University of Michigan Transportation Research Institute*. Retrieved from http://www.umtri.umich.edu/what-were-doing/news/driverless-vehicles-fewer-cars-more-miles

Voronov, M., De Clercq, D. & Hinings, C. R. (2013). Conformity and distinctiveness. *Journal of Management Studies* **50**(4), 607–645.

Williamson, O. E. (1985). *The Economic Institution of Capitalism*. New York, NY: Free Press.

Zott, C. & Amit, R. (2007). Business model design and the performance of entrepreneurial firms. *Organization Science* **18**(2), 181–199.

Zott, C. & Amit, R. (2008). The fit between product market strategy and business model: Implications for firm performance. *Strategic Management Journal* **29**(1), 1–26.

Zott, C. & Amit, R. (2015). Business model innovation: Toward a process perspective. In C. Shalley, M. Hitt & J. Zhou (Eds.), *Oxford Handbook of Creativity, Innovation, and Entrepreneurship: Multilevel Linkages* (pp. 395–406). New York, NY: Oxford University Press.

Zott, C. & Huy, Q. N. (2007). How entrepreneurs use symbolic management to acquire resources. *Administrative Science Quarterly* **52**(1), 70–105.

6 How to Design a New Business Model – A Dynamic Design Method

A Process Perspective on Business Model Design

Traditional car manufacturers, which long relied on a linear manufacturing value chain, are facing a serious challenge from disrupters with innovative business models, such as Tesla and Uber. From the move away from car ownership and toward ride sharing, to the development of self-driving cars, the automotive industry is undergoing a sea change. Ford Motor Company, which was founded in 1903, is facing these challenges head on, as it attempts to define and build the mobility business model(s) of the future – no small feat for a long-established car company. To do so, it is experimenting with numerous smaller initiatives and business models that are aligned with its overarching vision for the future, which is to "become the world's most trusted mobility company, designing smart vehicles for a smart world that help people move more safely, confidently and freely."[1] By investing in diverse mobility initiatives – such as a scooter share and an autonomous vehicle startup, among others – Ford is reframing its identity from being "just" a car manufacturer to becoming a player in connected mobility.

As Ford works toward achieving its vision for the future, a parallel change is taking place. This change accelerated with the appointment of a new CEO, Jim Hackett, in 2017. Under Hackett's leadership, Ford is applying the iterative, learning-based, and human-centered tenets of *design thinking* across the company – from designing innovative products (like a groundbreaking all-electric Mustang[2]) to designing entire new business models, as evidenced by Ford's hiring of "business model designers" who will "combine strategic thinking and human-centered design thinking processes to think differently about existing business models, or to craft and build new ventures"[3] (see Exhibit 6.1). Design thinking, as this indicates, is human-centered. It is about finding out the needs of real human customers and responding to these needs, whether through product design or business model design (or both!).

Prior to joining Ford, Hackett was the CEO at a furniture manufacturer, Steelcase, where he first learned about the design thinking process developed by California design firm IDEO – knowledge he brought with him when he was appointed chairman of Ford's new Smart Mobility division in 2016.[4] From early work with IDEO (a partnership that started in 2005) and now through a firm-wide learning program and a mobility design lab

[1] Ford Media Center (2017) and Johnson (2018)

[2] The car's innovative, user-centric entertainment system was developed by "a cross-functional team [that] was allowed to brainstorm, prototype, test, and try again" (Schwab, 2019).

[3] Ford (2018)

[4] Ford Smart Mobility was described as a "subsidiary formed to design, build, grow and invest in emerging mobility services . . . Ford Smart Mobility LLC is part of Ford's expanded business model to be both an auto and a mobility company. The company is continuing to focus on and investing in its core business – designing, manufacturing, marketing, financing and servicing cars, SUVs, trucks and electrified vehicles. At the same time, Ford aggressively is pursuing emerging opportunities through Ford Smart Mobility, the company's plan to be a leader in connectivity,

Exhibit 6.1 Job Ad from Ford Motor Company

D-FORD BUSINESS DESIGNER

Location: Dearborn, Michigan US

Job Number 35794BR
Dearborn, Michigan US

Our Business Designers combine strategic thinking and human-centered design thinking processes to think differently about existing business models, or to craft and build new ventures. You will collaborate with a broad team of designers and stakeholders to help define strategy and growth opportunities for projects through designing, prototyping and bringing to life new products and services.

As a Business Designer you will...

- Explore the business model possibilities behind new concepts using research and financial modeling to shape and influence design.
- Design business models that enhance and extend consumer experiences, and create new opportunities for revenue across time horizons.
- Translate business strategy and business models into actionable insights for the project team.
- Gain a deep understanding of external market context for future businesses or services.
- Guide teams through the business viability process to help assess investments in new products, services, or ventures.
- Collaborate with key project stakeholders to understand their strategic priorities, key challenges and opportunities.
- Be an ambassador for Ford, building relationships with external business partners in order to test product and service pilots.
- Create and deliver inspiring presentations to senior executives and external audiences.
- Support development of strategic priorities and initiatives.
- Partner with Business Development and Finance regarding invest/buy opportunities.

(D-Ford), design thinking has been institutionalized at Ford.[5] While its initiatives are quite ambitious, and it will take years to tell if its investments in innovative new mobility projects will pay off, Ford has embraced a different way of going about innovation, anchored in design processes.

In Chapter 5, we used a strategic design lens to better understand business models, in particular their antecedents and what makes them

---

mobility, autonomous vehicles, the customer experience and data and analytics." (Ford Media Center, 2016)

[5]Roberts (2019) and Gelles (2016)

robust. That lens, however, was largely static. In this chapter, we adopt a more dynamic approach, i.e., a process perspective. For many design thinkers, the *process* is the key to successful design: "What really matters for a modern company is building design processes – lightweight methods for problem-solving, creativity and iteration."[6]

The process perspective on business model design is concerned with the question, "How do new business models come about?" It centers in particular on the issue of how to design business model innovations. To understand this better, researchers have examined the parallels between business model design and product innovation design. They have conducted in-depth case studies of business model innovation in both established and new firms. These analyses have led to the development of process models with distinct phases. They have also yielded the insight that at a high level of abstraction there seems to be little difference between product innovation and business model innovation. At a more fine-grained level, however, there are significant differences among the concrete activities that need to be performed in business model innovation compared with product innovation.[7]

Design as a process broadly consists of two steps: an analytical step of finding and discovery, and a synthetic step of invention and making.[8] These steps allow designers to create new products, services, or business models by (i) developing a deep and holistic understanding of end users to ideate new solutions; (ii) visualizing, prototyping, and refining new possibilities in an iterative manner; and (iii) creating a new activity system to realize and implement the nascent idea in a profitable way.[9]

California design company IDEO has championed a design process that has become widely adopted. Although it was originally devised for the design of new products, it has also proven to be effective for designing new services, as well as entire new businesses.[10] As mentioned above, it is the design approach that Ford has adopted, not only in new product development but as a new way of approaching business model problems. In the

[6]Vassallo (2018, p. 75)
[7]Bucherer, Eisert, and Gassmann (2012); Frankenberger, Weiblen, Csik, and Gassmann (2013)
[8]Owen (1998)
[9]Brown (2008)
[10]See Bhavani and Sosa (2008) and IDEO website.

next section, we will explain how it can be adapted for the design of new business models.

The Business Model Design Process

Case studies of business model change have yielded rich insights into the process of *how to* design a new business model. Spanish firm Kiluva, for example, developed a franchised network of Naturhouse stores selling dietary supplements in Spain and abroad. The firm managed to transform its business model through a process of trial-and-error. It subsequently scaled up its new model for international expansion. There were two distinct phases in its transformation. First, there was a five-year period during which the company experimented and explored a nutrition advice store concept. This was followed by a high-growth exploitation phase, when the company replicated the new store concept and its associated business model across Spain and neighboring countries.[11]

Building on this and similar cases, observations and insights from past research, and the IDEO design process, we offer in this section a design process model that not only describes at a high level how business model design works, but is also rich and detailed enough to provide specific guidance to business model designers. Business model innovation and enhanced value propositions for business model stakeholders are possible design outcomes.[12] To acknowledge this context-specific approach, we relabel the

[11] See Sosna, Trevinyo-Rodríguez, and Velamuri (2010). Other useful case studies include Demil and Lecocq's (2010) study of Arsenal Football Club (London, UK), and the study by Aspara et al. (2011) of Nokia's corporate transformation between 1987 and 1995.

[12] Regarding the design of systems (e.g., activity systems) as opposed to products, design theorists and practitioners alike have called for a greater integration of systems theory and design theory. Dunne (2018, p. 140) notes that "for some problems, the idea of a single 'user' is inappropriate.... What matter[s is] not just the end-user, but the entire network of stakeholders and the relationships between them: the *system*, in other words." He goes as far as suggesting that the integration of focal firm members in the design process will promote the successful implementation of the design solution. Vassallo (2018, p. 90), based on the observation of increasingly

three generic IDEO process stages – ideate, iterate, and implement – as BM*Ideate*, BM*Iterate,* and BM*Implement*, respectively, where "BM" stands for "business model," and "BM*I*" suggests business model innovation as a possible outcome.

BM*Ideate*

The first business model innovation design phase is BM*Ideate*. This entails observing business models in use, synthesizing insights, and finally generating innovative new business model solutions.

Observing Business Models In Use

When Airbnb co-founders Joe Gebbia and Brian Chesky launched their new business model in 2009, things were not doing well at first. Rentals were slow, the founders were in debt, and potential investors were hesitant due to the poor business metrics. In fact, many people doubted that the Airbnb model would ever work, because it required strangers to trust one another. At one end of the model, you had to let complete strangers sleep in your home; at the other end of the model, you had to sleep in a complete stranger's home. However, rather than cutting their losses and shutting down the new venture, Joe and Brian decided that they wanted to give it another try and help property owners better market their properties. So, they rented a nice camera and traveled to New York City, where they met with early users and took attractive photos of the rental properties on offer. While working with the property owners, they were able to observe first-hand the user experience, through which they gained valuable insights: "The thing we thought took two clicks, took 12! We were way wrong. It felt like this moment of enlightenment, seeing the world through their eyes. We gathered all those sources, stimuli, observations, and came

---

dense interconnectedness among people, suggests that "design thinking . . . needs to look at a bigger whole by incorporating . . . systems thinking . . . [which] sees collections of interdependent components as a set of relationships and consequences that are at least as important as the individual components themselves."

back to San Francisco, and we got smart because of it."[13] From their observation of business model users, they gained the insight that they needed to not only build an online rental marketplace, but more importantly simplify and build trust in the Airbnb model. Based on this insight, they decided to enact a number of enhancements to the business model to address and overcome the psychological and emotional trust barriers. For example, they added high-quality, reassuring images and edited the user interface to eliminate sharp edges. Following these design enhancements, Airbnb took off; rentals began to grow at an exponential rate.

As this example shows, and as we have already seen in Chapter 5, the design process should be grounded in a deep understanding of the user's true needs and problems. This can be achieved by a thorough observation of users on the ground, followed by subsequent analysis.[14] Chinese firm Transsion Holdings, which was founded in 2006 by George Zhu, is a leading provider of mobile phones in Africa and an example of a business model and associated product being built pursuant to a precise, deep observation. Prior to starting the company, Zhu worked in Africa for almost a decade; from this experience, he observed first-hand that the mobile phones available for sale did not meet local users' needs. In response, Transsion (largely through its Tecno brand, which started in Nigeria) designed phones with features specifically relevant for consumers in Africa, such as dual SIM card slots, longer battery life, and camera phones optimized for African complexions. Importantly, they are also low-cost. To achieve this, the company buys

---

[13]Quoted in Vassallo (2018)

[14]Observation is a natural first step in a bottom-up business model design process. A bottom-up process is team-based, interdisciplinary, and cuts through organizational hierarchies and across organizational functions, often following a human-centered, "design-thinking" philosophy. It may also involve outsiders, such as customers or strategic partners. Nevertheless, in order to initiate and move such a project forward, it will need to have the support of the top management team. A top-down business model design process, by contrast, is anchored in engaging the CEO and the Top Management Team (TMT). If the starting point of the design process is at the very top of the organizational hierarchy, the sequencing of steps in the ensuing design process could be different than when the starting point is situated lower. In the top-down case, the observation step is likely to be cut short, and the generation of ideas is likely to occur earlier in the ideation process, maybe even before observing business models in use, especially if the goal is to come up with a completely disruptive new business model.

pre-made components before assembling the phones, including in a local Ethiopian facility.

In the context of the business model, observation has to be interpreted more broadly than just with respect to how end users (renters in the Airbnb case) interact with a product or service. First, the focus should be on all business model stakeholders, i.e., not only end users but also suppliers (property owners in the Airbnb example), partners, and the focal firm itself. Second, observation should be about how stakeholders play their respective roles within a given business model, not (just) on how customers use the products and services delivered as part of the business model. Thus, observation for the purpose of designing new business models is more encompassing and complex than for designing new products or services. It requires the business model designer to gain a profound understanding of the DESIGN drivers introduced in Chapter 5: Deployable resources, External environment, Stakeholders' activities, Incumbents' templates, Goals, and Needs of business model stakeholders. To provide an illustration for the Needs driver, consider the need for trust to engage in transactions with strangers on an online platform in the Airbnb example.

For firms with an established business model, observation should be preceded by careful documentation and analysis of the current model. This is not a straightforward exercise, as relatively few firms engage in such analysis – let alone on a regular basis. They are therefore not acquainted with the relevant concepts, tools, and methods. As explained in Chapter 3, most managers are used to thinking very carefully and methodologically about products and services, but few have experience in analyzing the activity systems of their firms. However, to improve their existing models, senior managers need to first carefully take stock of their business model's content (***What***), structure (***How***), governance (***Who***), and value logic (***Why***). They also need to examine whether these are still consistent with the value creation and value capture goals of all relevant business model stakeholders. The debates, conversations, and insights that such analysis generates are themselves valuable. As is the case with product innovation, understanding what problem the focal firm is facing ("problem finding") could be as important, if not more so, than the subsequent solution. As John Arnold, a Stanford professor of mechanical engineering and design pioneer, put it: "Each of man's advances was started by a question. . . . Knowing what questions to ask and how to ask them is sometimes more important than the eventual answers."[15]

Achieving a deep understanding of the advantages and drawbacks of existing business models through internal analysis should be supplemented by field research based on ethnographic research methods, contextual inquiry, and on-site observation.[16] Such field research involves engaging deeply and personally with stakeholders (i.e., vendors, customers, and strategic partners) to understand how they perceive the value that is created for them by the focal firm's business model (i.e., the value proposition they perceive). What tangible benefits do they derive from being a participant in the focal firm's business model? What are their goals regarding value creation and capture with respect to their participation in the focal firm's business model, and how are these goals currently met?[17] Field research may also involve observing *non*-participants, e.g., non-customers, to find out more about their needs, and why their needs are currently not met by the focal firm's business model. For example, IDEO designers working with Ford devised an "immersive research" project on "multimodal transportation" to understand how ordinary people in Chicago went about their daily commutes in the city and the constraints (and options) they faced. The designers went on learning "excursions," such as going to lunch without a car, with a set time constraint and a budget constraint – all while carrying shopping bags. They also conducted interviews and trailed locals, including a doorman who went to work via walking and using public transportation, to gain insight into their behavior and come up with "ways to improve their commutes."[18]

The essence of this first step in the business model design process is asking not only what business model (non-)participants are doing, but also why, in order to understand meaning-based needs, and to anchor the new design solutions on those needs. This is important, because data often provides clues to what is happening, but not always why it is happening. Specific

---

[15]Quoted in Vassallo (2018, p. 24)
[16]See Beckman and Barry (2007, p. 30)
[17]Zeisel (2006, p. 226) refers to the interactions among various stakeholders as "environmental behaviour" and asks: "Who does what with whom? In what relationship sociocultural context, and physical setting?"
[18]Gelles (2016)

techniques include (i) interviewing business model (non-)stakeholders, asking them to tell a story of how the business model fits (or not) with their own goals and needs; (ii) observing how the stakeholders interact with the focal firm, such as how they use or contribute to the production or delivery of the focal firm's services and products; and (iii) trying to understand the strategic partners' own business models and what role the focal firm plays in it (looking "from the outside in"). As illustrated by the Airbnb example, observation is especially powerful – and more likely to deliver valuable insights – when it is anchored on a working prototype or early version of a business model; in other words, when there is a chance to see the business model in use. As Steve Jobs once stated, "It's really hard to design products by focus groups. A lot of times, people don't know what they want until you show it to them."[19] A few decades earlier, reflecting on his decision to introduce the Model T, although there had been no established market for mass-produced automobiles, Henry Ford had famously quipped: "If I had asked people what they wanted, they would have said faster horses."[20]

Moreover, designers should aim at gaining a better understanding of internal and external constraints (e.g., financial constraints, technology adoption rates, the macroeconomic situation) by talking to business model stakeholders, as well as experts in the relevant ecosystems. Issues that might be addressed are the problems and requirements that these third parties see, and how these perceptions compare with the focal firm's own assumptions.

Lastly, since the focal firm will not be operating in a competitive vacuum, observation should also comprise an explicit acknowledgement and analysis of the templates that firms operating in the same product-market space have adopted. Inspiration regarding business model designs can also be gleaned from firms operating in other industries and product-market spaces which share important characteristics or visions with the focal firm. For example, Autonomic, a venture acquired by Ford Smart Mobility in 2018 and based in Palo Alto, California, is building an open, cloud-based platform, called the "Transportation Mobility Cloud." Sunny Madra, now vice president at Ford X (and former CEO of Autonomic), compared their platform to Apple's operating system: "If you look at the iPhone when it

---

[19]Valentino-DeVries (2011)
[20]Gelles (2016)

first came out, half the apps they created and half they had curated. But today Apple makes 0.002% of all the apps. The rest of the ecosystem, the Ubers, the Instagrams, everything else are developed on the platform that they've created. We strongly feel that same ecosystem is going to evolve in the connected car, connected city ecosystem."[21]

Synthesizing Business Model Insights

Following observation of business models in use, the designers need to "identify interesting nuggets or stories from the data collected, to find patterns of behavior . . . and to see what is missing within the use, usability, and meaning" of the current business model design solution.[22] More specifically, synthesizing in the context of the business model means gaining a comprehensive, holistic understanding of the design challenges and influences that the focal firm is facing. For example, what customers are we/should we be serving? What are their needs/goals? What are their problems? Where are we currently falling short in helping customers solve their problems? What could we do better? To what extent do we rely on strategic partners to conduct activities for us? In other words, the business model designer needs to develop a strong sense of the market gap that the focal firm is addressing, the problems that it is solving for its various stakeholders, and the forces that will shape the design solution, for example, what activities other business model stakeholders could perform that are currently performed by the focal firm.

Synthesizing key insights from a vast amount of data may be the most difficult task in the design process. It involves collecting, and communicating, the data gathered during the observation stage, then organizing it creatively into emerging themes that may relate to the DESIGN drivers and/or to the business model design elements (i.e., the ***What, How, Who***, and ***Why*** of the activity system). This is akin to the work that qualitative researchers perform when they sift through large amounts of ethnographic and field data in order to detect new variables and/or theoretically interesting relationships. Although this step in the design process seems fuzzy, vague,

---

[21] Seeking Alpha (2018) and Strader (2018)
[22] Beckman and Barry (2007, p. 6)

and hard to codify, qualitative methods could provide enhanced rigor, such as through tabulation techniques.[23]

Besides identifying and crisply articulating the problem to be solved (see Chapter 9 on the importance of defining a clear problem statement), synthesizing insights about the business model may also involve the formulation of a new preliminary value logic and its associated value propositions (see Chapter 8). These can be used to map out the potential "opportunity" space. This also renders explicit the resources and capabilities of the focal firm and those of current business model stakeholders and other players in the ecosystem. The overarching objective of this step is to creatively organize and lay out all the pieces of the puzzle from which the new business model will eventually be constructed.

Generating New Business Model Solutions

After synthesizing the insights derived from observing stakeholders, the business model designer needs to generate solutions. These solutions should address the problems identified previously, better serve the needs of the various stakeholders, and enhance the focal firm's value propositions to them. This either involves making modifications to an existing business model, or creating an entirely new activity system from scratch. Newness can refer to the content (***What***), structure (***How***), governance (***Who***), and/or value logic (***Why***) of the business model. It can be achieved by engaging in a disciplined brainstorming exercise, which, as mentioned earlier, represents a structured technique for unleashing creativity. Ideas for new business models are often rooted in the work conducted prior to the brainstorming, keeping in mind previously gathered facts, the themes identified, and the DESIGN drivers. If the result of one brainstorming round is not satisfactory (for example, the solution is not novel enough), several rounds may be required to achieve a desirable outcome.

To maximize their effectiveness, brainstorming sessions should be guided by rules that are conspicuously displayed. These rules can be written on a whiteboard or posters, so that every participant can see them.[24] Given the complexity of the business model as a design object, some of these

[23]See Miles, Huberman, and Saldaña (2013)

[24]See Osborn (1963); Sutton and Hargadon (1996)

rules, such as "encourage wild ideas" or "be visual," should be elaborated. What are wild business model ideas, for instance, and how can one be visual about a business model? For instance, wild ideas are those that go beyond the traditional mental models of managers in the focal firm's industry, or break the traditional frame of thinking (such as introducing a vertically integrated business model in an industry where outsourcing is the norm; an example of this is Spanish retailer Zara in the fashion industry).

As mentioned in Chapter 5, the likelihood of breaking the frame can be increased by considering templates from completely unrelated industries. For example, the business model of Nike, a sports apparel manufacturer, could be considered as a template for redesigning the business model of a pulp and paper manufacturer, by using the sports company as an inspiration for focusing on marketing/branding and outsourcing non-core activities. The use of such non-conventional templates can be seen as "looking from the outside in." To break out of existing mental models, it is desirable that the brainstorming team be interdisciplinary and carefully composed of domain experts, business model experts (academics, business executives, or consultants), and a diverse group of outsiders (non-focal-firm members) with the ability to adopt a higher-level, system-wide perspective ("bird's eye view"). As we will see in Chapter 9, researchers have also started to develop ideas about how to visually depict business models, which could be useful for the brainstorming.[25]

There are several caveats concerning the use of brainstorming for generating ideas for new business models. First, the systemic nature of business models suggests an important guiding rule is: "Look at the forest, not just the trees!" In other words, the participants of a brainstorming session should be constantly encouraged to adopt a broad, holistic perspective, to avoid getting stuck on particular details. Second, since business models are more complex and abstract design objects than consumer products (such as

[25] Amit and Zott (2002, Figure 1), for example, graphically depicted eBay's business model in the form of a flow chart, where boxes that represent activities performed by business model stakeholders are connected by arrows that represent exchanges between the activities. In a similar vein, Sánchez and Ricart (2010, Figures 1–4) use flowcharts that connect performance indicators of business models, such as economies of scale, willingness to pay, or high brand recognition, to depict value creation dynamics (i.e., value loops, or virtuous circles).

toothbrushes), participants of a brainstorming session should have been deeply immersed into the prior steps of observing and synthesizing. This will have fostered their business model mindset (Chapter 3) and helped them develop a thorough, holistic understanding of the design task at hand. Third, recent research has shown that business model innovation is often enacted by powerful individuals. By contrast, teams with consensus-based decision-making practices may not be as effective for realizing business model innovations.[26] This suggests that firms that favor team-based idea generation formats need to think carefully about roles and responsibilities, such as who decides which ideas will be evaluated positively and taken forward to the next stage, BMI*terate*. Last but not least, brainstorming may not provide a full-fledged business model solution, but identify various (sometimes conflicting) elements that still need to be combined and aggregated into a coherent whole.

BMI*terate*

In the context of business model innovation, the next stage after ideating new business models involves (i) consolidating the various ideas into a coherent whole to yield one or possibly several alternatives; (ii) evaluating these alternatives according to relevant criteria; and (iii) prototyping the highest-ranked alternative(s) to the extent possible, i.e., experimenting on a small scale and keeping expenditures low. By combining and repeating these steps in an iterative manner, the goal in this phase of the business model design process is to achieve higher focus and clarity on the details of the emerging design.

Consolidating Business Model Ideas: Crafting a Coherent Whole

Consolidation is a necessary step because otherwise the designers might get caught up in an endless loop of generating new ideas, without knowing exactly which ones to use and combine, or when and where to stop.

[26]Snihur and Zott (2020)

The DESIGN drivers elaborated in Chapter 5 can serve as guiding principles for clustering and consolidating ideas.

- **Deployable resources/External environment**: Consolidation might be based on specific constraints, and how well the new ideas address the constraints. In the case of a fintech venture such as Zopa or Prosper, for example, the key element of the external environment to consider is existing banking regulations. If the firm is more established, another possible classification scheme could be anchored on internal constraints, such as the differences between the new idea and the existing business model, while considering the difficulty and the expected cost of integrating the new idea into the existing model.
- **Stakeholders' activities**: Another possibility would be to cluster business model ideas that leverage stakeholders' activities to a similar degree. For instance, one set of business model ideas might be consistent with a highly vertically integrated structure in which the focal firm performs most of the activities, whereas another set of ideas could view the focal firm solely as an orchestrator with many activities performed by third parties (suppliers, partners, and customers).
- **Incumbents' templates**: Another clustering principle might be to order ideas around powerful and inspirational templates, like well-known online marketplaces, platforms, or specific firms, such as "Amazon for . . . ," "eBay for . . . ," "Zara for . . . ."
- **Goals and Needs**: Ideas for new business model designs that emerge during the generation phase could also be grouped around the specific problems that they will likely help to address. In other words, they could be clustered around the goals and needs DESIGN drivers, with the objective of creating the strongest possible value propositions for key business model stakeholders.

One should also not discard the possibility, however, that powerful and unexpected themes for clustering might emerge during the ideation phase. Regardless of the criteria used for consolidation, the task of the business model designer at this stage is to create a coherent and consistent whole – specifying the ***What, How, Who,*** and ***Why*** of the new activity system – by selecting a few ideas from among many possible ones, combining them, and fleshing them out to yield a complete business model solution.

Evaluating the New Design(s) and Rank Ordering Them

Following the consolidation of business model ideas, the various emerging alternatives need to be evaluated. Important questions need to be addressed:

- How much total value does the new model create compared to the old one?
- Are the value propositions to stakeholders strong enough to provide them with sufficient incentives to participate in the business model?
- Can one find a revenue and cost structure to allow for adequate value capture for all business model stakeholders, so that they can meet their incentive compatibility constraints?
- How well is the goal of balanced value creation and capture being met?
- How scalable is the model? Can it support fast growth?
- What are the vulnerabilities and bottlenecks of the business model? Where can it break down? What are the chief risks?
- Are constraints effectively being dealt with? What new constraints are created or brought to the forefront?[27]
- How does the new business model compare with those of competitors? In particular, what points of differentiation (basis for competitive advantage) does it offer?
- How adaptable is the new business model to future changes in the DESIGN drivers (e.g., changes in customer needs)? To changes in technology?
- How robust is the new business model – i.e., does it offer high legitimacy and at the same time protect against imitation from competitors?
- Are the resources and capability in place in the focal firm (or with partners) to make the new model a reality?
- How compatible is the new business model with the firm's corporate strategy? How compatible is it with the existing organizational structure, including compensation and incentive mechanisms?

Evaluation might proceed by developing a scorecard that considers these questions (or any subset thereof) and assigns them weights. Each business

[27] For example, consider a focal firm that wants to change its distribution model by using dealers instead of direct selling. However, if the dealers refuse to take title to the inventory, and at the same time the focal firm cannot afford to take title itself, a new financial constraint is being highlighted.

model alternative could then be assessed using the scheme. The most highly rated alternatives could subsequently be prototyped. (Note that in keeping with the highly iterative nature of the business model design process, prototyping could precede evaluation, in order to better assess the above questions.)

Prototyping a New Business Model

Prototyping involves building a mock-up of the business model at the lowest possible cost. "Go fast" and "no frills" are typical guidelines for prototyping services that could also apply to prototyping business models.[28] In its simplest form, a business model prototype is a graphical, verbal, and visual description of "how it works," mixing text, graphical illustration, and video. It explains how the business model is relevant to various stakeholders, how they are supposed to interact with each other, what they are supposed to contribute, and what benefits they will get from participating.

After building the prototype, the various business model stakeholders must be exposed to it and given the opportunity to experience it. "The prototype is an attempt to solve the problem, but its main value is as a vehicle for learning."[29] On this basis, feedback can be collected from stakeholders about whether the business model helps them fulfill their goals, and whether it effectively meets their constraints. In other words, the designers must get into observation mode and repeat (iterate) various observational methods; observing and prototyping are most powerful when they go hand-in-hand. Each time business model designers try something, they learn a little bit more about the problem they should solve.[30] The feedback and insights gained can be used to refine the model further.

For example, as a division within Ford Smart Mobility, Ford X aims to quickly prototype new transportation solutions. One of its projects, Jelly, was conducted as a research project in partnership with Purdue University. It had a working business model prototype, where 40 scooters were distributed and used on the campus via an app. Its objective was to study how

---

[28]See Bhavani and Sosa (2008)

[29]Dunne (2018, p. 20)

[30]This iterative process has also been referred to as "co-evolution or problem-space and solution-space," or as "reflection-in-action." See Dunne (2018, p. 18-19).

e-scooters can best be incorporated into an urban environment.[31] According to Sunny Madra of Ford X, the Jelly project helped his team "better understand what's required to succeed in the micro-mobility space, such as the importance of human-centered design, the critical importance of a reliable supply chain, and the need to work with cities and campuses to do scooter sharing responsibly."[32] This comparatively low-cost test was an important source of learning and insights.

Prototyping may thus involve implementing a crude, possibly modular version of the business model, thereby enabling online (as opposed to offline) learning.[33] New elements or modules can be prototyped and added over time. The extent to which this is possible, however, depends on the specific business model at hand. For example, business models that require significant investment in capital expenditures (CapEx), or involve many important strategic partners, could be difficult to "mock up" and more challenging to prototype in a modular fashion. It is, nevertheless, not entirely impossible to prototype the "bricks and mortar" elements of new business models. Consider the example of CredEx, a microfinance fintech based in Shenzhen, China, that was founded in 2010.[34] The founders identified a gap in the market, namely providing small-scale loans to individuals and small businesses. At the outset, the company was entirely offline, with shops in major malls where potential borrowers applied for loans by completing mountains of paperwork. To utilize its expertise in microloans, CredEx started with an "Asset Transfer Model." Under this model, CredEx took care of loan applications and approvals, providing loans to customers using its own funds. These loans were then sold to banks, a source of funding for subsequent loans. The company's second business model, which was adopted in 2011, was the "Assisted Loan Model." Here, both banks and CredEx provided capital for loans, at a specific ratio. While CredEx performed all the activities around providing the loans, banks had the final say on whether to actually approve them.

Eventually, the offline services provided by CredEx moved to an app. Borrowers could apply directly through the app for loans; the entire loan

[31] Tally (2018)
[32] Madra (2018)
[33] Gavetti and Levinthal (2000)
[34] Amit and Han (2016)

application and approval process was digital and lasted less than ten minutes. In order to test the new online model, the firm developed numerous prototypes of the online interface with applicants and the back-office electronic follow-up. The rollout was gradual; initially, it was only available in one district of a city. During an expansion period of several months, the system was refined and perfected.

In summary, prototyping helps test assumptions underlying the attractiveness of the business model and generates data to assess the validity of these assumptions. If, for instance, the hypothesized value proposition rests on the assumption that customers really care about (and will pay a premium for) convenience, "we had better find out as quickly as possible if that is in fact true."[35]

BM*Implement*

Implementation in the context of BMI requires putting together all the elements that are envisioned by the new design. This includes design elements that refer to the ***What*** of the business model (i.e., what are the activities?), the ***How*** (i.e., how are the activities connected to each other?), the ***Who*** (i.e., who is carrying out each of the activities?), and also the ***Why*** (e.g., why is value created and captured? What is the revenue model?). The demarcation with the previous design stage (especially prototyping) can be rather fleeting, as it may not be easy (or desirable) to say where trial-and-error stops, and where full-blown implementation begins. This is especially true when implementation is gradual and guided by feedback-based learning. Recall, for instance, the Jelly scooter R&D project that Ford conducted with Purdue University. The learning it facilitated paved the way for Ford to acquire Spin, a dockless scooter share startup. With the acquisition of Spin, Ford turned its hitherto experimental scooter-sharing business model into a more tangible part of its portfolio of mobility solutions.

In any case, attention must be paid at this stage to the focal firm's organization, and how it fits with the new business model. Organizational redesign may be required as part of implementation in order to make the new business model work. (For more on this, see Chapter 10.)

---

[35]Liedtka and Ogilvie (2011, p. 131)

Distinctive challenges may arise at this stage for new and existing firms. In the case of new firms, the implementation of the new business model entails the acquisition of resources (e.g., capital, human resources, legitimacy), as well as the creation of processes through which these resources are deployed. These processes form the basis of the activities that the focal firm carries out (business model content) and of the exchanges that weave these activities together (business model structure). Implementation also entails the forging of partnerships, and the creation of exchange and coordination mechanisms with the parties that are external to the focal firm (business model governance). In addition, the business model designer needs to consider other issues of focal firm design, which should be consistent with the business model. These include the design of the internal organization (including incentive structures, span of control, roles and responsibilities of organization members, HR policies, values, culture, and norms), and the design of a product-market strategy (e.g., product-market scope, market timing entry, and product-market positioning).

In the case of existing (incumbent) firms, the implementation of the new business model will likely entail changes to the existing business model and/or to the organization design and strategy. In certain cases, the organizational cost of making these changes will be relatively low (e.g., when the business model change simply involves adding some new activities to the existing system, as was the case for Apple iTunes). In other cases, however, the costs of making the changes will be more significant, because they imply profound changes to the status quo and significant organizational change (e.g., IBM's move from a computer manufacturer to an IT services provider). Specifically, if the new business model represents a radical departure from the existing model, implementing the new business model will require a number of changes that need to be carried out simultaneously. The implied magnitude and complexity of these changes can entail high – and maybe even prohibitive – costs (both monetary and in terms of the time needed to carry out the changes). Chapter 10 will provide more detail on this, but we note here that at the heart of the implementation challenge are (i) the potential magnitude and complexity of the implied changes, which are due

Exhibit 6.2 Business Model Design Process

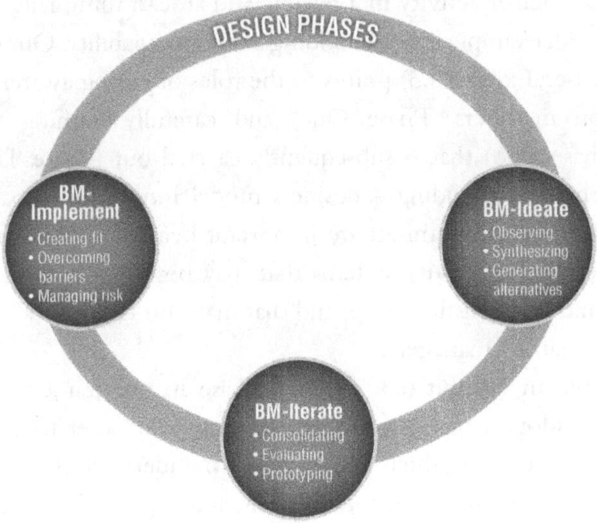

to the systemic nature of the business model; and (ii) the achievement of fit between the new business model, the organization, and the product-market strategy of the focal firm. Exhibit 6.2 summarizes the business model design process explained in this section.

Building a Business Model Innovation Capability

In this section, we present a process for building a business model innovation capability, and we highlight the strategic role of such a firm-level capability.[36] The section combines some of the key ideas from this and the previous chapter and extends them by moving from a one-time business model innovation to repeated business model innovation initiatives.

---

[36]This section draws on Amit, Giessen, and Zott (2019).

An organizational capability can be defined as "the capacity to perform a particular activity in a reliable and at least minimally satisfactory manner."[37] An example is Ford building a design capability. Our three-stage framework (see Exhibit 6.3) points to the roles of raising awareness among organization members (Phase One) and carefully framing the design process (Phase Two) that is subsequently carried out (Phase Three). The first two phases of building a business model innovation capability (i.e., raising awareness and framing) are important because business models are boundary-spanning activity systems that may be difficult to grasp due to their systemic and holistic nature, and that may also fall outside the familiar mental schemata of managers.

As shown in Exhibit 6.3, the first phase in our framework requires managers to adopt a business model perspective in order to complement their typical focus on products and services, to understand the strengths and weaknesses of their current business models, and to grasp the key dimensions along which the current business models can be innovated. We call this the "awareness stage." In the second phase, managers – as business model innovation designers – need to frame the design problem that they are facing. They do so by, for example, calibrating their aspirations with technological, financial, and human capital feasibility. We call this the "framing stage." In the third phase, managers need to carry out the creative business model (re-)design and implementation work in a well-defined design process. We call this the "design stage."

The key idea behind this framework is that building a business model innovation capability requires an initial spark provided in Phase One (awareness stage), then gradual development through iterative cycling between Phases Two (framing stage) and Three (design stage) across various business model innovation initiatives. Creating awareness (Phase One) helps framing (Phase Two), and vice versa. Enhanced awareness and framing then guide the design effort (Phase Three), which in turn heightens awareness of

[37] Helfat and Winter (2011, p. 1244)

Exhibit 6.3 Building a Business Model Innovation Capability

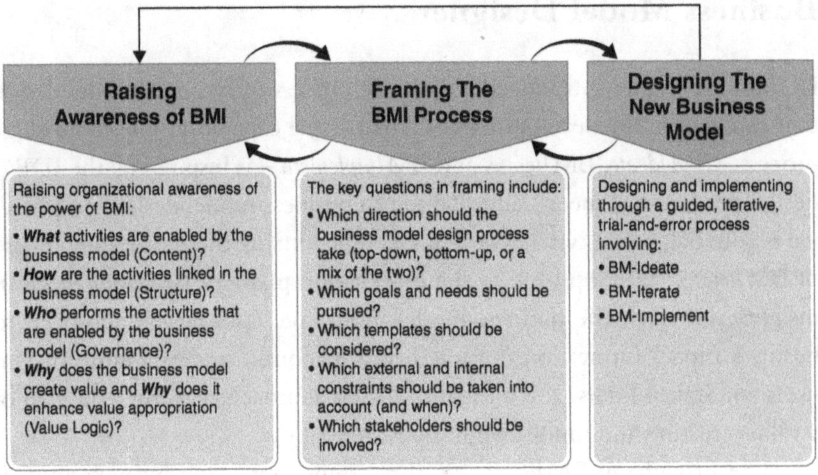

business model innovation (Phase One) and sharpens the attention paid to key boundary choices (Phase Two). These dynamic loops deepen managers' awareness of the design tasks at hand. They also allow them to develop their skills, build the right mindset, and refine the processes that form the basis of an organizational capability. When this is carried out repeatedly and mindfully over multiple business model innovation initiatives, a firm can build a business model innovation capability, which can be viewed as a dynamic capability.[38]

---

[38]A dynamic capability is a higher-order capacity that helps a firm integrate, build, and reconfigure internal and external resources to address and shape rapidly changing business environments (Teece, Pisano, and Shuen, 1997). Specifically, it refers to the "capacity of an organization to purposefully create, extend, or modify its resource base" (Helfat et al., 2007, p. 4). When designing a business model is performed repeatedly, in patterned ways, and embedded at least partly in organizational processes, it can be considered a dynamic capability (Amit and Zott, 2016). This higher-order capability characterizes how a focal firm develops a new business model, synchronizes the business model with its business environment, and/or shapes the business environment in its favor.

Summary of Key Takeaways for the Effective Business Model Designer

In this chapter, we introduced a dynamic process of business model design that can lead to the development of a firm-level capability. The three-stage process – BM*Ideate*, BM*Iterate*, and BM*Implement* – is inspired by the IDEO design process, but specifically adapted to business model design. Its phases are sequential, but also iterative. For example, during the prototyping phase of BM*Iterate*, you loop back to the observation phase of BM*Ideate* to glean insights and adapt the business model prototype. This design approach to business model innovation is rooted in a profound understanding of end users and stakeholders. It is a learning-based approach with the end goal of a value-creating and innovative business model.

The first phase, BM*Ideate*, has three steps: observing business models in use, synthesizing insights, and generating new solutions. In the first step, business model designers embark on a deep dive into the needs of all business model stakeholders, and the roles the stakeholders assume within the business model. The next step in the BM*Ideate* phase is synthesizing and making sense of the data and insights obtained in the first step, which requires translating the observations into clear, actionable insights. This stage helps flesh out the market opportunity, the problem(s) the solution addresses, and the forces behind the design solution. Finding links to organize data into different themes (such as the DESIGN drivers and the activity system elements) is a challenge that requires perseverance and creativity. During this step, the problem is also clearly defined and stated. A first version of the new value logic can be identified, along with the resources and capabilities of the focal firm and other stakeholders. In essence, the synthesis step spells out all the pieces that will form the new business model. The next step in BM*Ideate* is generating new solutions by brainstorming ideas for new business models. This may yield parts that need to be aggregated into a whole (in the BM*Iterate* stage), rather than a complete solution. It is important for brainstorming to be conducted by a diverse group that can think holistically and look from the outside in, and consider templates even from entirely different industries. At this stage, a graphical representation of the business model, such as a flow chart, can be constructed.

BM*Iterate*, the second phase of the business model design process, has three steps: consolidating business model ideas, evaluating alternatives, and prototyping the best ideas. The first step (consolidation) entails selecting a few ideas and creating a complete business model solution, which is guided by certain specification criteria (such as the DESIGN drivers). Next, these solutions are evaluated and ranked, the second step of the BM*Iterate* phase. Finally, the best choices can be prototyped (step three), which tests the assumptions that underpin the new solution. Prototyping can also happen before, or in conjunction with, the evaluation stage of BM*Iterate*. It entails building a mock-up of the business model that shows the role of each stakeholder, and the benefits they will achieve from participating in the business model. Feedback should be obtained from stakeholders on the prototype; the business model designers then go back into observation mode to iterate and refine the solution.

Finally, in the implementation phase (BM*Implement*), the elements of the new business model that have been identified in the previous steps are set into place. This phase often overlaps with prototyping of BM*Iterate*. For new companies, the relevant resources must be acquired, and the necessary processes (including exchange mechanisms with partners) set in place. The business model should be consistent with the internal organization and the firm's product-market strategy. For incumbent firms, the new business model often entails changes to the organization and firm strategy, which can be costly. These implementation challenges will be covered, along with others, in more depth in Chapters 10 and 11.

References

Amit, R., Giessen, E., & Zott, C. (2019). Building a business model innovation capability. Working paper.

Amit, R. & Han, X. (2016). *CredEx (A)*. Wharton Case Study 90. The Wharton School, University of Pennsylvania.

Amit, R. & Zott, C. (2002). Value drivers of e-commerce business models. In M. A. Hitt, R. Amit, C. Lucier, & R. D. Nixon (Eds.), *Creating Value: Winners in the New Business Environment* (pp. 15–47). Oxford, UK: Blackwell Publishers.

Amit, R. & Zott, C. (2016). Business model design: A dynamic capability perspective. In D. J. Teece & S. Leih (Eds.), *The Oxford Handbook of Dynamic Capabilities,* Oxford, UK: Oxford University Press. (Retreived from www.oxfordhandbooks.com)

Aspara, J., Lamberg J., Laukia, A., & Tikkanen, H. (2011). Strategic management of business model transformation: Lessons from Nokia. *Management Decision* **49**(4), 622–647.

Beckman, S. L. & Barry, M. (2007). Innovation as a learning process: Embedding design thinking. *California Management Review* **50**(1), 25–56.

Bhavani, R. & Sosa, M. (2008). IDEO: Service Design (A). Case study 10/2008-5276. INSEAD.

Brown, T. (2008). Design thinking. *Harvard Business Review* **86**(6), 84–92.

Bucherer, E., Eisert, U., & Gassmann, O. (2012). Towards systematic business model innovation: Lessons from product innovation management. *Creativity and Innovation Management* **21**(2), 183–198.

Demil, B. & Lecocq, X. (2010). Business model evolution: In search of dynamic consistency. *Long Range Planning* **43**(2–3), 227–246.

Dunne, D. (2018). *Design Thinking at Work: How Innovative Organizations are Embracing Design.* Toronto, CA: University of Toronto Press.

Ford (2018). D-FORD BUSINESS DESIGNER. Retrieved from https://ford.gr8people.com/index.gp?opportunityID=3133&method=cappportal.showJob

Ford Media Center (2017, October 3). Ford's Future: Evolving to become most trusted mobility company, designing smart vehicles for a smart world. Ford Media Center. Retrieved from https://media.ford.com/content/fordmedia/fna/us/en/news/2017/10/fords-future-evolving-to-become-most-trusted-mobility-company.html

Ford Media Center (2016, March 11). Ford Smart Mobility LLC established to develop, invest in mobility services; Jim Hackett named subsidiary chairman. Ford Media Center. Retrieved from https://media.ford

.com/content/fordmedia/fna/us/en/news/2016/03/11/ford-smart-mobility-llc-established--jim-hackett-named-chairman.html

Frankenberger, K., Weiblen, T., Csik, M., & Gassmann, O. (2013). The 4I-framework of business model innovation: A structured view on process phases and challenges. *International Journal of Product Development* **18**(3–4), 249–273.

Gavetti, G. & Levinthal, D. (2000). Looking forward and looking backward: Cognitive and experiential search. *Administrative Science Quarterly* **45**(1), 113–137.

Gelles, D. (2016, February 13). The commute of the future? Ford is working on it. *New York Times*. Retrieved from https://www.nytimes.com/2016/02/14/business/the-commute-of-the-future-ford-is-working-on-it.html

Helfat, C., Finkelstein, S., Mitchell, W., Peteraf, M., Singh, H., Teece, D., & Winter, S. (2007). *Dynamic Capabilities: Understanding Strategic Change in Organizations*. Malden, MA: Blackwell Publishing.

Helfat, C. & Winter, S. (2011). Untangling dynamic and operational capabilities: Strategy for the (n)ever-changing world. *Strategic Management Journal* **32**(11), 1243–1250.

IDEO website. Retrieved from http://www.ideo.com/expertise/business-design/

Johnson, M. W. (2018). How Ford is thinking about the future. *Harvard Business Review Digital Articles*, 2–6. Retrieved from https://hbr.org/2018/05/how-ford-is-thinking-about-the-future

Liedtka, J. & Ogilvie, T. (2011). *Designing for Growth: A Design Thinking Tool Kit for Managers*. New York, NY: Columbia University Press.

Madra, S. (2018, November 8). Let's go for a spin: Ford buys scooter company to provide customers a first-last mile solution. *Medium*. Retrieved from https://medium.com/cityoftomorrow/lets-go-for-a-spin-ford-buys-scooter-company-to-provide-customers-a-first-last-mile-solution-bbeae278d373

Miles, B., Huberman, A. M., & Saldaña, J. (2013). *Qualitative Data Analysis: A Methods Sourcebook*. Thousand Oaks, CA: SAGE Publications Inc.

Osborn, A. F. (1963). *Applied Imagination: Principles and Procedures of Creative Problem-Solving*. New York, NY: Charles Scribner's Sons.

Owen, C. L. (1998). Design research: Building the knowledge base. *Design Studies* **19**(1), 9–20.

Roberts, I. (2019, December 4). How design is driving Ford to reimagine what a car company can be. *IDEO*. Retrieved from https://www.ideo.com/journal/how-design-is-driving-ford-to-reimagine-what-a-car-company-can-be

Sánchez, P. & Ricart, J. E. (2010). Business model innovation and sources of value creation in low-income markets. *European Management Review* **7**(3), 138–154.

Schwab, K. (2019, November 17). Ford is betting its future on an electric Mustang SUV. *Fast Company*. Retrieved from https://www.fastcompany.com/90431339/ford-is-betting-its-future-on-an-electric-mustang-suv

Seeking Alpha (2018, September 12). Ford Motor Company (F) management presents at Morgan Stanley's sixth annual Laguna Conference (Transcript). Seeking Alpha. Retrieved from https://seekingalpha.com/article/4205876-ford-motor-company-f-management-presents-morgan-stanleys-sixth-annual-laguna-conference?part=single

Snihur, Y. & Zott, C. (2020). The genesis and metamorphosis of novelty imprints: How business model innovation emerges in young ventures. *Academy of Management Journal* **63**(2), 554–583.

Sosna, M., Trevinyo-Rodríguez, R. N., & Velamuri, S. R. (2010). Business model innovation through trial-and-error learning: The Naturhouse case. *Long Range Planning* **43**(2–3), 383–407.

Strader, R. (2018 January 9). Why we're working with Autonomic to create a platform that can power future cities. *Medium*. Retrieved from https://medium.com/cityoftomorrow/why-were-working-with-autonomic-to-create-a-platform-that-can-power-future-cities-96700c2824e6

Sutton, R. I. & Hargadon, A. (1996). Brainstorming groups in context: Effectiveness in a product design firm team. *Administrative Science Quarterly* **41**(4), 685–718.

Tally, S. (2018, October 23). E-scooters at Purdue are sweet as jelly. Purdue University. Retrieved from https://www.purdue.edu/newsroom/releases/2018/Q4/e-scooters-at-purdue-are-sweet-as-jelly.html

Teece, D. J., Pisano, G., & Shuen, A. (1997). Dynamic capabilities and strategic management. *Strategic Management Journal* **18**(7), 509–533.

Valentino-DeVries, J. (2011, August 24). Steve Jobs's best quotes. *Wall Street Journal.* Retrieved from https://blogs.wsj.com/digits/2011/08/24/steve-jobss-best-quotes/

Vassallo, S. (2018). *The Way to Design.* San Francisco, CA: Foundation Capital.

Zeisel, J. (2006). *Inquiry by Design – Environment/Behavior/Neuroscience in Architecture, Interiors, Landscape and Planning.* New York, NY: WW Norton & Company.

Zott, C. & Amit, R. (2015). Crafting business architecture: The antecedents of business model design. *Strategic Entrepreneurship Journal* **9**(4), 331–350.

7 How to Design a New Business Model – Methods Championed by Startup Entrepreneurs

Converting Design Ideas into Practice

In the previous chapter, we introduced a design-led process for envisioning and crafting a new business model. The strength of that process lies in its early stages, BM*Ideate* and BM*Iterate*, which help managers and entrepreneurs unveil the needs of customers and other stakeholders, in part through human-centered observation. Through a mix of analytical and synthesis techniques, they are able to craft a business model that utilizes these observations and meets the identified stakeholders' needs; is aligned with the long-term goals and vision of the focal firm; creates value for all stakeholders, not just the end users; complements the focal firm's product-market strategy; and fits with the firm's organizational structure. As such, the innovative business model contributes to the competitive advantage of the focal firm. If management develops a business model innovation capability, which enables ongoing, repeated business model innovations, the sustainability of the focal firm's competitive advantage is enhanced.

The last stage of the design process, BM*Implement*, however, is less well scripted and explained in theory and practice than the preceding stages. At this stage, business model designers and innovation managers often resort to employing techniques from other fields, such as entrepreneurship or organization, to identify and apply suitable processes for converting design ideas for new business models into practice. Entrepreneurial processes in particular have become increasingly popular for this purpose – not just with new ventures, but also within established firms. These processes are typically associated with the development of startups or corporate ventures under conditions of high uncertainty and resource scarcity.

Given their increasing importance, in this chapter we introduce and discuss three distinct entrepreneurial processes. Two of these processes (discovery-driven planning and effectuation) have been proposed by entrepreneurship scholars, and the third has been widely adopted in practice (lean startup). We elaborate on their basic principles, illuminate their intellectual roots, explain what they have in common and how they differ, and discuss their suitability for developing new business models. Together with the design process introduced in Chapter 6, they constitute a "process tool kit" for managers and entrepreneurs interested in developing new business models. In that sense, they also complement the analytical business model tool kit that will be introduced in Chapter 9, which helps to articulate, create, and communicate business model ideas to others.

The entrepreneurial processes presented below should be viewed as complements, rather than substitutes, for the design methodology laid out in Chapter 6. They should also be seen as complementary to each other. Indeed, pragmatic managers are often agnostic to pure-bred techniques. Instead, they often combine methods to obtain better results. Thus, when crafting their own innovation journey or building their own innovation process, managers mix and match discovery-driven, effectual, and lean principles.

Consider, for example, the innovation process of German multinational company Bosch. In recent years, Bosch has launched, in partnership with UC Berkeley, an internal accelerator program that supports new startups. It relies on an innovation framework for developing new products and business models, rapidly and at low cost. The framework incorporates and combines elements of lean startup and business model design. Because teams participating in the Bosch accelerator test and validate ideas before full-blown development, development costs are significantly reduced (up to 6–10 times).[1]

Discovery-Driven Planning – Fail Soon, and Fail Fast

The first of the three entrepreneurial processes we will cover is discovery-driven planning (DDP), which tackles the inherent uncertainty around designing an innovative new business model by proposing a framework for identifying and testing crucial assumptions.

Basic Principles of Discovery-Driven Planning

As the name suggests, discovery-driven planning (DDP) is a normative entrepreneurial technique that combines the discipline of planning with an openness to unexpected discoveries. Originally developed by Ian C. MacMillan, the Dhirubhai Ambani Emeritus Professor of Innovation and Entrepreneurship at the Wharton School, and Columbia Business School Executive Programs Faculty Rita Gunther McGrath, its goal is to facilitate entrepreneurship in established firms. It promises an increase in the expected performance of entrepreneurial initiative by lowering the probability and/or the cost of failure.[2] At its heart lies the imperative to test assumptions about an entrepreneurial project in a rigorous, comprehensive, and systematic manner. This enables a learning process fueled by planned experimentation,

---

[1]Innovation Leader (2019)

[2]McGrath, MacMillan, and Venkataraman (1995); McGrath and MacMillan (2000)

which gradually reduces uncertainty and increases knowledge about key elements of the business model. Discovery-driven entrepreneurs are guided through "enlightened trial and error" and learn their way into an uncertain future.

At every learning point (also called a "milestone" or "checkpoint"), the entrepreneurial managers need to ask themselves a range of questions about the business model opportunity, its underlying assumptions, and whether it truly makes sense to continue with the project in its considered form. The discovery-driven implementation process thus creates a series of decision points at which the project can be discontinued – or adapted in response to the improved information base. Put differently, testing assumptions at milestones creates a series of real options for the entrepreneurial manager that allows them to withdraw from the venture, or continue investing in it with an improved concept.[3] This real options logic underlying the discovery-driven technique is supported by empirical evidence, specifically the fact that the success of well-performing venture capitalists is partly due to their rigor and discipline in pulling the plug from (i.e., ceasing to supply further cash to) underperforming portfolio companies and concentrating on the better-performing ones.[4] The underlying philosophy could be summarized as "If you have to fail, then it is better to fail sooner, and more cheaply."

More specifically, discovery-driven planning consists of six interrelated steps: framing, benchmarking, specification of deliverables, testing of assumptions, managing to milestones, and parsimony.

Framing

Framing (step one) asks the entrepreneurial managers to define long-term success by asking a series of questions. For example, what would a successful project look like several years in the future? What would make the

---

[3]A real option refers to the opportunity to acquire or develop an asset. The corresponding investment has three characteristics: it is partially or completely irreversible; there is uncertainty over the future rewards from the investment; and one has some leeway about the timing of the investment (Dixit and Pindyck, 1994).
[4]Guler (2018)

project worthwhile for them? What metric would they use to measure success? Discovery-driven planning thus encourages entrepreneurial managers to first think about the end game for their projects, establishing a clear vision and long-term goal that is worth striving for. Then, like chess masters, the entrepreneurs should reason back from there (game theorists would call this "backward induction") to figure out what they need to do in order to maximize the likelihood of reaching their long-term goal.[5] For example, if the goal is to achieve high profits with a new business model, then based on the profit margin requirements a *reverse income statement* can be established that indicates the revenues that are necessary to deliver the required profit. In the context of strategically designing an innovative business model, framing in DDP corresponds to the "goal" design driver in the business model design process (see Chapters 5 and 6).

Benchmarking

Benchmarking (step two) asks the entrepreneurial manager to peg the key revenue and cost metrics (e.g., from the reverse income statement) against the market, and against the firms with the most comparable business models. The purpose of this step is to establish as realistic a starting point as possible with the new business model project. Like step one (framing), this is a purely conceptual exercise that does not yet require any significant investments in the project. Instead, it entails the identification of what we called "templates" (see Chapter 5) and benchmarking against them.

Specification of Deliverables

Specification of deliverables (step three) is also conceptual, as it involves laying out all the activities that are required to generate and deliver the customer experience; in other words, it involves being clear and specific about the operational requirements of the various activities (i.e., the ***What***)

[5]Backward induction is a powerful technique to solve multistage games. It consists in first solving the last stage for an optimal solution, then based on this the second-to-last stage, then the third-to-last stage, and so on (Aumann 1995).

that constitute the business model. For example, how many salespeople are needed to sell the new product or service, and to earn the required revenues determined in step one? How many sales calls do they have to make? How many leads do they have to generate? What conversion rate is necessary (i.e., how many sales do they have to close, and in what time period)? In the context of business model design, this step corresponds to the determination of the content of the business model, namely what activities are needed.

At this stage, key assumptions are made that should be carefully documented in a *Key Assumptions Checklist.* Establishing this list requires a conversation among all those involved with the project. Getting these parties to agree on the assumptions that are being made is critical, but not straightforward. Different managers often take different business model assumptions for granted (e.g., based on their specific experience or "gut feeling"). However, some of these assumptions later turn out to be wrong, which can be extremely costly. This step of carefully documenting and agreeing on assumptions should therefore not be skipped. It constitutes the essence of the discovery-driven planning approach: to acknowledge with the greatest possible honesty what one does not know for sure about the business model and its desired effects.

Chemdex.com, which was established in September 1997, is a well-documented example of what was then a new B2B e-commerce business model. It failed because the founders had made bold assumptions about the business model without carefully testing them, which later turned out to be fatal. The basic idea behind Chemdex.com was to facilitate trade in specialty chemicals, such as laboratory chemicals and enzymes. The company aimed to replace the catalogue-based business model of previous suppliers. It also sought to increase efficiency in the specialty chemicals supply chain by providing up-to-date information about products and prices, and reducing mark-ups from intermediaries. Chemdex.com went public in 1999, despite having obtained only $29,000 in revenue in 1998. It raised a total of $670 million from investors (including Kleiner Perkins Caufield & Byers, a top-tier US venture capital firm). At its peak, it boasted a market capitalization of $7 billion, with a stock price of $243 per share. By June 2001, however, barely four years after founding, its shares were worth only a few cents. Investors realized that key assumptions they had made – for example, about likely lack of competitive reaction, high speed of adoption by customers, low costs of technology implementation, etc. – were completely wrong and untenable. As a result, the business model was not commercially viable. In a discovery-driven implementation plan, these assumptions would have been identified and tested earlier, and without burning through so much money along the way.

Testing, Milestones, Parsimony

Testing of assumptions (step four), managing to milestones (step five), and parsimony (step six), are no longer merely conceptual steps of discovery-driven planning, but involve action. These steps, which refer to the careful use of resources and a reluctance to make large upfront expenditures, are most powerful when they are combined with each other. Key assumptions about the business model (identified in step three) should be tested (step four) early on in the business development process at milestones (or checkpoints, step five) that have been preselected or even created because they allow for maximum learning at the lowest possible cost (step six).

For example, assumptions about the value proposition of a new online insurance business model – such as for which customer groups it most resonates – could be tested by creating an experiment on Facebook targeted at various user groups. The data from the experiment could then be used to assess the validity of the assumptions. These could subsequently be adjusted if necessary, along with the reverse income statement and operational requirements. If the project no longer looks feasible or attractive enough, then the focal firm needs to ask whether it should invest more time and money into the project, change its business model (i.e., perform a "pivot"), or even abandon it.

Oil and gas firm Royal Dutch Shell, for example, decided *not* to launch an innovative car-hailing service, FarePilot, after an 18-month experiment in London (Europe's biggest car-booking market) revealed that demand for the service was simply not strong enough. The original idea was to help drivers on car-hailing platforms such as Uber find areas in which taxi demand was high. In a pivot, Shell changed the business model to one that would link drivers to other private hire taxi companies. However, it could not get that model to work profitably, either. In the end, the company made the decision to shut the project down.[6]

Conversely, enterprise messaging platform Slack resulted from a successful business model pivot by founder Stewart Butterfield, following the sale of another project, Flickr, to Yahoo in 2005. Butterfield co-founded Flicker's parent company, Ludicorp, which was initially focused on a multiplayer online game. While the game was not a success, the Ludicorp team turned one of the game features into Flickr. After this successful (first) pivot, and the subsequent sale of Flickr, Butterfield tried to again launch an online multiplayer game, Glitch, which was released in 2011. Glitch, however, was once again not a success. Undeterred, Butterfield shifted his attention to a tool his team had developed for sending internal messages, which was known as the "Searchable Log of All Conversation and Knowledge" (or Slack for short).[7] The (second) pivot by Butterfield clearly paid off, and by 2019 Slack had grown to 10 million daily users.[8]

Discovery-Driven Business Model Development: Pros and Cons

Discovery-driven planning applies to entrepreneurial and corporate venturing, which includes the design and implementation of a (sometimes novel) business model. Every venture and incumbent has a business model, with associated assumptions that must be identified and tested. The discovery-driven planning methodology is applicable to the identification and testing of business model-specific assumptions, especially when the goal is to innovate the business model (and not just to come up with a better mousetrap, such as the next generation of smartphones).

Business model assumptions are made about the design elements of the activity system, namely about the ***What***, ***How***, ***Who***, and ***Why*** dimensions (see Chapter 1). In addition, assumptions are made about how the

[6]Raval and Ram (2019)
[7]Griffith (2019) and Born Digital (2015)
[8]Kastrenakes (2019)

system functions as a whole.[9] These business model assumptions should be highlighted in the *Key Assumptions Checklist*. Examples include:

- Key activities can be performed at a reasonable cost (***What?***)
- We can get sufficient and reliable real-time information at low cost from our customers about their (changing) preferences, and we can feed this information into our production system so that new products can be designed rapidly (***How?***)
- We will be able to partner with the government to certify our services (***Who?***)
- Customers will accept a subscription-based model for ordering basic items (***Why?***)
- The business model ensures that new product designs that correspond to new customer needs are available in less than ten business days (*system-level property*)

Discovery-driven business model development is consistent with the experimentation-driven approaches for building new business models that seem to prevail in practice.[10] In contrast with general trial-and-error experiments, however, "with discovery-driven planning companies can model the uncertainties and update their financial projections as their experiments create new data."[11] More importantly, "one can experiment with business models conceptually before any investment is required."[12] Thus, discovery-driven planning constitutes a refined way to explore the validity and viability of a new business model. Like design thinking (Chapters 5 and 6), it represents reflection-in-action: steps 1–3 (framing, benchmarking, specification of deliverables) involve reflection (before taking potentially expensive action), and steps 4–6 (testing assumptions, managing to milestones, parsimony) involve action (to sharpen one's ability to reflect).

---

[9]Systems theory suggests that any system may exhibit emerging properties that do not arise directly and that cannot be predicted from the properties of the parts (Von Bertalanffy, 1972).
[10]E.g., Sosna, Trevinyo-Rodríguez, and Velamuri (2010)
[11]Chesbrough (2010, p. 362)
[12]McGrath (2010, p. 259)

Additional advantages of discovery-driven business model implementation include the following:

- It promises to increase the overall return on investment, especially over a portfolio of entrepreneurial projects, by reducing the probability and the expected cost of failure.
- It creates a series of decision (go/no-go) points that force a manager to explicitly consider adapting the concept, pivoting to another concept, or abandoning the project altogether.
- It requires extensive communication among all those involved in the business model project (for example, to reach consensus over assumptions made) and thus helps to create alignment around a common vision.
- It fits well with the systematic, disciplined, and process-oriented way in which many businesses are run, and with which many employees and managers feel comfortable. Discovery-driven planning is like a "Trojan horse" that enables the injection of entrepreneurial techniques and initiative "through the back door" into established firms. Packaged as a process, it asks employees to become keenly aware of the assumptions that they are making, and to creatively design experiments through which these assumptions can be tested in a smart and entrepreneurial fashion – namely, cheaply and early, as startup entrepreneurs would do.
- It sends an important message about failure to members of the organization. More specifically, it communicates to the team that failure in business model projects conducted under high uncertainty and severe resource constraints is "OK" when it is well-reflected, that is, when it is a result of learning from well-designed experiments that test crucial assumptions. Thus conceived, it is better to fail earlier and cheaply – rather than later and at greater cost.[13]

Of course, there are also a number of challenges with applying discovery-driven planning to business model development.

- First, as explained in Chapter 3, business models are sometimes difficult to grasp conceptually, because they are a system-level construct.

---

[13]Thomke (2003) makes a distinction between failures and mistakes. Failures are natural outcomes of intentional and well-designed experiments. As such, they are useful because they facilitate learning and reduction of uncertainty. Mistakes refer to thoughtless or poorly designed experiments, or to a lack of conscious tests of important assumptions; they impede learning.

In a related vein, it may be challenging to exhaustively identify all the assumptions that one is making about the business model, especially at the system level.

- Second, performing market tests of entire business models (as opposed to prototyping and/or testing particular products or services) can be challenging and requires careful thought.
- Third, it can be inherently difficult to admit that you do not know everything, and that you may even have significant knowledge gaps. But this is precisely what is required for discovery-driven planning. Without this precondition, the method will not work or deliver its desired results.
- Fourth, one of its main advantages – that it requires a great deal of communication among business model stakeholders and those involved in implementing the new model – could also be a main source of difficulty. Communication-intensive processes can lead to disagreements and promote interpersonal conflict, especially if those involved are not process-savvy or do not have the required soft skills.
- Fifth, despite its process-based and systemic nature, discovery-driven planning goes against the conventional planning philosophy behind linear, stage-gated, and history-based (rather than forward-looking) planning approaches that are prevalent in many established firms. This problem is exacerbated if the discovery-driven approach requires taking steps (like canceling a project) that could be perceived as threatening vested interests and undermining an individual's career and power.
- Sixth, last but not least, scientific evidence about the DDP approach is scant; as a whole, it has not been subject to rigorous empirical testing and scrutiny.

Other Planning Approaches That Are Related to Discovery-Driven Principles

Building on the key ideas and principles behind discovery-driven planning, scholars have proposed other closely related business model implementation approaches.[14] One of these approaches has been termed *Parallel Play*, because overall it resembles the ways in which preschool-aged children discover new things about the world by engaging in play.[15] Rather than competing with their peers when playing, young children take an active

[14]E.g., Gans, Stern, and Wu (2019); McDonald and Eisenhardt (2020)
[15]McDonald and Eisenhardt (2020)

interest in others around them and often mimic what they are doing. They also test different toys before choosing a favorite. Scholars have observed that such behaviors also characterize the ways in which effective entrepreneurs in nascent markets develop their business models. In a nascent market, the demand for new products and services is unclear. Only a few, often new firms strive to navigate the unchartered waters of a highly dynamic, uncertain, and ambiguous new market environment.[16] The *Parallel Play* process can be applied to effectively craft a working business model in such a challenging market environment. As Exhibit 7.1 shows, it combines elements of design and discovery-driven planning.

Specifically, *Parallel Play* helps entrepreneurs with their choice among various alternative business model designs. It entails entrepreneurs designing and prototyping their business models by borrowing ideas from startup competitors in the nascent market, and also by drawing on the templates of incumbents in adjacent markets that offer substitute products (see the box "Playful" Design in Exhibit 7.1). Before committing to one specific business model option, however, effective entrepreneurs have been shown to deliberately test major assumptions (the core of discovery-driven planning) about the various business model alternatives (see the box Discovery-Driven Learning in Exhibit 7.1).

The idea of searching for, considering, and testing *various* business models for the same opportunity *in parallel* represents a refinement of the basic discovery-driven process introduced earlier, which assumes the pursuit of a single preferred option. In a nascent market, however, business model designers should not commit too soon to a favorite design option due to the high uncertainty of the market environment. They also need to be aware that such commitment may entail significant opportunity costs, by putting the venture on a distinct path and thereby possibly foreclosing other business model options down the road (which may subsequently turn out to have been better choices). This is also known as the *Paradox of Entrepreneurship*.[17]

---

[16]According to Santos and Eisenhardt (2009, p. 644), nascent markets are "business environments in an early stage of formation . . . characterized by undefined or fleeting industry structure . . . unclear or missing product definitions . . . and lack of a dominant logic to guide actions . . . Thus, nascent markets constitute unstructured settings with extreme ambiguity."
[17]Gans, Stern, and Wu (2019)

Exhibit 7.1 *Parallel Play* Process for Designing Business Models in Nascent Markets

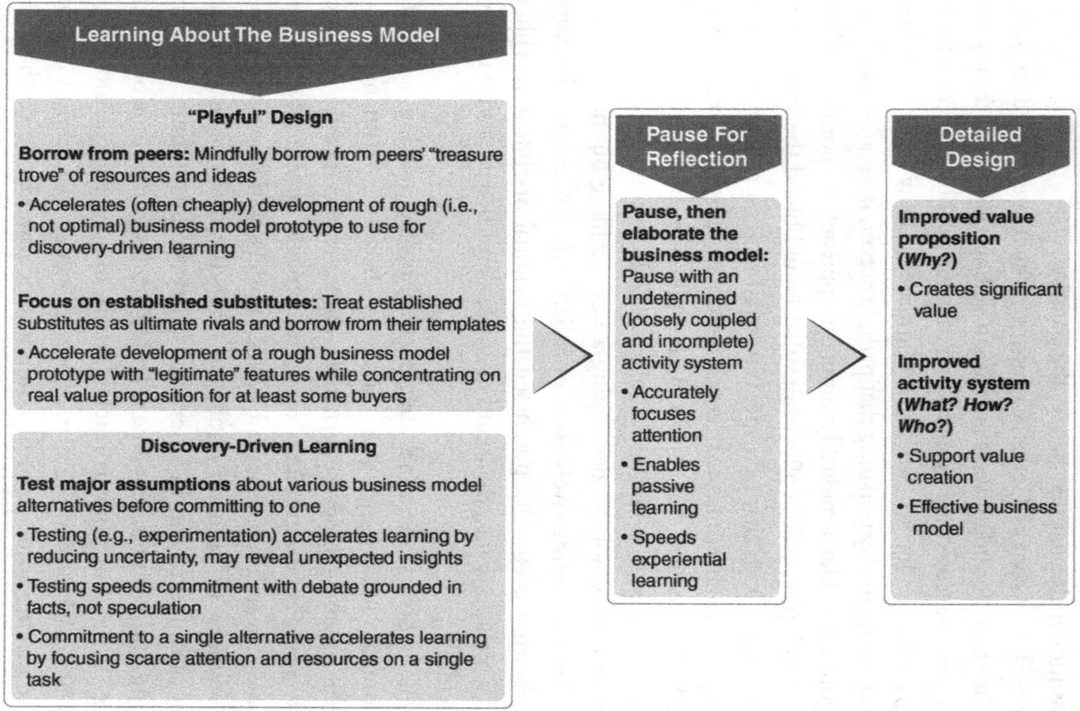

Source: Adapted from McDonald, R. M. & Eisenhardt, K. M. (2020). Parallel Play: Startups, Nascent Markets, and Effective Business-model Design. *Administrative Science Quarterly*, **65**(2), 483–523.

Ranking alternative viable business models requires knowledge that can only be gained through experimentation, but experimentation to resolve uncertainty ultimately results in some level of commitment that can shape the market and/or influence other paths, even to the point of foreclosing other business model alternatives; hence, the paradox.

Consider Starbucks Coffee Company, which was started in Seattle in 1971. Its three founders were intent on selling premium, freshly roasted coffee beans, because they thought that this was the best approach for introducing quality coffee to American consumers. They built their business model accordingly. By pursuing that path, however, it became less likely that they would consider a radically different approach to commercialization, such as developing retail coffee shops that would blend the Italian café bar business model with that of a specialty retail store, a gallery, and an office (for more on such conceptual combination of templates, see Chapter 3, especially the section "Cognitive Underpinnings of Business Models"). That is why employee Howard Shultz was able to leave the company and pursue his own vision by developing a new retailing business model that centered – counterintuitively – on an Italian-style coffee bar. The company Schultz started eventually purchased the original Starbucks (keeping the name), which grew into the brand of coffee shops that are today ubiquitous worldwide.[18]

Some scholars therefore suggest that before making a significant commitment and engaging in discovery-driven experimentation of a particular business model alternative, entrepreneurs should conduct an extensive, largely commitment-free search process. Specifically, they should continue to search for possible business model solutions to the perceived customer need or problem until they reach the limits of learning in the absence of commitment. In other words, they should continue until further searching and commitment-free learning no longer seem worthwhile or possible. When this point is reached, there may be two or more business model alternatives with similar expected values that cannot be ranked without making some level of commitment toward one of them. From these, the business model decision-makers will have to choose and commit

[18]Schultz and Jones Yang (1999)

to one based on their sound judgment, taking into consideration their own values, vision, intuition, and identity.[19]

In line with discovery-driven principles, entrepreneurs should thus avoid making important, costly, and potentially irreversible choices up front without properly considering the alternatives. This is because the resulting activity system and its concomitant commitments and responsibilities could be difficult to unwind. At the same time, however, they should not delay commitment for too long, because otherwise they will not learn fast enough what works and what does not work, especially in a nascent market. Such commitment involves the adoption of a basic structure regarding the ***What***, ***How***, ***Who***, and ***Why*** of the activity system, but it does not yet require having a fully formed business model in which all details have been unequivocally addressed. The basic principles and ideas should be in place. This not only allows for active learning via testing, but also for passive learning from observation of the "bare bones" (i.e., loosely coupled and under-determined) business model and how it works in practice (see box Pause for Reflection in Exhibit 7.1). Such learning enables the entrepreneur to further reduce uncertainty and proceed with completing and elaborating the business model. For example, a successful "social investing" startup, which connected seasoned investors to "followers," did not see its direct peers (startups in the same market) as competitive threats.[20] It observed these peers at the early stages, even borrowing from them useful, specific business model elements. As the startup experimented and tested its assumptions, it chose to focus on larger, established industry rivals such as UBS or Fidelity (who offered substitute products) as a greater competitive threat.

In summary, *Parallel Play* refines the discovery-driven planning method for developing a business model by suggesting more than one alternative for largely commitment-free staged experimentation first, and then by initially leaving the business model deliberately under-specified once a particular option has been chosen. This fosters both active learning through

---

[19]Gans, Stern, and Wu (2019)

[20]Example cited in McDonald and Eisenhardt (2020)

experimentation (assumption testing) and passive learning from observation, which mirrors a tenet of design thinking, namely the importance of human-centered observation.

Effectuation – Just Do It!

The key idea behind discovery-driven planning is to successively reduce uncertainty by engaging in active, deliberate, low-cost, and low-commitment experiments that make it possible to test key assumptions about business models. Discovery-driven planning is based on two main premises. The first premise is that managers know what they do not know (and hence what they need to test). The second premise is that they already have a pretty good idea of the market opportunity (a.k.a. customer needs) and possible solutions (specifically, business models) to address it. If these two requirements are not met, essential steps of discovery-driven planning such as framing, benchmarking, or specification of deliverables would be nearly impossible to carry out. What happens in practice if these preconditions are not met? What if, for example, managers do not know what they do not know; that is, they face non-quantifiable risk (also referred to as "uncertainty"[21]) instead of quantifiable risk (which refers to a situation in which the possible outcomes are known and can be associated with probabilities)? Or, what if they only have a vague hunch about a potential gap in the market? In situations such as these, where there is high uncertainty (as is often the case at an early stage of problem-finding), an entrepreneurial process known as *effectuation* may be useful for crafting a value-creating business model.[22]

---

[21] Knight (1921)

[22] Sarasvathy (2001) coined the term "effectuation" based on a study of 45 expert entrepreneurs, whom she interviewed and asked to solve problem sets by speaking out loud so that she could follow and study their thought processes. She found that a majority of the entrepreneurs she studied used effectuation, which she defined as processes that "take a set of means as a given and focus on selecting between possible effects that can be created with that set of means" (Sarasvathy, 2001, p. 245).

Effectuation Principles

Effectuation denotes a logic of entrepreneurial action that starts with a focus on means. Means are the resources that entrepreneurial managers and business model designers have at hand, and can use for imagining different effects, or possible ends toward which the resources can be deployed (hence the term *effect*uation).[23] Committing to one of these goals (for example, the goal of creating value by addressing a hypothesized customer need), the entrepreneurs take immediate action to implement a business model. That action is characterized by the following five main principles:

- Leveraging resources at hand: Resources at hand (also called the "deployable resources" of the focal firm in Chapter 5) include, first and foremost, the venture team members and their aspirations, knowledge, expertise, financial resources, personal networks, and so on.[24] In the case of a corporate venture, the resources and capabilities of the corporation are also included here. Unlike in design thinking, in effectuation such resources are not considered as constraints but as a starting point. In the context of building a business model, an important aspect is the focus not only on "who are we and what do we know?" but also on "whom do we know?" That is, to which other stakeholders (firms or individuals) could the venture team reach out for building a (possibly boundary-spanning) business model? (Note that this initial focus on means that are available in the present is very different from discovery-driven planning, which starts with a focus on the future by framing the end goal.)

---

[23]Effects correspond to the "goals" design driver discussed in Chapter 5. In effectuation, goals are short-term and frequently change, unlike in discovery-driven planning where they are long-term and largely remain stable (unless market tests conducted at a milestone strongly suggest that they should be modified).

[24]This is reminiscent of bricolage, an entrepreneurial process found in resource-poor environments where "making do with what is at hand" allows entrepreneurs to "create something from nothing by exploiting physical, social, or institutional inputs that other firms reject or ignore" (Baker and Nelson, 2006, p. 329).

- Keeping in mind affordable loss: Instead of adopting a profit-maximizing attitude, effectual business model designers are mindful about what they are prepared to lose in the worst-case scenario. They strive for cheap implementation and learning, and emphasize cautious use of the money, time, and other resources they (and their investors and partners) own. (Note that this is similar to the *parsimony* principle of discovery-driven planning.)
- Building partnerships: Instead of being obsessed with competition, effectual entrepreneurs seek to build strategic partnerships with the other firms and customers around them. This makes sense, given that effectual business model building often takes place in highly ambiguous environments where the market may not be well-defined, and hence the set of competitors may not be clear. (Note that this action principle is also present in the *Parallel Play* version of discovery-driven planning, as explained above, as well as in the *Stakeholders' Activities* design driver mentioned in Chapter 5.)
- Leveraging unexpected contingencies: Sometimes, uncertainty is so severe that possible outcomes, let alone the associated probabilities, cannot be identified. These situations have been labeled as "unknown unknowns," where things cannot be anticipated or expected. In other words, every now and then along the business development journey, something completely unexpected will happen. Effectual business model designers need to keep an eye out for these surprising events, and take advantage of them rather than view them as negative constraints. (In discovery-driven planning, *milestones*, i.e., checkpoints where assumptions are tested, represent planned opportunities for discovering such contingencies, but effectuation reminds us that they can happen anytime.)
- Controlling the near future: Given that the future, especially in highly ambiguous environments, is essentially unpredictable, effectual entrepreneurial action calls for focusing on its controllable aspects. This characteristic is based on the logic that, "to the end we can control the future, we do not need to predict it."[25] One example would be to conduct experiments and test assumptions deliberately (like in discovery-driven planning) at checkpoints that the business model designer determines, i.e., controls.

Exhibit 7.2 illustrates the effectuation approach.

---

[25]Sarasvathy (2001, p. 251)

Exhibit 7.2 Illustration of Key Effectuation Principles

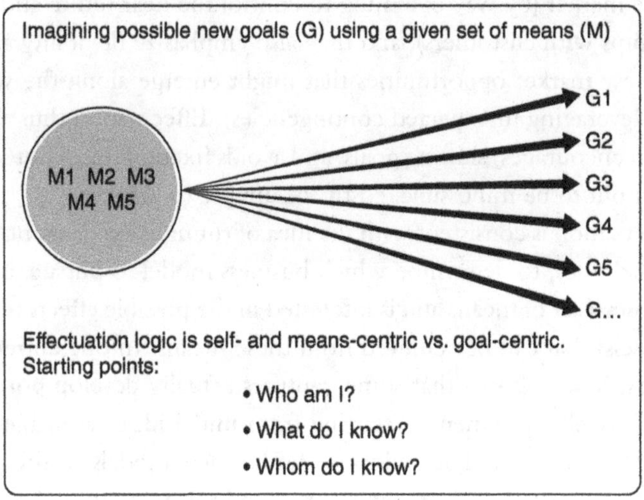

Effectual Business Model Development: Pros and Cons

The conditions under which effectuation as a logic of entrepreneurial action can be used to guide business model development are intuitive and simple. For example, entrepreneurs should draw on their available means and ideas as a starting point (i.e., short-term goal) for the implementation process. This implies that they can launch their entrepreneurial project even if they only have a vague hunch about a possible business opportunity. Indeed, the effectuation method is applicable in many situations, and with numerous constellations of founders, resources, levels of environmental uncertainty, available partnerships, and perceived market gaps. This lowers the hurdle that potential first-time entrepreneurs may perceive about building a new venture and/or a new business model, which may prevent them from taking the leap and starting a new (corporate) venture in the first place. Effectuation is reassuring in the sense that everybody should be able to perform it; it lowers the bar for taking entrepreneurial action.

Effectuation is reassuring in another sense, too: its main principles serve to lower both the cost and the risk of failure in entrepreneurial venturing. The five principles mentioned above guard against the imprudent use of resources (e.g., through their attention to available means, affordable loss, and building partnerships). They call for closeness to, and constant feedback from, the market (by way of aiming to control the near future and creating partnerships with customers), and they also emphasize flexibility and alertness to new market opportunities that might emerge along the way (e.g., through leveraging unexpected contingencies). Effectuation thus allows for (and even encourages) shifting goals, and avoids fixation on an outcome that may turn out to be impossible, costly, or unwise to achieve.

Effectuation is consistent with the idea of running experiments, including parallel ones, to determine which business model to pursue, because it presupposes a set of means and is interested in the possible effects (e.g., business models) that can be achieved from these means. In one entrepreneurship study, it was shown that some ventures actually develop portfolios of business model experiments, "starting from initial ideas, available capabilities, and experiences. They add specific business models to the portfolio and redefine others based on experiences and information gathered in the course of previous business model experiments."[26]

Although effectuation can be deployed in many entrepreneurial situations, it seems best suited for nascent markets and other environments characterized by especially high levels of uncertainty. In terms of business model development, effectuation lends itself particularly well to crafting boundary-spanning activities (i.e., those that are not internal to the focal firm). Researchers have also referred to this part of the business model as the *external value creation architecture*.[27] Effectuation encourages the active involvement of partners in order to leverage their complementary resources and capabilities.

It is not, however, an exclusive approach that precludes others. Effectuation principles can be combined with, say, more planning-based approaches, either sequentially or simultaneously. This helps business model designers adapt to a shifting environment, or to changes in the level of uncertainty. In later stages of business development, for example, uncertainty about what elements of a business model work is typically reduced, and other logics of action may be brought to bear.[28]

---

[26] Andries, Debackere, and Van Looy (2013, p. 306)

[27] Futterera, Schmidt, and Heidenreich (2018)

[28] Sarasvathy (2001) mentions "causation" as an alternative logic to effectuation. In a causal mode of action, business model designers focus on a given goal (rather than

Effectuation also has limitations. First, it is largely driven by coincidence and trial-and-error. For example, "whoever first buys . . . becomes by definition the first target customer." According to the methodology, entrepreneurs elaborate their business model "by continually listening to the customer and building an ever-increasing network of customers and strategic partners."[29] However, in reality entrepreneurs rarely just "go with the flow" and learn haphazardly along the way, but often consciously select and design business model experiments to test key hypotheses about them.[30] Such behavior is more consistent with the design and discovery-driven planning approaches explained earlier. Second, action implies commitment, and so the *Paradox of Entrepreneurship* mentioned earlier can apply. Effectuation can begin with a simple idea, and does not require the identification of a customer need that is highly likely to be significant and pervasive. Exploring that idea in an effectual mode involves a local (not global) search for a business model that works. Due to this myopic and constrained search behavior, the upside of the opportunity (financial or otherwise) will, on average, be limited. Effectuation, in summary, could be characterized as a "low risk, low return" search strategy.[31]

---

given means), such as a preferred business model, and aim at finding the best possible means (rather than goals), e.g., partners, or their own resources and capabilities that enable key activities in the business model.

[29] Sarasvathy (2001, p. 247)

[30] Andries, Debackere, and Van Looy (2013)

[31] Several recent studies have examined empirically the usefulness of "effectuation" vs. "causation" approaches in the context of business model innovation. Futterer, Schmidt, and Heidenreich (2018), for example, find that effectuation works better in high-growth industries, while causation is more effective in low-growth industries. Reymen et al. (2017) also compared effectuation and causation, finding that effectuation is used to identify a viable value proposition, while causation is used to flesh out other aspects of the business model; furthermore, under situations of resource shortages, an effectual logic tends to replace a causal one. Finally, relying on a longitudinal case study approach, Andries, Debackere, and Van Looy (2013) identify "focused commitment" and "simultaneous experimentation" (a manifestation of effectual logic) as two possible approaches to business model development. They theorize that focused commitment has a positive effect on initial growth but jeopardizes long-term survival, with simultaneous experimentation having the exact opposite effects, i.e., a negative effect on initial growth but enhancing the chances of long-term survival.

Lean Startup – Test, Test, Test

Lean startup is a methodology that builds on the central ideas behind the methods mentioned earlier (design thinking, discovery-driven planning, and effectuation). More broadly speaking, it draws from ideas on organizational learning, real options, product development, and technology evolution.[32]

The lean startup is anchored on the observation that entrepreneurs' subjective perception of a business model opportunity may be very different from a validated one. To highlight this, the method encourages entrepreneurs to explicitly formulate a series of empirically testable hypotheses about the opportunity, then test these hypotheses by conducting deliberate experiments in a lean, or non-wasteful, fashion. At its core, the lean startup method rejects strictly planning-based entrepreneurship processes and embraces an iterative approach driven by efficient experimentation with early customers. It has therefore also been characterized as hypothesis-driven entrepreneurship, and described as a scientific approach to entrepreneurship.[33]

Basic Principles of Lean Startup

The goal of the lean startup is to shorten product development and rapidly discover a viable business model.[34] The notion of "lean" refers to the method's focus on avoiding unnecessary resources and waste, and points to the roots of the concept in the lean manufacturing movement, with its emphasis on streamlined production systems.[35] The lean startup approach gleaned further inspiration from agile software development and the possibilities offered by open-source and free software to cut waste even beyond the typical capital efficiency and frugality of entrepreneurs.[36]

---

[32]Contigiani and Levinthal (2019)

[33]Leatherbee and Katila (2019)

[34]Blank (2003, 2013); Ries (2011, 2017)

[35]Womack, Jones, and Roos (1990)

[36]Today, software teams everywhere use agile, which was built on lean principles and has led to specific iterative frameworks such as Scrum and Kanban. The main tenets of agile were captured in a 2001 manifesto. While they are ubiquitous in software, agile principles have also been applied by other non-IT teams, including in companies such as ING and Siemens (Prats et al., 2018).

Although it is primarily aimed at startup firms, the lean startup method has also been suggested for use in established firms to build new business models and even entire new businesses.[37]

Exhibit 7.3 Lean Startup Process for Business Model Development

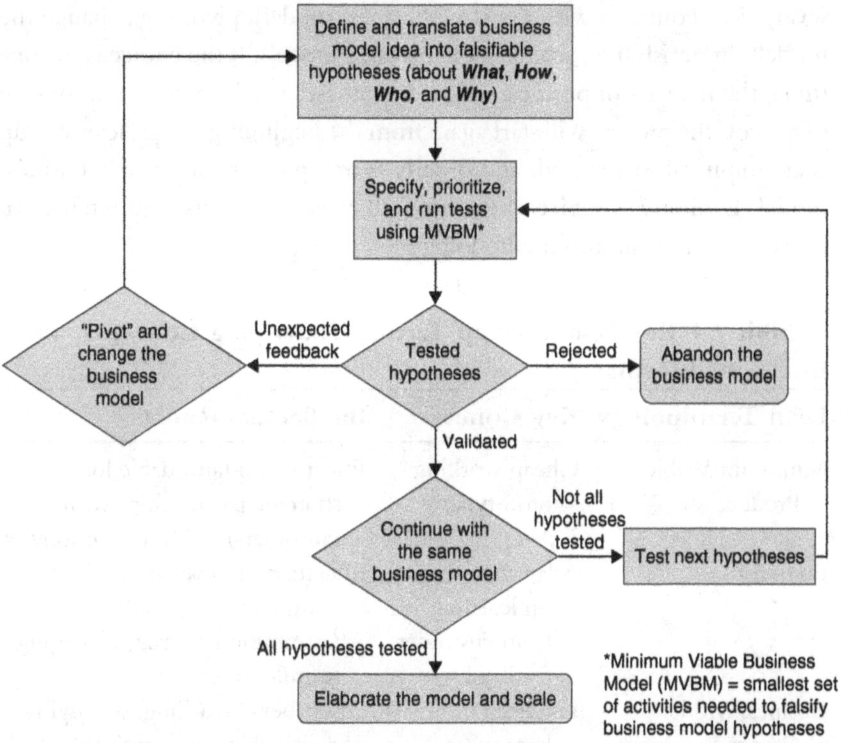

As Exhibit 7.3 shows, when applying this approach to building a new business model, managers and entrepreneurs are first asked to translate their idea about the business model into a series of falsifiable hypotheses (about the ***What***, ***How***, ***Who***, and ***Why*** of the envisioned activity system). Following that, they need to specify, prioritize, and run tests of these hypotheses

[37]See Ries (2017) and Lashinsky (2018)

using a *minimum viable business model*, or MVBM, as the basis for testing (note that since the method was originally developed for products, the original term used was *minimum viable product*, or MVP). An MVBM represents the smallest set of activities needed to falsify a business model hypothesis.[38] The key objective is to learn from these market-based tests in a fast and frugal way, and reduce the uncertainty about the viability of the business model. Based on the test outcomes, a decision needs to be made about whether to persevere (i.e., continue with the same business model), pivot (i.e., change the model), or perish (i.e., abandon the business model). If the choice is to continue, the next set of business model hypotheses needs to be tested. In case of a pivot, the process will start again from the beginning. Thus, lean startup is an empirical, structured, and orderly search process for a viable business model. Exhibit 7.4 depicts the terminology, key concepts, and intellectual roots of the lean startup methodology.

Exhibit 7.4 Key Lean Startup Terms, Underlying Concepts, and Intellectual Roots

Lean Terminology	Key Concept	Intellectual Roots
Minimum Viable Product	Cheap working prototype	Effectuation (affordable loss, strategic partnerships with customers), DDP (parsimony)
Pivoting	Adaptation based on learning from customer feedback	Effectuation (leveraging contingencies), DDP (assumption-testing, managing to milestones)
Business Model Canvas	Untested hypotheses	DDP (benchmarking, specifying deliverables, assumptions)
Agile	Rapid development	Effectuation (acting before planning), DDP (iteration between acting and planning)

One company that applied the lean startup methodology in its early stages is file sharing and synchronization service Dropbox, which was founded in 2007 by two former MIT students. Intent on satisfying a

[38]An MVP, according to Eisenmann, Ries, and Dillard (2011), is the smallest set of features and/or activities needed to falsify a product hypothesis.

need that "most people didn't know they had" (a seamless file sharing experience), the Dropbox team found early on it had to conduct a test of its "leap-of-faith question: if we can provide a superior customer experience, will people give our product a try?" When co-founder Drew Houston described the Dropbox solution to potential VCs, for example, they had difficulty grasping the concept. At the time, there were many companies and apps for file sharing, but they were clunky to use. Building a final (or even prototype) version of the product, however, would have been expensive and time-consuming in terms of development. Dropbox's solution was to release as an MVP a simple video targeted at savvy early adopters. The video was a short demonstration narrated by Houston, which showed how the final product would work. It was peppered with references and jokes that would appeal to the target audience, and it quickly garnered attention. This was a cheap way (i.e., without having to actually build a product) to actually demonstrate interest, gain crucial feedback from potential users, and build early visibility.[39]

Applying lean principles, such as building an MVP and having a learning-oriented mindset, allowed Dropbox to achieve scale and visibility in a highly organic way. In a presentation at the 2010 Startup Lessons Learned Conference, Drew Houston said that he and his team had learned that the biggest risk was "making something no one wants"; that "not launching" is painful, but "not learning" is fatal; that you should "put something" in the hands of users that is not necessarily code and "get real feedback ASAP"; and that you should "know where your target audience hangs out and speak to them in an authentic way."[40] Building a minimum viable product – and the associated business model to deliver this product – Dropbox was able to first establish there was market demand, then deliver an elegant tool that was quickly adopted by consumers.

Lean Startup Business Model Development: Pros and Cons

Essentially, the key promise of applying the lean startup method to building innovative business models is to search in an efficient and effective manner.

---

[39] *TechCrunch* (2011)

[40] Lean Startup Co. (2014, July 2). Dropbox @ Startup Lessons Learned Conference 2010 [video file].

It is efficient in the sense that it does not waste resources unnecessarily; speeds up development time; and proceeds in a rational, systematic manner that can be easily understood and communicated to others. It is effective in the sense that there is a high likelihood that a viable business model will be actually developed due to the close interaction and consultation with customers and other business model stakeholders.

Two associated benefits are:

Reduced market risk: Customer and stakeholder feedback during the development process ensures that one does not build a business model that customers do not want, or one for which stakeholders find little value in participating.

Reduced capital expenditure (CapEx) and initial funding needs: Through its emphasis on cheap experimentation, lean startup reduces the need for large amounts of project funding. It encourages delaying CapEx to bring the business model to life, until these costs cannot be avoided any further.

Given that the lean startup method is relatively young (it was originally articulated by Steve Blank and subsequently developed more fully by Eric Ries), scientific evidence about its performance effects is still scant. However, the early evidence is promising. In a study of early-stage venture teams, one set of teams was trained to use a scientific hypothesis-testing approach. The study showed that these teams performed better and pivoted more often than the control group teams, who used their preferred default approach.[41] A scientific approach helps entrepreneurs not only better understand their current situation, but also identify better possibilities. This suggests that the lean startup method is likely to facilitate the development of valuable business propositions and, by analogy, value-creating business models.

Although it seems promising and intuitive, in practice the lean startup is not so straightforward to apply, however, especially in large, established firms. In a recent study comparing the propensity of entrepreneurs to use "lean" versus "heavy" approaches for building a new business, researchers

---

[41] See Camuffo, Cordova, Gambardella, and Spina (2020). The trained teams exhibited on average 13.1% more pivots than the others, which suggests that a scientific lean approach enables them to adjust their ideas or envision new ones whose outcome distributions have higher expected returns.

found that potential entrepreneurs are slightly more likely to lean toward "heavy" approaches (i.e., those that require some degree of commitment and a significant investment of resources, for example, through creating and safeguarding intellectual property, or writing a business plan).[42] Indeed, it is worth considering the limitations of lean startup that mirror some of the disadvantages of discovery-driven planning and effectuation, especially within the context of an established firm. These include:[43]

Cost of experimentation: Although this cost is a function of the industry in which a new venture or business model is situated, and also of the complexity of the respective business model, the fixed cost of experimentation is often greater than zero, especially in the later stages of business model development. It includes the cost of building experimentation capabilities, for example, through training key personnel in the use of the scientific method. It also includes the cost of potentially foreclosing other business model options (see the *Paradox of Entrepreneurship* discussed earlier in this chapter).

Disclosure of strategically important information: Performing market-based tests and getting feedback on minimum viable business models from customers, strategic partners, or suppliers implies disclosing information about the business model that may be strategically relevant. This could, in turn, foster imitation by rivals. (For hints about how to make a business model more strategically robust against imitation, see Chapters 4 and 5.)

Cost of damaged reputation: Not all experiments that are conducted as part of a lean business model development process are viewed positively by stakeholders. Customers, for example, who are used to receiving near-perfect services or products from a focal firm, and who are used to flawlessly functioning business models, may be negatively surprised when confronted with a "minimum viable" customer experience.

Noisy signals: The testing of hypotheses may yield noisy signals instead of clear and unequivocal learning insights. This may be partly due to statistical challenges with the sampling process, such as selecting the right target group of early business model stakeholders (like early customers, likeliest suppliers, partners for distribution, etc.).

---

[42] Bennet and Chatterji (2017)

[43] See Contigiani and Levinthal (2019)

Cost of organizational change: Lastly, if the outcome of the lean business model development process suggests a new model that requires changing an existing one, and/or changing the organizational structure, processes, and strategy to support it, then this may be costly – both financially as well as in terms of the motivation, time, and attention of key members of the organization.

Summary of Key Takeaways for the Effective Business Model Designer

The last step of the three-stage business model design process introduced in the previous chapter, BM*Implement*, is also the most open-ended. In this chapter, we went over three complementary methodologies that are useful for taking a business model innovation from concept to reality in the BM*Implement* stage. Often used in entrepreneurship, these three methodologies – discovery-driven planning, effectuation, and lean startup – build on Chapter 6. They also complement the tools that will be explained in Chapter 9.

The first entrepreneurial methodology is discovery-driven planning, which seeks to lower the cost of failure by reducing uncertainty. It does so by breaking a project down into steps (framing, benchmarking, specification of deliverables, testing of assumptions, managing to milestones, and parsimony), and identifying and testing assumptions about the business model. This makes it easier to see at various points if the project should be continued, abandoned, or altered then continued. The first three steps are conceptual. In framing (step one), managers define long-term success (the "goal" business model design driver). The second step, benchmarking, requires identifying existing firms, including their business model templates. In step three, the operational requirements of the business model's activities are spelled out (in other words, the content is defined), and key assumptions are documented. The last three steps (testing of assumptions, managing to milestones, and parsimony) involve implementation action.

A concept related to DDP is *Parallel Play*, which is applicable to nascent markets, where entrepreneurs are faced with a high level of uncertainty and where they need to choose among various alternative business model options. When using *Parallel Play*, firms engage in a highly dynamic process of business model choice and elaboration. They create prototypes by blending incumbent templates and the business models of other startups, testing several business models "in parallel." This provides a method for balancing between the need to commit to a business model quickly and not committing to something without having considered the viable alternatives. Entrepreneurs are encouraged to learn by observing their competitors, and actively test their assumptions and early business model ideas.

The second entrepreneurial method is effectuation. Unlike discovery-driven planning, which assumes that managers understand customer needs and potential new business models thoroughly, effectuation works best in situations where there is non-quantifiable risk, and managers have only a preliminary or unclear sense of the market opportunity. Entrepreneurs deploy the means they have available to make the business model a reality. Their actions are characterized by five qualities: leveraging resources at hand, keeping in mind affordable loss, building partnerships, leveraging unexpected contingencies, and controlling the near future.

Finally, we went over the lean startup, a hybrid entrepreneurship methodology that has been widely adopted in recent years. Building on the main ideas behind design thinking, DDP, and effectuation, the lean startup helps entrepreneurs form hypotheses about the market opportunity and test them in a lean (fast, inexpensive, low-waste, and iterative) way. The business model equivalent of the minimum viable product known in the lean startup is the minimum viable business model. Following low-cost market tests, the business model designer can decide to persevere, pivot, or perish.

References

Andries, P., Debackere, K. & Van Loy, B. (2013). Simultaneous experimentation as a learning strategy: Business model development under uncertainty. *Strategic Entrepreneurship Journal* **7**(4), 288–310.

Aumann, R. J. (1995). Backward induction and common knowledge of rationality. *Games and Economic Behavior* **8**(1), 6–19.

Baker, T. & Nelson, R. E. (2006). Creating something from nothing: Resource construction through entrepreneurial bricolage. *Administrative Science Quarterly* **50**(3), 329–366.

Bennett, V. M. & Chatterji, A. K. (2019). The entrepreneurial process: Evidence from a nationally representative survey. *Strategic Management Journal*, 1–31.

Blank, S. (2003). *The Four Steps to the Epiphany: Successful Strategies for Products that Win*. Morrisville, NC: Lulu Enterprises Incorporated.

Blank, S. (2013). Why the lean start-up changes everything. *Harvard Business Review* **91**(5), 63–72.

Born Digital. (2015, September 25). A brief history of Slack. *Born Digital*. Retrieved from https://www.borndigital.com/2015/09/25/a-brief-history-of-slack-2015-09-25

Camuffo, A., Cordova, A., Gambardella, A. & Spina, C. (2020). A scientific approach to entrepreneurial decision making: Evidence from a randomized control trial. *Management Science* **66**(2), 564–586.

Chesbrough, H. (2010). Business model innovation: Opportunities and barriers. *Long Range Planning* **43**(2–3), 354–363.

Contigiani, A. & Levinthal, D. A. (2019). Situating the construct of lean start-up: Adjacent conversations and possible future directions. *Industrial and Corporate Change* **28**(3), 551–564.

Dixit, A. K. & Pindyck, R. S. (1994). *Investment Under Uncertainty*. Princeton, NJ: Princeton University Press.

Eisenmann, T., Ries, E. & Dillard, S. (2011). Hypothesis-driven entrepreneurship: The lean startup. HBS No. 812-095. Harvard Business Publishing.

Futterer, F., Schmidt, J. & Heidenreich, S. (2018). Effectuation or causation as the key to corporate venture success? Investigating effects of entrepreneurial behaviors on business model innovation and venture performance. *Long Range Planning* **51**(1), 64–81.

Gans, J. S., Stern, S. & Wu, J. (2019). Foundations of entrepreneurial strategy. *Strategic Management Journal* **40**(5), 736–756.

Griffith, E. (2019, June 2). As Slack prepares to go public, its C.E.O. is holding his tongue. *New York Times*. Retrieved from https://www.nytimes.com/2019/06/02/technology/slack-stewart-butterfield.html

Guler, I. (2018). Pulling the plug: The capability to terminate unsuccessful projects and firm performance. *Strategy Science* **3**(3), 481–497.

Innovation Leader (2019, September 23). Here's our list of 2019 impact award winners. *Innovation Leader*. Retrieved from https://www.innovationleader.com/heres-our-list-of-2019-impact-award-winners/1163.article

Kastrenakes, J. (2019, April 26). Slack plans to go public after hitting 10 million daily users. *The Verge*. Retrieved from https://www.theverge.com/2019/4/26/18518022/slack-public-offering-ipo-announced-sk-stock

Knight, F. (1921). *Risk, Uncertainty and Profits*. Boston, MA: Houghton Mifflin.

Lashinsky, A. (2018, February 22). How 'The Lean Startup' turned Eric Ries into an unlikely corporate guru. *Fortune*. Retrieved from https://fortune.com/2018/02/22/lean-startup-eric-ries/

Lean Startup Co. (2014, July 2). Dropbox @ Startup Lessons Learned Conference 2010 [video file]. Retrieved from: https://www.youtube.com/watch?time_continue=14&v=y9hg-mUx8sE&feature=emb_title

Leatherbee, M. & Katila, R. (2019). The lean startup method: Team composition, hypothesis-testing, and early-stage business models. Stanford University working paper.

McDonald, R. & Eisenhardt, K. (2020). Parallel play: Startups, nascent markets, and the effective design of a business model. *Administrative Science Quarterly* **65**(2), 483–523.

McGrath, R. (2010). Business models: A discovery driven approach. *Long Range Planning* **43**(2–3), 247–261.

McGrath, R. & MacMillan, I. (2000). *The Entrepreneurial Mindset*. Boston, MA: Harvard Business School Press.

McGrath, R., Macmillan, I. & Venkataraman, S. (1995). Defining and developing competence: A strategic process paradigm. *Strategic Management Journal* **16**(4), 251–275.

Prats, J., Siota, J., Gillespie, D. & Singleton, N. (2018). Organizational agility. Oliver Wyman and IESE Business School. Retrieved from https://www.oliverwyman.com/content/dam/oliver-wyman/v2/publications/2018/april/Organizational_Agility.pdf

Raval, A. & Ram, A. (2019, June 13). Shell puts the breaks on plan to launch London car-hailing service to rival Uber. *Financial Times*, pp. 13.

Reymen, I., Berends, H., Oudehand, R. & Stultiëns, R. (2017). Decision making for business model development: A process study of effectuation and causation in new technology-based ventures. *R&D Management* **47**(4), 595–606.

Ries, E. (2011). *The Lean Startup: How Today's Entrepreneurs Use Continuous Innovation to Create Radically Successful Businesses*. New York, NY: Crown Books.

Ries, E. (2017). *The Startup Way: How Modern Companies Use Entrepreneurial Management to Transform Culture and Drive Long-Term Growth*. New York, NY: Currency.

Santos, F. M. & Eisenhardt, K. M. (2009). Constructing markets and shaping boundaries: Entrepreneurial power in nascent fields. *Academy of Management Journal* **52**(4), 643–671.

Sarasvathy, S. D. (2001). Effectual reasoning in entrepreneurial decision making: Existence and bounds. *Academy of Management Proceedings* **1**, D1–D6.

Schultz, H. & Jones Yang, D. (1999). *Pour Your Heart Into It: How Starbucks Built a Company One Cup at a Time*. New York, NY: Hyperion.

Schmidt, J. & Heidenreich, S. (2018). The role of human capital for entrepreneurial decision-making - investigating experience, skills and knowledge as antecedents to effectuation and causation. *International Journal of Entrepreneurial Venturing* **10**(3), 287–311.

Sosna, M., Trevinyo-Rodríguez, R. N. & Velamuri, S. R. (2010). Business model innovation through trial-and-error learning: The Naturhouse case. *Long Range Planning* **43**(2–3), 383–407.

TechCrunch (2011, October 19). How DropBox started as a minimal viable product. *TechCrunch*. Retrieved from https://techcrunch.com/2011/10/19/dropbox-minimal-viable-product/

Thomke, S. (2003). *Experimentation Matters: Unlocking the Potential of New Technologies for Innovation*. Boston, MA: Harvard Business School Press.

Von Bertalanffy, L. (1972). The history and status of general systems theory. *Academy of Management Journal* **15**(4), 407–426.

Womack, J., Jones, D. & Roos, D. (1990). *The Machine That Changed the World: The Story of Lean Production, Toyota's Secret Weapon in the Global Car Wars That Is Now Revolutionizing World Industry*. New York, NY: Free Press.

8 Value Propositions – The NICE Framework for Measuring the Impact of the Business Model

In today's highly interconnected world, customers are no longer passive recipients and consumers of firms' products and services, and suppliers are no longer just arm's-length vendors of services and goods. Instead, customers are becoming increasingly involved in the development, production, and delivery of the very same products and services that are intended for their consumption, and suppliers are becoming tightly integrated into many firms' research and development (R&D) and production activities. This phenomenon can be described as the "co-creation" of value within a focal firm's business model.[1] Customers of eBay (and apps such as Letgo), for example, perform the central functions of marketing (writing product

[1]Prahalad and Ramaswamy (2004)

descriptions) and sales, and they hold inventory – in effect performing activities and incurring related costs that were previously assumed by retail firms. Technology companies like Microsoft involve their customers in the beta testing of early product releases, saving millions of dollars in R&D expenses every year. Firms and organizations as diverse as Apple, Lego, and NASA also tap into the creativity of their customer and supplier base to pursue models of open innovation, harnessing the power of crowds to solve tricky business issues, and sometimes even hard scientific problems, in record time and at low cost.[2] Crowdsourcing information to improve product quality is another form of digital co-creation. Consider Waze, a GPS-enabled navigation app for mobile devices bought by Google in 2013 for close to $1 billion.[3] Drivers share real time information on traffic and road conditions, such as accidents or other road hazards, which the software utilizes to update the suggested route in order to enable users of the app to reach their destination faster. Waze's network-based business model has strong direct positive network externalities: the more users are on the app at any given time, the more accurate the navigation guidance becomes and the greater the value created for all stakeholders.

The business model, through its integrated, holistic, and balanced consideration of value creation and value capture (see Chapters 1 and 2 of this book), brings the customer and other stakeholders such as suppliers and strategic partners back into the spotlight. Unlike other forms of innovation, such as product or process innovation, business model innovation rarely originates in a technological breakthrough, but begins with the question, "What customer needs will the new business model address?"[4] (see Chapter 4). This customer- (and more generally stakeholder-) centric view suggests important connections with the design field (see Chapters 5 and 6) and with the marketing domain. In marketing, an important construct has been suggested to capture the imperative of the focal firm to be sufficiently attractive to customers and other stakeholders. This is the notion of the value proposition. Indeed, the attention of managers and investors has turned

---

[2]Lakhani, Lifshitz-Assaf, and Tushman (2013)
[3]See United States Securities and Exchange Commission (2019, p. 19)
[4]Amit and Zott (2012, p. 45)

to the value proposition as a key consideration for creating a competitive advantage, complementing the traditional strategic concern about their firm's scope as well as the mode and timing of entry into its chosen market segments. But what is a value proposition in the context of a business model?

Business Models and Value Propositions

The marketing literature suggests that the value proposition to customers "explains the relationship among the performance of the product, the fulfillment of the customers' needs and the total cost to the customer over the customer relationship life cycle."[5] In other words, it reflects the net benefits that customers receive from a focal firm's attempts to address their needs. An early definition links the value proposition to focal firm strategy and performance by observing that "behind any winning strategy must stand a superior value proposition – a clear, simple statement of the benefits, both tangible and intangible, that the company will provide, along with the approximate price it will charge each customer segment for those benefits."[6] This is in line with the logic proposed by strategy scholars who suggest that the *realized* value proposition to customers (which they refer to as value created for customers) equals the customer's willingness to pay, minus the price paid for the product or service.[7]

---

[5]Payne and Frow (2005, p. 172)
[6]Lanning and Michaels (1988)
[7]See Brandenburger and Stuart (1996). Economists refer to the value created for customers as the consumer surplus. Note that value propositions could also be defined without consideration of costs, as the sum of all benefits that a stakeholder receives from a focal firm. For example, Osterwalder and Pigneur state that a value proposition is "an aggregation, or bundle, of benefits that a company offers customers" (2010, p. 22); it "describes the benefits customers can expect from your products and services" (2014, p. 6). Moreover, value propositions could be defined as the unique value a stakeholder receives from the focal firm compared to what they would receive from dealing with a rival firm. Conceived this way, they could be viewed as referring to "the communication of the unique benefits and utility

Building on these perspectives, and noting that focal firms that craft sustainable business models need to offer a value proposition not only to customers but also to all other stakeholders involved in the business model, we define a *value proposition* as follows:

A value proposition is a hypothesis formulated by a focal firm about how much value it creates for a stakeholder by way of providing tangible as well as intangible benefits that fulfill the stakeholder's needs, net of any costs that the stakeholder incurs and/or perceives.

Two observations follow from this definition. First, we deliberately use the word "stakeholder" and not "customer." In a business model, the focal firm needs to provide a strong value proposition to customers as well as suppliers and strategic partners, in order to create strong incentives to collaborate for all business model participants. Second, value propositions are subjective, not objective.[8] In other words, they are in the eyes of the beholder. Different stakeholders might perceive and evaluate the same benefit differently. For example, a busy top executive will place a different value on rapid order delivery than a retired employee. Value propositions are subjective in another sense as well. They are based on subjective assumptions that the focal firm's managers make about the subjective utility functions[9] of the various stakeholders.

---

obtainable only from the focal product in contrast to those from its competitors" (DeSarbo, Jedidi, and Sinha, 2001, p. 845).

[8]In this regard, Vargo and Lusch (2004, p. 11) state: "The enterprise can only offer value propositions; the consumer must determine value and participate in creating it through the process of coproduction. If a tangible good is part of the offering, it is embedded with knowledge that has value potential for the intended consumer, but it is not embedded with value (utility). The consumer must understand that the value potential is translatable to specific needs through coproduction. The enterprise can only make value propositions that strive to be better or more compelling than those of competitors."

[9]A consumer's utility function measures the consumer's satisfaction from a product or service. The utility function captures the consumer's ranking of preferences over a basket of products and services; that is, the order in which the consumer chooses one product/service over another.

Benefits may be derived from the core product or service and its associated features, but also from the business model, which enables the product or service development, production, and delivery. The distinction between a product and a business model has been explained in earlier chapters (e.g., in Chapter 4), and the distinction between the associated value propositions is not difficult to grasp. For example, the value proposition to a user of a Gillette razor is distinct from, yet complementary to, the value proposition associated with Gillette's cheap razor and expensive consumable blades business model.

Alternatively, consider Pinduoduo, a Chinese e-commerce platform started in 2015. Only four years after founding, it reached twelve-month gross merchandise values of $117.5 billion, with 536.2 million active annual users and 3.6 million merchants on its platform.[10] It has achieved this scale by employing a different business model than other leading Chinese e-commerce platforms, such as JD.com and Alibaba's Taobao. Using popular social networking platforms, such as WeChat, users form shopping teams to unlock group prices. They enjoy lotteries, free products, and other fun incentives for inviting friends. Items – which can be everything from low-ticket items to groceries and appliances – are shipped from manufacturers directly. This, along with the high-volume "viral" feature of the platform allows for steep discounts. Many of Pinduoduo's customers are in more rural areas, with the majority of its users from third- and lower-tier Chinese cities.[11] The value proposition of its business model is clearly distinct from the value proposition of individual products sold through its platform.

However, the distinction between the value proposition from a service and the value proposition associated with the business model enabling the service might be more challenging to see. In order to highlight the distinction, let us consider the definition of a service according to the OECD (Organization for Economic Cooperation and Development): "Services are outputs produced to order and which cannot be traded separately from their production. Services are not separate entities over which ownership rights can be established. They cannot be traded separately from their production."

---

[10] Pinduoduo Inc. website
[11] Lee (2018)

This is based on a definition provided by French economist Jean-Baptiste Say in the early nineteenth century.[12]

Using this definition allows us to highlight the difference between the value proposition of a service and the value propositions from its underlying business model (which enable the service). Together they constitute the aggregate, or total, value proposition to the customer (see upper right-hand side of Exhibit 8.1).

Exhibit 8.1 Value Proposition of Product and Business Model

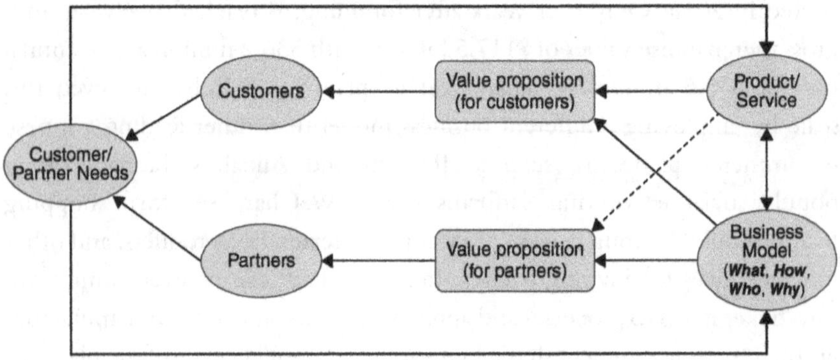

Consider a restaurant food delivery service, for example. A restaurant has the choice between two basic business models. It could provide the delivery itself (in-house delivery), or it could work with a delivery service such as Uber Eats. The value proposition of the service (for which production and consumption cannot be separated) is largely independent from the specifics of the enabling business model: customers typically value a hot, tasty meal delivered by a friendly delivery person on time; this does not depend on who specifically delivers the meal. The business model, however, could generate additional benefits for the customer. Uber Eats, for instance, is part of Uber's loyalty program, Uber Rewards. Through this program,

[12]Chapter XIII ("Of Immaterial Products, or Values Consumed at the Moment of Production") of Say's *Treatise on Political Economy* (1803)

Uber Eats customers earn points that can later be redeemed against other services provided by Uber, such as car rides. In this example, the production of the customer benefit through the business model (i.e., loyalty points) can be separated from its consumption.

In a similar vein, Amazon offers customers an Amazon credit card for buying products online and in physical stores at the same price (in other words, a case where the value proposition of the retailing service is the same whether the customer uses the online or offline channel) and earning loyalty points that can be cashed in later for the purchase of any product available for sale on the Amazon website. Again, the value proposition of the business model is distinct, and it enhances the value proposition of the service.

Alternatively, consider airline transportation. If an airline upgrades the quality of the food it serves in business class, it strengthens its value proposition to the customer associated with the core service (air transportation from location A to location B) without making any significant changes to the underlying business model. If, however, the airline leases planes from another company instead of operating its own planes, this represents a business model change that would not normally affect the core service (of offering punctual airplane transportation from location A to location B). For some passengers, however, the change might nevertheless affect their customer experience. For example, they might associate the leased plane with lower quality and safety, and the aggregate value proposition might therefore change. Hence, in this example the value proposition of the service may be diminished by the value proposition of the business model.

In many cases, though, the value proposition of the business model becomes an integral part of (and therefore cannot be distinguished from) the value proposition of the service. Consider the emerging ride hailing industry. With a company like Lyft, passengers might enjoy a basic transportation service (essentially the same as they would get by using an old-fashioned taxi), but at the same time they benefit from additional information provided as part of the service (e.g., about the driver's location at any point in time and how long it will take until they are picked up), as well as from a hassle-free and convenient payment process that saves time. These additional benefits that are enabled by Lyft's business model not only augment the value proposition of the basic service, but they become an integral part of the service. Similar to other forms of transportation, they are consumed as they are produced.

Exhibit 8.1 shows that the business model designer needs to think carefully not only about the value proposition for customers, but also the value proposition for partners. In the context of the business model, partners who carry out activities have their own needs. The focal firm needs to respond to these needs with a clear and distinct value proposition. That value proposition emanates from the business model (as indicated by the arrow from the business model to the value proposition from partners). To a certain extent, it also comes from the product or service that is delivered to the customer, even though the partners derive no use value from it. When customers perceive a product as far superior to all available substitute products, this clearly enhances the appeal for partners of participating in the business model, because it promises continuously high and steady demand for the product (hence the dashed arrow from product to value proposition for partners in Exhibit 8.1; it is dashed because, as a function of the value proposition for customers, the link is indirect).

A Formal Model of the Value Proposition

As shown in Exhibit 8.1, a business model needs to provide value propositions to all stakeholders involved, not just customers or the focal firm. It does so either directly (as indicated by the arrows from the business model to the respective value propositions in Exhibit 8.1), or indirectly through the product or service it enables (as indicated by the arrows from the business model to the product, and from there to the various value propositions). Value propositions, according to our definition, are promises of value creation for stakeholders. A business model therefore needs to be geared toward *total value creation*, i.e., value creation for *all* parties involved (see also Chapter 1, in particular Exhibit 1.5 on this point). To better understand this concept, and the difference between value created and value appropriated, it is worth considering a simple model of total value creation in a business model with one focal firm, one customer, and one supplier.

The straight line in Exhibit 8.2 represents the total value created in that model. Each participant (firm, supplier, customer) has a specific amount of the total value created that it is able to capture, which is a function of its individual bargaining power. The customer's share is the value they capture, which is equal to the customer's willingness-to-pay minus the price paid. Similarly, the focal firm's share is the amount of value it manages to capture, which is equal to the price the customer paid minus the cost paid to the supplier. Finally, the supplier's share is the value it captures, which is the price the firm paid, minus the supplier's opportunity cost. Four "value-based" strategies have been identified in this simple model. The first way is to increase the willingness-to-buy of customers of the firm (i.e., a classic differentiation approach). The second way is to lower the opportunity cost of suppliers (i.e., making it cheaper for a supplier to work with the focal firm). The third way is to lower the willingness-to-pay of customers for competing firms' products (such as by creating switching costs). Finally, the fourth way is to increase the opportunity costs to suppliers of working with other firms (such as through creating switching costs for suppliers).[13]

Exhibit 8.2 Total Value Created in a Simple Business Model

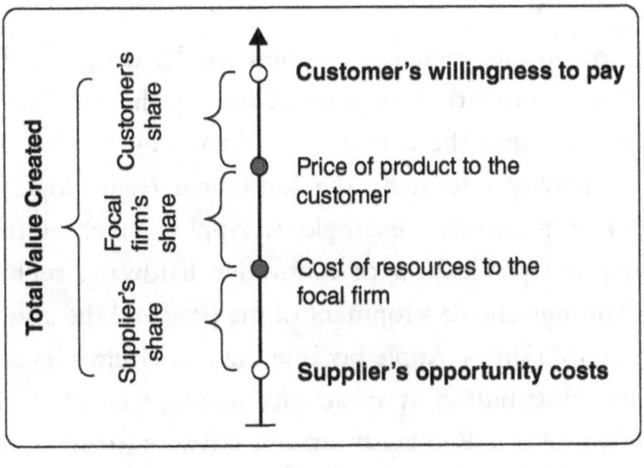

Source: Adapted from Brandenburger A. M. & Stuart H. W., Jr. (1996). Value-based business strategy. *Journal of Economics & Management Strategy*, **5**(1), 5–24.

[13]Information taken from Brandenburger and Stuart (1996)

How the Business Model Enhances Value Propositions: The NICE Value Drivers

With the distinction between the value propositions of products or services and business models in mind, we now take a deeper dive into the value propositions of business models. Viewed as an activity system, the business model can be characterized through "design themes," which refer to the system's dominant value creation drivers. Design themes are configurations of design elements, or the degree to which design elements are orchestrated and connected by distinct themes. Conceptual and empirical research has established that some of the common design themes that orchestrate and connect the elements of an activity system include **N**ovelty, lock-**In**, **C**omplementarities, and **E**fficiency (summarized by the acronym NICE).[14] The NICE value drivers represent value propositions of business models; business models can have one or more value drivers. We elaborate on each of these value drivers below.

Novelty

The essence of novelty-centered business model design is the adoption of new activities (content), new ways of linking the activities (structure), new ways of governing the activities (governance), and/or new ways to monetize the activity system by the focal firm (value logic). As shown in Chapter 4, a prominent example is Apple, which initially focused on the design and production of innovative hardware, such as personal computers. Through the development of the iPod and the associated music download business iTunes, Apple became the first electronics company that included music distribution as an activity (content novelty), linking it to the development of the iPod hardware and software (structure novelty). By adding the digital music distribution activity to its business model, Apple also innovated the value logic of its business model by extracting revenue from the sale of the iPod and from the use of the iPod, namely the digital

[14] Amit and Zott (2001)

distribution of music. This example illustrates how Apple expanded its locus of innovation from the product to its business model.

Schumpeter defined innovation as the introduction of new products or services; new methods of production, distribution, or marketing; or the tapping of new markets.[15] Yet this definition of innovation does not capture fully the essence of business model innovation. Specifically, it does not capture the business model innovations introduced by companies such as Uber or Netflix; peer-to-peer platform companies like LinkedIn, eBay, and Match; or marketplace companies such as Amazon. In each of these companies, the innovation was at the business model level, rather than (or in addition to) the product or service level. Each of these companies has innovated the way in which they conduct their business. Hence, for these and many other companies, the business model became the locus of innovation, in addition to the product, service, or process. Novelty became an important value driver.

The unique characteristics of virtual markets (i.e., the removal of geographical and physical constraints, the possible reversal of information flows from customers to vendors, and other novel information bundling and channeling techniques) make the possibilities for business model innovation appear almost endless. While there are a vast number of potential business model structures for a given set of activities, not every combination makes economic sense.

Digital firms can uncover latent sources of value by identifying and incorporating valuable new complementary products and services into their business models in novel ways. One dimension of innovation in business models refers to the appropriate selection of participating parties. For example, firms can direct and intensify traffic to their websites by initiating affiliate programs with third parties, who are compensated for enabling the execution of transactions from their own sites.

There can be substantial first-mover advantages for business model innovators. Being first to market with a novel business model makes it faster and cheaper to create switching costs by capturing "mindshare," and by developing brand awareness and reputation. Business model innovators can also gain by learning and accumulating proprietary knowledge through data analytic methods, and by preempting scarce resources.

---

[15]Schumpeter (1934)

Lock-In

Business models can also be designed for lock-in, the power to keep stakeholders such as customers and partners as business model participants. Lock-in can be manifested as switching costs, or as network externalities that derive from the structure, content, and/or governance of the activity system. For example, in eBay's business model, most of the marketing and sales activities (such as photographing and describing items for sale) are performed by the customers (sellers). What keeps them attracted to eBay and motivates them to perform these activities? What prevents them from switching to other service providers? Arguably, one very important factor is the strong positive network externalities inherent to the eBay activity system. With a massive base of potential buyers, sellers know that they are more likely to execute a trade at an attractive price on eBay than elsewhere. That's why they keep coming back – they are locked in. The same applies to social networking sites such as Facebook or LinkedIn. In addition to enjoying friendship-based networking externalities, Facebook members typically invest considerable effort in personalizing their profiles. These investments form strong impediments to switching to other providers.

The value-creating potential of a business model also depends on the extent to which it motivates customers to engage in repeated transactions. This characteristic can also be described as the "stickiness" or "lock-in" property of a business model. It prevents migration to competitors and increases transaction volume through repeat transactions.

There are several ways in which customer retention can be enabled by a business model. First, loyalty programs can be established that reward repeat customers with special bonuses. These programs are similar to airline frequent flyer reward programs and hotel chain loyalty programs. Second, firms can develop a dominant proprietary design standard for business processes, products, and services (e.g., Amazon's patented shopping cart). Third, firms can establish a trusting relationship with customers, such as by offering them transaction safety and reliability guaranteed by independent and highly credible third parties. For example, Zopa increases the credibility of its loan screening process by utilizing two well-known credit rating agencies (Equifax and Callcredit).

Switching costs might include the costs of switching firms after an Internet user has customized products, services, or information to his or her needs. The companies that participate in the business model often use specific methods to personalize goods (products, information, and services), and thus increase switching costs. These methods might include the ability to set up personalized product lists or conduct direct advertising, analyze submitted customer information, use cookies, analyze click streams, analyze past purchases, create a personalized interface, target emails, and target cross-selling on web pages. Furthermore, the creation of virtual communities bonds participants to a particular business model. Such communities enable frequent interactions on a wide range of topics and thereby create loyalty and enhance transaction frequency.

Familiarity with the interface design of a website or app represents customer learning and thus inhibits customers from switching to other sites. This argument gains strength when customization features such as "one-click ordering," a standard feature of many e-commerce sites, are available. Personalization can also be achieved with filtering tools that compare a customer's purchase patterns with those of like-minded customers and make recommendations based on inferred tastes. The more the customer interacts with the system, the more accurate the matching results become. Customers thus have a high incentive to use the system. This creates a positive feedback loop.[16] Notable for our discussion of business models is the idea that increasing returns and positive feedback may derive from network effects.[17]

Digital business models connect various parties that participate in exchanges and can thus be considered network generators. Networks may exhibit externalities in that the production or consumption activities of one party connected to the network have an effect on the production or utility functions of other participants in the network. This effect is not transmitted through the price mechanism. Network externalities are usually understood as positive consumption externalities in which "the utility that a user derives from consumption of the good increases with the

---

[16]Arthur (1990)

[17]Katz and Shapiro (1985), Shapiro and Varian (1999)

number of other agents consuming the good."[18] Henceforth, we will refer only to consumption externalities when discussing network externalities. In the context of a business model, network externalities are present when the value created for customers increases with the size of the customer base. Consider, for example, messaging application WhatsApp. Each WhatsApp user benefits from a larger number of WhatsApp users.

There may also be *indirect* network externalities that arise when economic agents benefit from the existence of a positive feedback loop with another group of agents. Consider, for example, the business models implemented by online auction companies such as eBay. As mentioned earlier regarding eBay, a buyer on one of these auction sites has no immediate advantage from the presence of additional buyers. However, the presence of more buyers (a signal of current and future market liquidity) makes it more attractive for potential sellers to put their products up for sale at that particular site, thus enhancing the site's attractiveness to potential buyers. Both buyers and sellers thus benefit indirectly from increasing numbers of other buyers and sellers. Another example of such indirect network externalities is a dating site, such as Match.com. The more women there are on the site, the more attractive this site becomes for men, and more men are likely to join. This in turn makes the site also more attractive to women as they have more men to choose from.

An indirect network effect can be attributed to the complementary nature of some of the major components of the network that constitutes a business model.[19] In an auction business model, the complementary components of the network would be the buyers and sellers. Here, the total value created is a direct function of network size.

Although some business models (for example, those revolving around online communities and auctions) are more likely than others (for example, those focusing mainly on direct, online sales) to exhibit important network externalities, e-commerce business models can be designed to harness the power of this lock-in mechanism. Amazon, for example, has incorporated several community features into its business model.[20] Among other things,

---

[18]Katz and Shapiro (1985, p. 424)
[19]Economides (1996)
[20]Kotha (1998)

it has created a "community of interests" by allowing its customers to write product reviews. Even stronger are the network effects created by certain online games where customers can interact with each other in complex virtual environments. A prominent example is *World of Warcraft*, a massive multiplayer online role-playing game (MMORPG) where individual players assume virtual characters. Through their avatars, players explore the fictional planet of Azeroth, acquiring gear and engaging in interactions (including trading) with other "characters." As more players join, they contribute to building an increasingly complex and engaging online community, boosting the game's appeal.

Novelty and lock-in, two of the four main value drivers in our model, are linked in two important ways. First, business model innovators have an advantage in attracting and retaining customers, especially in conjunction with a strong brand. Second, being first to market is an essential prerequisite to being successful in markets characterized by increasing returns. First movers are in a good position to initiate the positive feedback dynamics that derive from network externalities, and to achieve a critical mass of suppliers and/or customers before others do. In "winner-takes-most" or "winner-takes-all" markets, it is paramount to be the first to enter.

Complementarities

Complementarities are present whenever bundling activities within a system provides more value than running activities separately.[21] For example, in commercial banking, a deposit activity is an important source of funding that complements the banks' lending activity. Or consider the pharmaceutical industry, where R&D conducted by innovative biotechnology firms provides the drug pipeline for the marketing and distribution activities of large pharmaceutical firms. Similarly, in the diamond business, organizing polishing and distribution activities under one roof is advantageous because it enables the firm to tailor stones to the demand in each market segment.

Complementarities are also present whenever having a bundle of goods provides more value than the total value of having each of the goods

---

[21] Teece (2000)

separately. Strategy scholars have highlighted the importance of providing complementary outputs to customers.[22] "A player is your complementor if customers value your product more when they have the other player's product than when they have your product alone."[23]

Firms can leverage this potential for value creation by offering bundles of complementary products and services to their customers. These complementary goods may reflect vertical complementarities (e.g., after-sales service) or horizontal complementarities (e.g., one-stop shopping) that are often provided by partner firms. They are often directly related to the activities that are enabled by the firm's business model. For example, ebookers, a European online travel site, grants its customers access to weather information, currency exchange rate information, and information about immunization clinics. These services enhance the value of the core products (airline tickets and vacation packages) and make it convenient for users to book travel and vacations with ebookers.

Similarly, offline activities can complement online activities. Customers who buy products through online sites may value the possibility of getting after-sales service through bricks-and-mortar retail outlets, including the ability to return or exchange merchandise. This complementarity between online and offline businesses is the essence of "click-and-mortar" business models. A customer of a clothing retailer such as Zara, for instance, might buy a dress through Zara's online store, but return it to a physical location if it does not fit.

Business models may also create value by capitalizing on complementarities among activities (such as supply chain integration), and complementarities among technologies (such as linking the imaging technology of one business model participant with the Internet communication technology of another), thereby unleashing new value.

---

[22]Complementarities can be defined with respect to outputs or inputs, that is, with respect to the determinants of a firm's profit function. A profit function that is well-behaved (i.e., concave, continuous, and twice continuously differentiable) is complementary in its inputs if raising the level of one input variable increases the marginal return to the other input variable. See Milgrom and Roberts (1990, 1995) for a discussion of complementarity that is relevant for BMI strategy.
[23]Brandenburger and Nalebuff (1996, p. 18)

Efficiency gains made possible by information technology pave the way for the orchestration and profitable exploitation of complementarities. Weaving together activities enabled by distinct firms into the focal firm's business model is economically compelling when their incentives are aligned, that is, when both the focal firm and the partner are better off working together rather than independently. Such complementary activities often enhance the value proposition for customers. Customers may benefit from complementary products and services, for example, through reduced search costs and improved decision-making due to more complete information. For example, Edmunds.com, an online car search company, combines a broad range of information and related services that are provided by different vendors. This enhances the benefits for new or used car buyers and is incentive compatible.

Novelty is also linked with complementarities. The main innovation of some e-commerce business models refers to the complementary content of transactions. At Cars.com, an online platform for buyers and sellers of cars and vendors of complementary products (e.g., accessories) and services (e.g., repairs), buyers or sellers of new and used cars benefit from a range of complementary services associated with buying or selling a car.

Efficiency

Efficiency-centered design refers to the ways in which firms aim at achieving greater efficiency through the design of their activity systems. An efficiency-centered activity system aims at reducing transaction costs. For example, a focal firm may decide to integrate vertically into activities to avoid being taken hostage by its trading partners, who may have an incentive to exploit a situation of codependency. Or consider the reverse case, in which a firm manages to standardize the interfaces between activities in its system, and thereby lower its transaction costs by outsourcing some activities to third parties. This explains the rise of the business process outsourcing industry in India, where companies like Tata Consultancy Services (TCS), Wipro, and Infosys each have over 175,000 employees and revenues of at least $8bn globally. Another example is First Data Corporation (acquired by Fiserv in July 2019), a U.S. firm that handles crucial activities for credit card companies, such as dealing with applications, authorizing credit lines, or processing transactions. First Data employs about 24,000 people, and handles over 2,500 transactions per second in businesses located in 118 countries.[24] These are examples of efficiency-centered designs where the governance of the activity system is implied. Firms can also aim at achieving efficiency through their activity system content and structure. Some low-cost airlines dropped activities considered standard by regular airlines, like onboard catering or seat assignment, and changed the way activities are performed and linked to each other.

The greater the transaction efficiency gains that are enabled by a business model, the greater the value proposition of the business model. Efficiency enhancements can be realized in a number of ways. One way is by reducing information asymmetries between buyers and sellers through the supply of more up-to-date and comprehensive information. Improved information can also reduce customers' search and bargaining costs, enable faster and more informed decision-making, provide for greater selection at lower costs by reducing distribution costs, streamline inventory management, simplify transactions and thus reduce the likelihood of mistakes, allow individual customers to benefit from scale economies through demand aggregation and bulk purchasing, streamline the supply chain, and expedite transaction processing and order fulfillment. All of these implications of improved information benefit both vendors and customers. Marketing and sales costs, transaction processing costs, and communication costs can also all be reduced in an efficient business model.

Efficiency gains in highly networked industries are well documented. A study of highly networked Japanese firms, for example, suggests that information flows and reduced asymmetries of information, among other factors, are important in reducing the potential transaction costs associated with specialized assets.[25] More generally, information technology leads to a reduction of the costs of coordinating and executing activities. These arguments can be related to the efficiency gains generated by digital business models.

---

[24] Figures are for 2015; see First Data website.

[25] Dyer (1997)

There is an important relationship between the efficiency and novelty value drivers. Certain efficiency features of a business model may be due to novel activities (***What***). For example, Artnet.com, a European company that has adopted a business model that enables online art auctions, reduces the asymmetry of information between buyers and sellers of art (traditionally a source of severe inefficiencies) through maintaining and expanding a comprehensive database of transactions (including information on price) that is accessible to its clients. This information service, which allows participants in auctions to benchmark a current offering against historic art sales, was novel in the art auction business and increases business model efficiency. Efficiency can also derive from novel business model structures (***How***). That is, small reorganizations within existing business models may lead to considerable efficiency gains.

The efficiency value driver can also be helpful for fostering lock-in. A business model's efficiency features may serve to attract and retain customers and partners. The higher the relative benefits offered to existing and prospective participants, the higher their incentives to stick with or join the network established by the business model. The increasing return properties inherent to network effects then magnify the relative benefits offered, thus triggering positive feedback dynamics.

Conversely, when a business model creates lock-in, it can also have positive effects on its efficiency. For example, many retailing platforms allow buyers to rate sellers. This feature increases buyers' trust in the fairness of transactions and therefore fosters the stickiness of the respective business model. This feature also provides a strong incentive for repeat sellers to refrain from cheating, which clearly enhances business model efficiency. Moreover, the promise of high-volume (repeat) business generated by a business model's strong potential for lock-in also constitutes an incentive for high-profile partners to become contributors of complementary activities.

In summary, there are important relationships between novelty, lock-in, efficiency, and complementarities. The potential value created for all stakeholders in a business model depends to an important extent on the combined effects of all four value drivers (see Exhibit 8.3).

Exhibit 8.3 NICE Value Drivers of Business Models

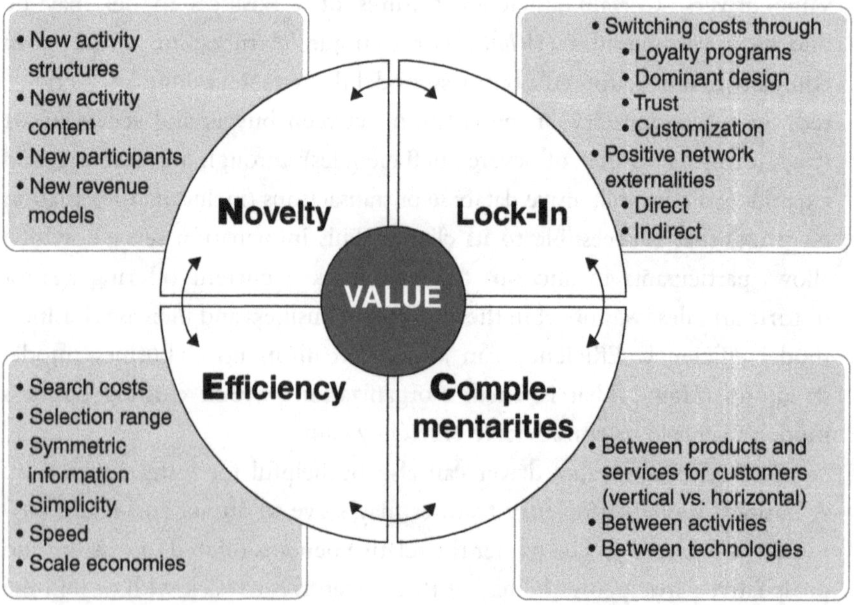

From Value Proposition to Value Appropriation

The business model's value creation, from which its value propositions are derived, lays the foundations for the focal firm's value appropriation in two ways. First, it does so by codetermining the overall total value created, which is the upper limit to the focal firm's value appropriation. Second, the business model also influences the focal firm's bargaining power vis-à-vis other business model stakeholders. The greater the total value that is created by the business model, the greater the focal firm's potential bargaining power, and the greater the amount of value that the focal firm may be able to appropriate.[26] We will explain this logic in more detail next, focusing on the novelty value driver.

---

[26]Zott and Amit (2007)

Business model innovation may give rise to entrepreneurial rents.[27] These monopoly-type rents may accrue to business model stakeholders between the introduction of an innovation and its diffusion. While we expect novelty-centered business model design to have a positive effect on the performance of a focal firm, we note that entrepreneurial rents may accrue to *all* stakeholders in the business model. In order to predict the overall effect of novelty-centered value propositions on the performance of the focal firm, we must also consider their effect on the firm's ability to appropriate the value that its business model generates. This ability depends on factors such as (i) the switching costs of other business model stakeholders, (ii) the focal firm's ability to control information, (iii) the ability of other stakeholders to take unified action vis-à-vis the focal firm, and (iv) the replacement costs of other stakeholders.[28] For example, the higher the switching costs of other business model stakeholders, the greater the focal firm's bargaining power vis-à-vis these stakeholders, and the greater its ability to appropriate rent.

We suggest that, *on average*, an increase in business model novelty will not decrease the focal entrepreneurial firm's ex-post bargaining power relative to other business model stakeholders. The focal firm is the innovator, and its business model is the locus of innovation. The higher the degree of business model novelty, the higher the switching costs for the focal firm's customers, suppliers, and partners, as there may not be readily-available alternatives to doing business with the focal firm. The other determinants of the focal firm's bargaining power are unlikely to be systematically affected in one direction or the other. The focal firm's bargaining power vis-à-vis these parties is unlikely to be diminished through novelty-centered business model design. Therefore, considering the positive effect of novelty-centered business model design, both on total value created and on the ability of the focal firm to capture that value, we expect a positive effect of novelty-centered business model design on the performance of an entrepreneurial firm.

---

[27] Rumelt (1987)
[28] See Coff (1999, p. 122)

Summary of Key Takeaways for the Effective Business Model Designer

In this chapter we defined the *value proposition* of a business model, by building on the marketing literature. The value proposition is a hypothesis that describes the value created for business model stakeholders (net of any costs incurred). Our definition once again highlights the importance of creating value for *all* business model stakeholders. Furthermore, we suggest that the value proposition of a business model is separate from, but complementary to, the value proposition of a product. While the value proposition of a service may not be as easy to distinguish from that of the associated business model, together, the two make up the *total* value proposition to the customer, in the same way that the value proposition of a product complements the value proposition of a business model. As digitization enables new links between firms and their suppliers and customers, new participants are becoming increasingly involved in the process of active co-creation of value, as manifested in open business models.

We also presented a framework that expands on the basic model of value creation with a single firm, a single supplier, and a single customer. Our framework presents four different drivers of value, which can be powerfully combined in different ways to maximize the value created for all stakeholders. They are summarized by the acronym NICE: *N*ovelty, lock-*In*, *C*omplementarities and *E*fficiency. The novelty value driver can be captured by the focal firm through first-mover advantage, for example, and defended through switching costs. Lock-in refers to the ability of a business model to retain key stakeholders; it can appear as switching costs or network externalities. Business models can lock in customers through mechanisms such as loyalty programs, design standards, trust, or personalization. The third NICE business model value driver is complementarities, which exist when bundling activities within a business model enhances the overall value (compared to adding up the value of each item separately). Finally, the efficiency value driver of business models captures how the design of the activity system reduces transaction costs; this is especially clear with digital business models that benefit from high efficiency at a relatively low cost.

References

Amit, R. & Zott, C. (2001). Value creation in E-business. *Strategic Management Journal* **22**(6–7), 493–520.

Amit, R. & Zott, C. (2012). Creating value through business model innovation. *MIT Sloan Management Review* **53**(3), 41–49.

Arthur, W. B. (1990). Positive feedbacks in the economy. *Scientific American* **262**(2), 92–99.

Brandenburger, A. M. & Nalebuff, B. J. (1996). *Co-Opetition.* New York, NY: Doubleday.

Brandenburger, A. M. & Stuart, H. W., Jr. (1996). Value-based business strategy. *Journal of Economics & Management Strategy* **5**(1), 5–24.

Coff, R. L. (1999). When competitive advantage doesn't lead to performance: The resource-based view and stakeholder bargaining power. *Organization Science* **10**(2), 119–133.

DeSarbo, W. S., Jedidi, K. & Sinha, I. (2001). Customer value analysis in a heterogeneous market. *Strategic Management Journal* **22**(9), 845–857.

Dyer, J. H. (1997). Effective interim collaboration: How firms minimize transaction costs and maximise transaction value. *Strategic Management Journal* **18**(7), 535–556.

Economides, N. (1996). The economics of networks. *International Journal of Industrial Organization* **14**(6), 673–699.

First Data website. Retrieved from https://www.firstdata.com/en_gb/about-first-data/media/first-data-facts.html

Katz, M. L. & Shapiro, C. (1985). Network externalities, competition, and compatibility. *American Economic Review* **75**(3), 424–440.

Kotha, S. (1998). Competing on the internet: The case of Amazon.com. *European Management Journal* **16**(2), 212–222.

Lakhani, K. H., Lifshitz-Assaf, H. & Tushman, M. (2013). Open innovation and organizational boundaries: Task decomposition, knowledge distribution and the locus of innovation. In A. Grandori (Ed.), *Handbook of Economic Organization: Integrating Economic and Organization Theory* (pp. 355–382). Northampton, MA: Edward Elgar Publishing.

Lanning, M. & Michaels, E. (1988). A business is a value delivery system. McKinsey Staff Paper No. 14. Retrieved from https://www.mckinsey.com/business-functions/strategy-and-corporate-finance/our-insights/delivering-value-to-customers

Lee, E. (2018, July 26). The incredible rise of Pinduoduo, China's newest force in e-commerce. *TechCrunch*. Retrieved from https://techcrunch.com/2018/07/26/the-incredible-rise-of-pinduoduo/

Milgrom, P. & Roberts, J. (1990). Rationalizability, learning, and equilibrium in games with strategic complementarities. *Econometrica* **58**(6), 1255–1277.

Milgrom, P. & Roberts, J. (1995). Complementarities and fit strategy, structure, and organizational change in manufacturing. *Journal of Accounting and Economics* **19**(2–3), 179–208.

Osterwalder, A. & Pigneur, Y. (2010). *Business Model Generation: A Handbook for Visionaries, Game Changers, and Challengers*. Hoboken, NJ: John Wiley & Sons.

Osterwalder, A., Pigneur, Y., Bernarda, G., Smith, A. & Papadakos, T. (2014). *Value Proposition Design: How to Create Products and Services Customers Want*. Hoboken, NJ: John Wiley & Sons.

Payne, A. & Frow, P. (2005). A strategic framework for customer relationship management. *Journal of Marketing* **69**(4), 167–176.

Pinduoduo Inc. website. Retrieved from https://en.pinduoduo.com/company

Prahalad, C. K. & Ramaswamy, V. (2004). *The Future of Competition: Co-Creating Unique Value with Customers*. Boston, MA: Harvard Business School Press.

Rumelt, R. P. (1987). Theory, strategy and entrepreneurship. In D. J. Teece (Ed.), *The Competitive Challenge*. Cambridge, MA: Ballinger Publishing.

Say, J. B. (1803). Of Immaterial Products, or Values Consumed at the Moment of Production. In Clement C. Biddle (Ed.), (trans. CR Prinsep), *A Treatise on Political Economy; or the Production, Distribution, and Consumption of Wealth*, (from the 4th ed. of the French). Philadelphia, PA: Lippincott, Grambo & Co, 1855. 4th–5th ed.

Schumpeter, J. A. (1934). *The Theory of Economic Development: An Inquiry into Profits, Capital, Credit, Interest, and the Business Cycle*. Cambridge, MA: Harvard University Press.

Shapiro, C. & Varian, H. R. (1999). *Information Rules: A Strategic Guide to the Network Economy*. Cambridge, MA: Harvard Business School Press.

Teece, D. J. (2000). Strategies for managing knowledge assets: The role of firm structure and industrial context. *Long Range Planning* **33**(1), 35–54.

United States Securities and Exchange Commission. (2019, January 13). *Form Q-10 of Google Inc.* Retrieved from https://www.sec.gov/Archives/edgar/data/1288776/000128877613000055/goog10-qq22013.htm.

Vargo, S. L. & Lusch, R. R. (2004). Evolving to a new dominant logic for marketing. *Journal of Marketing* **68**(1), 1–17.

Zott, C. & Amit, R. (2007). Business model design and the performance of entrepreneurial firms. *Organization Science* **18**(2), 181–199.

9 Evaluating Existing Business Models and Designing New Ones – Your Essential Toolkit

Business Model Analysis – Why Is It Needed?

Business model analysis refers to the set of practices and tools that enable managers to (i) define precisely how their current business model works; (ii) evaluate the current business model's strengths, weaknesses, and impact on firm performance; (iii) design, implement, and evaluate innovative new business models; and (iv) redesign existing business models. In this chapter, we present and describe some of the most prevalent tools for business model analysis that have been suggested in the literature, and some that are widely used in practice. In doing so, we draw on the material that we have developed over the past two decades; on the vast repertoire of design methods that exist; and on specific business model tools, such as the *Business Model*

Canvas from Alexander Osterwalder and Yves Pigneur, and the *Business Model Navigator* introduced by scholars at the University of St. Gallen.[1] We link these various analytical tools to our business model framework and the concepts used in this book.[2]

Our basic framework, which was introduced in Chapter 1 (see Exhibit 1.4), is a fundamental tool in and of itself. It helps, for example, to articulate and describe an existing business model. While it appears to be a simple tool, in practice it can be challenging to apply. Asked about the business model of their company, many managers struggle to give a concrete answer, and it is not unusual to hear different answers from different managers within the same company. This is partly due to unclear definitions of the term "business model," and the varying notions of it that people have. However, even when there is one commonly agreed upon, high-level definition (for example, that of the business model as an activity system), individual managers might have different views of their firm's business model. They might also find it challenging to articulate their firm's business model with precision and depth. That, of course, makes it extremely difficult to recognize the strengths and weaknesses of the current model (which model precisely?), and/or come up with a better one. It is therefore important to have a framework that clearly defines the various dimensions and components of a business model with sufficient breadth as well as depth. Beyond that, additional methods and tools are needed in order to apply the framework to better articulate and understand the existing business model, for better understanding the drivers of a new design to guide and optimize the design effort, for actually designing and

---

[1]See Gassmann, Frankenberger, and Csik (2014), and Osterwalder and Pigneur (2010). Note that other useful tools and analytical frameworks have been proposed, for example, by Afuah (2019), George and Bock (2017), or Johnson (2010).

[2]The central purpose of this chapter is to introduce a basic set of methods and tools that can be used to apply the concepts and ideas presented in this book and bring them to life. We do not aim at providing a full and exhaustive representation of business model design tools – this is beyond the scope of the book. Indeed, the core value of this chapter lies in helping the reader identify those tools and methods from among the many offered in the field that are truly essential for designing business model innovations.

implementing business model innovations, and, finally, for evaluating the pros and cons of new and existing business models. These methods and tools are addressed in the sections that follow.

Tools for Articulating and Understanding Business Models

As we have seen in previous chapters, in particular Chapters 1 and 4, business model innovation is realized at the activity system-level. It results from innovations in any one or more of the business model's key dimensions, with system-wide effects. As shown in Chapter 2, business model innovation is a new level of innovation. It is a distinct new source of value creation, which is different from, but complements, product, service, or process innovation. We also suggested (in Chapter 3) that business model innovation is not as easy to comprehend and relate to as other, more conventional forms of innovation. Therefore, in order to harness its full potential, managers need to raise awareness of the power of business model innovation. In Chapter 6, we argue that this is also an important precedent for building a business model innovation capability. In short, managers and employees involved in their firms' innovation efforts need to adopt a business model mindset (see Chapter 3 on how this can be accomplished). Managers also need to be able to articulate the business model of their firm in order to analyze it more deeply. Several techniques have been proposed for this: telling a high-level story of how the business model works; elaborating on the distinct dimensions of the business model in detail; and producing a chart that shows the main activities that constitute the firm's business model and the ways in which these activities are linked. We will next explain each of these methods separately.

Story of "How It Works"

According to author Joan Magretta, business models are "stories that explain how enterprises work . . . with precisely delineated characters [***Who***], plausible motivations [***Why***], and a plot [***What, How***] that turns on an insight about value."[3] Elaborating on this idea, she further explains that, "creating

[3]Magretta (2002, p. 87), terms in brackets added.

a business model is, then, a lot like writing a new story. . . . all new business models are variations on the generic value chain underlying all businesses."[4] The value chain encompasses all the activities associated with making and selling a product, service, or experience to customers (see Chapter 2). Thus, the business model told as a story revolves around activities, like our business model framework (Chapters 1 and 4). The story as a tool for articulating a business model is therefore perfectly consistent with our key concepts.

According to Magretta, a good story fulfills two conditions. First, it needs to make sense. For example, it needs to satisfy the incentive compatibility constraints of all business model stakeholders. Second, it should have a satisfactory "ending," in the sense of delivering a profit for the focal firm. Condition 1 refers to what we called the *value proposition* in Chapter 8. It suggests that the value proposition to any particular stakeholder in a business model must be strong enough for the stakeholder to "play along." Only then will the story be a plausible one. Condition 2 refers to what we called the *value logic* of the business model in Chapter 1, which is embodied in the question "***Why***." More precisely, ***Why*** does the business model create value, and ***Why*** does it enhance value appropriation for the focal firm? If the value logic for the focal firm is not compelling, the story is not convincing. At the end of the day, the for-profit focal firm should be able to enhance its value from its business model (or reach its value creation objectives in the case of a non-for-profit Non-Governmental Organization [NGO] or social enterprise).

As an illustration of a business model that violated these conditions, consider Priceline WebHouse Club. As mentioned in Chapter 2, Priceline introduced the reverse "name-your-own-price" auction mechanism to the airline travel industry. Encouraged by the enthusiastic early reception of their business model, the company's management was motivated to extend the concept from travel to other industries, such as groceries and gasoline. Their idea was to become a power broker for individual consumers vis-à-vis consumer goods brands. The story they told went something like this:[5]

---

[4]Magretta (2002, p. 88)
[5]See Magretta (2002, p. 90)

Via our Internet-based platform, millions of consumers tell Priceline Webhouse Club how much they want to pay for a specific consumer good, say, a jar of peanut butter. Customers specify the price, but not the brand. Webhouse Club then aggregates the bids and approaches companies like P&G to propose a deal: Take x% off the price of your product, and we'll order a million units this week. This is a win-win-win proposition: The consumer goods brand will get the advantage of increasing their sales dramatically, consumers will benefit from a lower price, and Webhouse Club receives a handsome fee in the process.

So the business model story goes. Unfortunately, this story grossly misjudged the value proposition to brand owners, by ignoring the importance they placed on their past investments in brand loyalty. The WebHouse Club model assumed customers would value price alone. It was thus prone to undermining brand loyalty, which dramatically weakened the *actual* value proposition to the brand owners. Since the brand owners refused to cooperate, the envisioned value logic of the business model could not be realized. Priceline WebHouse Club had to heavily subsidize discounts, and it eventually ran out of cash.

As this example shows, stories can be powerful tools for articulating, communicating, and accepting (or refusing) business models. Specifically, the storytelling tool consists of the following task:

Tool 1: Story of "How It Works" Write a one-paragraph story about how a business model works. In your story, explain the main activities that are conducted, who carries them out, and the order in which they are carried out. Also explain the logic of the new business model, why it is appropriate, and why it makes sense. What is the main source of value creation? What are the value propositions to customers and partners, and are they strong enough? How and why will you eventually make money?

The story as a tool to depict a business model is also a very good instrument to learn more about the business models of other firms (such as competitors). In particular, new firms anchored on a business model innovation often explain their story on their website (e.g., under the tab "about us," where you can often find another tab that explains "how does it work?"). For example, UK fintech company Zopa, which was referenced in previous chapters, has a short explanatory video on its website. This video, which is captioned "Understand Zopa in under 90 seconds," breaks down the Zopa business model into simple, easy-to-understand terms, using voiceover and brightly colored graphic animations.

Business Model Elaboration

Building on the holistic and compact narrative form of the business model story, it is useful to drill down further and elaborate on the different dimensions of the business model. In this more detailed mode of articulating and understanding a business model, the analyst methodically dissects the distinct dimensions, focusing on the pieces rather than on the business model as a whole (as the analyst would do when writing the story of the business model) – without, of course, losing sight of the whole. That is why Business Model Elaboration should be performed after, or in addition to, producing the Story of "How It Works," which it complements.

Tool 2: Business Model Elaboration Describe the ***What? How? Who?*** and ***Why?*** of the business model.

What are the key activities of the business model?

- What is being sold: A product? A service? A bundle of product(s) and service(s)? To which customer segment(s) exactly?
- What activities are required to generate and deliver that offering to the customer? Which ones are key?
- What resources and skills are required to enable these activities?

How is the customer experience created and delivered by the model?

- Adopt a systems perspective and describe the sequencing of activities.
- What are the key links between activities? E.g., through which channels are customers reached?
- What dynamic feedback loops are included in the model that allow for learning about, and reacting to, customer preferences?

Who are the key stakeholders in the new model?

- Which parties (including customers) perform which activities?
- Which activities are performed "in-house"?

Why does the business model enable value creation and capture?

- What is the main logic on which the business model turns?

- Are the value propositions to customers and other key stakeholders consistent with this logic? Are they strong enough?
- Do the value logic and the associated value propositions differentiate the focal firm from the competition?
- (In the case of a for-profit firm) How much value is captured by the focal firm? Is it enough to make a decent profit?

Activity Map

A single picture is worth more than a thousand words. In line with this conventional wisdom, it is helpful to represent the entire activity system as a chart, which we refer to as an Activity Map. In an Activity Map, the key activities (***What***) of the business model are represented as boxes. In each box, the respective activity is described verbally; it is best to use a verb to denote the activity. Arrows between the activity boxes represent the links and sequencing among activities. They therefore represent the structure of the business model (***How***). To denote the "owner" of each activity, i.e., the one who is carrying it out (***Who***), distinct colors can be used (e.g., green activity boxes for the focal firm, yellow boxes for customers, different shades of red for the various suppliers, etc.). The value logic (***Why***) can be written in text form into the graphic, although it should ideally be self-explanatory. Looking at the Activity Map as a whole should give you a good sense of the key idea(s) behind the activity system.

As an example, consider eBay, which was formed in September 1995. It was conceived as an online person-to-person auction platform, bringing together buyers and sellers of used goods. Auctions last 1, 3, 5, 7, or 10 days; eBay now also has a more traditional fixed price sale format for some listings. In 2002, it acquired payments provider PayPal; although PayPal was spun-off again from eBay in 2015, it continues to be available as a payment choice. To sell items, a user registers online by providing personal information and a credit card or bank account number, and by accepting the disclaimer and the rules set up by eBay. For a small fee, sellers have the right to auction and are granted space on the eBay site to display and describe their merchandise. They set parameters such as the auction length, the minimum bid level, and an optional reserve price. Buyers similarly provide a set of personal information before placing bids. The bidding function is used by a buyer to send eBay information about the amount he or she is willing to pay for an item. At the close of auctions, the highest bidder receives an email notification that they won, and their payment is processed. An automatic notification provides the seller with the buyer's email address, thereby enabling a discussion of shipment and payment details.

An affiliate program, the eBay Partner Network, increases eBay's visibility and brings profits to affiliates. Partners promote links that direct traffic from their sites to eBay. (Amazon has a similar program, where bloggers and other site owners promote Amazon products and direct traffic, receiving a small fee in exchange.) Exhibit 9.1 shows how all this information about eBay's business model can be captured visually using an Activity Map.[6]

Exhibit 9.1 Activity Map of eBay

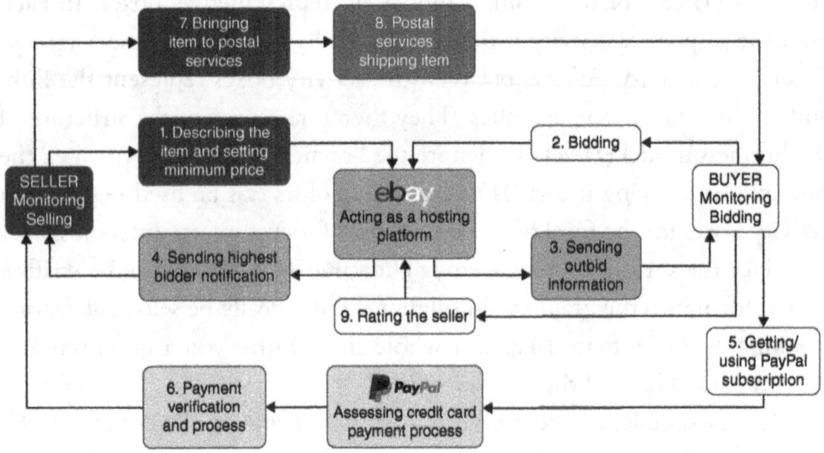

Thus, in summary:

Tool 3: Activity Map Visualize the business model through boxes (***What***), arrows between the boxes (***How***), different colors of boxes (***Who***), and additional text if necessary (***Why***).

Tools for Framing the Design Effort

By building on the discussion of the strategic design drivers (or design antecedents, as they are also referred to), which were described in detail in

[6]Amit and Zott (2002)

Chapter 5, we present a set of tools that can be used to frame the design of innovative business models. Specifically, to identify the Goals and Needs of customers, managers can formulate a problem statement or a questionnaire. As well, to identify Incumbents' templates, they can draw inspiration from incumbent business model templates (even from very different industries). Next, to evaluate the External environment, Stakeholders' activities, and Deployable resources, there are two important tools at the disposal of managers: environmental PEST scanning, and resource and capability scanning. These five tools are covered in more detail below.

Goals and Needs of Customers

Business model design and innovation are closely related. Business model designers need to understand customers' goals and needs, which can be formulated as problems, in order to come up with powerful and innovative solutions. This is consistent with the notion that designers-as-innovators deal with ill-defined problems, for which they attempt to find new and desirable solutions. "If solutions could be offered within the existing system, there would be no need to design. Thus, designers have to transcend the existing system. Their task is to create a different system or devise a new one."[7]

To accomplish this, identifying a compelling problem is quintessential. Unfortunately, many firms, especially large established ones, focus too much on finding new solutions in their quest for innovations. Consequently, they spend too little time asking themselves what problems they should actually be trying to fix for customers, and whether the underlying problems are truly the most important ones to solve. Albert Einstein was credited with saying, "If I had an hour to solve a problem I'd spend 55 minutes thinking about the problem, and 5 minutes thinking about solutions."[8] Although that might be an exaggeration, the sentence embodies the profound wisdom that thinking hard about the problem to solve may be at least as important (if not more so) than trying to figure

[7] Banathy (1996, p. 20)

[8] According to Quote Investigator website, Einstein actually never said this, although the quote is often attributed to him.

out a solution for it. That much is clear: if a great business model solution is found for a weak problem, or a business model solution is formulated that is more or less hypothetical and does not in reality capture well the existing needs and goals of customers, then much investment of effort, time, and money will have been wasted. Therefore, starting with a realistic, useful, crisp initial problem statement and attempting to refine it as time unfolds is extremely important. In this context, designers also talk about the "co-evolution of problem-space and solution-space."[9] Over time, as they test new solutions, they learn to understand the problem better, which in turn allows them to refine the solution, and so on.

Hence, we propose a simple, yet important, tool, the Problem Statement. This tool assumes a business model innovation project within a focal firm, a project sponsor (e.g., the focal firm's CEO), and an innovation team charged with carrying out the project.

Tool 4: Problem Statement (1) What is the problem that the innovation team should solve, according to the mandate from the project sponsor? (2) What is the problem that should be solved, according to the innovation team's own interpretation, after careful deliberation and discussion of its mandate? (3) If there are any discrepancies between (1) and (2), how can they be reconciled? Formulate a consolidated initial problem statement. (4) Get feedback from third parties on this statement: How could it be further refined?

A powerful problem statement is one that (i) is centered on key business model stakeholders, in particular customers, not the focal firm; (ii) considers customers as human beings, with all their goals, human needs, desires, and motivations; (iii) represents an important and meaningful issue for the customers; and (iv) is ambitious, yet feasible (i.e., it is possible to solve it in a way that makes economic sense). An initial problem statement serves as a starting point. As it rarely fulfills these four conditions perfectly, the problem statement needs to be improved, refined, and sometimes changed altogether in the early business model design stages. This process is called *problem reframing*, which involves seeing the problem from a different angle and asking a different question.

[9]Dorst and Cross (2001) quoted in Dunne (2018, p. 19).

To illustrate the reframing process, consider the following initial problem statement that was provided to a business model innovation team by its corporate sponsor, an interior hardware (in particular, bathroom) manufacturer: "*How can we make our company a leading supplier of services by leveraging our bathroom expertise?*" The question was important and meaningful for the focal firm. It was also quite ambitious, as it captured the intention – and difficulty – of changing from a product company to a services company. However, it neither focused on customers nor captured their needs, and so it did not fully satisfy the criteria laid out above. To better understand the issue at hand, the team conducted numerous interviews with managers from the focal firm, companies that were considered extreme users (e.g., McDonald's and Starbucks), cleaning companies, architects, plumbers, distributors, hotels, offices, public facilities, and end users (especially families and mothers). As a result of the insights gained from the interviews, in particular about the importance for facility managers of sustainable water solutions (e.g., early detection of water leakages in bathrooms), the team proposed to reframe the problem as follows:

> *"How can we help users solve their sustainability needs by not only letting them truly experience the social impact that they are creating, but also giving them monetary benefits?"*

This new problem statement represented an important advance compared with the earlier one, because it was now centered on customers, rather than on the focal firm that acted as a project sponsor. Enlightened by its deep understanding of customer and stakeholder needs, and guided by the new question, the business model innovation team went on to develop a B2B technology-based water management solution for facility managers that was delivered as an end-to-end service. It thereby not only identified a new business opportunity for the sponsoring firm, but was also able to meet the latter's initial request for a new business model that would leverage the firm's existing assets and resources, and help it transition into a services company.

As the example suggests, questionnaires are important auxiliary tools in the quest for identifying a compelling problem and asking a powerful question. To design a useful questionnaire for interviewing business model stakeholders, one needs to take the initial problem statement and develop a range of questions that probe it more deeply in terms of its relevance for the stakeholder. Questions need to be tailored to the respective interviewee. End users of bathrooms, for example, need to be asked different questions than facility managers. Possible questions to end users include the following: Could you describe to us your bathroom experience? What difficulties and frustrations have you experienced when using a bathroom? Which kinds of improvements have you desired, and why?

Good questions go below the surface and encourage interviewees to express themselves as human beings, articulating their emotions and values. This is best accomplished using open-ended questions (e.g., "How do you spend your day?"), for which the interviewer should take the time to let the interviewee express themselves. When interesting and unexpected points come up, or things are a little unclear, the interviewer should ask follow-up questions, in order to get to the bottom of things. It is important not to rush down the list of questions or ask them one-by-one in a mechanical way. Instead, the questionnaire should be interpreted as a flexible guide that helps to establish a meaningful, structured conversation with someone, with the objective of identifying a problem that truly matters.

It cannot be emphasized strongly enough that the central purpose of asking questions at an early stage in the business model innovation process is to achieve a better understanding of the problem to solve, rather than to find a solution for what could be a poorly defined problem. Therefore, the interviewer also needs to refrain from the urge to ask questions that superimpose the interviewers' assumptions and views on the interviewees, in particular about the problem to be solved. To resist this tendency, the interviewers should pretend they know nothing about the subject and treat their interviewees as the undisputed domain experts. Moreover, they should take ample – and accurate – notes about what the interviewees actually say (and not what they *think* they hear the interviewees say). Direct quotes and comments are valuable in that respect, as are verbs and feelings. Respondents should also be asked to articulate concrete actions and outcomes, and elaborate on what they mean when they use general terms, such as "culture," "relationships," or "resources." Such factual questioning and notetaking force the interviewers to listen carefully. It also helps prevent them from making premature interpretations and conclusions.

It also preserves their ability to come up with groundbreaking innovations. When you ask people directly about what they want, i.e., about solutions, often they will not be able to articulate their needs in terms of specific innovations that they desire. However, the purpose of a questionnaire in the context of business model innovation design is not to ask people what solutions they want. Instead, it is to identify and better understand their problems, which up until this point may have been under-appreciated, taken for granted, assumed to be insoluble, or simply gone unnoticed.[10]

Tool 5: Business Model Questionnaire Define who should be interviewed, when, and by whom. Given the current problem statement, formulate a range of open-ended questions that could be asked to probe more deeply into it. Keep the holistic perspective of the business model in mind when formulating questions to learn more about the motivations and issues of various stakeholders, not just customers. Prepare different versions of the questionnaire for different stakeholders (e.g., customers, suppliers, and partners). Identify questions that could be asked first in order to "break the ice" and establish a rapport with the interviewee. Be open to deviations during the interview, ask follow-up questions, and take comprehensive notes. After the interview, complement your notes with observations you have made during the interview, for example about non-verbal expressions and behaviors.

---

[10]Building on these very simple first steps of formulating a hypothetical problem and asking questions about it, a broad range of tools and techniques have been proposed that can also be useful for understanding business model stakeholders' goals and needs better, such as user profile, stakeholder journey, or shadowing. For an overview, see Liedtka and Ogilvie (2011). Pew Research Center, a non-partisan think tank based in Washington, DC, offers guidelines about good questionnaire design (see Pew Research Center website. Questionnaire Design.). For example, a questionnaire should be highly structured, and the order and phrasing of the questions should be carefully considered. It may be helpful to start with easy questions in order not to overburden respondents with several consecutive difficult questions. Early questions can also influence later responses in that they provide context for the questions that follow ("order effects"). Questionnaire development ideally is also a collaborative and iterative process. Finally, before bringing the questionnaire to real respondents, it should be pre-tested to better understand how respondents think about issues and comprehend questions.

Templates

In Chapter 5 (especially in the Incumbents' Templates section), we explained how managers can make use of examples, or templates, as a source of inspiration for business model innovation. Such examples could refer to the specific business models of individual firms (e.g., the business model of eBay, shown in Exhibit 9.1), or to more general principles, such as crowdsourcing, that characterize business models across a set of firms. The book *The Business Model Navigator*, for example, presents 55 models, called business model patterns, that can be used to challenge the dominant logic of any firm and stimulate the discovery of a new business model.[11] In addition, firms that have innovated strongly along any of the four dimensions (***What, How, Who,*** or ***Why***) could serve as templates. For example, the business model of Ryanair could be used to illustrate innovation along the ***What*** dimension (see Exhibit 9.2). Any of these various approaches can help in the ideation and solution-finding phases of the business model innovation process, when a new design needs to be crafted in response to a well-identified and crisply articulated problem.

Exhibit 9.2 Ryanair Business Model Template: *What?*

RYANAIR

- **Ryanair** combines frugality with additional offerings
  - The activity system and initial value proposition are trimmed down to a minimum, but there are add-on elements to the offering that yield additional revenues
  - For example, Ryanair customers often not only purchase a ticket, but also pay for checked luggage, allocated seating, priority boarding, food and drinks sold on the plane
- **Apple added** content distribution activities
  - The activity system is extended in such a way that new activities complement existing ones that can provide enhanced possibilities for monetization through selling small quantities of a very large range of products (e.g., iTunes, App Store)

[11] Gassmann, Frankenberger, and Csik (2014)

Tool 6: Business Model Templates Using visuals, videos, or stories, present examples of firms that have innovated their business models along the key dimensions (***What, How, Who, Why***). Do not be shy about presenting extreme examples from distant industries; these are often effective sources of inspiration.

External Environment, Stakeholders' Activities, and Deployable Resources

The industry-spanning nature of a business model requires the designer to review and assess which of the activities that are enabled by the focal firm's stakeholders might be accessible to the focal firm through partnering. Specifically, once a new activity system has been conceptualized by the designer, a comprehensive scan of activities that are enabled by current and potential stakeholders enables the designers to assess the desired governance of the envisioned activity system. Importantly, a systems perspective is needed in order to determine which activities should be enabled by the focal firm, and which activities are best enabled by others.

In a broader sense, the external environment in which the focal firm operates affects the feasibility and viability of intended business model designs. It influences the specific ways in which activities within the business model can be carried out. The focal firm's competitive landscape; the technological ecosystem within which the focal firm intends to operate; the legal and regulatory setting; and the overall macroeconomic environment present both opportunities and challenges to the designers. To enable business model designers to capitalize on the external conditions that may affect the focal firm, it is helpful to assess the Political, Economic, Social, and Technological environment (PEST)[12] of the focal firm's ecosystem. The Political aspect of a PEST analysis focuses on the areas in which a range of government policies, such as trade policies, and existing and pending regulations, such as taxes and tariffs, affect the firm. The Economic element of the PEST analysis targets key macroeconomic factors, such as interest and exchange rates, inflation, and the prospects of a recession. The Social factors in the PEST analysis are important demographics trends,

[12]See Aguilar (1967)

cultural attitudes such as the preferences of millennials (generation Y) versus generations X and Z, and workplace and lifestyle trends, to name a few. Finally, the Technological component considers the specific roles, development stage, and adoption of technologies within the ecosystem of the focal firm that may be essential to the intended business model.

Tool 7: Environmental PEST Scanning For each of the main external factors cited above (Political, Economic, Social, and Technological), write down a comprehensive list of the elements that shape the industry and firm. You can start by naming the most general and important factors (for example, that affect the entire industry), then narrowing these down to the most relevant ones. While it is useful to start with a more generic PEST analysis, it is necessary to then break it down into the more business model-specific factors, such as the required technological aspects of a firm's ecosystem.

In addition to the PEST analysis, a competitor and competitive analysis should be done in order to provide the business model designers a better understanding of the industry landscape. The Five Forces Industry Analysis[13] is a common tool used to perform these analyses. It considers the power of customers and suppliers, the barriers to entry, the threat of substitutes, and the intensity of competitive rivalry. Moreover, resources and capabilities enable the activities that are envisioned in the business model. These can be resources and capabilities owned or controlled by the focal firm, or by others. The following is a two-step simple capability scanning process, which enables the business model designer to assess the range of capabilities that can be deployed in the envisioned business model.

Tool 8: Resource and Capability Scanning (Step 1) Assess the capability gap. Evaluate the extent to which the focal firm's resources and capabilities can be redeployed in alternative uses in the envisioned business model, to determine the type of capabilities that the focal firm would need to access through partnering with other firms. (Step 2) Ecosystem capability scan: With the information on the type of capabilities that would need to be accessible to the focal firm established in Step 1, scan the ecosystem of the focal firm to identify potential partners whose capabilities can be embedded into the envisioned business model.

[13]See Porter (1980)

Tools for Designing and Implementing Business Model Innovations

This next section provides four tools that can help structure the design and implementation of business model innovations. These tools are in particular relevant to the processes outlined in Chapters 6 and 7.[14] A popular tool for generating, or ideating, creative new business model ideas is brainstorming. Next, recall the importance of experimentation when designing new business models. To this end, managers can use a storyboard to visualize and communicate the idea to others for preliminary feedback. They can then use a Test-Assumption-Matrix (TAM), which highlights the key assumptions of a low-cost business model experiment. Finally, for implementing innovative business models, the Business Model Canvas is a well-known tool that can help guide the development of a business plan from a business model design.

Generating New Business Model Ideas

As mentioned in Chapter 6, brainstorming is a well-established and widely used ideation method, which also works for generating new business model ideas. Most brainstorming formats follow a set of rules that are communicated to the participants ahead of time, such as "generate ideas spontaneously," "avoid discussing their merits," "do not criticize, do not mention negatives," "resist becoming committed to one idea," and "record all ideas."[15] Moreover, the appointment of a facilitator is crucial for keeping time, managing the discussion, and in particular for making sure that the rules are met.

Research on creativity has shown that individual brainstorming is more productive than brainstorming in a team in terms of the number of non-overlapping ideas generated per person.[16] However, team-based

---

[14]Zott and Amit (2015)

[15]See Bhavani and Sosa (2008)

[16]Some of the first brainstorming rules were laid out by Alex Osborn (1953), an advertising executive, in the 1950s. These rules (e.g., "Toss out as many ideas as possible. Don't worry if they're too crazy. Build on the ideas people generate. Don't criticize initially"), have, however, been called into question. In particular, teams

brainstorming rounds, especially on new business models, offer a number of advantages that might offset this expected loss in productivity:

1. Fostering a business model mindset within the organization.
2. Creating a sense of urgency and a common understanding about the importance of business model change.
3. Building an organizational memory of business model design solutions.
4. To the extent that business model stakeholders are involved in the brainstorming: getting them on board and encouraging them to endorse the new model.
5. Enhancing the skill set of participants involved in brainstorming, in particular for analyzing and designing new business models.

Research on brainstorming in design firms has revealed further benefits, such as impressing clients, providing income for the firm, creating a competition for status based on design skills, and supporting an attitude of wisdom (i.e., acting with knowledge while doubting what one knows).[17] Taken together, these benefits highlight the important role of brainstorming for business model innovation.

Tool 9: Brainstorming Establish a set of brainstorming rules, and appoint a facilitator to monitor and guide group behavior during the brainstorming session. Set a goal of creating the highest possible number of new business model ideas for the focal firm within a given time period. You may wish to center the brainstorming on the Problem Statement (Tool 4), or simply start without any constraints. Templates (Tool 6) can be used as a source of inspiration during the brainstorming session.

---

that use Osborn's rules of brainstorming have been found to come up with fewer ideas (and fewer good ideas) than individual team members would have developed alone. An HBR article written by Art Markman ("Your Team is Brainstorming all Wrong," 2017) offers some suggestions about how to fight this productivity loss, such as "let individuals work alone first," "take your time," and "let people draw" (see Markman, 2017). Other best brainstorming practices (e.g., take brief breaks, appoint a facilitator) are explained in a chapter by Paulus and Kenworthy (2019) entitled "Effective Brainstorming" in *The Oxford Handbook of Group Creativity and Innovation* (2019).

[17]See Sutton and Hargadon (1996)

Experimenting with New Business Model Ideas

As with generating innovative ideas via brainstorming, a host of techniques and tools have been proposed for prototyping and testing new business model ideas. In its most simple and basic version, a business model prototype can be constructed in the form of a storyboard – a set of visual frames or a brief video explaining *how the new business model works*, i.e., that highlight the essence of the new story (see Tool 1, Story of "How It Works"). A storyboard video could either be based on role play, or it could be animated (see the Dropbox example of a Minimum Viable Product mentioned in Chapter 7). There are many useful hints, instructions, and software tools for producing effective animated videos available on the internet. The common denominator of all these different versions of the storyboard is the focus on speed and simplicity, as opposed to a search for perfection. In other words, the KISS rule applies (KISS = Keep It Simple, Stupid).

This rough, cheap, and quick way of visualizing a new concept is perhaps most useful in the earliest stages of business model development, when the idea for the new model is still fresh and not 100% clear yet, even to those who have conceived of it. A storyboard helps crystallize the idea by articulating it to others. It is also a way to get feedback to learn more about the proposed business model solution, as well as the assumed underlying problem. It could also generate excitement, and promote alignment and a unified understanding among those involved in the innovation effort.[18]

Tool 10: Storyboard Draw a series of comic book-style frames to explain the essence of the new business model story, i.e., how the new model works. Give each frame a title and develop an accompanying narrative that explains what is happening in the frame. Present the frames to others (e.g., customers) to tell the story of the new business model and elicit feedback on it. Alternatively, or in addition, produce a short (animated) video about the new model.

Once the business model has been refined based on the feedback received on the storyboard, the next step in testing the new business

[18]For more practical advice on storyboarding, see IDEO (2015, p. 113)

model idea could be to develop a low-cost experiment to test it in the field. Low-cost means that the focal firm interested in the innovation sets an intentionally low budget (e.g., $500) for the test, which is consistent with the parsimony (frugality) principle of discovery-driven planning (see Chapter 7). This principle stipulates that in the early, non-revenue-generating stages of business model innovation, expenditures should be contained.

Due to the self-imposed budget constraint, and to the complexity that often characterizes business model innovations (at least compared with product or service innovations), it may not be feasible (or necessary) to test the entire model. Instead, the focus could be on the most critical assumption(s) behind the model (termed "key assumptions" in Chapter 7). Which assumptions to test, when to test them, and through which specific tests should be documented in a Test-Assumption-Matrix (TAM) table. In such a matrix, the rows represent the critical assumptions behind the business model, and the columns represent milestones (i.e., key events such as customer visits, or other experiments) at which assumptions can be tested. Checkmarks in the cells of the table indicate which assumptions will be tested at which milestones. Additional rows contain critical information about the envisioned test, for example: (i) type of test,[19] (ii) expected cost of test, (iii) parties involved in the test, and plan for making them participate, (iv) individuals responsible for executing the test, (v) test timing and deadline, (vi) expected test outcomes, (vii) realized test outcomes, and (viii) key learnings from the test.

Building and maintaining a TAM imposes a healthy discipline on the learning process. It also ensures that milestones are understood as learning opportunities. No milestone should be passed without learning as much as

[19]Possible tests for new business models, especially digital ones, include ad tracking, "fake" ads, landing pages, "fake" sales, pre-sales, split testing, and innovation games. They allow the designer and innovation manager to test business model stakeholder interest, customer willingness-to-pay, as well as detailed customer preferences and priorities. For more information on these test types, see, for example, Strategyzer's "Testing your business model: A reference guide" (2019).

possible about critical business model assumptions. In other words, the tool reduces the uncertainty underlying a new business model.

> **Tool 11: Test-Assumption-Matrix** Develop a test-assumption-matrix (TAM) in the form of a table that highlights the critical assumptions behind the new business model (in the rows), and the ways through which they can be tested at milestones using low-cost experiments (in the columns). In building and applying the TAM, make sure that the most critical assumptions will be tested as early as possible, at the lowest cost possible. Treat the TAM as a live, dynamic document, i.e., adapt it in real-time based on the learnings from each experiment, by rearranging columns (test priorities), adding or refining tests, adding/modifying/dropping assumptions (rows), etc.

Tests gradually reduce the uncertainty surrounding business model innovations by generating important empirical evidence about the validity of critical assumptions underlying the new designs. The TAM encourages and enables business model innovators to approach this task in a disciplined and structured manner. Of course, such a disciplined approach to testing needs to be guided and informed by human judgment, for example, when deciding which of the many assumptions behind a new business model are truly the most critical ones. In addition, human judgment is useful for crystallizing the key learnings from each test. This could be supported by asking the following questions (from DDP, see Chapter 7):

- What new evidence do we have about the validity of our assumptions?
- Do any of our assumptions need to be revised?
- What new assumptions need to be made?
- Have we discovered anything unexpected (e.g., a new need or opportunity, which allows us to refine or reframe our problem statement)?
- In light of the new evidence, what should the next milestone (test) be?
- What will it take to move to the next milestone?
- Can our objectives with respect to the new business model still be accomplished, or should they be revised?
- Regarding the business model innovation project in particular, should any of the following actions be considered: redesign, scale up or down, speed up or slow down, put on hold, form a joint venture, license, sell, abandon?

Implementing Innovative Business Models

Implementing a new, innovative business model either involves creating a new venture from scratch, or reshaping an existing organization. In both cases, it is advisable to develop a business plan in order to:

- Think through the business case for the new model in a systematic and comprehensive manner;
- Identify the key risks, and develop a mitigation strategy to address them;
- Explain or pitch the project to others (e.g., financiers) to get their feedback and/or buy-in and/or (financial) support;
- Decide whether it makes sense to go forward with the project, and, if so, in what way.

These benefits are further elaborated in Chapter 11. Here, we present a tool that can help translate a business model idea into a full-fledged business plan, namely the *Business Model Canvas* (in short, *Canvas*) developed by Alex Osterwalder and Yves Pigneur.[20] As already briefly mentioned in earlier chapters, the Canvas is a visual graphic that can be put on a poster. It contains nine distinct fields, each representing one of the following concepts: key activities (KA), key resources (KR), key partners (KP), value propositions (VP), customer relationships (CR), channels (CH), customer segments (CS), cost structure (C$), and revenue streams (R$). These concepts, taken together, are intended to depict the essence of how an organization as a whole – i.e., through its activities, products, services, and strategic choices – creates, delivers, and captures value. As such, they represent much of what needs to go into a business plan: general company description (KA), products and services (VP), marketing plan (CR, CH, CS), operational plan (KR, KP), management and organization (KR), strategy (KA, KR, KP, CS), and financial plan (C$, R$).[21] Thus, thinking through and applying the Canvas "is the perfect basis for writing a strong business plan."[22] The only business plan elements that the canvas does not address are environmental analysis (e.g., market and competitor analysis),

[20]On the difference between a business model and a business plan, see Chapter 2. The Canvas is explained in Osterwalder and Pigneur (2010).
[21]See Ford, Bornstein, and Pruitt (2007)
[22]Osterwalder and Pigneur (2010, p. 268)

risk analysis, implementation roadmap, and detailed financial spreadsheets as well as their underlying assumptions.[23] These elements could be added in a second step, however. In this sense, the Canvas can be viewed as a stepping stone toward developing a full-fledged business plan; it is truly a useful "tool for describing, analyzing and designing business models."[24] (See Exhibit 9.3 on how the Canvas maps onto the structure of a business plan.)

Exhibit 9.3 From Business Model Canvas to Business Plan

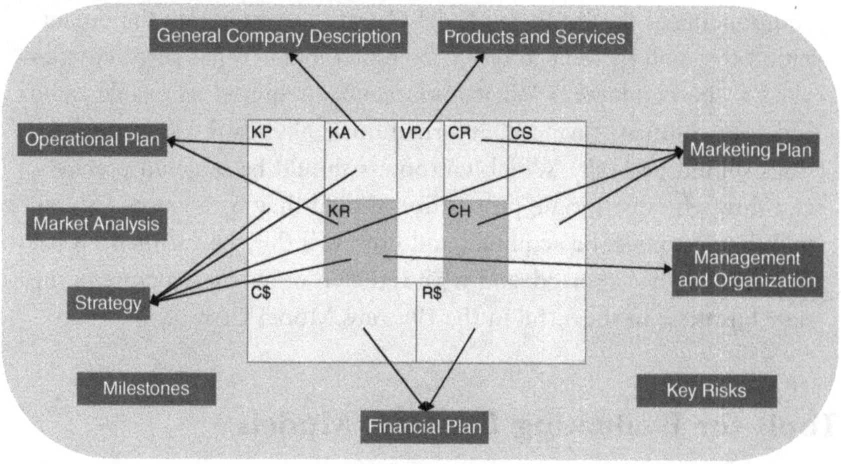

Recall that in this book we define the business model as the system of interdependent activities that are performed by a focal firm and its partners, and the mechanisms that link these activities to each other. Two out of the nine fields of the Canvas fit closely with this definition: key activities (KA) and key partners (KP). They capture the ***What*** and ***Who*** of the new business model, respectively. In addition, the ***Why*** is reflected in the Canvas fields value proposition (VP), cost structure (C$), and revenue streams (R$), and the ***How*** is at least partially addressed through the channels (CH) and customer relationship (CR) fields.

The Canvas can therefore be used as an instrument for taking the key elements of a business model innovation and turning them into a business

[23]See Osterwalder and Pigneur (2010, p. 269)

[24]Osterwalder and Pigneur (2010, p. 8)

case. It encourages business model designers to flesh out their idea. Specifically, it asks them to add important business elements (such as resources or customer segments) to translate their abstract, high-level idea into a concrete, nuts-and-bolts business proposition. Thus, a logical implementation sequence would be: Business model (***What, How, Who, Why***) → Canvas (KA, KR, KP, VP, CR, CH, CS, R$, C$) → Business plan.

Tool 12: Business Model Canvas Develop an actionable plan that maps the holistic idea for a business model innovation onto the key components of the Business Model Canvas characterizing the organization that will be built to enact the new model. What core activities need to be conducted? What resources are required to enable these activities (human, financial, informational, physical)? What partnerships should be built? Which customers should be targeted precisely, and through which value proposition should they be addressed? How will the customers be acquired, and how will they be retained? What revenues can be expected, and what is the ensuing cost structure of the new business? In short, fill in the Business Model Canvas.

Tools for Evaluating Business Models

The business model refers to a set of choices that a focal firm needs to make regarding the design of its activity system; it does not refer to *all* the strategic or operational choices that firm managers need to make. For example, decisions about what specific marketing policies to adopt (e.g., price, place, product, promotion) will have to be taken within a given business model. These decisions do not, however, affect the model as such, nor are they derived from it. This means that we should be wary about applying to the business model the same evaluation methods that are used to evaluate the firm as a whole, such as net present value, multiples, or breakeven analysis. Put differently, business model evaluation requires its own, specific approaches and techniques to complement the many other evaluation methods used to establish firm value.

In Chapter 8, we already introduced such an approach, namely value driver analysis. Recall the four NICE value drivers – Novelty, lock-In, Complementarities, and Efficiency – that explain the value creation potential of a business model.[25] These drivers can be used to assess the quality of a business model *distinct from* the many other firm choices, such as marketing policies or product-market strategy, that affect the firm's overall value. Hence, we propose the Value Driver Matrix as a tool for business model evaluation.

Tool 13: Value Driver Matrix Construct a matrix where the ***What, How, Who, and Why*** dimensions of the business model constitute the rows, and the Novelty, lock-In, Complementarities, and Efficiency value drivers form the columns. Fill in the cells of the matrix with a qualitative or quantitative assessment of how much the respective business model dimension leverages a particular value driver, e.g., on a scale from 5 (very strongly) to 1 (very weakly).

Of course, the ultimate arbiter of a business model's strength is whether it enhances the focal firm's ability to create value for its shareholders and employees, as well as for customers, partners, suppliers, and even society at large. Put differently, a good business model creates high total value (see Chapters 1 and 8) *and* it helps the focal firm capture a sufficient part of the total value that it creates. In the case of a for-profit enterprise, the business model should help the focal firm make a profit, because otherwise its long-term viability is in danger.[26]

Summary of Key Takeaways for the Effective Business Model Designer

This chapter introduced 13 distinct business model analysis tools, which offer a practical complement to the theory, cases, and information we have

---

[25] Amit and Zott (2001)

[26] Strategyzer, the company that was formed by Alex Osterwalder to leverage the success of the Business Model Canvas (Osterwalder and Pigneur, 2010), suggests seven criteria to evaluate new business model designs: degree of customer lock-in, percentage of sales that lead to recurring revenues, timing of earning versus spending, lower cost structure than competition, free value creation by external parties ("others who do the work"), scalability, and protection from imitation by competitors. Strategyzer, "Seven questions to assess your business model design" (2019, note that an online account is required to access this resource)

covered in prior chapters. We started with tools for applying our basic business model framework, which is foundational for clearly identifying and describing an existing business model. Only after mastering this capability – a deceptively simple task – is it possible to clearly communicate a given business model design to others. This capability is also a necessary prerequisite for critically assessing a business model design, and subsequently innovating it.

We included a selection of our own tools, tools that are widely used by practitioners, and tools that were developed by academics working in the field of business model innovation. All are compatible with our underlying conceptual ***What, How, Why,*** and ***Who*** framework, a system-level view of a business model as an activity system. More specifically, the tools in this chapter were organized into the following categories: tools for articulating and understanding business models (Tool 1: Story of "How It Works," Tool 2: Business Model Elaboration, Tool 3: Business Model Activity Map); tools for framing and guiding the design effort (Tool 4: Problem Statement, Tool 5: Business Model Questionnaire, Tool 6: Business Model Templates, Tool 7: Environmental PEST Scanning, Tool 8: Resource and Capability Scanning), tools for designing and implementing business model innovations (Tool 9: Brainstorming, Tool 10: Storyboard, Tool 11: Test-Assumption-Matrix; Tool 12: Business Model Canvas), and a tool for critically evaluating business models (Tool 13: Value Driver Matrix).

In summary, this chapter offers a tangible toolkit for tackling problems you may encounter in a structured way, in order to develop a rigorous, well-rounded, and stakeholder-centric business model mindset and business model innovation capability.

References

Afuah, A. (2019). *Business Model Innovation: Concepts, Analysis, and Cases.* Second Edition. New York, NY: Routledge.

Aguilar, F. J. (1967). *Scanning the Business Environment.* New York, NY: McMillan.

Amit, R. & Zott, C. (2001). Value creation in e-business. *Strategic Management Journal* **22**(6–7), 493–520.

Amit, R. & Zott, C. (2002). Value drivers of e-commerce business models. In M. A. Hitt, R. Amit, C. Lucier, & R. D. Nixon (Eds.), *Creating Value: Winners in the New Business Environment* (pp. 15–47). Oxford, UK: Blackwell Publishers.

Banathy, B. A. (1996). Information-based design of social systems. *Systems Research* **41**(2), 104–123.

Bhavani, R. & Sosa, M. (2008). IDEO: Service Design (A). Case study 10/2008-5276. INSEAD.

Dorst, K. & Cross, N. (2001). Creativity in the design process: Co-evolution of problem–solution. *Design Studies* **22**(5), 425–437.

Dunne, D. (2018). *Design Thinking at Work: How Innovative Organizations are Embracing Design.* Toronto, CA: University of Toronto Press.

Ford, B. R., Bornstein, J. M. & Pruitt, P. T. (2007). *The Ernst & Young Business Plan Guide.* Third Edition. Hoboken, NJ: John Wiley & Sons.

Gassmann, O., Frankenberger, K. & Csik, M. (2014). *The Business Model Navigator: 55 Models That Will Revolutionise Your Business.* Harlow, UK: Pearson Education Limited.

George, G. & Bock, J. A. (2017). *The Business Model Book.* Harlow, UK: Pearson Education Limited.

IDEO (2015). The field guide to human-centered design. Retrieved from www.designkit.org//resources/1

Johnson, M. W. (2010). *Seizing the White Space: Business Model Innovation for Growth and Renewal.* Boston, MA: Harvard Business Press.

Liedtka, J. & Ogilvie, T. (2011). *Designing for Growth: A Design Thinking Tool Kit for Managers.* New York, NY: Columbia University Press.

Magretta, J. (2002). Why business models matter. *Harvard Business Review* **80**(5), 86–92.

Markman, A. (2017, May 18). Your team is brainstorming all wrong. *Harvard Business Review.* Retrieved from https://hbr.org/2017/05/your-team-is-brainstorming-all-wrong

Osborn, A. F. (1953). *Applied Imagination: Principles and Procedures of Creative Thinking.* New York, NY: Scribner.

Osterwalder, A. & Pigneur, Y. (2010). *Business Model Generation: A Handbook for Visionaries, Game Changers, and Challengers.* Hoboken, NJ: John Wiley & Sons.

Paulus, P. B. & Kenworthy, J. B. (2019). Effective brainstorming. In P. B. Paulus & B. A. Nijstad (Eds.), *The Oxford Handbook of Group Creativity and Innovation* (pp. 287–306). New York, NY: Oxford University Press.

Pew Research Center website. Questionnaire design. Retrieved from https://www.pewresearch.org/methods/u-s-survey-research/questionnaire-design/

Porter, M. E. (1980). *Competitive Strategy: Techniques for Analyzing Industries and Competitors.* New York, NY: The Free Press.

Quote Investigator website. Retrieved from https://quoteinvestigator.com/2014/05/22/solve/

Strategyzer AG. (2019). Testing your business model: A reference guide. Retrieved from https://assets.strategyzer.com/assets/resources/testing-your-business-model-a-reference-guide.pdf

Strategyzer AG. (2019). Seven questions to assess your business model design. Retrieved from https://www.strategyzer.com/vpd

Sutton, R. I. & Hargadon, A. (1996). Brainstorming groups in context: Effectiveness in a product design firm. *Administrative Science Quarterly* **41**(4), 685–718.

Zott, C. & Amit, R. (2015). Business model innovation: Toward a process perspective. In C. Shalley, M. Hitt, & J. Zhou (Eds.), *The Oxford Handbook of Creativity, Innovation, and Entrepreneurship* (pp. 395–406). New York, NY: Oxford University Press.

PART III

Making Business Model Innovation Happen

10 Implementing Business Model Innovation in Established Firms – Organizational Barriers and How to Overcome Them

Changing the Model: The Importance of Fit

Chinese company Haier started out as a refrigerator manufacturer in the port city of Qingdao. In 1984, Zhang Ruimin was named the manager of a plant that had existed since 1920. The plant was state-owned, and it suffered from low productivity, quality problems, and high debt.[1] Under Zhang's direction, the company quickly entered into a joint venture with Swiss-based Liebherr Group, importing their technology and equipment. It then began expanding internationally as a contract manufacturer of refrigerators. This strategy not only returned Haier to profitability but set it on track to grow revenues 1,000-fold in the period from 1984 to 2000. By 2018, Haier Group Corporation had become the largest maker of appliances globally, with revenues of $35 billion and 75,000 employees worldwide.[2]

Haier achieved its stunning track record of profitable growth through a combination of classic product innovation and market expansion strategies, management innovation, and business model innovation. In 2005, it began changing its hierarchical, organizational, and management structure to an innovative new one known as "rendanheyi." This new system favors increasing autonomy of small corporate units called "microenterprises." Some of these microenterprises are market-facing, while others incubate new businesses. Still others provide vital activities, such as design, manufacturing, and human resources, to support the market-facing units.

Haier's internal reorganization thus facilitated a parallel transformation, starting in 2007, of its business model.[3] It went from being a traditional technology- and product-centered wholesale manufacturer to a customer-centric home appliance service provider.

---

[1] This section draws on Frynas, Mol, and Mellahi (2018); Hamel and Zanini (2018); and Han (2016), from which the direct quotes are taken.

[2] Hamel and Zanini (2018)

[3] On April 26, 2007, Haier launched a 1,000-day restructuring program to carry out its corporate transformation. The program was anchored on (now CEO) Zhang Ruimin's analysis that Haier "failed to make and deliver the products that customers really want" and that they faced challenges in "how Haier created value for its customers together with distributors and suppliers." Furthermore, "the development of information technology calls for new ways in which firms can discover and meet the demand of its customers" (Han, 2016).

Under Haier's old manufacturer model, market research and product design were conducted by separate business units. The manufacturing of parts and products was often outsourced to arm's-length suppliers. Products were delivered to Haier's outbound warehouses and sold through third-party sales channels (like chain stores and exclusive Haier shops) that had ordered them in advance. After-sales services (like delivery, installation, maintenance) were outsourced to third-party providers, and Haier had buyer-supplier contacts with its external stakeholders (such as OEM factories and sales channels). Although it enjoyed a strong bargaining position with these external stakeholders, it was also far removed from the true needs and preferences of the end customers. This entailed high inventory costs and low margins.

In contrast, Haier's new business model aimed to enable the customization of products for end customers ("make-to-order" or "mass customization"). It also aimed to facilitate relationship-based interactions with end customers to enhance their user experience ("servitization"). For example, Haier, like Dell, let customers select from a set of predetermined features and assemble their own products (e.g., television sets) on its online store. It also launched an online platform (iHaier) to engage customers and other stakeholders more directly in R&D, manufacturing, assembly, and services. Furthermore, the firm added new services, like bill payment and housekeeping, to be closer to its customers, and to get unique and intimate access to information about their needs. Delivery and installation services were bundled and improved through a 24-hour delivery guarantee for online sales. Interestingly, Haier also began to provide sales, warehouse, logistics, and after-sale services to competitors such as Siemens or Philips.

Two features of Haier's business model transformation stand out. First, Haier fundamentally transformed its business model while keeping its existing scope largely intact (i.e., manufacturing household appliances). Business model innovation in other firms such as IBM often involved changes to the scope of their businesses by adding new activities (such as consulting services) while de-emphasizing other activities (e.g., building mainframe computers or laptops). Second, Haier innovated its business model in tandem with its internal organizational structure and management system, which created enormous complexity (from many interrelated moving parts) and challenges in creating fit among the various systems: business model-business and corporate strategy-organization.

Haier's transformation was not seamless. New business model activities related to mass customization (e.g., conducting market-specific research and prospecting) competed with elements of the old business model, which was geared toward standardization (e.g., forecasting demand through the product development department). In addition, elements of the old organization (such as incentivizing salespeople through wholesale numbers) were not consistent with the customer-centric philosophy of the new business model (where sales staff are incentivized through retail numbers and customer satisfaction). Other new business model elements (like e-commerce activities) were at first affiliated with elements of the existing organizational structure; the resulting lack of structural independence, however, undermined their capacity to obtain resources and support.

The head of Haier's e-commerce division explained that "we started as a small department of 'Haier University' and then became a sub-unit of the advertising unit in the marketing department. Later on, we became a sub-unit of our Digital Products Group and were then transferred to be part of the exclusive shops division."[4] As a result, growth of the new e-commerce business model was constrained. Another challenge was noted by Haier's head of strategy, who reported on behavioral constraints and inertia: "Our employees were used to the old system of standardization and not willing to break their routines which they were comfortable with. Once they came across a little difficulty in adopting the new elements, they were more likely to lean back to the old practices."[5]

Another company that seems to have managed well the transition from old to new business model despite many obstacles is Suning.com, a Chinese conglomerate that was established in 1990. Like Haier, it initially just sold air conditioning units. It has kept traditional retail channels (stores), while also creating a dual model leveraging both its offline and online e-commerce

---

[4]Han (2016, p. 21)
[5]Han (2016, p. 20)

capabilities, describing itself as "China's largest online-to-offline (O2O) smart retailer."[6] Now, offline growth complements online growth for Suning, with its online segment experiencing 64.45% growth in 2018, and the business as a whole achieving annual revenues of $86 billion in 2019.[7] The company is an example of an "old economy" retailer leveraging its incumbent position to cement its (dominant) position in the "new economy."

So, What Does Implementation Mean Precisely?

Our definition of business model innovation (BMI) implementation in this chapter and the next goes beyond merely putting new business models into practice as working prototypes (which was the focus of earlier chapters). Here, we define BMI implementation as *all the choices that need to be made to ensure that the new business model can be fully operational and fulfill its main objective in the specific context of the focal firm.* In this context, the focal firm can be an established company, a new venture, or a non-for-profit social enterprise.

These choices can be broadly grouped around the following questions:

1. How should the firm be (re-)organized internally? In other words, how can *internal fit* be created between the focal firm's business model and its internal organizational design?
2. How should the focal firm, and its new business model, be embedded into its ecosystem? For example, which specific external stakeholders (customers, partners, suppliers) should be enlisted, and how can positive relationships with them be created, managed, and maintained? In other words, how can *external fit* be created between the business model and its ecosystem?
3. How can *strategic fit* be created? That is, how can fit be achieved among the focal firm's business model, its competitive strategy, and its corporate strategy? This entails considering the product-market positioning of the focal firm (with its new business model) against existing and potential competitors (e.g., product differentiation vs. cost leadership), its market

[6] Suning Holdings Group (2019)
[7] Suning Holdings Group (2019) and Suning Holdings Group website. Company Profile.

entry strategy (e.g., timing and location of entry, international expansion), and its corporate strategy (e.g., degree of diversification and scope of the firm).

Exhibit 10.1 summarizes and depicts our framework for BMI implementation.

Exhibit 10.1 Important Choices for Implementing the New Business Model

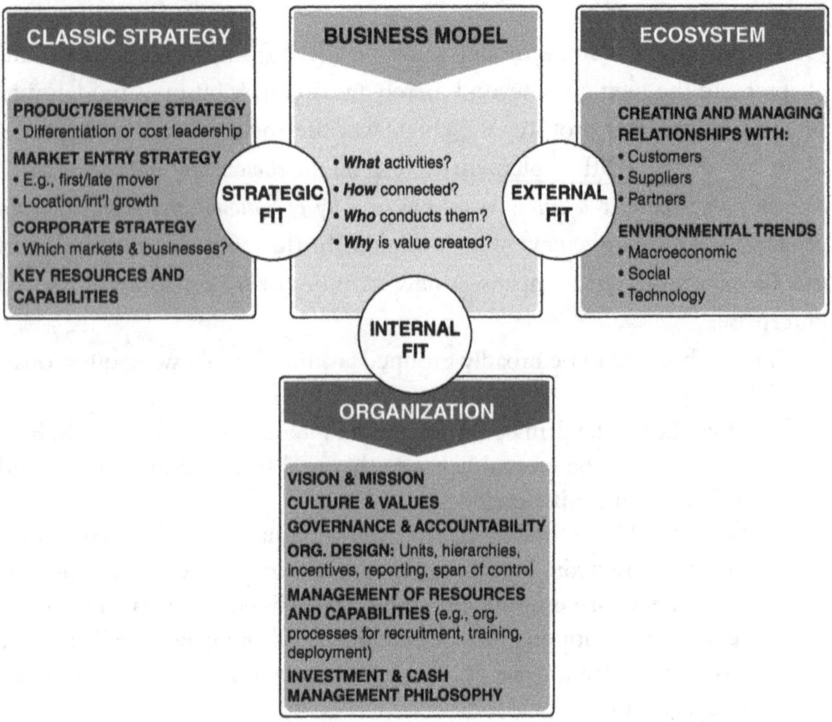

Exhibit 10.1 suggests that business model implementation encompasses the steps involved in moving from a business model prototype to a full-fledged, thriving organization that works well with the new business model (creating internal fit); making sure that the new business model and the organization mesh fluidly with their ecosystem (creating external fit); and adapting and aligning strategies (creating strategic fit). In other words, successful implementation implies the comprehensive creation of fit, so the new business model can be fully operational and fulfill its intended purpose for the focal firm.

Implementation Challenges in Established Firms

Our definition implies that implementing business model innovation is a highly complex and comprehensive change management task that requires careful management of people and processes within and across focal firm boundaries. It certainly involves challenges around how to create external fit (e.g., breaking with old partners and onboarding new ones) and strategic fit (e.g., investing in new capabilities required to support the new business model, and divesting from old ones that are no longer essential). However, the chief barriers to business model change in established firms – resistance to change and organizational inertia – refer to the creation of internal fit, as further explained and elaborated below.

Creating Internal Fit: Resistance to Change

Resistance to change from business model innovation in established firms refers to the *active* refusal by certain individuals to support the implementation of the new model, such as by withholding resources, engaging in political campaigns against the new model, or otherwise boycotting its implementation. Such active resistance from organization members may stem from: (i) lack of familiarity with the new model, along with its low perceived legitimacy; (ii) potential cannibalization of the mainstream business; (iii) perceived threat for one's own career and/or envy; (iv) probable lack of efficiency of the business model innovation; or (v) uncertainty about its scalability (i.e., growth potential) and future profitability.

When an established firm works toward adopting a new business model, the new model typically does not replace the old one right away, but the two models coexist side-by-side for some time. This situation has been described as "dual business models."[8] An example would be an established car manufacturer like BMW that also operates a car sharing business such as Share Now. The challenge with attempting to manage two different business models simultaneously in the same market is that the two models could conflict with each other in many different ways, for example

---

[8]See Markides and Charitou (2004), on which this paragraph draws.

in terms of value logics, activities, stakeholders, performance expectations, time horizons, etc. As a result, managers who have been operating within the old model might not take the new one seriously due to a lack of understanding, familiarity, or perceived legitimacy. Consider the chemical industry, where buyers and sellers of chemical substances long relied on well-established personal relationships within a stable supply chain that was not transparent to outsiders. The emergence of business-to-business (B2B) chemistry marketplaces in Europe, such as CheMondis, Chemberry, GoBuyChem, KEMGO, or Asellion, in parallel to the established channels, raised concerns among industry players about price transparency, the possible revelation of sensitive data, and legal liability.[9] In addition to such concerns, managers often view a new model as a threat to the established business, and to their own compensation and careers, which might lead them to engage in attempts to constrain, sabotage, or even kill the initiative.

Another important reason for active internal resistance to the implementation of business model innovations in established firms is uncertainty about their future efficiency and effectiveness. New business models are often designed for new customers that an incumbent does not currently serve (so-called "noncustomers"), in market segments and at price points that the incumbent might currently perceive as unattractive. They may also rely on resources and capabilities that the incumbent does not yet possess or is unable to access. In other words, these opportunities face significant market risks and might therefore appear unattractive and undesirable from the perspective of an incumbent manager.[10]

Creating Internal Fit: Organizational Inertia

A second barrier to creating internal fit, organizational inertia, refers to the forces that constrain the mindset and behavior of firm managers, motivating them to keep doing what they have done in the past.[11] It refers to *passive*

---

[9]Schmitt (2019)

[10]See McGrath (2010), and Kim and Mauborgne (2005) on the concept of noncustomers.

[11]Organizational inertia was originally defined by organization ecologists Hannan and Freeman (1977) as internal and external organizational constraints. Internal

resistance to BMI implementation from organization members, which may be rooted in:

- Past investments in assets, capabilities, routines, relationships, and contracts that are difficult to redeploy or unwind, and that therefore create strong path dependencies;[12]
- An organizational culture that does not support experimentation with new business models, and which may even be characterized by a deep-rooted fear of failure;
- A strong "dominant logic" of the existing business model within the focal firm that imposes cognitive constraints on managers, preventing them from switching collectively to a new mindset and embracing a new model.[13]

Path dependencies that arise from past investments imply persistence in decision-making patterns over time. New, innovative business models often require different asset configurations than the existing ones. Firm managers, however, tend to allocate resources to what they perceive are the most profitable uses. These are often associated with the old business model, because the legitimacy, scalability, and/or profitability of the new model are unproven. As a result, the established business model will be disproportionately favored, and the new (and potentially disruptive) one is likely to be starved of resources. Thus, organizational inertia from past investments (which has also been referred to as an "asset trap" or a "sunk cost") can

---

constraints stem from investment and sunk costs, limited availability of information for decision makers, established organizational culture, and organization history. External constraints refer to legal and fiscal barriers to market entry and exit, availability of information about the environment, external legitimacy, and collective rationality.

[12]The concept of path dependence is rooted in evolutionary economics and denotes a process that evolves as a function of its own history; it embodies the general principle that "history matters." For the importance of path dependencies in business models, and how they may play out differently for incumbent firms and new entrants, see Bohnsack, Pinske, and Kolk (2014).

[13]See Prahalad and Bettis (1986, p. 490): "A dominant general management logic is defined as the way in which managers conceptualize the business and make critical resource allocation decisions – be it in technologies, product development, distribution, advertising, or in human resource management."

be a major impediment to successful BMI implementation and adoption in established firms.[14]

Moreover, cultural and cognitive constraints within organizations may give rise to inertia. As we have seen in Chapter 3, business models as activity systems are not just objective organizational realities based in contracts, routines, and relationships, but they also exist as collective cognitive representations (the firm's "dominant logic") of "how we do business around here." An example would be the strong belief in analog photo making within Kodak or Polaroid. As such, existing business models tend to be naturally stable, and they are notoriously hard to change.[15] This is reinforced by their perceived efficiency and predictability, which slows incumbents' reaction times.[16] Consider the ongoing upheaval of the U.S. entertainment industry due to the emergence of on-demand streaming services. Despite the runaway success of Netflix in signing up customers, and declining subscriptions in traditional cable TV services, it took Disney a full twelve years from when Netflix was founded in 2007 to introduce its own streaming service, Disney Plus, in 2019.

Business Model-Specific Barriers to Implementation

Although they have been recognized by business model scholars and practitioners alike as detrimental, internal resistance to change and organizational inertia are barriers that need to be overcome in *any* corporate change project with significant organizational implications, not just when implementing a new business model. However, the particular characteristics and systemic, boundary-spanning nature of business models create additional challenges that need to be addressed. These are (i) high complexity and number of changes due to internal and external interdependencies, (ii) lack of specific business model know-how, (iii) lack of able and willing leaders who can drive business model change within the focal firm, and (iv) confusion or lack of agreement about the right model going forward.

---

[14] Chesbrough (2010)
[15] See Snihur and Zott (2020)
[16] Doz and Kosonen (2010)

As shown in Exhibit 10.1, the adoption of a new business model in an established firm entails changes to the existing business model, as well as to the firm's organization and strategy. The costs of making these changes depend on the degree of newness of the new model, and on the complexity and number of required changes. The complexity and number of required changes are, in turn, a function of the relevant interdependencies among the firm's business and corporate strategy, business model, organization, and ecosystem. If the new business model represents a radical departure from the existing one, for example, implementing the new business model will require a greater number of changes that need to be carried out simultaneously. Consequently, the magnitude and complexity of these changes can imply uncertainty and high costs. Consider the aforementioned B2B chemistry marketplaces. Their potential introduction raised a number of questions among established players: Will there be more orders? Do we need to hire new staff? Can we (as buyers or suppliers of chemicals) trust the platform operator regarding data security and the protection of sensitive data?[17] In other words, there was substantial uncertainty surrounding the new models.

In earlier chapters of this book (e.g., Chapters 3 and 5), we argued that a business model mindset, an astute knowledge of business model concepts, and an awareness about the value creation potential of business models are important prerequisites for business model innovation. Such know-how includes the ability to think holistically, to understand system dynamics, and to synthesize, i.e., to be able to put the various components of a business model together and make them function in concert. These are also critical skills for BMI implementation. They are, however, typically more concentrated at the top of the organizational hierarchy, which is why BMI projects are more likely to fail without sufficient active involvement (and not just moral support) from top leaders during the implementation phase. Business model innovations often call for difficult and risky personal adjustments and collective commitments, and they sometimes entail gut-wrenching decisions for executives. That is why a top management team, which is well-educated on business model matters and willing to consider a business model redefinition, is crucial for achieving the collective

[17]Schmitt (2019)

commitment necessary to take the risk to venture into a new business model and if necessary abandon the old one.[18]

Unfortunately, such able and willing leaders, who can drive business model change in an established firm, are not always available, due to functional specialization or short tenure (or both).[19] The resulting lack of able leaders willing to drive business model change has been referred to as the "business model innovation leadership gap"; it represents a major impediment to BMI implementation.[20]

Furthermore, there might be a lack of agreement about what should be the right model going forward. For example, of the two basic marketplace business models in the B2B chemistry industry, which one is the better model? The first possibility is the "matchmaker model," an electronic marketplace that brings together supply and demand, but is not necessarily the contracting party. The second possibility is the "one-stop-shop" model, where the electronic marketplace is also the contracting party. Both models offer pros and cons for the marketplace operator, as well as for marketplace participants; it is not clear per se which one is superior to the other.[21]

---

[18]Chesbrough (2007); Doz and Kosonen (2010)

[19]See Chesbrough (2007, p. 16): "Who within the company, other than the CEO, is responsible for all the ways the business creates value in its products and services and captures that value in the form of revenue from its customers?... The marketing leadership focuses on brand development and channels of distribution. The chief legal officer has a role to play, particularly when intellectual property is an important contributor to the ability to capture value from the model. But no one of these people has the ability to drive the entire business. In some businesses, a general manager or division president may have complete responsibility for the financial performance of a business unit. Even here, though, there often are sharp limits to the ability of these managers to innovate their business models. Some companies, for instance, put their general managers through two-year to three-year rotations running specific businesses, increasing the size of the businesses the managers run over time. This is too short a time frame to create new business models. It takes more time than that to develop business-model experiments, obtain clear results, interpret and understand the results, and then carry out a broad deployment of those results. Little wonder, then, that most general managers simply stay with the current business model."

[20]Doz and Kosonen (2010)

[21]Schmitt (2019)

Lastly, although business model thinking should be a *sine qua non* in modern management, it is cognitively challenging (see Chapter 3). R&D managers, for example, need to make the connection between the technical domain of inputs (and its associated activities) and the economic domain of outputs (with its associated activities), typically in the face of high technical and market uncertainty. Under such conditions, what is the right business model going forward is not always clear. This lack of clarity can give rise to confusion or cognitive dissonance.[22] It can also foster unproductive disagreement and conflict in management teams. In the example of CEWE (a former analog photo finishing company that became a digitally driven photobook provider), despite strong support from the founder there was initially high skepticism about whether the technology-focused spin-off that the company had created to explore digital photography would ever be able to define and implement a successful business model. It was not entirely clear, in other words, where the journey would lead. The lack of cognitive alignment between corporate sponsors of business model innovation and the implementation teams often presents a barrier to effective decision-making.[23]

Overcoming BMI Implementation Barriers in Established Firms

As we have seen above, active resistance to change, passive organizational inertia, and cognitive misalignment are major impeding forces that can stand in the way of successful business model innovation in established firms. These problems can be rooted in leadership and knowledge gaps, managers' fears about their compensation and careers, past investments in assets and capabilities, an organization culture that seeks to preserve the status quo and is alien to experimentation, and/or a dominant (old) business model logic. Complexity, uncertainty, and confusion about the new business model only add to these concerns. Since the precise nature and extent of implementation challenges may vary from firm to firm, however, there is no

---

[22]See Chesbrough and Rosenbloom (2002) and Chesbrough (2010). The term cognitive dissonance refers to the mental discomfort or psychological stress experienced by someone who holds contradictory beliefs, ideas, or values.
[23]Bosbach et al. (2019)

boilerplate solution. Overcoming barriers to BMI implementation requires a sound, case-specific analysis to identify the "problem behind the problem," such as why exactly middle managers resent the introduction of a business model innovation. However, conditional on such an analysis being conducted, some general hints can be offered on how to address these issues.

Addressing Leadership and Knowledge Gaps

In general, successful business model innovation requires two things. First, it requires strong and decisive leadership. Second, it requires a specific set of attitudes and skills among the firm's managers and employees. A high degree of involvement from top management is indispensable given the potentially profound, strategic, and wide-reaching consequences of business model innovation for the focal firm. Swedish furniture retailer IKEA is a case in point. It is changing its traditional, long-standing business model from the top. Originally conceived as a network of vast out-of-town furniture showrooms and inventories to which customers could drive, pick their preferred products from the shelves, and assemble them at home, IKEA has embarked on a broad overhaul of its business model since Jesper Brodin became CEO of IKEA's main retail arm, Ingka Group, in 2017. Under his leadership, IKEA is turning its out-of-town stores into distribution centers for home delivery to serve its increasing online customer base. At the same time, IKEA is offering furniture rentals and investing in smaller stores in city centers to become more accessible to consumers, which represent deviations from its original business model.

To address potential leadership and knowledge gaps, incumbent firms interested in business model innovation need to systematically identify, educate, and empower internal leaders, specifically with respect to their openness to considering innovation in a broad sense (and not just in terms of technology, product, or process innovation). As we have seen, business model innovation also often involves far-reaching changes with many moving parts. It therefore requires that managers and employees alike are able to think holistically and to keep the "big picture" in mind; embrace partnerships (e.g., with customers); consider technology as an enabler of new ways of doing business, not as an end in itself; remain flexible and adaptive to rapidly changing customer preferences and competitive landscapes; and embrace, rather than fear, uncertainty. In other words, the firm's human capital not only needs to be selected for, and trained in, business model analysis and change management, but it also needs to embrace a more entrepreneurial mindset. Such a mindset views uncertainty as a source of opportunity rather than as a threat. It also emphasizes playful and cheap – yet disciplined – experimentation over traditional planning approaches, and encourages autonomous initiative-taking from individuals to change the status quo.

Moreover, given that business model innovation implies a change process that can take several years to play out, as shown by the Haier example, avoiding fast management rotations is desirable. Otherwise, accountability may not be clear. Also, the nurturing of internal leaders may have to be supplemented by the hiring of new ones with the desired skill profiles from the outside, and by the creation of separate organizational units and rewards for business model innovation. These units need to be carefully structured, so they are not too much at odds with the parent corporation. Otherwise, a later reintegration into the mainstream business could become difficult.

German photo finishing company CEWE illustrates these leadership and management imperatives.[24] It is one of the very few companies that managed not only to survive the market storm that swept away analog photography and replaced it with digital photography, but even to thrive. Founded in 1961, CEWE had become Europe's largest photo printing company by 1996, printing over 2.1 billion color photos that year alone. Ten years later, however, the analog photo business had practically ceased to exist, forcing the world's largest company in this space, Kodak, to declare bankruptcy in 2012. CEWE managed to avoid the same fate by experimenting with digital technologies, and by proactively introducing them into the market. For example, as early as 1997 the company installed terminals in drugstores and supermarkets that allowed customers to print out digital photos themselves, thereby essentially cannibalizing CEWE's prevailing business model, which relied on a network of photo finishing labs with state-of-the art printing technology. These steps were supported by heavy investment in research and development (R&D).

---

[24]This example is based on Frankenberger et al. (2012).

CEWE's new approach was explicitly endorsed by the firm's top management. At the presentation of the digital photo terminal prototype, the founder and then chairman of the board, Heinz Neumüller, apparently scolded his digital team that they were destroying his life's work. However, he then immediately asked them, "When will you have built the first 100 terminals?" To do so, the company hired new people from the outside, rather than rely on its long-time employees who were steeped in (and attached to) the analog photo finishing business model. The new employees brought digital skills and a fresh mindset to the company. These were important steps to master the swift – and radical – transition from analog to digital in the photo printing business. CEWE eventually became a leading provider of photo books and other printed and personalized products, such as brochures, flyers, posters, cups, T-shirts, and mobile phone covers.

Anticipating and Overcoming Resistance to Change

There is a vast repertoire of knowledge and suggestions on how to overcome the resistance to change among managers and employees. The proposed solutions often focus on a combination of soft skills (e.g., communicating, convincing, coercing) and structural measures (e.g., adjusting incentives, hiring outsiders, and creating separate organizational units).[25] A favorite structural approach for business model innovation is to separate the new business model from the old one structurally or spatially through distinct organizational arrangements, organizational members, geographic locations, and/or physical infrastructure.[26]

---

[25]According to Cummings and Worley, both intrapersonal (or "self-management") and interpersonal skills are necessary skills for organization development. Intrapersonal skills refer to the ability to know your "own values, feelings, and purposes as well as the integrity to behave responsibly in a helping relationship with others." Important interpersonal competencies include "group dynamics, comparative cultural perspectives, and business functions as foundation knowledge, and managing the consulting process and facilitation as core skills." These competencies help build relationships, which "start with a grasp of the organization's perspective and require listening to members' perceptions and feelings . . . This understanding provides a starting point for joint diagnosis and problem solving" (2009, p. 52).
[26]Frankenberger and Zott (2018)

A case in point is Nespresso, which started as a new business model initiative within the Nestlé corporation. Although Nespresso, like Nestlé's core business, Nescafé, also involved selling coffee, the two business models were notably different. Nescafé sold instant coffee to the mass market through supermarkets, whereas Nespresso specifically targeted wealthy young urban professionals. Furthermore, Nespresso chose an exclusive club to act as its distributor. In other words, Nescafé followed a typical fast-moving consumer goods business model, whereas Nespresso adopted a business model more akin to a luxury goods manufacturer. Not only were the two business models different, but they also conflicted with each other. Nespresso coffee was in effect cannibalizing sales of Nescafé. For these reasons, Nestlé set up Nespresso as a new unit in a different town in Switzerland, assigned one of its rising stars as its CEO, and gave the venture the freedom and autonomy to compete in its market as it saw fit. The approach proved to be a great success, and Nespresso has become one of the most profitable units within Nestlé.

Structural separation also has important drawbacks, however, such as redundancies or underexploited synergies between the two business models; a potential build-up of different organizational cultures, governance, and incentive systems; and deferred and essentially unresolved decisions about how and when to transfer from the old to the new model. It can be particularly difficult to assess whether, when, and how to integrate the old and the new business models.

Countering Organizational Inertia

The main recommendation from the business model literature about how to counter the stifling effects of organizational inertia inside established firms is to experiment continuously with new business models; this seems paramount for overcoming business model implementation barriers.[27] Some ways to experiment include "probing" (attempting to "experience the future" by visiting "lead locations" or establishing development centers

[27] Sosna, Trevinyo-Rodríguez, and Velamuri (2010); Andries and Debackere (2013)

in cities that are "innovation hotspots"), local experiments and in-market tests, and corporate venturing.[28]

Running experiments provides valuable information about the viability of a business model innovation and thus reduces the market uncertainty associated with it. It also sends a powerful message inside the organization about the importance of embracing an entrepreneurial mindset and entrepreneurial processes. The entrepreneurial spirit and energy transmitted by members of a business model innovation team that dare to experiment and thereby defy conventional corporate perfectionism can be passed on to other organization members, increasing their enthusiasm and willingness to embrace the innovation. Formal programs dedicated to promoting experimentation with new business models and entrepreneurial initiatives by employees, such as accelerator programs, can be helpful in this respect.

Take, for example, German engineering giant Bosch. Since 2017, Bosch has invested in hundreds of internal teams that work together for six to twelve months and receive funding to test their new business model ideas. A little more than two-thirds of these projects are stopped by the participants themselves after three months, and another two-thirds (of the remaining third) after twelve months.[29] In other words, less than 10% of projects survive the first twelve months. One important lesson and deliberate cultural message from this program is that "failing is ok, it is part of the process." It is therefore important to try often, and if the experiment does not work out, it is better to fail soon and cheaply.

Corporations are increasingly adopting diverse institutionalized approaches for systematically promoting innovation from within. These approaches, which also work in the context of business model innovation, include: accelerators, incubators, innovation labs, cross-functional teams, scouting missions, and challenges (e.g., hackathons).[30] Such organizational solutions can be exclusively designed for BMI. Alternatively, BMI can be added to existing arrangements as one possible (but not exclusive) form of innovation.

---

[28]Doz and Kosonen (2010)

[29]Osterwalder, Viki, and Pigneur (2019)

[30]See Prats et al. (2018) for an excellent overview.

Accelerator

Accelerators are entrepreneurial programs that last a fixed period of time (usually three months). They are focused on learning (e.g., validating and refining the offering) and offer new ventures extensive consultation with mentors, program directors, customers, guest speakers, alumni, and peers.[31] These programs can be part of a corporation, or they can be stand-alone. Notable stand-alone accelerators include Y Combinator (in Silicon Valley), Techstars (originally in Boulder, Colorado, but now a global franchise), and Seedcamp (in London). Independent accelerators sometimes work in close partnership with corporates. In such cases, only startups that match both partner and accelerator requirements are selected for the program, and there is an emphasis on facilitating a bridge (e.g., information and resource exchange) between partners and startups. Corporate accelerators can admit a mix of internal and external startup projects; the specific requirements for admissible projects depend on the strategic objectives of the corporation. The higher the proportion of admitted external projects, the greater the corporation's strategic emphasis on "outside-in" innovation.

Accelerator programs aim at helping startups grow and develop in a much shorter time frame than if they were on their own. The mentoring and education that these venture participants receive helps them refine their business model and strategy prior to field tests, and improves their understanding of the entrepreneurial landscape. It also helps them prepare for external fundraising. One-third of venture-backed companies in the U.S. that raised a Series A financing round in 2015 had previously gone through an accelerator program.[32] Several of these accelerator participants, including Airbnb, SendGrid, and Dropbox, subsequently exhibited substantial growth. Research also indicates that some (but not all) accelerators achieve their intended objectives and manage to speed up relevant business growth indicators for new ventures such as funding, web traffic, or employee

---

[31] This section draws on Hallen, Bingham, and Cohen (2014); Weiblen and Chesbrough (2015); Tom (2016); and Seed-DB website. Seed Accelerators.

[32] Tom (2016)

growth. In short, accelerators promise to help business model innovators by significantly shortening their time to market.

Incubator

Like accelerators, incubators also target ventures that are at an early stage of development (e.g., shortly before or after the first product or service launch). Compared with accelerators, however, which strongly emphasize rapid learning through intense mentoring and peer-consulting, traditional incubators primarily help ventures by providing physical infrastructure (e.g., office spaces, an internet connection, printers) and professional services (e.g., legal, accounting, administrative support) at discounted rates. Their goal is to provide ventures with the time and resources necessary to build a value-creating business model. They also admit ventures at different times, and their venture-tenants spend varying lengths of time in the incubator. In contrast, accelerators admit a cohort of ventures that all start and end together, over a fixed (and short) period of time.

Corporate incubators, like independent incubators, provide young ventures with funding, co-location, expertise, and contacts. The general intention is to provide founding teams (that could be composed of existing employees) with a startup-like environment that protects them from the often slow and bureaucratic parent organization. At the same time, incubated ventures can benefit from the resources (e.g., customers or technological assets) and capabilities of the parent firm. This provides them with significant advantages that can foster the early implementation of entrepreneurial business model innovation projects. However, incubated projects might also receive too much support from the parent company and protection from market forces, which might increase the cost of failure at later stages of implementation. Moreover, closeness to the parent corporation might limit their possibilities in terms of pursuing partnerships with competitors, or developing business models that could threaten to cannibalize or disrupt the corporate sponsor.[33]

---

[33]Hallen, Bingham, and Cohen (2014); Weiblen and Chesbrough (2015); Prats et al. (2018)

Innovation Lab

An innovation lab is a dedicated physical environment or facility with a shared workspace in which employees can engage with each other to explore new product, service, or business model ideas. In contrast to traditional workspaces, innovation labs are designed to be stimulating and non-threatening work environments with an ambience that fosters creativity. "In addition to the architectural uniqueness of these spaces, these centers have varying processes in place to facilitate individual and team creative thinking such as thinking of existing problems in a new ways, generating new ideas and thinking about how these ideas could be implemented."[34] This means that in the context of business model innovation, innovation labs can be particularly useful in the early stages of the process. They can also be quite useful during the implementation stage, when problems occur that call for creative approaches to come up with effective solutions.

An innovation lab can be part of an established firm (for-profit or not) that has sufficient resources to run its own internal program to encourage employee creativity and innovation. It is a fast and flexible tool to address the host organization's specific innovation requirements. An innovation lab can be set up for just a few days, or it can run over the course of a few months. It can also be an ingrained part of a firm's innovation process and as such contribute to providing a constant stream of innovations.

Cross-Functional Team

Cross-functional teams consist of organization members from different functional areas, such as marketing, engineering, manufacturing, and purchasing. Members can also be recruited from outside the organization, for example, from among customers, suppliers, or partners; this is how a cross-functional team could mirror the boundary-spanning nature of a business model. Such teams have traditionally played an important role in product innovation, where they increase creativity and reduce

---

[34]Magadley and Birdi (2009)

"groupthink." Their creative collaboration processes promote innovative outcomes, especially when the following conditions are met: (i) strong sense of team identity (as opposed to team members identifying primarily with their functional areas); (ii) encouragement to take risks; (iii) involvement of customers in the team; and (iv) active monitoring of the cross-functional team's project by senior management. In contrast, strong social cohesion (i.e., interpersonal attraction, comfort, and commitment to maintaining close interpersonal relationships) among team members has a negative effect on the output of creative teams. Interestingly, it has been observed that functional diversity as measured by the number of team members from different functional areas has no significant positive (or negative) effect on innovativeness.[35]

Cross-functional teams are likely to play an important role for business model innovation, too, especially in the early design and late implementation phases. During these phases, innovative outcomes are desirable, and the participation and buy-in from the corporation's various functional areas and business units need to be ensured. According to recent research involving over 140 business model innovation projects in 44 corporations in Germany, Austria, and Switzerland, the key parameters of success (where success is defined as the degree of innovativeness of the resulting business model) are as follows:[36]

- High level of *task differentiation* between the BMI initiative team and the respective business unit (BU), i.e., low degree to which the BMI initiative team members draw on the existing knowledge and skills of the BU. They instead look outside the BU for new skills, knowledge, technology, systems, and processes.
- High level of *social integration* – not among team members (which could be detrimental, as research on product innovation has shown), but between team members and the business unit. Such social integration refers to the quality of relationships (i.e., how close you are to someone and how frequently you contact them), the number of relationships, and the alignment of vision between the various parties to the relationship. In other words, even though business model innovation teams should not overly rely on the firm's existing capabilities and

[35]Sethi, Smith, and Park (2001)
[36]Frankenberger and Zott (2018)

strive for high task differentiation, they should not entirely "cut loose" from the "mother ship" either, but maintain cordial and good social relations with managers operating within the established business model.

- Lastly, the joint positive effect of task differentiation and social integration on the degree of innovativeness of a business model is enhanced when the right form of *initiative governance* is adopted. Consistent with the literature on cross-functional teams, this happens when (i) the team is self-directed, i.e., when team members are granted a high degree of autonomy "to do their jobs well"; and (ii) the team is embedded in a challenging performance context, i.e., the work ethic among team members is strong, and ambition runs high.[37]

Besides the structural setup of cross-functional teams, it is also important to consider the processes by which they are run. As briefly mentioned in Chapter 7, examples of such processes include Agile, Kanban, Scrum, and other lean processes.

Scouting Mission and Challenges

Scouting missions are temporary projects set up by firms with the objective of gathering timely and relevant information on interesting new developments (e.g., business model innovations) in domains that are of central interest to the focal firm. The team members or expert professionals commissioned ("scouts") typically seek input from startups, inventors, specialized consultancies, and/or university researchers. They also attend conferences and trade shows that are believed to be at the vanguard of innovation. A variant of this organizational approach would be a "think tank," which is a more permanent institutional arrangement focused on performing research, organized either as a stand-alone institute or as part of a corporation. Samsung, for example, has an interdisciplinary internal think tank, Think Tank Team, which includes scientists, engineers, strategists, researchers, and designers.[38]

---

[37] Glaser, Stam, and Takeuchi (2016)
[38] Think Tank website.

A more direct and proactive way of gaining insights into innovative business models and related technological trends would be for a company to organize a competition, more specifically, a business model challenge. This involves publishing an open invitation to internal and/or external participants to solve a particular business model issue for the focal firm. By focusing on a specific problem, such a challenge provides innovators (individuals, teams, or startups) with the opportunity to craft and submit original concepts to the focal firm. These concepts not only promise to create value through a business model innovation, but they can also stimulate new thinking and learning inside the established corporation. In other words, challenges can be effective vehicles for changing company culture and employees' mindsets. For example, Giesecke and Devrient, a 170-year-old family-owned German company known for its reliability and technology leadership in cash and security technologies, uses challenges (called "hackathons") to tap into the entrepreneurial drive and potential of its employees, and to change the company culture.

Summary of Key Takeaways for the Effective Business Model Designer

In this chapter we took a comprehensive view of business model implementation in established firms, examining the numerous associated challenges, and some ways to tackle them. Given the complexity of a business model, and its boundary-spanning nature, business model innovation implies a host of far-reaching changes. Overall, the firm must ensure the new business model fits with its existing strategy (competitive and corporate), with its internal organization, and with its ecosystem.

Two of the most salient BMI implementation challenges are internal resistance to change from members of the organization (active resistance), and organizational inertia (passive resistance). Active resistance to change can be countered through the application of managerial soft skills. It can also be countered by more "structural" measures, such as creating separate business units or hiring outsiders. Having a strong separation between the old and new business models is tricky, however, and comes with an important set of potential setbacks. Organizational inertia, meanwhile, can be countered through continuous experimentation with new business models. Firms can more formally institutionalize this experimentation in several ways, including accelerators, incubators, innovation labs, cross-functional teams, scouting missions, challenges, or hackathons.

Overcoming business model implementation challenges in general requires a mindset that is holistic and entrepreneurial; this is required to grasp the business model at a high level, as well as tackle its many intricate, interrelated moving parts. Comprehensive and astute change management is also needed, particularly as a new business model can be highly disruptive, even to the point of cannibalizing the established model. It is imperative, therefore, that the top management of the firm is highly involved in the process, placing decisive strategic importance on the new business model.

References

Andries, P., Debackere, K. & Van Loy, B. (2013). Simultaneous experimentation as a learning strategy: Business model development under uncertainty. *Strategic Entrepreneurship Journal* **7**(4), 288–310.

Bohnsack, R., Pinkse, J. & Kolk, A. (2014). Business models for sustainable technologies: Exploring business model evolution in the case of electric vehicles. *Research Policy* **43**(2), 284–300.

Bosbach, K., Bidmon, C., Brillinger, A. S. & Rohrbeck, R. (2019). New business model implementation in corporate settings: The importance of cognitive alignment work. *Academy of Management Proceedings* **2019**(1).

Chesbrough, H. (2010). Business model innovation: Opportunities and barriers. *Long Range Planning* **43**(2–3), 354–363.

Chesbrough, H. W. & Appleyard, M. M. (2007). Open innovation and strategy. *California Management Review* **50**(1), 57–76.

Chesbrough, H. & Rosenbloom, R. (2002). The role of the business model in capturing value from innovation: Evidence from Xerox Corporation's technology spin-off companies. *Industrial and Corporate Change* **11**(3), 529–555.

Cummings, T. G. & Worley, C. G. (2009). *Organization Development and Change*. 9th Edition. Stamford, CT: South-Western Cengage Learning.

Doz, Y. L. & Kosonen, M. (2010). Embedding strategic agility: A leadership agenda for accelerating business model renewal. *Long Range Planning* **43**(2–3), 370–382.

Frankenberger, K., Gassmann, O., Sauer, R., Lee, J. Y. & Meister, C. (2012). CEWE business model innovation – when disruptive technologies hit you. University St. Gallen, Case Study.

Frankenberger, K. & Zott, C. (2018). The role of differentiation, integration, and governance in developing innovative business models. *Academy of Management Proceedings* **2018**(1).

Frynas, J. G., Mol, M. J. & Mellahi, K. (2018). Management innovation made in China: Haier's rendanheyi. *California Management Review* **61**(1), 71–93.

Glaser, L., Stam, W. & Takeuchi, R. (2016). Managing the risks of proactivity: A multilevel study of initiative and performance in the middle management context. *Academy of Management Journal* **59**(4), 1339–1360.

Hallen, B. L., Bingham, C. B. & Cohen, S. (2014). Do accelerators accelerate? A study of venture accelerators as a path to success. *Academy of Management Proceedings* **2014**(1).

Hamel, G. & Zanini, M. (2018). The end of bureaucracy. Harvard Business Review November–December, 51–59.

Han, H. (2016). The co-evolution of business model and internal management in corporate transformation. Working Paper Draft, The Wharton School, University of Pennsylvania.

Hannan, M. & Freeman, J. (1977). The population ecology of organizations. *American Journal of Sociology* **82**(5), 929–964.

Kim, C. W. & Mauborgne, R. (2005). Value innovation: A leap into the blue ocean. *Journal of Business Strategy* **26**(4), 22–28.

Magadley, W. & Birdi, K. (2009). Innovation labs: An examination into the use of physical spaces to enhance organizational creativity. *Creativity and Innovation Management* **18**(4), 315–325.

Markides, C. & Charitou, C. D. (2004). Competing with dual business models: A contingency approach. *Academy of Management Perspectives* **18**(3), 22–36.

McGrath, R. (2010). Business models: A discovery driven approach. *Long Range Planning* **43**(2–3), 247–261.

Osterwalder, A., Viki, T. & Pigneur, Y. (2019, November 15). Why your organization needs an innovation ecosystem. Harvard Business Review Digital Articles. Retrieved from https://hbr.org/2019/11/why-your-organization-needs-an-innovation-ecosystem

Prahalad, C. K. & Bettis, R. A. (1986). The dominant logic: A new linkage between diversity and performance. *Strategic Management Journal* **7**(6), 485–501.

Prats, J., Siota, J., Gillespie, D. & Singleton, N. (2018). Organizational agility. *Oliver Wyman and IESE Business School.* Retrieved from https://www.oliverwyman.com/content/dam/oliver-wyman/v2/publications/2018/april/Organizational_Agility.pdf

Schmitt, L. (2019). Challenges affecting the adoption of B2B electronic marketplaces. *Journal of Business Chemistry* **2019**(3), 154–164.

Seed-DB website. Seed accelerators. Retrieved from https://www.seed-db.com/accelerators

Sethi, R., Smith, D. C. & Park, C. W. (2001). Cross-functional product development teams, creativity, and the innovativeness of new consumer products. *Journal of Marketing Research* **38**(1), 73–85.

Snihur, Y. & Zott, C. (2020). The genesis and metamorphosis of novelty imprints: How business model innovation emerges in young ventures. *Academy of Management Journal* **63**(2), 554–583.

Sosna, M., Trevinyo-Rodríguez, R. N. & Velamuri, S. R. (2010). Business model innovation through trial-and-error learning: The Naturhouse case. *Long Range Planning* **43**(2-3), 383–407.

Suning Holdings Group website. Company profile. Retrieved from http://www.suningholdings.com/cms/companyProfile/index.htm

Suning Holdings Group (2019, March 29). Suning.com reveals 30.35% year-on-year growth in 2018. Cision PR Newswire. Retrieved from https://www.prnewswire.com/in/news-releases/suning-com-reveals-30-35-year-on-year-growth-in-2018-861652258.html

Think Tank website. Retrieved from https://thinktankteam.info/

Tom, M. (2016, February 5). One-third of U.S. startups that raised a Series A in 2015 went through an accelerator. *Pitchbook.* Retrieved from https://pitchbook.com/news/articles/one-third-of-us-startups-that-raised-a-series-a-in-2015-went-through-an-accelerator%20

Weiblen, T. & Chesbrough, H. W. (2015). Engaging with startups to enhance corporate innovation. *California Management Review* **57**(2), 66–90.

11 Implementing Business Model Innovation in New Ventures – Balancing the Prospects of Shooting for the Stars with the Risks That Can Sink the Ship

The Importance of BMI Implementation for New Ventures

In 1989, British entrepreneur Mark Dixon founded Regus (later renamed International Workplace Group, or IWG). He was responding to the increasing need among companies to outsource their real estate. The business model of the new venture was anchored on providing serviced office space with flexible terms for professionals and businesses; it could succinctly be described as "space as a service." Key activities in this business model were finding, designing, building, and operating office space. Headquartered in Brussels, the Belgian capital, the venture began expanding internationally in 1994 into Latin America, Asia, and the U.S. Buoyed by strong demand from internet-based startups, the company opened up many new spaces and completed an IPO on the London Stock Exchange in 2000. Following the sudden "dot-com crash" later that year, however, IWG began to struggle. In 2003, it put its U.S. operations under Chapter 11 bankruptcy protection. This came as a shock, and brought into sharp relief several key challenges in implementing a new business model in a new venture:

- Building a strong balance sheet and financial position with positive cash flows and low debt (e.g., by growing moderately, and not too aggressively);
- Justifying new investments into growing the business by engaging beforehand in careful business planning and considering worst-case scenarios;
- Diversifying risk, e.g., by aiming for a sound mix of customers;
- Ensuring a path to profitability by choosing a viable revenue model (e.g., right mix of revenues from space rentals and services such as office staff and tech support).[1]

As a result of heeding these implementation imperatives, IWG was able to grow and further expand internationally. In 2018 (nearly 30 years after founding), it had established a presence in over 120 countries, with 3,500

[1] IWG CEO Mark Dixon referred to the hotel business model as a template for his own shared workspace model. If you do not charge for services, it is "like having a hotel where you give all the food and drink away, and room service is free. You might have a full hotel, but you just cannot make any money." Eavis (2019).

locations in 1,100 cities, reaching close to $4 billion in revenues and $200 million of operating income. Furthermore, IWG's market capitalization in the fall of 2019 was about $4.5 billion.

This compares sharply with the American company WeWork, which was co-founded in New York in 2010 by Adam Neumann and Miguel McKelvey, on almost all implementation dimensions and performance indicators. Having a very similar business model to the one of IWG, WeWork was valued at over $40 billion, before it was forced to pull its planned Initial Public Offering (IPO) in September 2019. The documents it had filed with the U.S. Securities and Exchange Commission (SEC) revealed heavy losses and gave rise to severe investor concerns about its approach to implementation. As of September 2019, WeWork had raised a total of $12.8 billion in funding since founding; it lost $1.9 billion in 2018 alone on revenues of $1.8 billion.[2] This was partly due to its rapid and aggressive investment into prime locations in the U.S. (such as New York, Boston, and San Francisco), as well as its heavy expansion into China and Southeast Asia starting in 2017. The young company was also harshly criticized for other practices, including its corporate governance; its purchase of a corporate Gulfstream G650 jet for $60 million; investing in unrelated projects, such as a private school in Manhattan run by the wife of the founder and then-CEO, Adam Neumann; and Neumann's employment of close friends and family. Neumann's otherwise brash and overconfident leadership style was also criticized, leading to his forced resignation in late 2019. Exhibit 11.1 compares IWG and WeWork on some selected implementation choices.

Given that IWG and WeWork both espoused very similar business models ("space as a service"), the striking disparity in the performance of these two firms was largely due to differences in their age and maturity; to their different implementation choices in terms of revenue model, real estate, growth, location, and product strategy (as shown in Exhibit 11.1); and to

---

[2] United States Securities and Exchange Commission (2019) and Powell (2019)

Exhibit 11.1 Implementation Differences Between IWG and WeWork in 2019

	IWG (2019)	WeWork (2019)
Revenue Model	28% of revenues from services, rest from rentals	5% of revenues from services, rest from rentals
Real Estate Strategy	Short-term leases with landlords; increasing use of franchising model in which partners operate under the IWG brand and take the risk of leasing	Long-term leases with landlords (as a result, $47bn in outstanding lease obligations)
Growth Strategy	Moderate, carefully planned growth	Rapid expansion, both nationally as well as internationally
Location Strategy	"Spreading offices around," e.g., nationwide coverage in the U.S. in every town and suburb to match customers' new digital work patterns (and diversify business risk)	Focus on prime areas in large cities
Product Strategy	Multi-brand approach with different price points (like hotels) to appeal to different customer segments, from freelancers to large corporates	Focus on freelancers and startup entrepreneurs, providing them with shared workspaces and incubation services, actively promoting collaboration among them

governance and leadership issues (as mentioned above). This example points to the importance of thoughtfully addressing the implementation issues of novel business models in new ventures.

Implementing BMI in New Ventures – Challenge or Opportunity?

Since new ventures have by definition had a short history, the inertial forces that could derail BMI implementation in these firms are typically much weaker than in established firms.[3] Similarly, founders and employees working in new ventures are used to frequent changes (so-called "pivots") on key strategic dimensions to ensure the survival of their young firms. Active internal resistance to change in new ventures is therefore in general less pronounced than in established firms (although exceptions are of course possible). More importantly, perhaps, implementing an innovative business model is likely viewed more as an opportunity than as a challenge in young ventures.[4] Indeed, conceptualizing and defining the business model is one of the most fundamental strategic decisions that every founder needs to make. Furthermore, the possibility of adopting an *innovative* business model offers *all* founders a lever to create value. Viewed that way, business model innovation levels the playing field. This is because founders no longer need to rely on factors such as exclusive access to valuable scarce resources (like patents or technological know-how) in order to come up with a groundbreaking innovation that may disrupt entrenched incumbents and

[3]However, ventures exhibit other organizational mechanisms and cognitive processes that can impede business model innovation, as Snihur and Zott (2020) have found. For example, consensus-based decision-making among members of a founding team is likely to inhibit business model innovation because it favors "the lowest common denominator," i.e., a relatively standard, widely accepted business model.

[4]Note that there has been less research conducted on business model implementation in new ventures compared to established firms, which may be a consequence of actual or perceived lower internal implementation hurdles.

open up entirely new market opportunities. As a result, internal hurdles to BMI implementation can be expected to be lower in younger firms than in older ones.

Business model innovation plays into the cards of entrepreneurial firms in other important ways, too. Some conditions discussed earlier in this book that favor business model innovation – such as adoption of an entrepreneurial mindset, design mentality, willingness to embrace experimentation, openness to external partnerships, and focus on customer needs – are likely to be met (at least to some degree) in new ventures. Their leaders, as owners of the business, are often willing and able to drive business model innovation, especially when they have sufficient decision-making power, thus overcoming the business model innovation leadership gaps mentioned in the previous chapter.[5]

Interestingly, the business model innovations of *other* firms (for example digital platforms such as Instagram, Amazon, and Google Search) can also open up new opportunities for entrepreneurs to launch their businesses. Quite a few direct-to-consumer firms (e.g., selling shaving blades, socks, or mattresses) were born online using third-party digital platforms to perform critical activities. At Amazon, 58% of the gross merchandise value of sales (about $160 billion) in 2018 was carried out by independent vendors, a business segment that is growing more rapidly than Amazon's own sales.[6] In the same year, Apple paid its vendors in the App Store $34 billion.

Still, business model innovation in new ventures requires astute management of risks during the implementation phase to ensure strategic and external fit (see Exhibit 10.1 in the previous chapter), and it may bring about unwanted and risky unilateral dependence on external business model stakeholders. It is also saddled with its own specific leadership and governance problems, as we explain below.

---

[5]Snihur and Zott (2020)
[6]Bezos (2019)

It Is About Managing Risks, Not Taking Them

Risk and uncertainty are inherent characteristics of the entrepreneurship process.[7] Although some people believe that entrepreneurs are risk takers and, like gamblers, enjoy situations in which the stakes are high and the odds are against them, in general this is not the case (and certainly not supported by scientific evidence).[8] Most entrepreneurs are risk-averse. They are keenly interested in minimizing risks in order to increase the likelihood of survival (and success) of their ventures.

Although there can be many types of risk, startup risks generally cluster around five types (see Exhibit 11.2): (i) demand-side risks (e.g., customer acceptance of the offering may not be as expected); (ii) supply-side risks (e.g., risk associated with the management team, the product/service, the technology, partners, and vendors); (iii) competition risks (e.g., imitation of the offering by competitors); (iv) capital market risks (e.g., funding, timing, and value at exit); and (v) environmental (e.g., macroeconomic, regulatory, and political) risks. Some of the risks of starting up a new venture may be accentuated through business model innovation, while others may be reduced (see Chapter 4 sections on the pros and cons of business model innovation). Others may not be affected at all.

Exhibit 11.2 Types of Risk in Startups

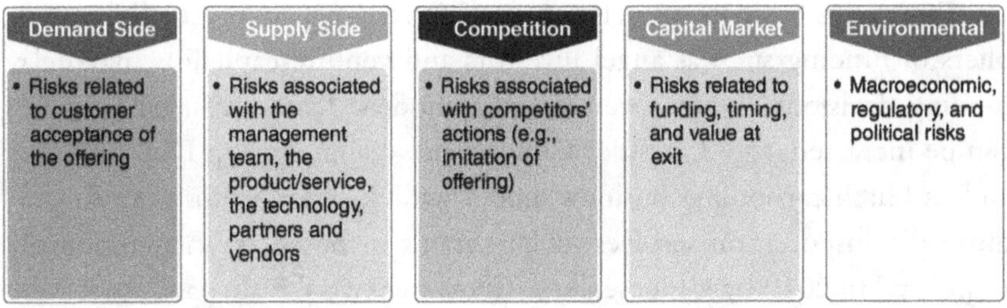

[7]According to Knight (1921), the notion of "risk" refers to a situation in which the probability of alternative outcomes can be determined, and therefore risk can be insured. "Uncertainty," however, refers to a situation in which the probability of alternative outcomes cannot be determined, and so it cannot be insured. Knight believes that the key function of entrepreneurs lies in bearing uncertainty.
[8]MacCrimmon and Wehrung (1988)

For example, radically new business model innovations can increase *demand-side risks*, because customers may have doubts about the legitimacy of the new model, at least initially. Consider how many years it took for e-commerce firms like Amazon to finally take off, simply because many customers were initially reluctant to use their credit cards for online payments. Business model innovations can also bring about increased *supply-side risks*, for example, when they involve complex partnership arrangements and investments in assets that generate strong path dependencies. Moreover, they could be easy to imitate, thus increasing *competition risks*, as shown by Disney's move into streaming entertainment services with Disney Plus, which is similar to Netflix's streaming service, yet Disney has a running start since it owns a huge movie library.[9] A particularly strong form of competition risk results when dominant firms engage in unfair competitive practices. For example, in early 2011 Google apparently changed its search algorithm to favor its own online price comparison service over rival offerings such as Kelkoo (a European firm founded in 1999). From then on, Google's service was shown at the top of customers' search queries, and customer traffic from Google to other sites dried up. As a result, the share of Kelkoo's revenues that came from Google search engine referrals dropped by over 90%. Google was fined $2.7 billion by the European Union for this anti-competitive practice, but only six years later. It was therefore essentially able to crush an early pioneer and business model innovator. This example highlights the importance of business model innovation strategy for new ventures.[10]

Innovative business models can also increase *capital market risks*, as suppliers of funding such as angel investors and venture capitalists may delay funding decisions on unproven business models. Lastly, *environmental risks* can be increased, too. Consider Chinese ride-hailing group Didi Chuxing and its Hitch carpooling business model, which offers a substitute for traditional transportation services such as trains or buses. It was temporarily suspended in 2019 by Chinese authorities after two female passengers were murdered by drivers, thus raising regulatory concerns over the public safety of the business model.

While some of the risks from business model innovation can be partly addressed through designing the business model in a robust way

---

[9] Barnes (2019)
[10] Satariano (2019)

(see Chapter 5), others have to be addressed through entrepreneurial risk management techniques like business planning or discovery-driven planning (see Chapter 7). Accordingly, the importance of risk management for new ventures has not diminished in the digital age of business model innovations. On the contrary, it is as relevant as ever: the financial implications of ignoring or mismanaging basic business risks can be disastrous. Underestimated costs, overestimated demand, and overly aggressive investment into growing the business (e.g., through rapid and ambitious international expansion) can yield strongly negative cash flows that may require a restructuring of the business (as in the case of WeWork), or even result in bankruptcy (as in the case of Better Place).

Dependence on External Third Parties: The Sharks Dilemma

A particular risk that needs to be highlighted for new ventures implementing business model innovations is their potential dependence on third parties. As we have seen throughout the book, business model innovations are often boundary-spanning, which means that not all of the activities in the business model are performed by the focal firm, but some (including important ones) are outsourced to external providers. This creates a tension between the need for partners on the one hand, and the potentially damaging use of market power and misappropriation of the venture's own ideas, intellectual property, and other valuable resources by these very same partners (or "sharks") on the other hand. New ventures thus face the so-called "sharks dilemma," namely, under which circumstances do they choose partners with high potential for abuse of market power or misappropriation over less risky partners?[11]

One example of how the "sharks dilemma" might play out in the digital economy is the increasing dependence of new ventures on powerful digital platforms such as the Apple and Google app stores, Amazon Marketplace, eBay, or Facebook and Instagram.[12] These platforms are changing the ways

[11] Katila, Rosenberger, and Eisenhardt (2008)

[12] Kenney and Zysman (2016)

in which founders launch and operate their ventures. The unique dependencies that entrepreneurs experience when transacting through digital platforms seem contradictory to the traditional independence of entrepreneurship. Scholars have coined the term "dependent entrepreneurship" to reflect the dependencies that entrepreneurs must successfully navigate on digital platforms, and to emphasize the new form of entrepreneurship that such platforms create.[13] The increasingly tight grip of tech giants like Apple and Alphabet (the parent company of Google) over the distribution of digital offerings to individual consumers is purported to have contributed to a distinct shift from B2C to B2B over the past decade.[14]

Internal Governance and Leadership Problems That Can "Sink the Ship"

In addition to their young age, entrepreneurial ventures possess several unique characteristics that distinguish them from established firms, especially publicly traded ones, and that have implications for their governance and leadership.[15] First, in new ventures there is less separation of ownership and control, a prime driver for established firms to adopt governance practices such as disciplined board monitoring. The financial interests of CEOs and owners (shareholders) are typically more aligned in new ventures than in established firms. Thus, the agency problem that calls for monitoring executives with misaligned financial incentives is typically less pronounced in new ventures than in established firms.

Second, with respect to leadership there are often challenges that relate to the composition and size of the founding team. Common trouble spots include a lack of clear definition of roles and responsibilities, which leads to conflicts among founders; a lack of mission-critical competencies among the co-founders; role confusion when co-founders feel betrayed or lost as the venture scales; and poor communication by founders that results in frustration and inefficiencies.

---

[13]Cutolo and Kenney (2019)
[14]Lohr and Griffith (2019)
[15]This section draws on Garg (2013)

Third, entrepreneurial ventures are often resource-constrained, especially at the early stages of firm development. They also operate under high uncertainty, in particular when in nascent markets and/or when they are focused on business model innovations. This implies that venture boards have fewer reliable and meaningful financial metrics at hand, such as profit or return on equity, for assessing venture performance. In addition to focusing on firm strategy, board members may therefore have to turn to more detailed operational activities and decisions, such as product introductions, or employee recruitment and dismissals.

Fourth, it is common for members of the board of directors (BOD) of a new venture to have significant financial stakes in the business, especially when they are representatives of professional investors. They also often possess significant knowledge of the relevant industry, which helps them guide the venture and add value to it. For these reasons, they again may interpret their task more as helping the management team create value, rather than monitoring them and ensuring proper venture governance. One negative side effect of this might be that directors get "too cozy" with the management team. The incentive alignment between directors and managers, and their common financial interests, may create governance voids that could come back later to haunt the venture.

Stark examples to illustrate leadership challenges include business model innovators Uber and WeWork. Uber co-founder Travis Kalanick served as CEO until he was pressured by investors to resign in 2017. During Kalanick's tenure, Uber was plagued by allegations of a toxic, undisciplined corporate culture that tolerated discrimination and sexual harassment. Many of these allegations were seen as somehow linked to the behavior and persona of Kalanick.[16] Uber more generally became known for engaging in overly aggressive measures widely seen as troubling or immoral. These included ignoring local regulations to quickly enter a market, implementing surge pricing during crises and natural disasters (such as Hurricane Sandy), attempting to undermine competitor Lyft by hiring independent contractors to "sabotage" the company (by ordering and

---

[16] Isaac (2017)

canceling rides), and covering up a major data breach.[17] With WeWork, the founder and CEO, Adam Neumann, similarly had an outsize role in setting the company culture. WeWork's biggest financial backer, Masayoshi Son of the Softbank Vision Fund, later admitted he had ignored negative aspects of Neumann and ensuing governance issues. Son stated, "My own investment judgment was really bad. I regret it in many ways." Speaking about Adam Neumann, he said, "I shut my eyes to a lot of his negative aspects."[18]

Finally, governance problems can exacerbate leadership problems (and vice versa). Prior research has identified problematic entrepreneurial leadership traits such as narcissism and hubris that, if left unchecked, can lead to dysfunctional top management teams and precipitate the collapse of young and small firms. Narcissism is a double-edged sword that can lead to "bold actions" by managers,[19] but it has been shown to be harmful for entrepreneurial firms.[20] Specific leadership behaviors, such as overpromising and underdelivering, reckless risk-taking, or cronyism, have also been identified. These can have similarly damaging effects on the development of young firms, and thus endanger the successful implementation of business model innovation.

Business Model-Specific Barriers to Implementation

The previously mentioned business model-specific barriers for established firms – complexity, inertia, lack of business model know-how, lack of able and willing leaders, and lack of agreement about the right model (see Chapter 10) – also apply to new ventures, in particular to the challenge of managing complexity. The probability a business model innovation will be successfully implemented in a new venture may be inversely related to the number and variety of business model stakeholders involved in its design. This is due to the stakeholders' diverse and often diverging preferences, incentives, bargaining power, and possibilities for value appropriation

[17]Popper (2013); Newton (2014); Newcomer (2017)
[18]Dvorak and Fujikawa (2019)
[19]Chatterjee and Hambrick (2007)
[20]Engelen, Neumann, and Schmidt (2016)

that need to be considered and balanced. The greater the number and diversity of stakeholders, the higher the risk that some of them will mount opposition or even drop out of the business model at some point during implementation. Given that young focal firms in general do not have direct managerial control over their surrounding network of partners and suppliers, and suffer from low brand recognition, lack of legitimacy, and/or low bargaining power, they may become increasingly dependent on this network. This in turn heightens the risk that the business model will encounter problems – or even fall apart – during implementation.[21]

A case in point is the business model of Israeli startup Better Place (see Chapter 4), which centered on transportation as a service. The business model relied on a system of environmentally friendly battery swapping stations and charging spots for electric cars, and on the active and willing participation of car makers, battery producers, clean energy providers, energy distributors, infrastructure builders and maintenance providers, national governments, and end-users. One of the reasons why the startup eventually failed was the sheer complexity of its business model, which made it extremely difficult to implement. Eventually, key partners such as car manufacturer Nissan-Renault refused to cooperate and pulled the plug on their partnership with Better Place.

Approaches to Overcoming BMI Implementation Barriers in New Ventures

The precise nature and extent of implementation challenges may vary for each venture. In order to effectively address barriers to BMI implementation in new firms, a thorough analysis must therefore first be conducted to identify the relevant issues. Conditional on the results of this analysis, tailored solutions can then be crafted to address the specific problems. A common denominator of all these solutions, however, is that they aim at de-risking the new venture. In what follows, we explain some effective risk management approaches, such as business planning, building trust with external stakeholders, lowering dependence on third parties, using strategic considerations in adopting a revenue model, and improving internal governance.

[21] Sandström and Osborne (2011); Berglund and Sandström (2013)

Business Planning: An Effective Way to Manage Risk

There are many different ways in which founders can manage the general risks from starting a new venture anchored on a business model innovation. Examples include investing in their own education (e.g., learning about general management and/or about specific business model knowledge and skills; see Chapters 3 and 4), carefully selecting the target industry, surrounding themselves with capable people (e.g., co-founders), lining up investors with deep pockets, and producing a business plan. Producing a business plan can be viewed as a particularly important way of managing the risk inherent in a new business venture, because doing so increases the chances of venture survival significantly.[22] Even though factors that lie outside the control of founders, such as developments in the industry, the passage of time, or the nature of the opportunity, seem to matter more for venture success and survival chances than business planning, of all the factors that are under the control of founders, business planning seems to matter most. Why is that?

First, business planning facilitates venture development and organizing. Surprisingly, many founders do not organize their ventures in an orderly manner (i.e., identifying an idea, acquiring resources, developing a business model, testing it deliberately and mindfully, developing and marketing products and services, etc.). This harms their chances of being successful.[23] A lack of organizational activities can be particularly problematic in the case of a venture with an innovative business model, because (by definition) the model is not yet tried and tested in the marketplace, and therefore faces a high risk of failure.

Second, business planning refers to the process of thinking through a new venture with an innovative business model in a thorough and systematic fashion. This process may be more important than its actual outcome (the business plan), because it promotes a holistic mindset that (as we have seen in earlier chapters) is an important precursor of business model innovation. It also allows founders to recognize gaps in their knowledge, document

---

[22]According to Delmar and Shane (2003), the chances of survival are improved by up to 60%.

[23]See Shane (2008, Chapter 7)

risks that need to be mitigated, and discover assumptions that need to be articulated and tested. In other words, it injects a healthy dose of discipline into the entrepreneurial process and thereby makes it less unpredictable and more manageable. In sum, business planning as a cognitive activity provides an important risk-reducing function.

Third, to be effective, business planning should not be restrained to armchair theorizing at a purely conceptual level. On the contrary, entrepreneurial best practice involves going out into the field, talking with people (customers, industry experts, regulators, competitors, suppliers, and others) and asking for their feedback, and collecting data to corroborate the viability of a perceived business model opportunity. Based on this research, the resulting business plan will be a carefully prepared, cohesive, and concise description, analysis, and evaluation of the venture. The document (a text, slide deck, or series of spreadsheets), loaded with facts and figures, provides critical information about the founders, the market (customers, competitors), the business model (innovation), the product, the strategy, the financial prospects, and the risks involved.

As such, the business plan constitutes an important decision-making tool for entrepreneurs (informing them about whether and how to take the venture project forward); an important means for communicating and "selling" the opportunity to others (e.g., prospective investors, employees, or board members); and a crucial risk management tool, because the assumptions made in the business plan can be contrasted with observed data from the marketplace and updated accordingly. In other words, business planning is a valuable complement to, and input for, the dynamic business model innovation design and development processes described in Chapters 6 and 7 (e.g., Discovery-Driven Planning).

It is therefore puzzling why many entrepreneurs never write a business plan, and why some entrepreneurship advisors even passionately argue against it, despite the strong and ample scientific evidence documenting its benefits. It is true that business planning takes time, may otherwise be costly, can only reveal a static and incomplete snapshot of reality (i.e., never fully uncovers all relevant facts), and may lead to a false sense of security and "having things under control." At the same time, however, the forfeited upsides can be substantial, and the risks of abstaining from planning potentially immense.[24]

Building Trust with Business Model Stakeholders by Using Symbolic Actions

New ventures exhibit high mortality rates in the earliest stages of their life cycle. This phenomenon has been described as the "liability of newness,"[25] and it is rooted in two main factors. First, it can be caused by a lack of experience with internal organizational issues such as new roles and new incentives, which can cause worry, conflict, and inefficiency among organization members who do not trust the new system. Second, new ventures rely on social relations among strangers (e.g., between the firm and its customers) characterized – at least initially – by low trust. This makes the social relations fragile for at least some period of time (the time it takes to build trust). Business model innovations potentially magnify these vulnerabilities. A new activity system exacerbates the lack of experience of business model stakeholders that operate within the new system, and it may reinforce doubts that external business model stakeholders, such as suppliers or customers, might have with respect to the appropriateness, efficiency, and viability of the new venture, along with its new business model.

How can the lack of trust be overcome in early-stage ventures? Entrepreneurship research suggests that founders can engage in a range of behaviors aimed at establishing legitimacy and credibility with internal (and external) stakeholders. One particularly potent type of behavior is symbolic management.[26] Symbolic management actions are actions that are deployed in a business setting and involve symbols. A symbol, in turn, is something that stands for or suggests something else; it conveys social

[24]Business planning should not be confused with a lack of flexibility; planning does not prevent acting flexibly and adapting to a changing reality (and vice versa). Importantly, preparing a business plan does not imply that the entrepreneurs need to stick to the plan at all costs. Interpreted this way, business planning is consistent with the lean startup method and can complement it.
[25]Stinchcombe (1965); see also Chapter 4.
[26]The following section draws on Zott and Huy (2007) and Zott and Huy (2009).

meanings beyond its intrinsic content or obvious functional use.[27] The intrinsic dimension of entrepreneurial actions (such as developing a business plan) aimed at setting up a new venture with a business model innovation could be to explain the new concept to investors, early employees, or first customers. Meanwhile, the symbolic dimension of these actions can make the new venture more credible and trustworthy to these and other stakeholders. Exhibit 11.3 shows some exemplary actions and explains both their intrinsic and symbolic aspects.

Exhibit 11.3 Intrinsic and Symbolic Dimensions of Management Actions

Intrinsic Dimension	Symbolic Dimension
Emphasizing management degree (e.g., MBA)	From prestigious (high-ranking) MBA school
Speaking at conferences to disseminate information and knowledge	Established people recognize our expertise and invite us
Building up market and product expertise	Labeling such effort as "research" to enhance its social respectability
Reducing salaries to cut costs	Strong belief in (or commitment to) the venture
Negotiating hard with investors to get superior benefits for one's venture	Displaying strong conviction about the future success of one's venture, and about own abilities as a business leader
Having a work office	With prestigious address (display desirable social belonging or social success)

Symbols suggest categorizations that help people frame social situations or interpret ambiguous (and thus potentially confusing) ones. They are particularly important for entrepreneurial managers who need to secure resources (e.g., funding) and/or get the buy-in from skeptical third parties (e.g., suppliers), especially in highly uncertain contexts. Until a new company with a new business model becomes more broadly accepted, no one knows whether it will be successful. Because of this uncertainty, perceptions of the credibility of a prospective course of action will depend on subjective social beliefs and on executives who shape these beliefs through the symbolism of their actions. The same uncertainty, incidentally,

[27] Merriam Webster Dictionary. Symbol.

also applies to successful, established corporations such as banks and automakers whose business models are increasingly challenged by fintech and car sharing startups, respectively.

Research on entrepreneurship has identified at least four types of symbolic action strategies that entrepreneurial managers in both new ventures and large businesses can use to create the right impression and establish trust with internal and external stakeholders. These are symbolic actions that convey: (i) personal credibility, (ii) professional organization, (iii) organizational achievement, and (iv) stakeholder relationship quality.

Personal Credibility

The first important category of symbolic management actions is related to the personal credibility of the entrepreneurial leaders. Are they the kind of persons able to build a company with an innovative business model? In an existing company, are they the kind of persons who can manage a major and complex business model innovation project? How personally committed are they to the project? An example would be a founder accepting a low salary, or forgoing one altogether. On a substantive level, this action helps the venture save scarce resources. On a symbolic level, however, it also demonstrates the entrepreneur's commitment and thus sends a compelling signal to investors.

Professional Organization

In addition to building personal credibility, entrepreneurs (or intrapreneurs, in established firms) need to impress upon resource providers the professional qualities of their project, both in terms of structure and processes. Their challenge is to convince others that the business model innovation project is worth their time, money, and effort, especially in the absence of tangible proof or a track record. For example, using deliberately rigorous methods to select people working on the business model innovation project sends a powerful signal of professionalism. Being ruthless in screening people suggests that the entrepreneurial managers do not compromise on people quality now. More importantly, it also suggests that they will not compromise in the future. A 2019 survey of over 5,000 adults in the U.S.,

U.K., France, and Germany has shown that job applicants are attracted as much, if not more, by organizational attributes such as organizational culture, innovation, and other expressed values, than by compensation packages or opportunities for advancement.[28]

Organizational Achievement

A third category of symbolic actions attempts to convey organizational achievement, which refers to past accomplishments on important issues. This represents a real challenge for startup entrepreneurs, and it can be particularly important in the case of largely unproven business model innovations. For example, rather than merely pitching the business model verbally, effective innovators actually develop a prototype (see Chapters 6 and 7) or use controlled demos, to convey an early idea of how the business model might work. Moreover, being able to endure a certain period of time is a major credibility test (and proof), just to be able to show that they are no longer "fly-by-night." Established companies have a lot more experience and more evidence to prove it. Business model innovation projects, however, may face similar challenges as startups due to their newness, even when they are embedded in an established firm with a proven track record.

Stakeholder Relationship Quality

Lastly, symbolic actions can convey the quality of stakeholder relationships by way of association. Successful entrepreneurs know that they can boost their credibility by emphasizing favorable associations where and when it counts. This can happen through effective name-dropping (without exaggeration) in conversations or presentations, or (even better) through actually securing the backing of high-profile investors and industry experts who join the project's board and thereby become an important symbol of prestige.

---

[28]See Glassdoor (2019)

The truly successful way to cultivate relationships with reputable resource providers and business model stakeholders is by being attentive to them. Symbolic actions such as sending inexpensive gifts with the ventures' logos, or sending inexpensive but personalized e-mails or handwritten notes of appreciation act as reminders of reliability and continued existence. Such gestures of personal attention can distinguish thoughtful entrepreneurial executives from their peers. Most people are capable of doing this, but many simply do not take the time or think it is important enough to take the trouble to do so. However, inexpensive symbolic management actions can make all the difference in new, unproven ventures with new, unproven business models, especially if they are used frequently, skillfully, and in varied ways.[29]

Countering the Sharks Dilemma: Defense Mechanisms That Work

Recall the "sharks dilemma:" Why would ventures choose partners with high potential for abuse of market power or misappropriation over less risky partners? Research shows that the answer to this question depends on the venture's specific resource needs and its available defense mechanisms.[30] Founders tend to choose risky partners when they urgently need partners' unique resources and capabilities (i.e., when they have little other choice), and/or when they have effective defense mechanisms in place to protect their own resources and knowledge. These defense mechanisms are legal protection (e.g., from patents), secrecy (e.g., trade secrets), and timing (i.e., involving risky partners at a later stage, when the costs of knowledge

---

[29]Variety of symbolic management actions refers to the use of different action categories (i)–(iv), i.e., conveying (i) personal credibility, (ii) professional organization, (iii) organizational achievement, or (iv) stakeholder relationship quality. Skillfulness of symbolic management refers to high awareness of resource constraints and willingness to work around them; tailoring the message to the audience; and delivering it using a complementary delivery style (e.g., face-to-face conversation). See Zott and Huy (2007) for details.

[30]Katila, Rosenberger, and Eisenhardt (2008)

and resource leakages are smaller). Since some of these defense mechanisms may be less effective in the context of business model innovations for which effective patent protection, for example, is not available, the sharks dilemma remains a valid concern.

Other protection mechanisms that could help lower the risk of misappropriation through external business model partners are having a "plan B" (i.e., alternative providers lined up) and strengthening the ownership of key managers (e.g., by investing in the startup). The latter measure could serve to increase managers' commitment not to disclose corporate secrets, thus reducing the risk of knowledge leakages. Salaried managers tend to adopt a more opportunistic approach, which increases the risk of leakage, as they might be hired by partners or by competitors.[31]

Choosing a Revenue Model Strategically

Adopting a revenue model influences the cash flow and the profitability of the focal firm both directly and indirectly. Since profits are defined as revenues minus costs, the direct effect is clear. However, a revenue model can also be used to differentiate the venture from the competition and thus indirectly influence its profitability. In other words, it can fulfill an important strategic function.

To illustrate, consider Hawaii-based event-planning firm Hobnob, a venture founded in 2015 that lets users create personalized invitations sent by SMS and MMS. It has deliberately adopted a revenue model that differs from Facebook's (which offers a competing event invitation service to Hobnob), in that it does not rely on advertising or sharing user data.[32] Instead, it relies on charging fees for specific features like pre-designed templates for invitations. The purpose of this is twofold. First, the venture seeks to avoid entering into head-to-head competition with Facebook. Second, it seeks

[31]See Colombo, Croce, and Murtinu (2014). For a discussion of further protection mechanisms, see Bonakdar et al. (2017).

[32]Lohr and Griffith (2019)

to attract users who are tired of "social tools that are focused on increasing 'time in app' to sell your data to ad networks."[33]

As another illustration, consider Netflix in its earliest days, when it competed directly with established video rental companies such as Blockbuster. To complement its mail-order DVD rental service, Netflix adopted a subscription-based revenue model that allowed customers to rent out as many DVDs per month as they wanted (although they could only rent a maximum of three DVDs at a time). From a cash flow and profit-maximizing perspective, that revenue model in the DVD rental business was inferior to the transaction-based model of the incumbents, as it shifted much of the value created to customers. However, the subscription model allowed Netflix to gain market acceptance of its business model innovation, and differentiate itself further from the competition. As marginal streaming costs are very low in the movie streaming business of Netflix, the attractiveness of the subscription revenue model is that it offers predictability and serves as a signal of continued quality.

Three main revenue model types have been identified.[34] The first is the straightforward paid revenue model, where a product or service is provided in exchange for a stated price. Paid models can be further broken down into subscription revenue models, where payments are made on a recurrent and stable basis, and transaction payments models, where payments are made per transaction. Past studies have shown a positive relationship between product quality and the effectiveness of a paid revenue model; consumer awareness and low advertising rates have also been cited as factors. The second type of revenue model is the advertising revenue model. Under this model, users do not pay for a product, but revenue is earned through the ads that are bought by advertisers and shown to users. Prior work has shown this model to be more effective when the advertising rate is higher, and aversion to ads is lower. This revenue model has also been linked to lower product quality. Finally, the third dominant revenue model is the freemium model, where two products are offered – a premium paid version and a more basic (and/or ad-sponsored) free version. Spotify and Dropbox are two examples. Some positive aspects of freemium models cited in the literature include

---

[33] Hobnob website

[34] See Tidhar and Eisenhardt (2020)

the segmentation of customers and the "trial" aspect prior to purchase. Self-cannibalization is a potential concern, however.

Establishing Good Governance from Day One

Digital ventures with new business models need to prevent governance and leadership crises by adopting strong governance principles from day one. This is, however, not as easy as it may sound, for various reasons. First, business model innovations are often boundary-spanning, since they rely on the active participation of external stakeholders (suppliers, partners, and customers) in the activity system of the focal firm; the importance of external stakeholders is therefore high. Digital business models increasingly rely on ever-greater numbers of external stakeholders, especially when they are "born digital and global," that is, when they digitally reach broad and large markets (on both the supply and demand sides). Furthermore, the wide reach and digital characteristics of business model innovations profoundly change the nature of interactions between the focal firm and its external stakeholders. These interactions happen primarily (and sometimes exclusively) through digital interfaces. This implies a loss of human touch and increased anonymity of interactions. Finally, many companies with substantial equity valuations (such as Airbnb) choose to remain private for longer periods of time than in the past. They continue to raise money from private equity sources rather than in the public markets through an IPO, which makes it "important to assess whether they are likewise maturing their governance structures and internal control environments to match their size and market impact."[35]

These factors, taken together, point toward an increased need and a greater role for corporate governance in new ventures, especially those that have adopted digitally driven business model innovations. Corporate governance in an entrepreneurial business model context refers to the mechanisms, rules, and processes by which new firms are controlled and operated, and that concern the distribution of rights and responsibilities among different stakeholders in the focal firm and its business model (both internal

---

[35]U.S. regulator cited by Chair Mary Jo White (2016).

stakeholders such as the board of directors, managers, employees, and owners, as well as external ones such as customers, suppliers, and partners). The business model perspective thus calls for an expanded view of corporate governance, far beyond its traditional focus on principals (shareholders) and agents (managers). At the same time, the principles of sound governance in *any* entrepreneurial firm continue to hold, notably with respect to boards of directors, ownership, and top management leadership.[36]

Boards of Directors

A venture should establish a board of directors (at early stages of venture development also called a "board of advisors"). A venture's board of directors often consists of both inside and outside directors. Inside directors usually include the founders and/or the CEO, and possibly one or two other top executives, all of whom may also be co-founders. Outside directors include representatives of professional investors (e.g., venture capital firms), former co-founders who no longer work at the venture, and independent directors who are often former entrepreneurs, or senior executives from relevant industries.[37] The responsibilities of the board are summarized in the OECD principles of corporate governance.[38] The importance of these principles is accentuated through recent examples of poor governance (e.g., at WeWork), which may also signal the need to better tailor these principles to the specific circumstances and challenges of venture boards (explained in the internal governance section above).

Ownership

The owners of a venture range from the founders and early employees (to whom restricted common shares were sold shortly after the formation of the company), to family members and friends, angel investors, and institutional investors. The more diverse the owner base of a company,

---

[36]According to Li, Terjesen, and Umans (2018), these are the key corporate governance variables in entrepreneurial firms.
[37]See Garg and Furr (2017)
[38]OECD (2015)

the more likely it is that there will be divergent interests and incentives among the owners. One potential source of conflicts of interest, between institutional investors who serve on the board of directors of a venture capital-backed company and the founders, is that investors (as BOD members) are fiduciaries for all shareholders. They are therefore obligated to make decisions that are in the best interest of all shareholders of the company. On occasion, however, what is best for the company and all its shareholders may not be in the best interest of the limited partners who invested in the fund that in turn made an investment in the company. Such conflict emerges when the BOD discusses the timing and mode of a liquidity event, and an investor pushes for liquidity sooner than what founders/management believe is in the best interest of the company. Other sources of conflict between investors and founders emerge in the context of fundraising and C-level senior hires. There may also be divergence of interests among different institutional investors in a focal venture. In general, such conflicts among owners (so-called "principal–principal" conflicts) may be harmful to the development of the venture.

To minimize this risk, managers of such ventures may use process behaviors that follow a logic of "divide and conquer" to reconcile (to the extent possible) the diverging interests among owners, and obtain resources and advice from them. These behaviors include (i) engaging in role-based dyadic interactions with owners, usually those that have representation through a board seat; (ii) proposing a single decision alternative (not presenting multiple proposals) in board meetings; (iii) using board meetings mainly for updates, and holding separate meetings for brainstorming on business model and other strategy issues; and (iv) using political action (e.g., forming political alliances with certain owners, framing issues strategically, using information selectively and symbolically) to close the strategy-making process.[39] Another mechanism that can be used to mitigate potential conflicts among owners is engaging in deep discussions at board meetings that lead to the formulation of a shared vision and the mission of the company. In addition, social activities can greatly contribute to strengthening the trust and respect among BOD members and thereby mitigate to some extent potential misalignments of interests.

---

[39] Garg and Eisenhardt (2017)

Top Management Leadership

A venture's top management team is ultimately responsible for adopting sound corporate governance practices, complying with laws and regulations, and in general ensuring high ethical standards of behavior. One element relates to the shared values and beliefs of the leadership team and its ability to develop a corporate culture that is solidly anchored in a set of shared values that will guide behaviors and decision-making throughout the organization. Governance and leadership principles are indeed often reflected in a set of values that are meant to be representative of organizational culture. To limit the damaging effects of narcissistic or hubristic entrepreneurial leaders, for example, experts recommend building highly functional teams that can isolate and buffer the negative effects of individual dysfunctional leaders.[40] Empowering employees, adopting flatter organizational hierarchies, and encouraging bottom-up decision-making to distribute power more equally among organization members should also help in this regard. These measures favor monitoring, and they facilitate the alignment of objectives.[41]

As a general rule, measures that aim at establishing good corporate governance should be adopted sooner rather than later – ideally from day one. In a corporate governance sense, then, private firms should be run like public firms. This will also ensure a smoother transition from private venture to public firm, which typically brings with it new outward-facing processes, for example, toward public shareholders. But here again, ventures with business model innovations that take their responsibilities toward external stakeholders seriously will have less trouble with this transition, as they will ideally have developed at least some of these processes already.

Summary of Key Takeaways for the Effective Business Model Designer

In this chapter, we covered some of the most important business model implementation challenges facing young ventures, which are in general less subject to inertial forces than ventures created within incumbent firms.

---

[40] Kets de Vries (1985)
[41] Colombo, Croce, and Murtinu (2014)

Although younger firms usually already have the underlying conditions in place that favor – rather than work against – BMI implementation, certain types of risks are acute and need to be managed. Young ventures implementing BMI may become dangerously dependent on partners, for instance, and they are especially susceptible to experiencing leadership and governance problems. These are on top of the usual risks impacting young firms, such as demand-side risks, supply-side risks, competition risks, capital market risks, and environmental risks.

The first especially salient BMI implementation risk for startups is the potential dependence on larger, more established third parties. The term "dependent entrepreneurship" captures the dynamic between platform-dependent young firms and large digital platforms such as Amazon. Another especially salient risk for young firms is the potential for governance and leadership issues, which may stem from the blurring of the lines between ownership and control of the firm. In turn, this may lead to the tolerance of poor behavior, since the disciplining mechanism of an independent board may be weaker than in a more established, publicly traded company.

We also went over some risk mitigation strategies for young ventures implementing innovative new business models. The first strategy is business planning, a crucial step that imposes discipline, helps develop a business model mindset, and results in a tangible document with valuable information. The second strategy is building trust with external stakeholders; an effective way to do this is by using symbolic actions. The third strategy to manage business model implementation risk is lowering dependence on third parties. Some protection mechanisms that firms can engage in include traditional measures such as legal protection, secrecy, and timing, as well as measures more specific to business models, such as having backup partners and taking measures to decrease knowledge leakages. The fourth strategy is using strategic considerations in adopting a revenue model (such as a paid, advertising, or freemium revenue model). Finally, business model implementation risks can be mitigated by improving internal governance to help prevent leadership and governance crises that can escalate into serious scandals. This is a serious challenge, as a boundary-spanning activity system (especially a digital one) can involve many stakeholders. Some measures to improve governance are to establish a board of directors, minimize principal-principal issues, and set in place measures to monitor and counteract the effects of poor-quality leaders.

References

Barnes, B. (2019, November 11). Disney's debut shows streaming force. *New York Times*, pp. B1.

Berglund, H. & Sandström, C. (2013). Business model innovation from an open systems perspective: Structural challenges and managerial solutions. *International Journal of Product Development* **18**(3–4), 274–285.

Bezos, J. (2019, April 11). 2018 Letter to Shareholders. *The Amazon Blog Dayone*. Retrieved from https://blog.aboutamazon.co.uk/company-news/2018-letter-to-shareholders

Bonakdar, A., Frankenberger, K., Bader, M. A. & Gassmann, O. (2017). Capturing value from business models: The role of formal and informal protection strategies. *International Journal of Technology Management* **73**(4), 151–175.

Chatterjee, A. & Hambrick, D. C. (2007). It's all about me: Narcissistic chief executive officers and their effects on company strategy and performance. *Administrative Science Quarterly* **52**(3), 351–386.

Colombo, M. G., Croce, A. & Murtinu, S. (2014). Ownership structure, horizontal agency costs and the performance of high-tech entrepreneurial firms. *Small Business Economics* **42**(2), 265–282.

Cutolo, D. & Kenney, M. (2019). The emergence of platform-dependent entrepreneurs: Power asymmetries, risk, and uncertainty. Berkeley Roundtable on the International Economy. Working Paper.

Delmar, F. & Shane, S. (2003). Does business planning facilitate the development of new ventures? *Strategic Management Journal* **24**(12), 1165–1185.

Dvorak, P. & Fujikawa, M. (2019, November 6). SoftBank founder calls his judgment 'really bad' after $4.7 billion WeWork hit. *Wall Street Journal*. Retrieved from https://www.wsj.com/articles/softbank-books-loss-of-4-7-billion-on-wework-investment-11573024776

Eavis, P. (2019, October 2). As WeWork slows down, biggest competitor says it's thriving. *New York Times*. Retrieved from https://www.nytimes.com/2019/10/02/business/iwg-mark-dixon.html

Encyclopedia Britannica website. Association test. Retrieved from https://www.britannica.com/science/association-test

Engelen, A., Neumann, C. & Schmidt, S. (2016). Should entrepreneurially oriented firms have narcissistic CEOs? *Journal of Management* **42**(3), 698–721.

Garg, S. (2013). Venture boards: Distinctive monitoring and implications for firm performance. *Academy of Management Review* **38**(1), 90–108.

Garg, S. & Eisenhardt, K. M. (2017). Unpacking the CEO-board relationship: How strategy-making happens in entrepreneurial firms. *Academy of Management Journal* **60**(5), 1828–1858.

Garg, S. & Furr, N. (2017). Venture boards: Past insights, future directions, and transition to public firms. *Strategic Entrepreneurship Journal* **11**(3), 326–343.

Glassdoor (2019, July 10). *Culture over cash?* Glassdoor multi-country survey finds more than half of employees prioritize workplace culture over salary. *Glassdoor.* Retrieved from https://www.glassdoor.com/about-us/workplace-culture-over-salary/

Hobnob website. Retrieved from https://hobnob.app/about/

Isaac, M. (2017, June 21). Uber founder Travis Kalanick resigns as C.E.O. *New York Times.* Retrieved from https://www.nytimes.com/2017/06/21/technology/uber-ceo-travis-kalanick.html

Katila, R., Rosenberger, J. D. & Eisenhardt, K. M. (2008). Swimming with sharks: Technology ventures, defense mechanisms, and corporate relationships. *Administrative Science Quarterly* **53**(2), 295–332.

Kenney, M. & Zysman, J. (2016). The rise of the platform economy. *Issues in Science and Technology* **32**(3), 61–69.

Kets de Vries, M. (1985). The dark side of entrepreneurship. *Harvard Business Review* **63**(6), 160–167.

Knight, F. (1921). *Risk, Uncertainty and Profits.* Boston, MA: Houghton Mifflin.

Li, H., Terjesen, S. & Umans, T. (2018). Corporate governance in entrepreneurial firms: A systematic review and research agenda. *Small Business Economics* **54**(1), 43–74.

Lohr, S. & Griffith, E. (2019, November 24). Start-ups shift focus to business ventures. *New York Times International Edition*, pp. 23.

MacCrimmon, K. R. & Wehrung, D. A. (1988). *Taking Risk: The Management of Uncertainty.* New York, NY: Free Press.

Merriam Webster Dictionary. Symbol. Retrieved from https://www.merriamwebster.com/dictionary/symbol

Newcomer, E. (2017, November 21). Uber paid hackers to delete stolen data on 57 million people. *Bloomberg*. Retrieved from https://www.bloomberg.com/news/articles/2017-11-21/uber-concealed-cyberattack-that-exposed-57-million-people-s-data

Newton, C. (2014, August 26). This is Uber's playbook for sabotaging Lyft. *The Verge*. Retrieved from https://www.theverge.com/2014/8/26/6067663/this-is-ubers-playbook-for-sabotaging-lyft

OECD. (2015). G20/OECD principles of corporate governance. *OECD Publishing, Paris*. Retrieved from https://www.oecd.org/daf/ca/Corporate-Governance-Principles-ENG.pdf

Popper, B. (2013, December 18). Uber surge pricing: Sound economic theory, bad business practice. *The Verge*. Retrieved from https://www.theverge.com/2013/12/18/5221428/uber-surge-pricing-vs-price-gouging-law

Powell, J. (2019, September 26). WeQuit: Problems mount for WeWork. *Financial Times*. Retrieved from https://ftalphaville.ft.com/2019/09/25/1569411666000/WeQuit--problems-mount-for-WeWork/

Sandström, C. & Osborne, R. G. (2011). Managing business model renewal. *International Journal of Business and Systems Research* **5**(5), 461–474.

Shane, S. (2008). *The Illusions of Entrepreneurship: The Costly Myths That Entrepreneurs, Investors, and Policy Makers Live By*. New Haven, CT: Yale University Press.

Satariano, A. (2019, November 12). He beat Google. Yet it crushed him. *New York Times International Edition*, pp. 7.

Snihur, Y. & Zott, C. (2020). The genesis and metamorphosis of novelty imprints: How business model innovation emerges in young ventures. *Academy of Management Journal* **63**(2), 554–583.

Stinchcombe, A. L. (1965). Social structure and organizations. In J. P. March (Ed.), *Handbook of Organizations* (pp. 142–193). Chicago, IL: Rand McNally.

Tidhar, R. & Eisenhardt K. M. (2020). Get rich or die trying . . . finding revenue model fit using machine learning and multiple cases. *Strategic Management Journal* **41**(7), 1245–1273.

United States Securities and Exchange Commission. (2019, August 14). Form S-1 registration statement under the Securities Act of 1933 of The We Company. Retrieved from https://www.sec.gov/Archives/edgar/data/1533523/000119312519220499/d781982ds1.htm

White, M. J. (2016, March 31). Keynote address at the SEC-Rock Center on corporate governance Silicon Valley Initiative. Retrieved from https://www.sec.gov/news/speech/chair-white-silicon-valley-initiative-3-31-16.html

Zott, C. & Huy, Q. N. (2007). How entrepreneurs use symbolic management to acquire resources. *Administrative Science Quarterly* **52**(1), 70–105.

Zott, C. & Huy, Q. N. (2009). How to convince sceptical stakeholders: Display symbols with substance. *IESE Insight,* No. 3, Fourth Quarter 2009, 50–57.

12 Business Model Innovation Strategy in the Digital Age – What Does It Mean for You?

Business Model Innovation in the Digital Age: A Key Strategic Issue

Business model innovation centers on renewal and rejuvenation through opportunity creation, development, and exploitation. New and innovative business models explain how new entrants disrupt incumbents, and in turn offer a way for these same incumbents to invigorate their firms and mitigate the effects of disruption. Emerging and established technologies – such as 5G, artificial intelligence, the Internet of Things, blockchain, cloud computing, and connected mobility, along with real-time digital data and data analytic tools – open a wide range of innovative ways for entrepreneurial leaders to conceive of, design, implement, and manage novel and transformative business models with new activities, business processes, ways of connecting activities, and/or ways of governing activities. By designing their firm's boundary-spanning exchanges and activities, utilizing digital technologies, these leaders create a networked system of interdependent activities – namely their business models. The business model has thus become an important lever for enhancing the focal firm's "ecological fitness," i.e., for improving its fit with a continuously shifting technological and product-market environment.

As a result of the exponentially falling costs of information processing and telecommunication, both direct and indirect transaction costs have decreased. This has shifted the balance from tangible resources and capabilities to intangible resources and capabilities. It has also opened up new possibilities for entrepreneurial leaders to conceive of, and implement, innovative business models. Since focal firms can now outsource almost anything to anyone, the combinatorial possibilities for constructing systems that combine in-house activities (i.e., those performed within focal firm boundaries) with those performed by other parties have exploded. In other words, the number of possible combinations of activities, which are enabled by different tangible and intangible resources, and capabilities, which are owned and controlled by different parties, has multiplied dramatically.

The question of whether and how to innovate the business model has therefore become a strategic imperative for incumbent firms digitizing their businesses, as well as for digital native firms and startups (who need to be mindful of changes in their competitive landscape as well as technological changes). A business model innovation mindset has indeed become a prerequisite for transformative innovation, and entrepreneurial leaders of all firms need a business model innovation strategy.

The Strong Case for Having a Business Model Innovation Strategy

A business model innovation strategy refers to the choices entrepreneurial leaders must make with respect to:

- The design of a new system of activities (***What? How? Who? Why?***);

- The processes, including their antecedents, by which a new activity system is created; and
- The implementation and ongoing adaptation of the new activity system to ensure coherence (i.e., internal, external, and strategic fit), with the objective of sustaining and improving the focal organization's key performance metrics.

The business model innovation strategy complements the traditional scope and product market strategic issues that every firm must address. It has become a strategic imperative for large and small incumbent firms as well as for startups. Consider, for example, the Walt Disney Company. Disney is a multinational media and entertainment company known globally for its TV channels, movies, and theme parks. The development and rapid growth in the past decade of movie and TV streaming services, such as Netflix, Amazon Prime Video, HBO Go, Hulu, and YouTube TV, have presented a significant threat to Disney's business model. At the same time, shifting to a digitally anchored business model and developing its own streaming platform was perceived as a risky move for Disney, as it would disrupt its legendary TV and movie businesses. Nevertheless, the pressure resulting from the rapid increase in the pace of "cord-cutting" by cable subscribers led Disney's management to announce a radically redesigned business model innovation strategy in 2017. This new strategy included adding new activities (***What***) to complement and leverage its established TV and movie businesses. ESPN Plus, a digital streaming sports platform, was commercially introduced in April of 2018, and Disney Plus, a family-oriented movie streaming platform, was formally launched in the U.S. and Canada in November 2019.[1]

Or consider Swedish company Inter Ikea Holding B.V., the holding company of furniture retailer IKEA. It has a well-established worldwide network of large furniture retail stores. The rapid changes in the retail landscape, however, coupled with the exponential growth of e-commerce prompted a radical rethinking by management about how IKEA does business and suggested the need for a business model innovation strategy. As a result of this process, IKEA's business model is currently undergoing a significant transformation. IKEA is testing new retail formats, such as opening smaller stores

---

[1]Barnes (2019)

and pop-ups in city centers, and experimenting with "circular economy" initiatives such as refurbishing.[2] New activities are being added to its business model, including e-commerce and services such as furniture assembly (new ***What***). These activities require resources and capabilities that are accessed through new partnerships (new ***Who***). IKEA is also embracing partnerships with technology firms, which enable it to offer smart home products that are integrated into IKEA's traditional product line. One example is its partnership with Sonos, a California-based firm that makes smart speakers. Sonos speakers have been integrated into select IKEA products, creating, for instance, an innovative speaker lamp that can be controlled through a smartphone app.[3]

A business model innovation strategy, however, is not only important for traditional, for-profit firms such as Disney or IKEA. It is relevant for both for-profit firms and non-for-profit firms, for organizations that pursue a primarily social objective (e.g., social entrepreneurs), for governmental as well as non-governmental organizations, and for organizations such as schools and hospitals. Each and every firm or organization today faces unprecedented new threats and opportunities in the digital era. These threats and opportunities are anchored in the simple fact that innovations are no longer restricted to technological innovations. Innovations may also hail from new combinations of resources and managerial choices, which are often (but not always) enabled by digital technologies. These combinations can result in new business models, such as low-cost airlines, free newspapers that are only funded by advertising, or even hospitals for cataract surgery modeled after a fast-food chain.

Aravind Eye Hospitals is a chain of specialized hospitals that was founded in 1976, in the Indian state of Tamil Nadu. It was started by ophthalmologist Dr. Govindappa Venkataswamy (or "Dr. V"), who applied the efficiency of McDonald's fast-food business, which he took as a business model template, to healthcare in order to ramp up the number of patients his organization could treat.[4] Applying its innovative business model, Aravind was able

[2]Milne (2018)

[3]Milne (2019)

[4]According to Dr. V, "All I want to sell is good eyesight, and there are millions of people who need it ....[if] McDonald's can sell billions of burgers, why can't Aravind sell millions of sight-restoring operations, and, eventually, the belief in

to grow into a large, self-funded network of 13 eye hospitals, as well as numerous outpatient and training facilities. In the period 2017–2018 alone, it conducted over 4 million outpatient visits and over 478,000 "surgeries, lasers and intra ocular injections,"[5] as it works toward the goal of eradicating "needless blindness"[6] in India. Remarkably, half of its patients receive free or low-cost treatment.

Aravind is able to achieve this by employing a novel approach to providing a high volume of eye surgeries at a low cost. It streamlined ancillary activities and helped fund the surgeries of those patients who could not pay by charging the patients who could (new ***Why***). In addition, it worked with partner organizations (new ***Who***) to provide vision screening in more isolated villages (new ***What***); these organizations also helped coordinate and bring patients to Aravind. Aravind utilizes its scale, and its assembly-line approach (new ***How***) "increases productivity tenfold."[7] To access an even greater number of people, it has started to screen people for diabetic retinopathy, a serious degenerative condition related to diabetes, using an AI developed by Google.[8] Over the past four decades, Aravind has undertaken over 6 million surgeries.[9]

Business Model Innovation Strategy: Think Digital Platforms

The opportunities and threats presented by the emergence and growth of digitally enabled multisided platform business models, which enable digital interactions, exchanges, and commercial transactions among multiple parties, further strengthen the case for having a business model innovation strategy. The online travel reservation platform Expedia, the social

human perfection? With sight, people could be freed from hunger, fear, and poverty. You could perfect the body, then perfect the mind and the soul, and raise people's level of thinking and acting" Fast Company Staff (2006).

[5]Aravind Eye Care System (2018)

[6]Aravind Eye Care System website

[7]Aravind Eye Care System website

[8]Metz (2019)

[9]Aravind Eye Care System website

media platform Facebook, the dating platform Match.com, and the marketplace platform Amazon.com are examples of how advanced computing and communication technologies created new business opportunities that were captured by entrepreneurial leaders. The innovative business models they crafted enabled the creation of value for the stakeholders of the platform, and the capture of value by the focal firm (the platform).

Each of these digital platform business models is robust, scalable, and offers a compelling value proposition to the stakeholders who are incentivized to participate in it. Such digital platform business models can be stand-alone businesses, such as music streaming service Spotify and video platform YouTube, where both the financial transactions (e.g., subscribing to the service) and the delivery of the service are digital. Alternatively, they can complement a brick-and-mortar retailing business; examples of this are e-commerce retail sites such as Walmart.com and Macys.com, where the financial transaction (e.g., purchasing the product) is digitally enabled but the delivery is physical.

In addition to considerations about how to organize the platform and combine it with the existing business, an important aspect of a business model innovation strategy is the alternative ways of monetizing the traffic on the digital platform. The value capture of digitally enabled business models is facilitated through a range of (often novel) revenue models. Examples of different revenue models include subscription-based revenue models, such as the *New York Times*' online media platform, music streaming platform Deezer, and movie streaming platform Netflix; advertising-based revenue models, such as search engines Google and Yahoo; or commission-based revenue models, such as different types of marketplace business models, including CtoC (e.g., LendingClub.com), BtoB (e.g., Faire.com) or BtoC (e.g., Cars.com) companies. Commissions may also be generated through affiliate marketing programs, which are realized through digital referrals to an e-commerce site or digital marketplace; one example of this is Credit Karma, a personal finance digital platform that derives commissions from credit card issuers. E-commerce platforms use a range of revenue models, including sales revenue (e.g., Italian retailer Zegna's online site), transaction fees (e.g., parking payment app meterUp), razor/blade revenue models (e.g., the men's grooming companies Gillette and digital native Harrys.com), and more.

How to Develop a Business Model Innovation Strategy

Recall our definition of business model innovation strategy as *the pattern of choices of entrepreneurial leaders with respect to (i) the design of a new system of activities (**What? How? Who? Why?**); (ii) the processes, including their antecedents, by which the new activity system is created; and (iii) the implementation and ongoing adaptation of the activity system to ensure coherence (i.e., internal, external, and strategic fit) with the objective of sustaining and improving the focal organization's key performance metrics.*

Regarding the design of a new system of activities (the first part (i) of our definition), the development of a business model innovation strategy starts by embracing a business model mindset (see Chapter 3). A business model mindset is a state of mind and perspective that helps entrepreneurial leaders consider the firm's entire activity system as a way to capture business opportunities. Moreover, the development of a business model innovation strategy must be anchored on identifying clear and pressing needs in the market (see Chapter 4). This entails recognizing the perceived problems of customers, along with the needs of other potential stakeholders, and then addressing the following four questions to guide the development of a new and better model: ***What*** (activities)? ***Who*** (conducts them)? ***How*** (are they linked)? and ***Why*** (do they allow for value creation and capture)? (See Exhibit 12.1.)

With respect to the processes, including the antecedents, by which the new activity system is created (the second part (ii) of our definition), adopting a design perspective to business model innovation offers entrepreneurial leaders a content and process-based lens for crafting their BMI strategy. As we have argued in Chapter 5, a BMI strategy needs to aim for business models that are both legitimate and difficult to imitate. Furthermore, the development of a BMI strategy needs to consider the relevant internal and external antecedents, or drivers, that affect the design of a novel business model. These drivers can be summarized by the acronym DESIGN (see Exhibit 12.2).

Exhibit 12.1 BMI Strategy – Design of a New System of Activities

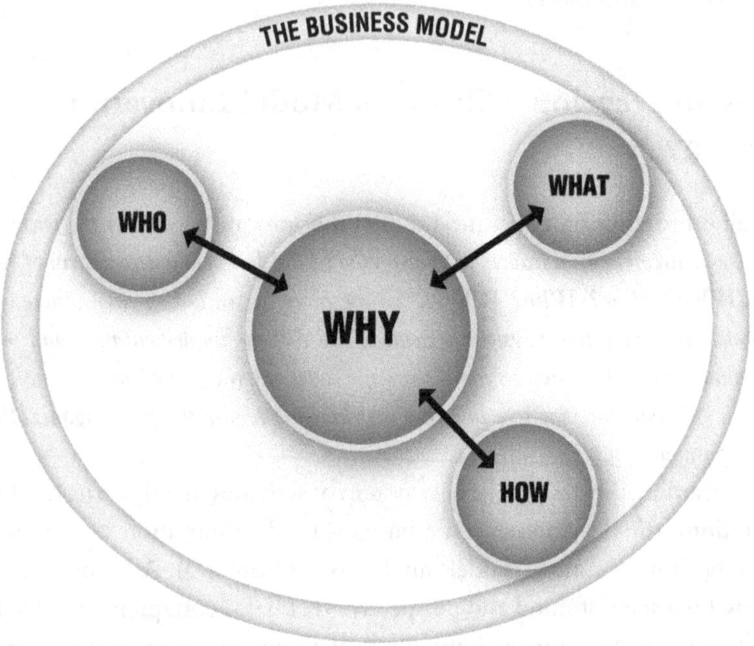

Exhibit 12.2 BMI Strategy – Antecedents

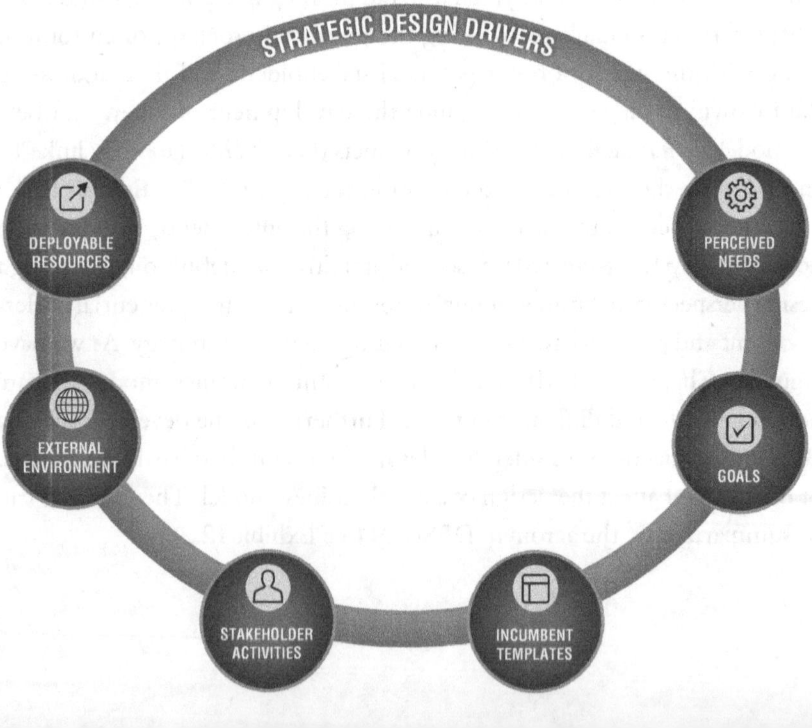

Importantly, a BMI strategy also needs to consider the processes for creating the novel business model. These processes include three iterative phases that we have labeled BM*Ideate*, BM*Iterate*, and BM*Implement* (see Chapter 6 and Exhibit 12.3).

Exhibit 12.3 BMI Strategy – Process

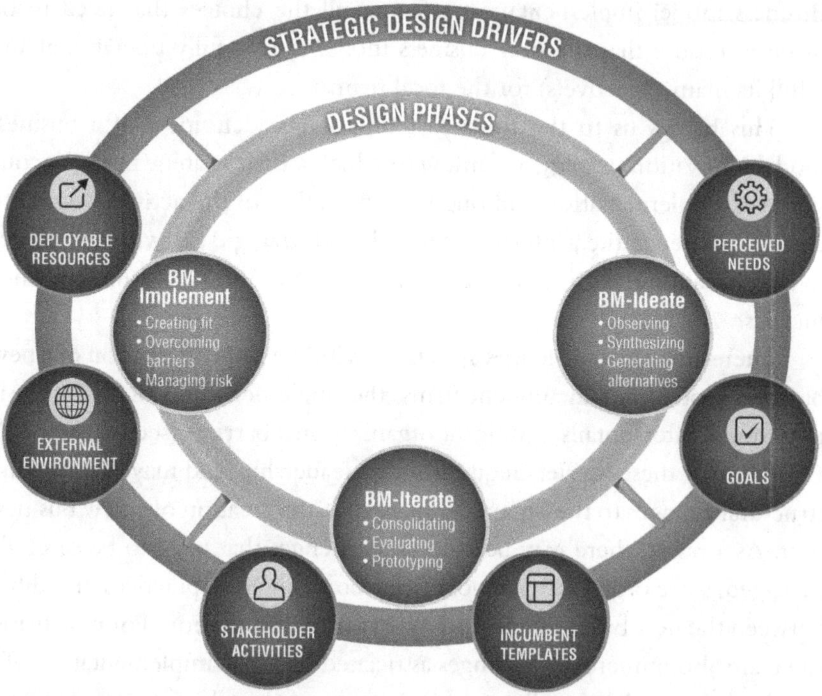

The first phase in the design of a new business model, BM*Ideate,* refers to observing and gaining a deep understanding of business models currently in use and their stakeholders' needs. It also refers to synthesizing and organizing the data gathered in the observation phase to identify themes that emerge with respect to the design elements, which in turn informs the generation of new business model solutions.

The BM*Iterate* phase in the design process of a new business model includes consolidating the various ideas into a coherent whole, evaluating the new design solutions, and prototyping the highest-ranked alternatives. When evaluating new business model designs and specifying the value propositions to the various stakeholders, it is important to identify clearly the drivers of value creation according to the NICE model (introduced in Chapter 8): Novelty, lock-In, Complementarities, and Efficiency.

The BM*Implement* phase of the design process, finally, involves scaling the prototype business model and engaging in full-blown implementation. Business model implementation refers to all the choices that need to be made to ensure that the new business model can be fully operational and fulfill its main objective(s) for the focal firm.

This brings us to the third part (iii) of our definition of a business model innovation strategy, according to which a BMI strategy needs to consider the implementation and ongoing adaptation of the activity system to ensure coherence (i.e., internal, external, and strategic fit) with the objective of sustaining and improving the focal organization's key performance metrics.

There are many challenges associated with the implementation of a new business model. For incumbent firms, the implementation of a new business model often entails significant organizational barriers (see Chapter 10). Overcoming these barriers requires strong leadership, and may also demand structural changes to the organization, such as the creation of a new business unit. As a result, there may be cultural challenges that need to be carefully managed, since organizational norms and compensation practices may differ between the new business unit and the existing organization. For new firms, there are also numerous challenges associated with the implementation of a new business model (see Chapter 11). In startups, the relevant resources must often be marshalled through partnerships, which may create mission-critical dependencies on others. Weak governance structures and inexperienced senior leaders are also factors that may impede the successful implementation of novel business models in young companies.

Last but not least, an innovation-oriented organizational culture and behavioral norms that embrace business model innovation as a continuous process enable the organization to proactively recognize environmental trends and pivot its business model. (See Exhibit 12.4 for an overview of BMI strategy at a glance.)

Exhibit 12.4 BMI Strategy at a Glance

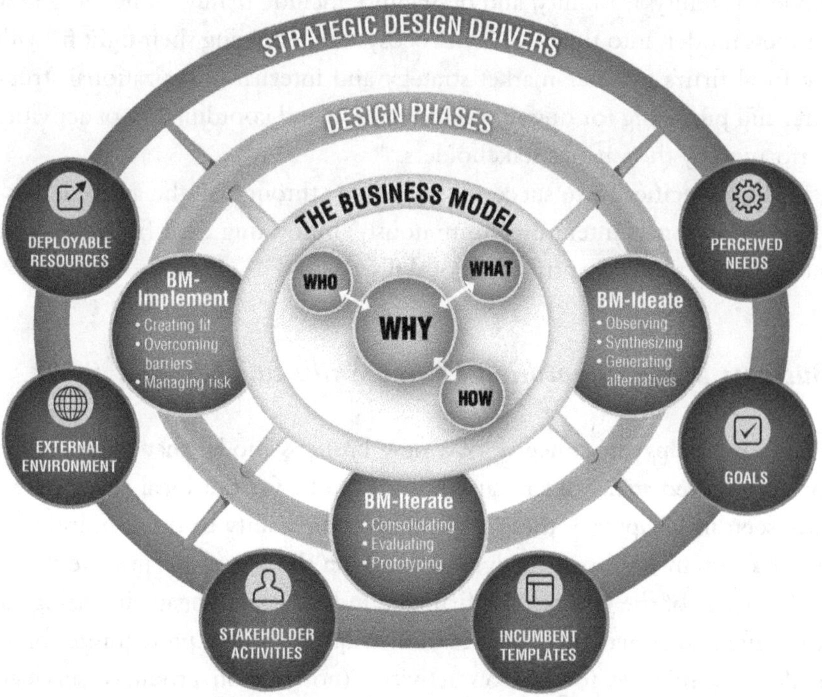

Business Model Innovation Strategy: What Does It Mean for You?

The capability to instill an innovation-oriented culture and behavioral norms in an organization – which enable it to innovate its business model regularly and adapt it to a continuously evolving external environment – resides to a large extent with individual managers and leaders, i.e., with you.[10] Managerial insight, vision, and leadership play a pivotal role for developing a business model innovation strategy.

The distinctive function of entrepreneurial leaders lies in recognizing market and technological trends, then conceiving, designing, and implementing innovative, robust, and scalable business models (and revenue models that enable them to profit from their innovation) that create value for

[10]See Adner and Helfat (2003) and Teece (2014)

all involved stakeholders. Essential managerial tasks to ensure the business model's viability, feasibility, and desirability include firmly embedding new business models into the focal firm's ecosystem, ensuring their tight fit with the focal firm's product-market strategy and internal organizational structure, and providing for ongoing orchestration and coordination of activities performed by the various stakeholders.[11]

More specifically, to successfully navigate through all the available possibilities, managers intent on (continuously) innovating their firms' business models need three essential types of skills.

Business Model Innovation Design Skills and Mindset

These will help you conceive of a new business model that creates value for all involved stakeholders, and ensures profit for the focal firm. As we have seen in Chapter 3, these skills include the ability to think holistically, adopt a system-level perspective (focusing on the forest not just the trees), look outside of the box of your firm and industry, and engage in analogical reasoning and conceptual combination. A quintessential prerequisite for all of this is a mindset focused on activities (not just on products, services, organizational functions, or operational processes).

The good news is that these cognitive skills can be learned and improved. Importantly, as a business model designer you need to focus on the problem before jumping (perhaps prematurely) to the conclusion (i.e., problem-finding should precede solutions-finding; see Chapter 9). In order to understand the problem better, you need to adopt a design attitude, which means observing and listening carefully and empathetically to others (see Chapter 5). And, finally, in designing winning business model innovations you need to ensure that everybody will gain, and the value proposition for each business model stakeholder is adequate (see Chapter 8). In other words, you need to embrace a philosophy of total value creation, which accepts that value co-creation with others can only work if you compensate them adequately, and do not just focus on value capture for yourself.

---

[11] Brown (2007)

Business Model Innovation Implementation Skills

These skills will help you bring the new model to life, integrate it with the old model (in the case of an established firm), and introduce the new business model into the marketplace. Since business models in the digital era typically span firm and industry boundaries, they often involve numerous third-party stakeholders who conduct key activities. Building, negotiating, and nurturing partnerships has therefore become a competence that you need to develop and perfect. The ability to build and project trust and credibility, which can be achieved through techniques such as symbolic management (see Chapter 11), helps with winning over partners, and also with acquiring many other kinds of valuable resources.

Other valuable skills for making business model innovation happen in new as well as established firms include recognizing, mitigating, and managing risks (e.g., having a business plan); adopting and adhering to sound governance standards (e.g., having a board of directors) from day one; identifying and adopting effective defense mechanisms against corporate "sharks"; and being strategic in your choice of revenue model.

Specifically, in the context of an established organization (see Chapter 10), as a successful business model innovation leader you need to be able to manage and drive change. This can be through creating awareness about the need for business model change with other organization members by sharing your vision, educating peers about the business model innovation so that they actually understand your vision, and anticipating and managing the fears that may stem from the uncertainty surrounding the new model. In general, you should take others along with you on the business model innovation journey by communicating openly and clearly at each and every step. In this context, you also need to be able to build, coach, and lead cross-functional teams that are differentiated from the main organization, yet socially integrated with it, and properly governed and incentivized. Such teams are an important vehicle for developing a truly innovative new business model. More broadly speaking, you need to help create an environment that encourages experimentation, tolerates failure, and promotes learning, so that organizational inertia and resistance to change can be successfully overcome.

Business Model Innovation Management Skills

This skillset involves the ongoing monitoring of the activities that encompass the business model and of the incentives of all the stakeholders who participate in the business model. It also involves the ongoing orchestration and coordination of activities performed by the various business model stakeholders, as well as the continuous adaptation of the entire system to changes in its environment. For example, intangible assets and other resources need to be continuously coordinated within the new business model to enable and conduct activities, and thereby fully realize their potential for value creation.

The acquisition and nurturing of these business model innovation design, implementation, and management skills comes on top of the demands placed on managers by traditional management tasks, such as organization design or product management, and the requirements imposed on them to manage the interactions between their firm and internal as well as external stakeholders. In this sense, it has become significantly more complex and demanding to manage and lead organizations today. In the past, the business model could be largely taken as a given. For example, banks, as financial service institutions, all basically functioned according to the same template, and taxi services essentially looked the same all over the world. This has profoundly changed, however. In the twenty-first century, the so-called "digital age," the business model has become one crucial variable (which is not a given) to consider for value and wealth creation.

The Bottom Line: What Is Your Business Model Innovation Strategy?

A business model innovation strategy has become one of the core strategic choices that entrepreneurial leaders of all kinds of organizations need to consider. For leaders of for-profit firms, it complements the firm's corporate strategy, namely issues that relate to the scope of the firm and include such questions as: What industries and product market segments should the firm be in? How and when should the firm enter/exit these markets (i.e., through mergers and acquisitions, joint ventures, or de novo entry)? A firm's business model innovation strategy also complements its business strategy, which centers on establishing and sustaining the competitive advantage of a firm in its product market(s). The focal firm's business strategy addresses such questions as how to compete in the firm's selected product market, and what resources and capabilities to acquire or develop to enable the profitable execution of its business strategy.

Entrepreneurial leaders are therefore faced with an indispensable and complementary strategic choice, namely the conceptualization, design, implementation, and management of transformative digitally enabled business models.

The resulting business model is a strategic asset that contributes to a firm's sustained competitiveness and profitability.[12] The conception, introduction into the marketplace, and ongoing management of your business model should not be left to chance; rather, it must be guided by a business model innovation strategy, which is anchored in a rigorous design process that combines organizational practices (e.g., regular brainstorming sessions) with creative insight at the individual managerial level (e.g., insight required for synthesizing the lessons learned from intense and comprehensive observation of stakeholders). In order to effectively navigate through the possibilities enabled in part by technological developments, your business model innovation strategy must depict the design and organizational processes of developing, implementing, managing, and continuously updating your firm's business model in a way that creates value for all the stakeholders in its activity system, while also capturing some of the value that is created.

The promise of innovative business models, however, goes beyond mere economic value creation and capture. Aravind Eye Hospitals in India and Grameen Bank in Bangladesh (a business model innovation in micro-lending to poor rural women, for which the founder, Muhammad Yunus, received the Nobel Peace Prize in 2006) serve as shining examples and sources of inspiration for social entrepreneurs who want to make the world a better place. They remind us that the big problems facing humankind, such as poverty, inequality, hunger, disease, or climate change, can be tackled through scalable business model innovations. To address climate change, for example, we need more sustainable business models, not just cleaner technologies, products, services, and processes. Innovations in business models can help us chart a path into a better and brighter future for all.

---

[12] See Amit and Schoemaker (1993)

References

Adner, R. & Helfat, C. E. (2003). Corporate effects and dynamic managerial capabilities. *Strategic Management Journal* **24**(10), 1011–1025.

Amit, R. & Schoemaker, P. J. H. (1993). Strategic assets and organizational rent. *Strategic Management Journal* **14**(1), 33–46.

Aravind Eye Care System (2018). Activity report 2017-18. Retrieved from https://aravind.org/wp-content/uploads/2019/04/Aravind_Annual-Report-2017-18.pdf

Aravind Eye Care System website. Retrieved from https://aravind.org/our-story/

Barnes, B. (2019, November 10). Netflix was only the start: Disney streaming service shakes an industry. *New York Times*. Retrieved from https://www.nytimes.com/2019/11/10/business/media/Disney-Plus-streaming.html

Brown, T. (2007). *Change by Design: How Design Thinking Transforms Organizations and Inspires Innovation*. New York, NY: HarperCollins Publishers.

Fast Company Staff (2006, July 20). And then there's Dr. V. *Fast Company*. Retrieved from https://www.fastcompany.com/675800/and-then-theres-dr-v

Metz, C. (2019, March 10). India fights diabetic blindness with help from A.I. *New York Times*. Retrieved from https://www.nytimes.com/2019/03/10/technology/artificial-intelligence-eye-hospital-india.html

Milne, R. (2018, February 1). Ikea unpacked: How the furniture giant is redesigning its future. *Financial Times*. Retrieved from https://www.ft.com/content/8a8bb9a0-0613-11e8-9650-9c0ad2d7c5b5

Milne, R. (2019, October 2). Ikea assembles software engineers in smart home push. *Financial Times*. Retrieved from https://www.ft.com/content/440249c8-e41e-11e9-9743-db5a370481bc

Teece, D. J. (2014). A dynamic capabilities-based entrepreneurial theory of multinational enterprise. *Journal of International Business Studies* **45**(1), 8–37.

Acknowledgments

We thank Claire Peeters, Xenia Kouteva and Adeline Abou-Ali, Jack Lee Zhang, and Amy Weiss for their valuable assistance in the development of this book. Both authors are grateful to their respective institutions (the Wharton School, UPENN, and IESE Business School, respectively) for providing financial support and the time necessary for this project. As well, we wish to express our sincere gratitude for the inspiration that we received from numerous entrepreneurial leaders around the world, many of whom are alumni of our current or previous institutions: Wharton, IESE, INSEAD, the University of British Columbia, and the Kellogg School, Northwestern University.

About the Authors

Raphael ("Raffi") Amit is the Marie and Joseph Melone Professor and a Professor of Management at the Wharton School. He has served as the Academic Director of *Wharton Entrepreneurship*, which encompasses all of Wharton's entrepreneurial programs, between 1999 and 2015. Professor Amit holds BA and MA degrees in Economics from the Hebrew University in Jerusalem, Israel, and received his PhD in Managerial Economics and Decision Sciences from Northwestern University's Kellogg Graduate School of Management.

For more than 20 years, Professor Amit's research and teaching has centered on the design and implementation of innovative business model strategies in both startups and incumbent firms. Professor Amit has published widely cited, award-winning research on a broad range of issues that relate to business model innovation strategies, entrepreneurship, and venture capital, and on a range of issues that relate to ownership, management, and control of Family Businesses. He is frequently quoted in practitioner outlets.

Professor Amit has held a range of management and board of directors positions in various companies around the world. He served as Chair of the

Board of Directors of Creo Products Inc. for six years (NASDAQ: CREO until May 2005 when it was acquired by Eastman Kodak). Professor Amit helped form the *Korean Global IT Fund*, a $100 million VC fund, and has served as the first Chairman of the KGIF Advisory Board. He has been serving on the boards of directors of numerous technology and family business firms for the past 25 years and consults globally to a range of private and public organizations.

Christoph Zott is a Professor of Entrepreneurship at IESE Business School. He holds a PhD in Commerce and Business Administration from the University of British Columbia, Canada, a DEA in Industrial Engineering from the Institut National Polytechnique de Grenoble, France, and a Masters in Industrial Engineering from the Karlsruhe Institute of Technology in Germany. For the past 25 years, Professor Zott has worked and lived in Canada, France, Germany, Spain, and the U.S. He coaches and consults with entrepreneurial leaders all over the world, and is passionate about helping people realize their dream to "create something from nothing."

Professor Zott designs and delivers workshops, courses, and programs on entrepreneurial leadership and business model innovation at the Executive Education, MBA, and PhD levels. He advises startups and growth ventures, as well as large established multinational firms interested in business model design, growth, innovation, entrepreneurial strategy, and change. Professor Zott's advisory work is anchored deeply in his own research; he has written over 50 articles, which have been published in top journals and books. His publications on business models in particular have won numerous awards. According to the Web of Science Group, Professor Zott is among the top 1% most impactful researchers in Economics and Business worldwide.

In addition to being an experienced academic, consultant, and public speaker, Professor Zott has served in various professional leadership roles.

For example, he currently serves as a Co-Editor of the *Strategic Entrepreneurship Journal*, the leading global academic journal on entrepreneurship. Professor Zott was also elected Chair of the Strategic Management Division of the Academy of Management, the world's largest organization of management scholars, and he is a Fellow of the Strategic Management Society.

He is a happy and proud father of four marvelous daughters and in his spare time loves to spend time with his family and practice sports, most notably triathlon and skiing.

Index

Page references followed by *e* indicate an exhibit.